# USA
# TODAY

# Teatime
# Crosswords

**Can't get enough of USA TODAY puzzles?**

You can play:

- In the USA TODAY newspaper

- At puzzles.usatoday.com

- By downloading the FREE USA TODAY app (Get it on Google Play or iTunes)

- By downloading the FREE USA TODAY Crossword app (Get it on Google Play or iTunes)

# USA TODAY

## Teatime Crosswords

## 200 Puzzles

Andrews McMeel
PUBLISHING®

Andrews McMeel Publishing
a division of Andrews McMeel Universal
1130 Walnut Street, Kansas City, Missouri 64106

www.andrewsmcmeel.com
puzzles.usatoday.com

22 23 24 25 26 PAH 10 9 8 7 6 5 4 3 2 1

ISBN: 978-1-5248-6992-2

ATTENTION: SCHOOLS AND BUSINESSES
Andrews McMeel books are available at quantity discounts with bulk purchase for
educational, business, or sales promotional use. For information, please e-mail the
Andrews McMeel Publishing Special Sales Department:
specialsales@amuniversal.com.

# Teatime
# Crosswords

# 1
# PLAYING IT SAFE

By Erik Agard

**ACROSS**

1 Like internships, ideally
5 Internship follower, ideally
8 Removes coding errors from
14 Besides that
15 "___ Maria"
16 Tie, as a score
17 "You sure 'bout that?"
19 Fir tree's dropping
20 "I'll take a ___ at it"
21 Palindromic detector
23 "___ Town Road"
24 Fat for cooking
26 Notion
28 Quinceanera, for one
33 Arthur of "The Golden Girls"
35 Malicious
36 Got under control
37 Peach ___
39 Sofa mishap
42 Sheet of glass
43 ___ Loops
45 Stereo protrusion
47 School of Buddhism
48 Place for bigs and littles
52 Many an image from "SpongeBob SquarePants," on the internet
53 Chlumsky of comedy
54 Georgia's capital, for short
57 Draped garment whose name comes from Persian
59 Martial artist's blow
62 Fold mark

64 Yale city
67 Impressive soccer shot
68 ___-country (dude-centric music subgenre)
69 Depend
70 Journalistic tell-all
71 Pose a question
72 Part of a.m.

**DOWN**

1 Church bench
2 Rueful word
3 "Who ___?"
4 "Molly of ___" (Alaska-set kids' show)
5 Punch in the ring
6 Fail to practice moderation
7 Early stage of an app
8 "No prob," in Spanish
9 8,848-meter-high mountain
10 Spelling competition
11 Revert
12 Shore squawker
13 Went fast
18 Tail off
22 Queso, for one
25 Cranks up, as an engine
27 "Don't dillydally!"
28 Shaving need
29 Likely to bail on plans
30 Blow away
31 It might be mapped or spliced
32 ___ Prairie, MN

**33** Ppl with heart emojis on Snapchat
**34** Belgian coin
**38** Camera function
**40** Asthma-treating devices
**41** Lunchtime, perhaps
**44** Locks of Love donations
**46** Quantity of plantains
**49** "Present!"
**50** Word after "black" or "bubble"
**51** World's largest hot desert
**54** Feel yesterday's workout

**55** Predator whose full name means "king tyrant lizard," briefly
**56** Faith-based action
**58** Washington Mystics org.
**60** Roast venue
**61** Bombard, as with snowballs
**63** "It's ___-or-die situation"
**65** Stir-frying vessel
**66** 12/31, for short

# 2

## PIG IT

By Erik Agard

**ACROSS**

1 Threaded fastener
6 Storm preceder
10 Injection
14 Marsupial mascot of the Queensland Reds
15 Neck of the woods
16 Per unit
17 Hatha practitioners
18 "Beautiful ___" (Beyonce & Shakira song)
19 Flour that's a palindrome
20 One indignity too many
23 Word after "color" or "rhyme"
26 ___ the cows come home
27 Day before a holiday
28 Islamic holiday
29 Ticklish Muppet
32 Crucial
34 Gobbles up
36 *throws hands up*
38 Advancing, in football lingo
44 Disturbed the peace, perhaps
45 Eldest Braxton sister
46 EGOT winner Rita
49 Kitchen, for one
52 Number of Canadian provinces
53 Greek letter that sounds like part of a spreadsheet
54 Airline org.
56 Pay increases
58 Bounce
62 With 6-Down, "I'm indifferent"

63 Timeline sections
64 Mizrahi of fashion
68 Great ___ (dog)
69 Triplicate ___ (three-body superhero)
70 Health care pro
71 Wraps up
72 Delight
73 Geico spokeslizard

**DOWN**

1 Dove's place
2 Dove's cry
3 Shred of old cloth
4 Top-tier
5 Words written on a dusty car
6 See 62-Across
7 Apt name for an opera buff
8 Diminutive superlative
9 Cocktails that might be dirty
10 Candidate's goal
11 Severe dislike
12 One of five in Mariah Carey's range
13 Unfrozen
21 Unagi or anago, in sushi
22 Part of a wintry mix
23 Appear to be
24 "Peace!" in Pisa
25 1080p device
30 Oven glove
31 Catchall category on surveys
33 Proofreader's suggestion
35 Horse's dad

**37** Overhaul

**39** Second-to-last out of 52-Across

**40** Avian synonym for "zero"

**41** Simple beds

**42** It might be taken or skinned

**43** Subjects of repentance

**46** Dr. Jekyll's bad side

**47** Columbus resident, e.g.

**48** Like a sphere

**50** Fantasy beast

**51** "___ my way downtown, walking fast . . ."

**55** Month following marzo

**57** Magazine release

**59** Number following dos

**60** Uncommon

**61** Word with no etymological relation to "island," surprisingly

**65** Rainbow's shape

**66** "Why do you ___?"

**67** Corporate highest-up

# 3
## PUT YOUR HAPPINESS FIRST
By Erik Agard

**ACROSS**

1 Shellfish restaurant
7 Deploy
10 Meatball ___ sub
14 In short supply
15 MLK's title
16 Skating jump
17 Parking lot
18 School singing group
20 Falafel bread
21 Baking show competitor
23 Profound
24 "You're not wrong"
26 Snake shape
28 Pep rally leaders
33 Tennis court surface
35 "___ You the One?"
36 Stage item
37 Homophone of 35-Across, to some
38 Conversational detour
42 Poem with a devotee
43 Smell
45 Eggs on sushi
46 Had possession of
48 "Rogue One" star
52 "Yes, ___!"
53 One of the Great Lakes
54 Untidiness
56 Cooler brand named for a legendary creature
58 BTS genre
62 U.S. Poet Laureate appointed in 2019

64 Atlantic and Pacific, for two
66 Cookie brand with many flavors
67 Prefix for "disclosure"
68 Bent-knee exercises
69 Try out
70 Crunches can make them shredded
71 First in line for the throne, perhaps

**DOWN**

1 Say whether you'll show up
2 Fruit served "na tigela"
3 "Breaking Bad" criminal
4 Meditation focuses
5 Segment of a play
6 Bail out
7 Impulse
8 Mental health day practice
9 "Killing ___" (Sandra Oh show)
10 Car racer's warmup
11 Car bar
12 Go back for more
13 Nationals' org.
19 Spruce up grammatically
22 Grammy-winning singer whose name spells out a pronoun
25 Partner of relaxation
27 ___-and-shut
28 Sing Christmas tunes
29 Not forthcoming

**30** You might have a lot of them in the fire
**31** Part of a network
**32** Drove too fast
**33** Silly error
**34** "Excuse you!"
**39** "This Strange Awakening" from the opera "Mota," e.g
**40** Buck-passing phrase
**41** "Sula" author Morrison
**44** Percussive punctuation for a joke
**47** What "TGIF!" anticipates

**49** Spanish for "house"
**50** Vehicle that might be jumbo
**51** Baltimore bird
**54** "Encore!"
**55** "Behind These Hazel ___"
**57** Seemingly forever
**59** Part of a newspaper
**60** Small bills
**61** Attention-getting sound
**62** Write quickly
**63** Single-stranded molecule
**65** ___-de-sac

# 4
## COOL IT!
By Fran & Lou Sabin

**ACROSS**

1 Type of track
6 Stinging blow
10 Bit of praise
14 Kegler locale
15 Take on
16 China placement
17 "Cool it!"
20 House vote
21 Where many arrive just to split
22 Fussy couple?
23 "___ She Sweet"
24 Tuning fork's output
26 "Cool it!"
32 Police blotter types, slangily
33 Texas hold 'em holding, perhaps
34 Penultimate letter
35 Vientiane is its capital
36 "Fantasia" dancer
38 Young salmon up to two years old
39 It may have several cups of coffee
40 Retina receptor
41 Letter flourish
42 "Cool it!"
46 Artificial bait
47 Worrisome thing
48 First-stringers
51 Small town
52 PC alternative
55 "Cool it!"
59 Definitely not well-done
60 Word with throat or loser
61 Bat maker's machine
62 Puppies' plaints
63 Clark of the comics
64 Command on 52-Across

**DOWN**

1 Duke's daughter
2 Cosmetics additive, often
3 Humerus neighbor
4 Garner
5 They are of mixed origin
6 Japanese religion
7 CEO carrier, perhaps
8 Dada co-founder
9 It can be split
10 Type of roll
11 Applications
12 Eat by candlelight, perhaps
13 Stable fare
18 Start of a counting-out rhyme
19 Certain voice range
23 Mann's "The Magic Mountain" locale
24 Word with fly or speed
25 17th of 50
26 What the Tin Man wanted
27 Home of Maine's Black Bears
28 Good hand to have
29 Hive activity
30 Condor's nest (Var.)
31 One in a condition of servitude

**Across / Down clues:**

32 "What's more . . ."
36 Billing unit, for some
37 Heading for a memo subject
38 Wooden pins
40 Good buddies
41 Cuddle together
43 Dental items
44 "Absolutely!"
45 Cross inscription
48 Twisted
49 Chiang Mai citizen, often
50 Holliday partner
51 Capital on the Aare

52 Jeff's sidekick
53 U.S. court star
54 "Half-Breed" singer
56 Word of reproval
57 Long-handled tool
58 Displayed fear, in a way

# 5
## LIFE PARTNERS
By Erik Agard

**ACROSS**

1 Some Pennsylvania Dutch speakers
6 Supermarket section
10 Scott-Young who created "Love & Hip Hop"
14 Color in old photos
15 Choose not to include
16 Very large-scale
17 Window-opening figures
19 Like bulls and bucks
20 Workplaces for some nurses, for short
21 Award for a show
22 Cider fodder
24 ___ and turning
26 Air kiss sound
27 Package-shipping option
28 Nobel laureate who said "If I tried to write a universal novel it would be water"
32 Ridged pants, for short
35 Hip-hop duo Salt-N-___
36 Achy
37 During
38 Mint cocktail
39 Side dish with cabbage
40 Frilly fabric
41 Apple music device
42 Diving board places
43 "Respect" singer
45 Promise of repayment
46 Pickling herb
47 Positioned

51 Start of a scale
54 Get off ___-free
55 Massage
56 ___ 51
57 Positioned perilously
60 Robin's home
61 Palindromic bread
62 Jazz bandleader Count
63 Dark aesthetic
64 Hardens
65 Blow through the budget

**DOWN**

1 Liability's counterpart
2 Transit option in D.C. or L.A.
3 "Skip me"
4 Respectful address
5 Acknowledgments
6 "You're ___ amazing, sweetie"
7 Award for a show
8 "Somebody told a ___ one day . . ." (MLK)
9 Words of finality
10 Music of '60s Tennessee
11 Australia's national gemstone
12 River in Egypt
13 Unreturned serves
18 Large units of weight
23 Golf hole number
25 Overtime format
26 Two-wheeled vehicle
28 Honeydew, e.g.
29 Song for one person

**30** Word before "hygiene" or "history"
**31** Breaking stuff
**32** Leg muscle
**33** Ilhan of Congress
**34** Costa ___
**35** Student
**38** Too many to count
**42** Soda can pieces
**44** Common Korean family name
**45** Privy to, as a plan
**47** Little pictures
**48** Come up

**49** Garam masala spice
**50** Waned
**51** "Rats!"
**52** Android version between Nougat and Pie
**53** Repay a sleep debt, say
**54** Piece of data
**58** Country whose capital is Abu Dhabi, for short
**59** Drink like a cat

# 6

# WHERE ARE MY BACKGROUND SINGERS?

By Erik Agard

## ACROSS

1 Interpersonal distancing
5 Reason for seasonal shots
8 Curved-guard swords
14 Slimy side
15 Dashed
16 Two-digit prime
17 Distributed
19 Like some of the characters on "The Casagrandes"
20 "The Purple People ___"
21 Messes up
23 Far from elevated
24 Actor Centineo
26 "They don't think it be ___ it is, but it do" (Oscar Gamble quote)
28 Good and honest
34 Boxer in the documentary "What's My Name"
35 Desperate appeal
36 Parts of drum kits
38 Phone sound
40 "Messenger" or "transfer" letters
42 Make available for purchase
43 Strongly opposed
46 Husband of Frigg, in Norse mythology
49 Pie ___ mode
50 Fun learning tool
53 Yawn-evoking person
54 Cover with asphalt
55 "Knew it!"

58 Small nocturnal bird
60 "Have fun!"
64 Was defeated by
66 Phone sound
68 1946-1964 birth
69 46-Across, for one
70 15th-century Peruvian
71 Validate
72 Final part
73 Falsehoods

## DOWN

1 Biked, say
2 Swedish furniture chain that owns TaskRabbit
3 Kappa Alpha Psi, e.g., for short
4 Aptitude
5 To's opposite
6 It might end in tears
7 "Do ___ others . . ."
8 Many Instagram posts
9 Person from Anchorage
10 Wager
11 Good's opponent
12 Casino city near Lake Tahoe
13 Skiing surface
18 Group of Girl Scouts
22 "You go, goalie!"
25 Org. that merged with the CIO in 1955
27 Geologic stretches
28 Singer Bareilles
29 Not out of the running

**30** Like some paper
**31** Capital of Vietnam
**32** Reward for a dog
**33** "Anyone there?"
**37** Perform excellently
**39** Chow
**41** Subject of the Nicole Chung memoir "All You Can Ever Know"
**44** E-bike alternative
**45** Song that's hard to get out of your head
**47** "All ___ day's work"

**48** Piercing site
**51** ___ Aviv
**52** Legume in masoor dal
**55** Jessica of "Honey"
**56** Part of a horse
**57** Since
**59** Defeat by a small margin
**61** "River" singer Mitchell
**62** A single time
**63** They negate nays
**65** "Eww, stop talking!"
**67** Combine

# 7
# BRILLIANT!
By Erik Agard

**ACROSS**

1 Novelist's rep
6 ___ shui
10 Poet's tribute
13 ___ Lama
14 Drink with tiny marshmallows
15 Word before "favor" or "supuesto"
16 Concept of mutual investment among women
18 "Tea you later," for one
19 Spanish for "water"
20 Kenyan capital
22 Percussive dance
25 Ever so slightly
27 Social division
28 An optimist might cling to one
32 Hot-button ___
33 Graffiti supply
34 Latte art medium
35 Los Angeles neighborhood
37 "This doesn't bode well"
41 Overly bold
43 "I might know the answer"
44 One-hit wonder, say
47 Something you might want to catch up on
49 Fly high
50 Hosp. parts
51 Necktie knot type
54 Soccer fans' shouts
56 "The Bachelorette" channel
57 Nickname for a good dancer
62 "The Catcher in the ___"

63 Assistants
64 Housewarming, e.g.
65 Some graduate degrees, for short
66 Remainder
67 "Whoops, sorry"

**DOWN**

1 In-app interruptions
2 Cry of frustration
3 Actor Wallach
4 Grammy, by another name
5 It has no winners or losers
6 Nemesis
7 Supply-and-demand class, for short
8 Author Roberts
9 Harvey Milk, for one
10 Be against
11 Uncertainty
12 Muppet with a No. 16 Billboard hit
14 Head of a department
17 Container of toothpaste
21 Bliss
22 End-of-workweek exclamation
23 "And another thing . . ."
24 Leaning Tower city
26 Bar-raising words
29 Didn't enunciate
30 Part of the translation of "Mardi Gras"
31 He/him/___

35 Used to be
36 Cigar remains
38 Buzz
39 Sharif of "Funny Girl"
40 Egg layers
42 Hip-hop luminary
43 Afternoon hour
44 August Wilson play with a 2016 movie adaptation starring Viola Davis
45 Cozy breakfast spots
46 Towering
47 Mass of bees

48 Tripoli's country
52 Boo-boo
53 Disencumbers
55 "Don't go!"
58 Brooklyn baller
59 Spherical figure
60 Projected fig. on a seatback screen
61 Lead vocalist for The Internet

# 8

## A BEAST OF A CRUSH

By Erik Agard

**ACROSS**

1 Bottom part of a semicolon
6 Fast-food chain HQ'd in Louisville
9 ___-Saxon
14 Heartless
15 Boat-rowing tool
16 Talked to a pet, perhaps
17 Decline
18 Spanish for "river"
19 Extra
20 Jitters experienced during a crush
23 Hawaiian wreath
25 It might be toxic
26 "It's the end of an ___"
29 "Star Trek" assent
32 Teatime treats
35 Devices that detect
37 Letters to mind
38 Youthful crushes
40 No longer obsessed with
43 Traffic-parting sound
44 Coat of ___
48 Used for sustenance
50 Org. with restrictions on liquids
51 Bugged
52 They hold lenses
54 Like 54-Down
55 Rhyming phrase for someone with a crush
59 Sheep sounds
60 Olympics category
61 Snippy response to "You asleep?"
63 Apex
64 Impersonate
65 Prefix for "physics" or "data"
66 Homeowner's document
67 One of the deadly sins
68 Old Testament garden

**DOWN**

1 Includes on an email thread
2 Singer Rita
3 "Como estas?" response
4 List of dishes
5 Oodles
6 The K in K-Town
7 Craft gatherings
8 "Tomb Raider" protagonist Lara
9 Three-syllable fruit
10 Lymph ___
11 Something that arrives just when you need it most
12 Painter Krasner
13 Peculiar
21 Puny people
22 A teacher might create a plan for one
23 Part of UNLV
24 Take a look at
27 Mandatory (Abbr.)
28 Jerk
30 "Here it is, just like we discussed"

**USA TODAY**

**31** Long u
**33** Cleveland NBAer, for short
**34** Single file
**36** Dentist's instruction
**37** Heartfelt request
**39** Century hundredths (Abbr.)
**40** Light switch position
**41** Designer Donatella
**42** Pod snack
**45** Got a library due date pushed back
**46** Titan of industry
**47** Pig's place

**49** Volleyball divider
**51** ___-rock
**53** Parts of mushrooms
**54** Scenario, for short
**56** Apt anagram of "vile"
**57** Fictional anemonefish found somewhere in this clue
**58** Make sweaters
**59** "___ Guy" (Billie Eilish song)
**62** Part of UCSF

# 9

## PART TIME

By Erik Agard

**ACROSS**

**1** From Gwynedd, say
**6** "___ the night before Christmas . . ."
**10** Matures
**14** Banishment
**15** Helpful clue
**16** Anna Zhigalova's sport
**17** Country near Australia
**19** The sun, for one
**20** Male deer
**21** Tennis official
**23** Be a good match
**24** Painting and such
**26** Painting supporters
**28** Bachelorette after Becca
**31** Mass times acceleration, per Newton's second law
**32** Royal flush card
**33** Aussie animal
**36** "Sadly . . ."
**39** Heist planner's holy grail
**43** Literary alter ego who inspired the Hulk
**44** Fashionably nostalgic
**45** Org. with a Slam Dunk Contest
**46** Musical pace
**49** Beginning
**51** Player who gets points
**53** Fed a signal to
**54** Talk up a storm
**55** "Is a ___ a sandwich?" (polarizing question)

**58** Person with legendary status
**62** Simone who sang "Sinnerman"
**64** Send it into extra innings, say
**66** Horse gait
**67** Unbusy
**68** Collections of leaves
**69** Imitate a wolf
**70** Some apartments don't allow them
**71** Period of time

**DOWN**

**1** Moistens
**2** Lit sign in a theater
**3** Peru's capital
**4** Advertising tagline
**5** "How Stella Got ___ Groove Back"
**6** "___ the breaks!"
**7** Bit of smoke
**8** Prefix akin to "contra-"
**9** Music player
**10** Donkey, biblically
**11** Intuition
**12** Inbox Zero target
**13** Categorizes
**18** Lex who hates Superman
**22** Organ with a lobe
**25** Leaf-collecting tool
**27** "The Lion King" uncle
**28** Possesses, old-style
**29** "___ Breaky Heart"
**30** Classified

**31** Fiction counterpart
**34** ___-textured hair
**35** "I'm Sorry" singer Brenda
**37** Prefix for "dextrous"
**38** "Hot Ones" host Evans
**40** Possible source of pressure
**41** Livestock drinking spot
**42** Apple's middle
**47** "Not impressed"
**48** Bit of expert advice
**50** "Impressive!"
**51** ___-pop (music genre)

**52** Egyptian city where the Arab League is headquartered
**53** French for "coasts"
**56** Detergent brand
**57** Muscle near a lat
**59** Compton's state, for short
**60** Sign for a seer
**61** Home observed by a birder
**63** Georgia airport code
**65** TV show supervisors

# 10
## USA NETWORK
By Zhouqin Burnikel

**ACROSS**

1 Movie ticket remnant
5 Flower that's an anagram of "tears"
10 "You should know better!"
13 "That's horrible!"
14 Put on, as a play
15 Game played on horseback
16 Cookie brand since 1975
18 Off in the distance
19 Even score
20 Basic unit of heredity
21 Some wall posters
23 Leave in the lurch
25 Suffers a defeat
26 Industrious bug
27 Competed in sprints and such
30 Howled at the moon
33 Spill cleaners
34 Sunscreen additive
35 Kerfuffle
36 Piques, as curiosity
39 Tan on a bookshelf
40 Praise highly
42 Rice on a bookshelf
43 Writes a program
45 "That's great news!"
47 Source of light
48 Nimble
49 Resistance group
52 Unlikely to support a crowdfunding project
54 Forum wrap
55 Go on and on

57 Verdi opera set in Egypt
58 Big-top performances
61 Take hold of
62 Similar
63 Camera lens part
64 All ready
65 Sneaky tactics
66 Long blog comment, perhaps

**DOWN**

1 Tender-hearted
2 Some Bangkok Post readers
3 Not yet achieved, as goals
4 Haunted house scream
5 Green light
6 Witness's place
7 Get under control
8 Source of hubris
9 "Aah," to a back rub, say
10 Healthy lunch
11 Wordless "How dare you?!"
12 Fashion designer Michael
15 First national restaurant chain to post calorie counts
17 Country south of South Sudan
22 Believer's suffix
24 Issa of "Insecure"
25 Error in judgment
27 Part of a bout
28 Order to Rover
29 Insert and Delete, for two
30 Island east of Java
31 Sistine Chapel ceiling figure
32 "Right on!"

**USA TODAY**

**33** Janelle of "Moonlight"
**37** Superstitious fan's backward garment
**38** Goes diving
**41** Steal, as a toy
**44** Number on a foam finger
**46** Short-term job
**47** Seamless transitions
**49** Far from smooth
**50** Stretchy fabric
**51** Glossy fabric
**52** Gives in to gravity
**53** Goodyear product

**54** Tony! Toni! Tone!, e.g.
**56** Furtive "Hey!"
**59** Down with something
**60** Make public

USA TODAY

# 11
# METALHEADS

By Caitlin Reid

**ACROSS**

1 Fashionable
5 Spanish appetizers
10 Place for a hat
14 Fallon's "Tonight Show" predecessor
15 Representative
16 Objectify with a look
17 Spoken
18 West African nation home to Accra
19 Hammer or handsaw
20 Shiny reward for a job well done
22 "I'm a ___, I'm in distress, I can handle this. Have a nice day." ("Hercules" line)
24 Skiing locales
25 iPhone assistant
26 Luxury item in a wallet
31 Nightmare, e.g.
33 ___ jeans
34 Beam of light
35 Intended
36 Police alert, briefly
37 Number on a store shelf
39 Actor Mahershala
40 ___ chart
41 Fuzzy leather
42 Bright side of an unfortunate situation
46 Cupid's Greek counterpart
47 Signing, as a deal
50 Word by a coin slot
53 Speed demon's body part
55 Like lemons and limes
56 Official decree
58 Reusable grocery bag
59 Stories passed down
60 Apple drink
61 Grandson of Eve
62 ___ out a living (got by)
63 "Westworld" actress Thompson
64 Fender flaw

**DOWN**

1 Plumber's target
2 ___ journey (arc that begins with a call to adventure)
3 Counting everything
4 Segment before the title sequence
5 Tackle together
6 Filled with horror
7 Partridge's tree, in a Christmas carol
8 TV journalist Curry
9 Sports venue
10 It might make a private remark public
11 They may clash at work
12 Natural soother
13 Big name in computers
21 Sound of spilled milk
23 Asset for a quarterback
25 Snooty type
27 Dallas City Hall architect

**USA TODAY**

**28** Very dry
**29** Triathlon, for one
**30** Change the color of
**31** Meat-slicing locale
**32** Stairwell rod
**35** More, en Califas
**36** Feels unwell
**37** Prank show first hosted by Ashton Kutcher
**38** Passed along, as an unwanted present
**40** Keep safe
**41** "Ol' Blue Eyes" Frank

**43** Swerved
**44** Make a mistake
**45** Counterparts of nephews
**48** Not a soul
**49** Boarded, as a train
**50** Speck in the sea
**51** Cozy breakfast area
**52** "OK, why not"
**53** Container toppers
**54** Reason to cram
**57** Casino cube

# 12
## PARTY TIME!
By Mark McClain

### ACROSS

1 Big simian
4 Youngest of the Obamas
9 Greenish-blue tint
13 Trash heap emanation
14 Sneeze sound
15 "___ noted!"
16 Single person hanging out with a couple
18 Enjoy a fine meal
19 Heavy weight
20 Checked out
21 The ___ Brothers ("Sucker" band)
22 C-to-C span
24 Adamant refusal
26 What you're wearing when you're not wearing anything
31 Talent
34 Devours
35 Dog's "hand"
36 Chip in for a hand
37 "Quiet!"
38 "Flights" author Tokarczuk
39 "What do you want?"
40 Anglo-___
41 Black-and-white sleeveful
42 Web-scouring tool
45 Bank transactions
46 Update, as a classic film
50 Dole out
52 "Amazing!"
54 Back muscle, for short
55 Opposite of a make
56 Signal to proceed
59 Swimming event
60 Busy Chicago airport
61 In ___ land (detached from reality)
62 Double play pair
63 Like washboard abs
64 Astrological feline

### DOWN

1 Latin phrase describing some committees
2 "That's beside the ___"
3 Mess up
4 TV journalist Diane
5 Dull pain
6 Leave hair everywhere
7 Manual weed-whacker
8 ___ Instant Messenger
9 Extra features
10 Multiply by five
11 Bone near the radius
12 "The ___ have it!"
13 Name that's a palindrome
17 New Jersey NHLer
21 Pleasures
23 Willing and ___
24 Not doing anything
25 Float on the air
27 Chocolate-and-caramel candy bars
28 Invitation from a motorcyclist
29 Villain hiding out in the east of Santiago

**30** Contraction in a Christmas poem

**31** Puts into words

**32** Body part where the patella is found

**33** "Everything's ready to go!"

**37** TV journalist Paula

**38** Utah city next to Provo

**40** Improvised jazz singing

**41** "Paper Moon" star Tatum ___

**43** Perches for birds

**44** Did some pressing

**47** Aquarium scum

**48** "Four Inhabitants of Mexico" artist Frida

**49** Grammy winner ___ James

**50** Snowballs, rotten tomatoes, etc.

**51** "In ___ of gifts . . ."

**52** Gradually withdraw

**53** In this location

**56** Came down with

**57** 17th Greek letter

**58** Under the weather

# 13
## HUSH-HUSH DOCUMENT
By Gail Grabowski

**ACROSS**

1 Strengthener of abs
6 Fill with joy
11 Missouri city, for short
14 Airport whose code is ORD
15 Sports Emmy winner Katie
16 Bathwater tester
17 Trustworthy words of wisdom
19 Gothic novelist Radcliffe
20 ___ out (withdraw)
21 Skin lotion ingredient
22 Muscat natives
24 Gusted
25 Ford car named for a legendary creature, for short
26 Fruit stand items
29 Supplier of birches and beeches
32 Puffy sight in the sky
33 Workshop array
34 "Go Set a Watchman" author Harper
35 Sierra Club founder John
36 Supper for swine
37 Purchases, in slang
38 Suffix for "lion"
39 Milk mishap
40 Striped Christmas candies
41 Scarcity
43 Only just
44 Societal expectations
45 Pucker-inducing
46 Herbal brew
48 Sunny spot for a houseplant
49 Unreturned serve
52 Historical time
53 When congresspeople get picked
56 Cedar relative
57 Bottom-line amount
58 "Time is money," e.g.
59 Collector's collection
60 Look without blinking
61 Identified

**DOWN**

1 Just average
2 Chain offering Belgian waffles
3 Tightly stretched
4 Commercial coffee holder
5 Rode a bike
6 Provide funding for
7 Valentine card sentiment
8 Boxer nicknamed "The Greatest"
9 Chain offering burritos
10 Antagonists
11 Self-contained
12 "Un-Break My Heart" singer Braxton
13 Camera part
18 Some craft beers
23 Barking sound
24 Become fuzzy
25 Bridge guard of folklore
26 Pinnacles
27 Luxurious

**USA TODAY**

**28** "Raiders of the Lost Ark" projectile
**29** Decoratively patterned fabric
**30** Fight off
**31** Like a cluttered room
**33** Nest material
**36** Musical that parodies Arthurian legend
**37** Online store icon
**39** Spots with potholes
**40** Auto buyer's need, perhaps
**42** Become inedible
**43** Indonesian island

**45** Proof of ownership
**46** WNBA officials
**47** Buffalo's Great Lake
**48** Brawl souvenir
**49** Actor Driver
**50** Hamster's home
**51** Looked at closely
**54** Frat letter
**55** Confidentiality contract initials found in this puzzle's four longest answers

**USA TODAY**

# 14
## CHOCOLATE CHOICES
By Patrick Jordan

**ACROSS**

1 Get the fuel gauge to F
6 Surprising setback
10 Strike abandoner
14 Draw ___ in the sand
15 Result of puncturing
16 Bike racer's challenge
17 Curves
18 Tons
19 Activewear brand with a Vanessa Hudgens collection
20 End of a date, perhaps
23 Potter's "M*A*S*H" rank (Abbr.)
25 Luau instrument, for short
26 Builds
27 Present-giver's prompt
30 Toilet paper layer
31 Data storage item
34 Paper quantity
38 Attends to wrinkles
39 Allow
40 Alabama city in an Ava DuVernay film
41 Was in attendance
42 Place with drinks and mics
44 Chesapeake ___
45 Traffic cones
46 The North Pole's ocean
50 He wears jersey number 16 in the Nationals' Presidents Race
52 Crying infant's sound
53 Plane-to-ground jump

57 One of Eden's outcasts
58 "Ah, gotcha"
59 Soccer star Kelley
62 ___ of passage
63 Tidy
64 King with a transforming touch
65 Flip-flops bare them
66 Liberal ___
67 Blog updates

**DOWN**

1 Talk a lot
2 Frothy tavern order
3 Nicole in "Raising Dion," for one
4 Reverse
5 Piece of change in Chihuahua
6 Meat case choice
7 "It's true!"
8 Easy as falling off ___
9 Obtain assistance
10 Protein drink
11 Palindrome meaning "citizenship-related"
12 Top-tier invitees
13 Fashion designer Bill
21 Job description part
22 "I'll ___ anything once"
23 Funny performer
24 Show with a libretto
28 "___ of your business!"
29 Org. that takes many forms
30 Pocket bread

**32** Modeling substance

**33** That woman

**34** Word after "gag" or "highlight"

**35** Skateboarder's protective pair

**36** Household appliance brand

**37** Reed-filled wetland

**40** Sight through a sunroof

**42** Hopi doll

**43** Slanted column

**44** Lighter brand

**46** Separated

**47** WKYS medium

**48** Wooden box

**49** Makes less wild

**50** Bothered ceaselessly

**51** Purple salad ingredients

**54** Reader of a manual

**55** Absurdly easy victory

**56** State with a swallowtail flag

**60** Chinese zodiac animal for 2020

**61** Pompous person, perhaps

# 15
## SO-CALLED
By Zhouqin Burnikel

**ACROSS**

1 Magician's garment
5 Missile thrown from behind the oche
9 Greektown sandwich
13 Everest's continent
14 "Such awful news!"
15 Sing the praises of
16 Former "The Talk" co-host
19 Really long time
20 "Seize the ___!"
21 Impersonated
22 "That's enough!"
24 Bouncer's concern
25 Cubes in a raw bar
28 "Nothing Compares 2 U" singer
32 Capital of Georgia, on scoreboards
33 Landscaper's turf
34 Papers, magazines, etc.
35 Like some golf tourneys
37 Relay race segment
39 Capital ___ tax
40 Show your feelings
41 Part of a semicolon
43 Aides for profs
44 "Matter of Fact" host
48 Workplaces for some 7-Down
49 Tuna holder
50 Burger chain with an arrow in its logo
53 Brewing ingredient

55 File type for many scholarly articles
56 2000s CBS forensics drama
57 "Inside the NBA" analyst
61 Country that borders Chile
62 Part of speech of "part" and "speech"
63 Remarked
64 175.2 square miles, for Tampa
65 Blast of wind
66 Queen Boleyn

**DOWN**

1 Viola holders
2 Give it ___ (try)
3 Bench alternatives, for some musicians
4 Piece of corn
5 Supports Americares, say
6 "Hey, sailor!"
7 Some hosp. workers
8 Island northeast of Trinidad
9 Model builder's adhesive
10 Three-foot unit
11 Finish an aquathlon
12 Complimentary verse
17 Ruler in "Thor"
18 Oil grp. formed in 1960
23 Pontius ___
24 Appended
25 Madagascar locale
26 Quarters, e.g.
27 Periods often named for monarchs

**USA TODAY**

**Down / Across (partial clue list)**

29 Dial-up pioneer
30 "wow, rly?!"
31 Tidy up
32 Knight's protective outerwear
35 Currency of Cuba or Mexico
36 Word before "school" or after "Club"
38 Lump
42 Spear with three prongs
45 Legal rights org. turning 100 in 2020
46 Going out with
47 Details, for short

51 Track legend Bolt
52 Squiggly mark
53 Female horse
54 Color akin to turquoise
55 "Also . . ."
57 Place to enjoy a mud mask
58 She/___ pronouns
59 Singer Rawls
60 Org. that's Edward Snowden's only Twitter follow

# 16
## PURSE FIRST
By Stella Zawistowski

**ACROSS**

1 Small glob
4 Infomercial's "Hurry!"
10 Khrushchev's country
14 Birmingham's state (Abbr.)
15 Beer with a crown logo
16 California wine region
17 Arachnid that might be found near train tracks
19 Effective insult, in slang
20 Hawaiian gathering
21 Computer port letters
22 "___ it!" ("Love that!")
23 Star pitcher for the Kansas City Monarchs
28 Weightlifter's helper
31 Corp. bigwigs
32 Na+ or Cl-
33 Got the heck out of Dodge
35 Airline whose name is a Greek letter
39 Buy and quickly resell, as a house
41 Directs followers
44 First light
45 Sacred object
47 Restaurant handout
49 Jaden Smith, to Jada and Will
50 Intergovernmental agreement
53 Skillful maneuvering
55 Asset in the ninth inning
59 20-Across dance
60 Dispenser of joe

61 Org. with film ratings
65 Worldwide (Abbr.)
66 Odds displays
70 Brown songbird
71 Was worthy of
72 Acorn producer
73 Nest egg parts
74 Expressed in words
75 Non-morning times (Abbr.)

**DOWN**

1 Author Roald
2 Baseball surname hidden in "cantaloupe"
3 ___ ghanoush
4 They keep houses cool in summer (Abbr.)
5 ___-out (unsatisfying answer, say)
6 Swim-bike-run race, for short
7 "Obviously!"
8 "Just a moment!"
9 Sing like a bird
10 Impartial
11 Riyadh resident
12 Piece of parsley
13 "Home on the ___"
18 Get rid of, as a ruler
24 Part of the DOJ
25 Pray ___ ("Pose" character)
26 People of Canada
27 Pea holder
28 Use a strainer

**29** Game that becomes another game if you swap its last two letters
**30** Working at a task
**34** River barrier
**36** Scottish girl
**37** Terrible ___
**38** Queen in "The Favourite"
**40** Locker room speeches
**42** Skillful
**43** Agitated state
**46** Apple computer
**48** A in French

**51** ___ and Ladders
**52** Vocal cords' location
**54** Humorist Bombeck
**55** Cook-off dish
**56** Moon-based
**57** Prefix with "violet"
**58** Prefix with "mural"
**62** Item on a movie set
**63** Eve's man
**64** Queries
**67** Sinusitis treater (Abbr.)
**68** Quilting social
**69** Not even

# 17
## LET'S MAKE A DATE!
By Claire Rimkus

**ACROSS**

1 Mr. ___ (former soft drink name)
5 Get going
11 Sports ___
14 Diva's memorable moment
15 "Don't think so"
16 Immeasurably long time
17 Old West mail system
19 Plop down
20 Embeds
21 Mr., Ms., or Mx.
23 Native of Colorado
24 Lines on a map
26 "Top Chef" host Lakshmi
29 Long fishes with distinguishing dorsal features
33 Suffix for "lemon" or "Gator"
34 Reason for a Boston "party"
36 Sunburn soother
37 Fully matured
39 Pepper used in some chilis
40 Tedious task
41 Many a "Trinkets" character, age-wise
42 Soaks in hot water
44 Large flightless bird
45 Photobomber's hand gesture
47 Not verbose
49 One-on-one swordfights
50 ___ bracket
51 Be behind
53 Glass ceilings, e.g.
58 Spider's creation
59 Color named after a fruit
62 ___-advised
63 Calendar listings
64 Activist Gonzalez
65 Initialism found in 17-, 29-, 45-, and 59-Across
66 "Oh, shucks!"
67 Handwashing substance

**DOWN**

1 Big ___ (David Ortiz nickname)
2 Metal with the chemical symbol Fe
3 Sweet cherry variety
4 Fragrance made from leaves and alcohol
5 Paper cup brand
6 "NBA Countdown" channel
7 Stats for golf holes
8 Opposite of "nay"
9 Workers in wards (Abbr.)
10 "For here" equivalent
11 Literary chart-topper
12 Disturb
13 Opening poker bet
18 Patronize, as a restaurant
22 "Any ___?"
24 Considerable wealth
25 Ahead
26 Heading for a second section
27 Goodbye that's bidden
28 Not flaky
29 Some mall attractions
30 Indiana NBAer

**31** Weaving devices
**32** Smoothly transition
**35** Painter's support
**38** Listless feeling
**43** Intense gaze
**46** Sang along at a concert, perhaps
**48** Banishes
**50** Lovers' rendezvous
**51** Bed size
**52** "On that you can ___" (lyric from "As Time Goes By")

**53** German city with a double letter
**54** Oppositional prefix
**55** Wasabi-loving Muppet
**56** Tomato type
**57** Trade
**60** "___ Luna" (Allende novel)
**61** French for "sea"

# 18
## WHERE THEY'RE AT
By Lynn Lempel

**ACROSS**

1 Smiles radiantly
6 Cheese's pasta partner
9 Tournament victor
14 Host with a mic
15 Brownie ___ mode
16 Video's complement
17 Wonder Girl, or any member of her teen team
18 Spot for skipping stones
20 Periods on a job
22 Spilled the beans
23 "No kidding!"
24 Actress Davis
26 At-bat stat
27 Miscalculate, say
28 Military advisor
32 Chats on a PC
33 Young horse
34 Boxers' weapons
38 Many "Peppa Pig" viewers
40 ___ donna (opera star)
43 FBI dude
44 Lengthy test answer
46 AP math class
48 Pharmacist Lilly
49 Pill with a protective covering
53 Some advanced degrees, for short
56 Colorado people
57 "The ___ Wears Prada"
58 MLB World Series mo.
59 King of Skull Island
61 ___ value (real estate stat)

64 Knight's garb
67 Single-use drink freebie
68 "Hi there"
69 Court org.
70 Mighty mad
71 Out of kilter
72 ___-Mex
73 What the ends of 18-, 28-, 49-, and 64-Across may contain

**DOWN**

1 They're placed on sporting events
2 Radiate
3 Workers for social change
4 Malicious sort
5 Ejected, as from a soccer game
6 Ruin
7 Landed
8 Frolic
9 Capital of Wales
10 Busy airport
11 Memorable maxim
12 One going for the gold, perhaps
13 Game for a good bluffer
19 "Thor" actor Idris
21 Water vessel, or some bodies of water backward
25 Quite a distance
28 Mention as a source
29 Networks of drs.
30 Piece of pizza

**USA TODAY**

**31** Fruit associated with Newton
**35** Be suspicious, so to speak
**36** "The Handmaid's ___"
**37** Grouchy mood
**39** Spider's egg holder
**41** Org. advocating for safe-ride programs
**42** Change
**45** Filler phrase
**47** Collapses under pressure
**50** Basic particle
**51** Rent payer

**52** Establishment that's an anagram of "orbits"
**53** Chocolaty coffee
**54** Reasons for rubdowns
**55** Edible rhubarb part
**60** Taunting remark
**62** Past the expected time
**63** Some wool coat wearers
**65** Suffix for "infant" or "percent"
**66** Lenient with rules

# 19
## SINGSONG SYLLABLES
By Rachel Fabi

**ACROSS**

1 Gal in the movies
6 Melody
10 Repeating sound effect
14 Texas cemetery site
15 "A Visit From the Goon Squad" author Jennifer
16 Every ___ and cranny
17 Alliterative sporting equipment
20 Key that can lead to a quick exit
21 Arguments in favor
22 ___ of honor
23 Pittsburgh NFLer
25 "I'd rather not talk about it"
28 Christmas carol contraction
29 Come to a ___ in the road
30 ___/her pronouns
31 Loads
33 Painting of Venus, often
34 Actor McKellen
35 Alliterative prank
39 Sty denizen
40 Traveled upon
41 "Here ___ nothing!"
42 Chuckle syllable
43 Phoenix ballers
44 Sept. preceder
45 Result
47 2019's Outstanding Comedy Series Emmy winner
51 Some Korean cars
52 Feeling your ___ (horse-inspired idiom)
53 Word outgrown by Romeo and Bow Wow
54 Alliterative Halloween getup
58 Southeast ___ (region home to Laos)
59 Folktales, e.g.
60 Warning sound
61 Series in which Gandalf appears, for short
62 Has debts
63 Havens

**DOWN**

1 Stares
2 Upper echelon of celebrity
3 It may be interpretive
4 "wut!?"
5 Causing to fall
6 Voice below 44-Down
7 Sheepskin boots
8 Short sleep
9 Head over heels
10 Break things off
11 Heartless
12 Long-handled gardening tool
13 Green-lights
18 Metal deposits
19 Unpleasantly damp
24 School founded by Henry VI
25 Evade
26 Palindrome in Iranian political history

**USA TODAY**

**27** Documentarian Burns
**29** Sums of savings
**31** French farewell
**32** Like close friends
**33** Lowest possible attendance
**36** Percussionist's time to shine
**37** "Um, sure?"
**38** Caesar wrap
**39** Noodle soup from Vietnam
**43** Drench
**44** Voice above 6-Down
**46** "Close, but no ___"
**47** Stands up to
**48** Fast-moving objects, in cartoons
**49** Singer Mann
**50** Secluded valleys
**52** Fairy-tale beastie
**54** Actor Penn who taught at Penn
**55** Prefix for "metric" or "morphic"
**56** Feminist org. with an urgent-sounding acronym
**57** Miembro de una familia

# 20
## CLAPBACKS
By Zhouqin Burnikel

**ACROSS**
1 Rattlesnake's warning
5 Not as much
9 Prize for a good picture
14 Ring of water around a castle
15 Show with booths
16 Role in "Popeye" or "South Side"
17 Venues for some civil cases
20 Tiny amount
21 Iran's former name
22 Longoria of "Overboard"
24 Place to get drinks on a train
27 Foul things up
28 Garden hose problem
30 Male turkey
31 Stroll
33 "Dennis the ___"
36 Jeans brand
38 Meeting where the pope is elected
42 Pico de gallo ingredient
43 Entertain
45 Distorts, as data
48 Shortest-named zodiac sign
50 Stone of "The Favourite"
51 Gore-___ (fabric)
52 Hid in the hand
55 Plant holder
56 Fix up
59 Face blowing a kiss, e.g.
61 Anglican denomination
66 Like a graveyard under fog
67 Pentathlon blade
68 View as
69 Weightlifting exercise
70 Folk singer Seeger
71 Norwegian Military Academy city

**DOWN**
1 "Let me think about that . . ."
2 Promise-to-pay note
3 Orange County city
4 Mix in a bowl
5 German camera brand
6 Panelist, often
7 Place to get a facial peel
8 Costa del ___, Spain
9 One-consonant instrument
10 Fail to articulate
11 Puts a hex on
12 Dress-code subject
13 String of prayer beads
18 ___ Sauv
19 EMT's lifesaving technique
22 Dartboard wood
23 Julia Louis-Dreyfus comedy
25 Corny-sounding rank
26 "My feelings exactly!"
29 Punch sound in comics
31 Marathon division
32 "August: ___ County"
34 Six-pack units
35 Name that's a shorter version of Felix (in a sense)
37 TiVo forerunner
39 Fountain choice

**40** Bloodsucking beings
**41** Red "Sesame Street" puppet
**44** Enjoy some shrimp dumplings, say
**45** Acting legend Meryl
**46** Person worth holding on to
**47** Run out
**49** Dish often filled and folded
**52** In favor of
**53** Game show host
**54** "Silly me!"
**57** Yard sale caveat
**58** Puts frosting on

**60** Discipline with throws
**62** Energy
**63** Primatologist's study
**64** Animation sheet hidden in "Justice League"
**65** Med. care provider

# 21
## AA BATTERY
By Gail Grabowski

**ACROSS**

1 North Pole surname
6 Brooch adornments
10 Phone downloads
14 Specialized vocabulary
15 Completely engrossed
16 You're reading one now
17 Namesake of the world's largest tennis stadium
19 Struggling to decide
20 "What had happened ___ . . ."
21 Talk wildly
22 Made revisions to
24 Battery fluid
25 "Where to Begin," author ___ Wade
26 Mahalia Jackson's music
29 Specialist in the study of plant life
33 Posteriors
34 Pilot's rite of passage
35 From scratch
36 Brief list shortener
37 Michigan or Minnesota, for example
38 Convenience store inconvenience
39 "Meet the Parents" star Polo
40 That woman's
41 Not relaxed
42 Blood vessels
44 Flea ___
45 Actress Lily-Rose
46 It might contain an emoji

47 Reliable
50 "Brown Skin ___" (Beyonce song)
51 Rowing implement
54 Sound of feline bliss
55 Math measurement that's less than 90 degrees
58 Somewhat
59 Honest-to-goodness
60 "___ fail me"
61 Biological pouches
62 Planetarium part
63 Workout byproduct

**DOWN**

1 Paw protrusion
2 Currency of Turkey
3 Aardvark's meal
4 "That's awful!"
5 Journalists' assets
6 Majestic
7 Rightmost point on a compass rose
8 NASCAR stat
9 Work boot feature
10 Mobilizing message
11 Parcel of land
12 ___ Barre (fitness studio chain)
13 Email button
18 Train track part
23 Anti-narcotics org.
24 They're not fine
25 Future stallions
26 Movie legend Garbo

**27** Word before "space" or "limits"
**28** ___ aleck
**29** Male razorbacks
**30** Confident way to solve crosswords
**31** Have a hunch
**32** Communicate with followers, perhaps
**34** Sharply inclined
**37** Where a liner may be repaired
**41** Legislation regarding levies

**43** Wine selection
**44** ___ mortals
**46** Championship
**47** Rejuvenation destinations
**48** Hefty horn
**49** Ex-A.G. Holder
**50** Largest of the Mariana Islands
**51** Shrek's species
**52** Alan of "M*A*S*H"
**53** Take it easy
**56** Business VIP
**57** "I don't have all day!"

# 22
## ADVANCING AGE
By Mark McClain

**ACROSS**
1 Half-melted snow
6 Temporary condition
11 Lowest of the three-letter body parts
14 2020 Summer Olympics city
15 Less often seen
16 "You know I ___ to do it to 'em"
17 Marvel TV show whose protagonist's first name was Peggy
19 "Now I get it!"
20 Pear variety
21 Tub top
22 Conductor's stand
24 ___ Angeles Lakers
25 Have the courage
26 Over-the-top
31 Graduating senior's decoration project
34 Guiding principles
35 Furnish with new parts
38 Take a sip of
39 "It Ain't Over ___ It's Over"
40 Come into existence
41 Not to be taken seriously
43 Upscale Honda cars
44 ___ Diego Padres
45 Word after "civic" or "prior"
47 Land measure
49 Young fellow
50 Salad with croutons
53 Papa Pope's first name on "Scandal"

54 Avoid
58 Elbow location
59 Softball practice enclosure
62 Luau garland
63 Furious
64 Some House of Lords members
65 Wrestling surface
66 Canceled
67 Regina King has won four

**DOWN**
1 Attempt
2 Corporate emblem
3 Luau instruments, for short
4 Align, as devices
5 Scorching
6 Heap compliments on
7 Far from easy
8 Kimberly Drew's field
9 Intentionally overlook
10 Blunder
11 Tom kha cuisine
12 Honolulu's island
13 Gouda's countrymate
18 Folk dancing shoes
23 Appropriate behavior
24 Fully loaded
25 One-on-one battle
26 Prefix meaning "eight"
27 Mountain range between Europe and Asia
28 Electric car brand
29 Eye parts that receive images

**USA TODAY**

**Down**

**30** Letter-shaped gasket also known as a toric joint
**32** In flames
**33** Person who lives near the Leaning Tower
**36** Went in a hurry
**37** Teacher's creation
**39** "Name That ___"
**42** Upscale Italian car
**43** Once more
**46** United by treaty
**48** Airplane compartment
**50** Not nervous

**51** General vicinity
**52** Give off
**53** Suffix for "kitchen"
**54** Many a robocall
**55** "First, do no ___"
**56** Like an eyesore
**57** Loch ___ monster
**60** ___ evasion
**61** Word of astonishment

# 23
## SNAKES ALIVE!
By Tracy Gray

**ACROSS**

1 They often wear black
6 Play for ___
11 Tobacco-regulating grp.
14 Nook or Kindle download
15 Dried poblano
16 Sushi bar selection
17 British comedy group with a "Flying Circus"
19 Picnic pest
20 Ooze through a crack
21 Baseball's "Hammerin' Hank"
22 Encouraging lead-in to "boy" or "girl"
23 "___ Star" (1983 Madonna hit)
25 Artist M.C.
27 App releases containing bug fixes
30 Duke or Duchess
31 Emulated an owl
32 Prong on a pitchfork
33 How oysters may be eaten
36 ___ times (the past)
37 Banana Republic's parent company
38 Torah teacher
40 Monopolize
41 Hearty drink from a flask
43 Like a sponge
44 Perrier competitor
46 Atmospheric science study
47 Jesmyn Ward creations
49 Fly-by-night
50 Leave out

51 Mirren with many royal roles
53 Makeshift seat at a barn dance
57 Genre for Nicki Minaj and Cardi B
58 "The Fast and the Furious" competitor
60 ___-crab soup
61 Some heels
62 Flower hidden in "Michaelmas term"
63 Organ with a stirrup
64 Taper off
65 Classroom furniture

**DOWN**

1 Jade and jasper, for two
2 Instrument used for tuning
3 Vocal inflection
4 Dorm room appliance
5 Pie in the ___
6 Summer Olympics vessels
7 Contest submission
8 Navigation aid for a bat
9 Not devote much effort to
10 Ronan, to Mia Farrow
11 Fluffy accessory
12 Al ___ (pasta phrase)
13 Place to exchange vows
18 Walked anxiously
22 Knee part, for short
24 Ladle or grater
26 Pro sports no-no
27 "I'm toast!"

**USA TODAY**

**28** Collared shirt
**29** Car with a V10 engine
**30** Felt-___ pen
**32** Game with "it"
**34** Share a boundary
**35** Prudent
**37** ___ rummy (card game)
**39** Fort Bragg or Fort Bliss, e.g.
**42** Basin for clothes
**43** Place secretly
**45** Doc for a collie or calico
**46** Pizza type
**47** Like Thor

**48** City on the Missouri River
**49** Took a catnap
**52** Singer Franklin
**54** Plays a role
**55** Vichyssoise veggie
**56** Hits "reply all" instead of "reply," say
**58** Place for eyebrow threading
**59** Cool

# 24
## VOWEL TERRITORY
By Evan Kalish

**ACROSS**

1 Anti-vaping spot, say
4 iPhone voice
8 Fedoras and such
12 "___ a Shame" (Spinners hit)
13 Chasm
15 Londoner, for one
16 Cheeseburgers on bread
19 Prefix meaning "all"
20 Cultural value system
21 Enjoys some almojabanas, say
23 Participated in a 5K
24 Amounts of money
25 Opposite of heavy lifting, in a sense
28 North African expanse
30 "___ are red . . ."
31 Drug officer, for short
33 Like cured meats
34 Wallowers throw them
37 Truck treats
38 Gwendolyn Brooks or Ocean Vuong
39 Philosopher Kierkegaard
40 Dismays
44 "Body part" prone to profanity
48 The "A" in UAE
50 Control-___-Delete
51 Grammy winner Aimee
52 Give a speech
53 MLB 14-Down
55 Paint removal tool
58 ". . . and then ___!"
59 First half of an LP
60 Parking area
61 One in upper mgmt.
62 Catch sight of
63 Most promgoers (Abbr.)

**DOWN**

1 Church organ components
2 "Stick to the ___ Quo"
3 Breathing condition
4 Articulates
5 Co. that developed the floppy disk
6 16-Across bread
7 Speck of land in the ocean
8 Cable channel home to "Watchmen"
9 Airplane seat dividers
10 "30 Rock" creator
11 Job durations
14 Bit of data
17 Reggae singer Peter
18 Pig's spot
22 In dire ___
25 Appeals to a higher power
26 SyFy's "Wynonna ___"
27 Nit to pick with a plot
29 "Early," to "late," e.g.
32 Upper limit
33 Hoops star Curry
34 Like a 10-hour-a-week job
35 Rapper who plays Fin Tutuola
36 Competition that's not close
37 Repairperson's organizer

**39** Few and far between
**41** Merit
**42** Hiker's paths
**43** Took, as an exam
**45** Atlas page
**46** Burden
**47** Release from ropes
**49** Red veggies from Schrute Farms
**52** "I approve"
**54** "Just a ___!" ("Be there momentarily!")

**56** Six-point football feats, for short
**57** "Uh-huh"

# 25
## HIDDEN CAMERAS
By Zhouqin Burnikel

**ACROSS**

1 Black-and-white whale
5 Cheesy sandwiches
10 Visibility problem
14 Perceive by touch
15 Greek salad tidbit
16 Spelunker's hangout
17 Has-been
19 Flat-pack furniture store
20 South American pack animal
21 "Harper Valley PTA" star Barbara
23 Get it wrong
24 Part of an egg used in mayonnaise
26 Oscar night slights
28 "Just ___ feared!"
31 Android counterpart
33 Go off-script
35 Lamb's dad
36 Barbecue remnants
38 Slalom course markers
40 Jazz quartet, for one
43 Condescending sort
44 Comes to a standstill
45 Not well
46 "The Addams Family" star John
48 "Where Did ___ Love Go" (Supremes hit)
49 Shaving goop
50 Christmas candy shapes
52 Lobster part
55 Luxury resort amenity
57 Transcript stats
59 "In my bag," e.g.
62 Long-lasting hairdo
64 Fastener with a hexagonal socket
67 Length times width, for a rectangle
68 Parental ___
69 McKinnon or Micucci in "Nature Cat"
70 Wearing nothing
71 "Grr . . ."
72 Vehicle for Blair Braverman

**DOWN**

1 Not scheduled to work
2 Bona fide
3 Honeycomb part
4 Lessen, as fears
5 Portrait stolen in 1911, with Picasso as a suspect
6 Golfer Ernie
7 Miller ___
8 Small-screen commercials
9 Williams with seven Wimbledon wins
10 Poli ___ (college major)
11 Achieves huge success
12 Finished
13 Equipment
18 Genre hidden in The Movielife
22 Elbows gently
25 JCPenney competitor
27 "Kapow!"

**28** Kept at ___ length
**29** Steamy room
**30** Sarcastic response to a threat
**32** Look after
**34** Book-loving Disney princess
**36** Performing in a movie
**37** Pig's nose
**39** Unload
**41** Vowel that follows theta
**42** Injured, perhaps
**47** Kathmandu native
**51** State capital on the Willamette River

**53** Cards in wallets
**54** Signs of canine affection
**55** Stretch across
**56** Lima's country
**58** Close with a bang
**60** Like some arguments
**61** Anagram and homophone of "meet"
**63** Sallie ___
**65** "Deliver Us From ___"
**66** Get married

## 26
# BEFORE BED
By Martha Kimes

**ACROSS**

1 "Look what I did!"
5 Pollution portmanteau
9 Period of sudden growth
14 Refined, like some cheddar
15 There's no place like it
16 Vietnam's capital
17 Party where you might eat haupia
18 "Z ___ zebra"
19 The "Pokemon" TV series, e.g.
20 S.Pellegrino or LaCroix
23 BMW competitor
24 "A Nightmare on ___ Street"
25 Band aid
28 Moguls
31 Palindromic term of address
34 Depart
36 Explosive material
37 "Roll Tide" school, for short
38 Soap set in Port Charles
42 "Look ___ this way . . ."
43 "Get it?"
44 Saying
45 Key in the top left
46 Toilet paper that Mr. Whipple begged shoppers not to squeeze
49 Sycophant's answer
50 ___'s Homemade pasta sauce
51 "So true!"
53 Clown's accessory
61 Mixologist's measure

62 Morrison who wrote "Beloved"
63 Actor Malek
64 Greek god of the dead
65 Bible garden
66 Excursion
67 Scents
68 ___ out (distribute)
69 Roll-call response

**DOWN**

1 Mineral low on the Mohs scale
2 Fire : fuego :: water : ___
3 "___ diary . . ."
4 Uzo who voiced Bismuth in "Steven Universe"
5 Beer-and-lemonade drink
6 Artwork made of tesserae
7 Not mention
8 ___ pool
9 Warm wraps
10 The ___ Games
11 Squad
12 Italy's capital
13 Seating level
21 External
22 Fender-bender results
25 Pond scum
26 Is introduced to
27 Lose your cool
29 Catchall category
30 Priscilla of makeup
31 Indonesian skewer dish
32 Publicist's concern

**USA TODAY**

**33** Auction actions
**35** Lab doc
**37** Auction action
**39** Equally trendy
**40** Actress/comedian DeLaria
**41** Team of judges
**46** Affectionate touch
**47** Fridge ornament
**48** "Everything's OK"
**50** Utensil with small holes
**52** Up, on a map
**53** Neighborhood in Manhattan or London

**54** Campus courtyard
**55** Reverse
**56** Big-ticket ___
**57** Connecting point
**58** Suffix for "soft" or "share"
**59** Dubai dignitary
**60** Ready to be picked

# 27
## IN THE WAY
By Gail Grabowski

**ACROSS**

1 Feels sore
6 Towns, on maps
10 Skyline haze
14 Sipped or swigged
15 Tidbit from a think tank
16 Goldie of "The First Wives Club"
17 Time for cake, perhaps
19 Swedish megastore with a museum
20 Grabbed a bite
21 Misfortunes
22 Completely tired
23 Maintains, as a lawn
25 Unruly demonstrations
27 Budgetary indiscretion
31 In search of
34 Certain lunch spot
35 Investment initials
36 "C'est la ___!"
37 Spine-tingling
39 Nanny ___
40 Breakfast beverages, briefly
41 Substandard
42 Williams who played Scooter on "Living Single"
44 At once
48 Sounds from a Siamese
49 Can't tolerate
53 Scrunchie's place, at times
55 Snorkeling gear
56 Museum display
57 Sword handle
58 Mickey Mouse co-creator
61 Object of adoration
62 Bar soap additive
63 Damage beyond repair
64 Tennis player Sampras
65 Have to have
66 Digging tool

**DOWN**

1 Marketing showdown
2 Largest Greek island
3 Mythical netherworld
4 Put a stop to
5 Garb for tackling moguls
6 Condensed magazine
7 "What are the ___?"
8 Drink with crumpets
9 Utter
10 Words on a package label
11 Tries to appease someone
12 "A Prayer for ___ Meany"
13 Pesky flying insect
18 Head-moving assents
22 Vague amount
24 Fleecy female
25 Have a hearty laugh
26 Far from certain
28 Online birthday greeting
29 Periods named for music genres, at times
30 Thanksgiving side dish
31 Proclaim publicly
32 Pacific island nation
33 Person trying out a new plane

**37** Tart-tasting
**38** No-frills beds
**41** Cruise stopover
**42** Looks after a Siamese
**43** Reuben bread
**45** Work hard
**46** Changed, as crossword clues
**47** Provide temporarily
**50** Seasonal mall hiree
**51** Pattern on a sole
**52** Fashion sense
**53** Miracle ___
**54** Roller coaster, e.g.

**55** Floating sheet of ice
**58** Obi-___ Kenobi
**59** Pub beverage
**60** How it's always done, initially

# 28
# WINDOW BOXES

By Patrick Jordan

## ACROSS

1 Silent-letter obligation
5 "I double-dog ___ you!"
9 Pajama halves
13 Hemmed in by
14 Decongestant spray brand
15 Comprehending reply
16 Moves back and forth
17 Diagonally cut pasta
18 "You gotta help me!" for one
19 ___ it in the bud
20 Streaking celestial event
22 Step-in-and-go shoes
24 CNBC interviewee's title, maybe
25 Chunk of earth
26 Battle involving markdowns
31 Prepared to ride
33 School day segment
34 "The truth is out!"
35 Have a common edge with
36 Truce outcome, ideally
37 Team that might serve two-masters
38 Part of rpm or mpg
39 Easter egg bringer
40 Bribers grease them
41 Driver's license prerequisites
43 Scrabble formation
44 "___ about time!"
45 Camp shelter securer
48 South Florida lagoon
53 "___ to Dalya's Bald Spot" (Angel Nafis poem)

54 "Check that out!"
55 Apply dye to
56 Identical ___
57 Unexpectedly missing
58 Intense pain
59 Faith-based breakaway
60 The ___ of my existence
61 Muscle or voice quality
62 Crafts' counterparts

## DOWN

1 Early times
2 Spam, e.g.
3 The forest, vis-a-vis the trees
4 Football successes (Abbr.)
5 Eating regimens
6 "Agnes Grey" author Bronte
7 City in Grenoble, in a sense
8 Pole dancing, e.g.
9 Step surreptitiously
10 Capital south of Lillehammer
11 Equal in society
12 Sewing join
14 Blow some dough
20 Orbiter with phases
21 Min. fragments
23 Secret scheme
26 They're made for the future
27 Risque
28 Influential country
29 Throat-clearing sound
30 Seating sections
31 Show amazement
32 Take orders from

**33** Candy price, once

**36** "The Owl and the ___"

**37** Golf vehicle

**39** ___ version

**40** Animal that might know one trick

**42** Throat annoyance

**43** Ready to rest

**45** Pricey steak

**46** Monarch's order

**47** Chaps

**48** Spill the secret

**49** "The Music Man" state

**50** Any moment now

**51** Nonstarter

**52** North Carolina university

**56** Bag-screening org.

# 29
## LINKEDIN
By Zhouqin Burnikel

**ACROSS**

1 Boca ___, Florida
6 Word associated with both "ore" and "roe"
11 Browser subwindow
14 Weasel out of
15 All fired up
16 Palette choice
17 Pension, e.g.
19 "Chances ___" (Johnny Mathis hit)
20 Prefix for "gruntled"
21 Docs' degrees
22 General Motors emergency service
24 Gets droopy
26 Brought to a close
27 City in the Dallas-Fort Worth metroplex
29 Sports bar fixtures
30 Agitate
33 Antagonist on "Power"
34 "My Cousin Vinny" star Marisa
36 "___, vidi, vici"
37 Personal stakes
41 Two tablets, e.g.
42 Pong maker
43 Nest egg for the golden yrs.
44 X-Ray ___
45 Some world leaders, for short
46 "___: Battle Angel" (2019 action film starring Rosa Salazar)
48 Diameter halves

50 Like most flea market items
51 Grad student's paper
53 Actor Vigoda
54 "Yuck!"
57 Crank up, as an engine
58 Banquet for a diplomatic visit
62 "BMO" singer Lennox
63 "The ___ Purple"
64 Drum kit item
65 Amigo
66 Shuts with force
67 Lugged around

**DOWN**

1 Hockey official
2 Like a diehard fan
3 Airport vehicle
4 Setting of the movie "Friday Night Lights"
5 Nancy Drew's boyfriend
6 Drops in the mail
7 Apples discussed on AppleInsider.com
8 Braggart's attribute
9 "When life gives you ___ . . ."
10 Latest fashion
11 "I've had enough!"
12 Preternatural glow
13 Pub crawl beverage
18 "No thanks"
23 Start a tennis game
25 Stud poker bet
26 "Buenos Aires" musical
27 Before surgery, for short

**28** Better of two bad choices
**29** Campground shelters
**31** Prefix for "venous"
**32** "The Comeback" star Kudrow
**33** Music : CDs :: movies : ___
**35** Little Havana's city
**38** State home to 27-Across and 4-Down
**39** Wiped away
**40** Make angry
**45** Water ___ (toy)
**47** "No clue!"
**49** Frisbee golf equipment

**50** Airport vehicles
**51** Chess ruse
**52** Greek equivalent of Juno
**53** Part of a molecule
**55** Buzzing pest
**56** "Present!"
**59** Arroz ___ valenciana
**60** Suffix for "loyal" or "royal"
**61** Unwanted tape hue

# 30
## SHE SHE
By Rachel Fabi

**ACROSS**

1 Backdrops for meteorologists
5 Wheat is separated from it
10 Feathery scarves
14 Setting of the graphic novel "Persepolis"
15 Center-to-circumference lines
16 "Yeah . . . that's wrong"
17 Gospel singer with 12 Grammys
19 "Do you ___?!"
20 Respects
21 Part of an Arnold Palmer
23 Stat governed by MLB Rule 9.04
24 Cliched
25 Has
28 "The Real Housewives of Atlanta" star
33 Letter after pi
34 Cast a ___ over
35 Influencer's goal
36 Scarf or wolf
37 Type
38 Fitting
40 Pristina-born pop star Rita
41 Genetic copy
43 They may get bruised or inflated
44 Colorful pond fish
45 "Hustlers" star who coined the phrase "Sorry to this man"
48 Space Race rival of the U.S.
49 Luigi rescues him in Luigi's Mansion 3
50 Try to win a seat

52 Start to knead?
55 Singer Nancy or Frank
59 Magnum ___
60 Rock star known for "Take Me Away" and "Ghost"
62 Bus price
63 By means of
64 Most recent
65 Poses the question
66 Singer with the album "Melodrama"
67 Time periods

**DOWN**

1 Cinderella's helpers
2 Violent Greek god
3 Treaty
4 Derisive looks
5 ___ justice
6 "Die Hard" villain Gruber
7 Org. whose seal appears on toothpastes
8 Countable
9 Finance-related
10 Short end of the stick
11 Redact, perhaps
12 Name before "of Cleves" or "of Green Gables"
13 Pop
18 Internet
22 Chooses
24 NBC sketch show
25 Vacuum brand

26 Big blue creature in the American Museum of Natural History
27 Unacceptable
29 Deer also known as wapiti
30 Eccentrics
31 French money
32 "Life for me ain't been no crystal ___" (Langston Hughes line)
34 Baking tin
38 Number in a bio
39 Bear food, in a fairy tale
42 Sworn enemies
43 Something Corporate genre

46 Skilled
47 In this manner
48 Lacking the skill
51 Card game with a 2019 Braille version
52 Couch
53 Some bitter brews, for short
54 Stay in the shadows
55 Mail
56 Old Russian ruler
57 Activist Parks
58 Insects in formicaries
61 Many a Christmas tree

# 31
# DOUBLESPEAK

By Caitlin Reid

**ACROSS**

1 Number of winks in a nap
6 Strikebreaker
10 Symbol on the Texas flag
14 Scott Joplin's "Treemonisha," e.g.
15 Food in a hard or soft shell
16 Smoothie seeds
17 Escorted over the threshold
18 Hairstyle for a special occasion, perhaps
19 Pay to borrow
20 "Can I come in?"
22 The "A" of STEAM education
23 Brewery barrels
24 Completely erase
26 Tabloid subject, for short
28 Place for a welcome mat
32 They might be e-filed
33 Accessory for a prom queen
34 ___-haw (donkey's bray)
35 Marching insects
36 Cloud of bees
37 Shelter that's pitched
38 In favor of
39 Successors
40 Hoops game named after an animal
41 Occasion to dine with dolls
43 Mariah whose first four singles all topped the Billboard chart
44 Freedom from worry
45 Bump on a toad

46 Sly
48 "Sleep tight"
54 Deeds
55 Fruit with as many syllables as vowels
56 Patchwork elephant of kidlit
57 Drive-___
58 Result of a fender bender
59 Video replay effect
60 Substance in bars
61 Slight advantage
62 Spunky

**DOWN**

1 "The Souls of Black ___"
2 Word before "seas" or "season"
3 Try again
4 Slowly drips
5 Big Apple baseball team
6 Leaves speechless, maybe
7 Tool for a guitarist
8 "Back in Black" band
9 Frequent library patron
10 Leftovers
11 "Everything's going to be OK"
12 "If it ___ broke . . ."
13 "Aw, darn!"
21 USSR agency
25 Type of savings plan, for short
26 Lake vessel
27 "Read all about it!"
28 Private log
29 Rowboat needs

USA TODAY

**30** Itty-bitty
**31** Pilot ___ ("The Bachelor" nickname)
**32** President after Roosevelt (the first one)
**33** Fool
**36** Sing to
**37** Soup ingredient
**39** Owns
**40** Control, as energy
**42** Settles a debt
**43** "Breaking ___ News" (comic strip about furry reporters)
**45** Like some teeth and lies
**46** Nutrition label listings
**47** Cuatro + cuatro
**49** Applied a freezer pack to
**50** Kool's backing
**51** Results of some modern engineering (Abbr.)
**52** Sewing finishes
**53** "Iliad" setting

# 32
## AT YOUR BIG AGE?
By Gail Grabowski

**ACROSS**

1 Work hard
6 Kibbles 'n Bits competitor
10 "___ was I ere I saw Elba"
14 La Scala performance
15 Pitcher Doolittle
16 Quick haircut
17 Parks and such
19 Borscht veggie
20 "___ there's a will . . ."
21 Auditions for a part
22 Astronaut's assignment
26 Halloween costume part
27 Get some air
28 Devices for streaming
32 Almost bring to a boil
33 Vehicle for Bessie Coleman
34 Cut with an ax
35 Golfer's warning
36 Skeptical
37 "The Ghost and Mrs. Muir" star Tierney
38 "If you ask me," in tweets
39 Former fillies
40 Tour leader
41 Reacted to a stressful situation
43 Wavee Dave, for Jackson State University
44 Obedience school command
45 Headgear for horses
46 NBA exec Brand
48 ___ peppers
50 Bouncer's post
51 Portable wrinkle remover
56 Not even one
57 In need of a massage, perhaps
58 Person handling the intros
59 Tailless primates
60 Some coding projects
61 Style of Bridget Riley paintings

**DOWN**

1 Ship diary
2 Earth Day mo.
3 "Full Frontal" host Samantha
4 Source of lead
5 Got out of hand
6 Quaking tree
7 Shakespearean king
8 Tempo
9 Ace's value, at times
10 If all goes right
11 Strike up a conversation, say
12 Twisted the truth
13 Defib experts
18 Sandal or clog
21 Quite uncommon
22 Square peg in a round hole
23 ___ tax
24 Best Actress nominee for "Casino"
25 Realtor's goal
26 Numerous
28 Get some shut-eye
29 Planned destination of the Rosalind Franklin rover

---

**30** Ballpark hot dog seller, e.g.
**31** Candy and cookies
**33** Chile's northern neighbor
**36** "A Black ___ Sketch Show"
**37** Burst of wind
**39** Like the Grinch
**40** Astronomer who clashed with Pope Urban VIII
**42** Puts away for later
**43** Rooster or gander
**45** Honeycomb sites
**46** "Show Boat" author Ferber
**47** Out of the ___

**48** Farmer's plant
**49** Plucked instrument
**51** PreCheck org.
**52** Little rascal
**53** Brand of 28-Across
**54** "___ the fields we go . . ."
**55** Tennis court divider

# 33
## PLAY PLACES
By Evan Kalish

### ACROSS
**1** Mont Blanc's mountain range
**5** ___ bran
**8** Flavor-enhancing additive, for short
**11** Saltwater expanses
**13** Mythical creature in "Puss in Boots"
**15** ___ out a living
**16** Landmark near Waikiki
**18** "It's Raining ___"
**19** Unusual
**20** Shearing target
**21** Spry
**23** Comedian Rudner
**25** Savage X Fenty buys
**27** Prefix for "arm" or "cast"
**28** Suffix for "micro" or "stetho"
**30** Some strays
**33** Mining target
**35** Hoops asset
**36** String snarl
**37** Breakfast meat
**41** Insulating handwear
**43** Sneaky "Hey, you!"
**44** America's national tree
**46** Pekoe, e.g.
**47** Outside-the-classroom adventure
**50** "See ya in the morning"
**54** Family diagram
**55** Ginger ___
**57** Spreader of falsehoods
**58** Admits a shortcoming, say
**60** Bit of rain
**62** Compete
**63** Wasabi-coated legume
**64** Commands from a judge
**67** Ulna's place
**68** "You're something ___"
**69** Follows incessantly
**70** Singer Kodi
**71** ___ jokes
**72** Just alright

### DOWN
**1** Like orange juice and vinegar
**2** Result in
**3** Cooking spray brand
**4** Winter precipitation
**5** "Look at you, all fancy-schmancy!"
**6** Get older
**7** "Sorry for Your Loss" star Kelly Marie ___
**8** Cellular barrier
**9** "Why did the ___ cross the road? To get to the body shop"
**10** Scientific inheritance
**11** Stenches
**12** Hoity-toity type
**14** Enlighten
**17** "___ the Explorer"
**22** Nojito or Virgin Mary
**24** New Testament disciples
**26** Like 100-to-1 odds
**29** Are backward

**31** Radiate, as light
**32** Ave. crossers
**34** Four-award feat, for short
**37** 30 or 50, often
**38** So to speak
**39** Something to type on a login page
**40** Units of corn
**42** Number of amendments in the Bill of Rights
**45** Octavia Butler novel
**48** Remove frost from an airplane's wings

**49** Role for an actor
**51** "Boomerang" actress Robin
**52** Stylist's creation
**53** 52-Down curl
**56** Winnie the ___
**58** Gemstone with a "fire" variety
**59** Informed verbally
**61** Positives, in decision-making
**65** "Born in the ___" (Springsteen song)
**66** Twosome

# 34
## OPEC MEETING
By Zhouqin Burnikel

**ACROSS**

1 Short records, for short
4 Cookware brand hidden in "crestfallen"
8 Pool hall triangles
13 Take a tumble
15 "If all ___ fails . . ."
16 Without a companion
17 Cedar-lined piece of furniture
19 ___ mignon
20 "Who you tellin'?"
21 Letters on a sunscreen bottle
23 ___ Moines, Iowa
24 Camp bed
25 "Super" grps.
27 Snowman in "Frozen 2"
29 She played Donatella Versace
33 Runner-up in a race
36 Commercials
37 Spanish for "bull"
38 The British ___
39 Ginger ___
40 "Exactly!"
41 "That's ___ blow!"
42 Big-leaguer
43 Gets the pot started
44 Gym class exercise
48 Machu Picchu's country
49 Perform in a glee club
50 "What ___ I tell you?"
53 Sneaky
55 Concert device
57 Fondue cheese
59 Like some gumbo and jambalaya
61 Basketball competition won by Dinamo Sassari in 2019
63 Squirrel's nut
64 Stat measured in square miles
65 Jazz player's showcase
66 Itsy-bitsy
67 Youthful-sounding surname
68 So far

**DOWN**

1 Moral code
2 Show preview
3 Nurse, as a drink
4 National Library of Iran city
5 Warm jacket
6 Rude person
7 "I'm game!"
8 Fundraising lottery
9 Stand-up comedian Wong
10 It ushers in chilly weather
11 Silent-letter body part
12 Stage backdrops
14 Cathedral bench
18 Silly antics
22 Dad
26 Zigzags downhill
28 Embodying a character
29 Rhyming youth sports level
30 "___ to Gossips" (Safia Elhillo poem)
31 Strong desire

**USA TODAY**

32 Chaotic scenes
33 Teller of tall tales
34 Home to Norway's Royal Palace
35 Ground beef sandwich
39 Grande's nickname
40 Do a ___ job
42 Fruit used to make duck sauce
45 Nook's counterpart
46 Brand of cinnamon gum or cream soda
47 Bit of progress
50 Wooden duck, e.g.

51 "When ___ the World" (LIZ song)
52 Train terminal
53 Improvise like Ella Fitzgerald
54 Lingerie material
56 High point
58 "I'd be glad to!"
60 Caterer's dispenser
62 Ocean State sch.

# 35
## PARK IN THE BACK
By Mark McClain

### ACROSS
1 European mountain range
5 ___ Verde National Park
9 Bleating youngster
13 Kindle competitor
14 Chilling in a bucket, say
16 Scent
17 Drink mixer that contains quinine
19 Underground habitat
20 Word after "loose" or "tight"
21 Grain for paella
22 Wandered around
24 Graphic design choice
25 Saint ___, Minnesota
26 TV shoot
29 Gave professional guidance
33 Boot-shaped country
34 Tournament ranking
35 Horror
36 Glossary item
37 "___ to Your Beautiful" (Alessia Cara song)
38 "The Read With Kid Fury and Crissle West" channel
39 Shopper's document
40 Foldable beds
41 Trends upward
42 Forever
44 School break
45 Aid and ___
46 In this very spot
47 Boulevard divider
50 Neighbor of Missouri

51 Put some ___ in your step
54 Like unwritten contracts
55 Absorbent sphere
58 Part of a fork
59 ___ beaver
60 In addition
61 With 23-Down, listen to
62 Traditional music genre
63 Take to heart

### DOWN
1 Prefix for "chamber"
2 Bird on the Canadian dollar coin
3 Small body of water
4 Bit of Winter Olympics equipment
5 Lawn care chore
6 Pass into law
7 Webpage
8 Quick tennis point
9 Mayor or councilwoman
10 Journalist Serwer
11 Chess turn
12 Born and ___
15 Personal assistants might run them
18 Partner in crime
23 See 61-Across
24 Hollywood preview
25 Equals
26 Screenplay starter
27 Faceplanted, say
28 Analyze grammatically

**29** Substantial
**30** Reduce, ___, recycle
**31** Makes less strict
**32** Put on clothes
**34** "The Way" singer Jill
**37** Physics, e.g.
**41** Showed again
**43** League in which Lusia Harris was drafted in 1977
**44** Overhaul
**46** B&B alternative
**47** Insect in an evolutionary "arms race" against bats

**48** Pennsylvania city
**49** "Phoebe and Her Unicorn" author Simpson
**50** "Don't let ___ to your head!"
**51** The "P" of IPA
**52** Other than this
**53** Proceed slowly
**56** Clumsy person
**57** "___ gawd, that's [insert pro wrestler]'s music!"

# 36
## MLK DAY
By Caitlin Reid

**ACROSS**

1 Yellow-orange hue
6 Knocks
10 Items at tire shops
14 Boxer Ali
15 Indonesian vacation destination
16 Thought
17 City where King wrote about "shallow understanding from people of good will"
19 Standard
20 Not tied, as shoelaces
21 Cozy up to
23 Septiembre o mayo
24 Short-lived craze
26 Talk indiscreetly
27 Glossy material
29 Franklin, Queen of Soul
33 Shoulder covering
36 Expansive
38 Shrunken Asian sea
39 Accepting this award, King spoke of "the known pilots and the unknown ground crew" of the civil rights movement
42 "___ upon a time . . ."
43 Black-and-white predator
44 Witch's works
45 Grant, as a gift
47 ___ commitment
49 "How do you like ___ apples?"
51 Very long period

52 Snarling sound
55 Left speechless, maybe
58 ___ roast
60 "And, I might add . . ."
61 Spiritual referenced in King's "I Have a Dream" speech
63 Defeat
64 Campus near Hollywood
65 Adjust for fit
66 "Late Night" host Meyers
67 Melodious accent
68 Long-winded

**DOWN**

1 Musician's project
2 State bordering Quebec
3 Frequent tweeters
4 Red Muppet
5 Desert rarity
6 "Notorious" SCOTUS member
7 Oohs and ___
8 Backup strategy
9 Mimic
10 Wedding party member with a pillow, maybe
11 Person put on a pedestal
12 More than a ___ coincidence
13 "Stay With Me" singer Smith
18 "Cool!"
22 Fish hidden in "kangaroo"
25 Scuba enthusiast
27 Dessert lover's "body part"
28 Spingarn Medal org.
30 "Silly rabbit! ___ are for kids!"

**31** Smog, for example
**32** Pub purchases
**33** Elitist
**34** Sharpen, as skills
**35** Preschool basics
**37** Terrify
**40** Really poignant, say
**41** "Game" of swapping voicemail messages
**46** "Well, looky here!"
**48** Des Moines state
**50** Parisian "thank you"
**52** Tiny pests

**53** Goes up
**54** Have another go at
**55** Make an escape
**56** Future atty.'s exam
**57** Farmer's location in a nursery rhyme
**59** SNCC activist Baker
**60** Six-pack muscles
**62** Grab grub

# 37
## DOUBLE A
By Zhouqin Burnikel

**ACROSS**

1 Glitzy fundraiser
5 ___ your stuff
10 Untidy person
14 Mooring spot
15 Surfaced
16 Fruit with fuzzy skin
17 In circles
20 "___ and Soul"
21 "Guy walks into ___ ..."
22 Messy bagel variety
25 To boot
29 Whisper tenderly
30 Performing in a theater
34 "Keep It" host ___ Madison III
35 Conclude through logic
37 "___ Miserables"
38 Discourage
40 Practically forever
43 "Star Trek" antagonists
45 In first place
46 Fails to keep pace
49 Org. with many schedules
50 Hardwood floor cover
51 Microbrewery option, for short
53 ___-la-la
54 "Warmer"
56 Catch in a sting operation, perhaps
58 Repeatedly
62 Haughty sort
63 Creme-filled cookies
64 GOT7 genre

66 Person who's looked up to
67 Dame, e.g.
68 "Boo'd Up" singer ___ Mai
69 Took the bus
70 Made less difficult
71 Make leakproof

**DOWN**

1 College transcript figure
2 Lung filler
3 Sign before Virgo
4 Island near Curacao
5 Make glum
6 Breakfast-in-bed holder
7 "Kim Possible" character ___ Stoppable
8 Letters on packages of meat
9 Oolong holder
10 Golf garment
11 "Elementary" star Lucy
12 Totally dominate
13 eBay action
18 "Enough already!"
19 Like "Monsters, Inc."
22 ___-fi
23 Billion-year period
24 "Early signs are encouraging"
26 Gets three RBIs, perhaps
27 "___ you with me?"
28 Road repair substance
31 Challenge for new immigrants
32 Carnival shelter
33 "Same here!"

**36** Item in an Easter basket
**39** Fish often grilled with sweet soy sauce
**41** Musician's mishap
**42** Mollified
**43** Ballpoint brand
**44** Disney World city
**47** Bar food
**48** Maple tree output
**50** Chain that sells camping gear
**52** "Brokeback Mountain" director Lee
**55** Relative of the pine marten
**57** Personal points of view
**59** Soprano's solo
**60** Tennis court fixtures
**61** Mete substitute
**62** Address for a knight
**65** Friend

# 38

# SOLID REASONING

By Patrick Jordan

## ACROSS

1 Spanish for "mother"
6 Play energetically
10 Put whipped cream on, say
13 Aquatic Disney princess
14 Like some chords
15 Megalomaniac's problem
16 27 or 64
18 Curator's stuff
19 Become baggy
20 Coastal inlets
21 Cabbies collect them
23 Follow through on
25 Keep ___ on (monitor)
26 Mauna Kea formation
32 Traffic light color
35 Sierra ___
36 Mukimo veggie
37 Irish equivalent of John
38 Iraqi city
39 Brewery product
40 "Also . . ."
41 ___ noir
42 ___ off (repels)
43 Realm of open discourse
46 Ski resort courses
47 Spanish small plates
50 Castle-storming strategy
52 "X-Men" mutant with claws
55 "___ am I kidding?"
57 D.C. is its capital
58 Dietary diagram
61 Animal on Michigan's flag
62 Musical blast from the past
63 Chicago airport
64 "You have my permission"
65 "___ assured . . ."
66 Desires

## DOWN

1 Navigational aids
2 Regions
3 Mournful song
4 TKO declarer
5 Member of a voting college
6 Paddy-grown grain
7 Word from the Latin for "burden"
8 Unruly crowd
9 Book's introduction
10 Unwraps impatiently
11 Fearsome folklore figure
12 Some cookware
14 "Are You the One?" channel
17 Like the proverbial cucumber
22 As easy as ___
24 Like 64 but not 27
25 "Mean Girls" screenwriter Fey
27 Families
28 Author of a hare racing story
29 Spring migration direction
30 Requirement
31 Body parts that might ring
32 Initials indicating urgency
33 List of options
34 Unlucky occurrences
38 Popular pens
39 Message-prompting sound

**41** Miss a lot
**42** Bro's place
**44** Carry laboriously
**45** Website with crafts
**48** "Dang it!"
**49** Its tail may be tucked in
**50** Chop ___
**51** Silent-letter landmass
**52** Physiques, for short
**53** Polish up for English class
**54** Hairy rainforest dweller
**56** Poetic salutes
**59** Futbol fan's chant

**60** Word of sudden comprehension

# 39

## IT'S SIZZLING INSIDE

By Gail Grabowski

**ACROSS**

1 Wing measurement
5 Rupi Kaur creation
9 Felt pain
14 Food associated with Tuesdays
15 Farmland measure
16 Clip wool from
17 Has a bug
18 Herbal beverages
19 Hard to lift
20 Kentucky's nickname
23 "You can't be serious!"
24 Trike rider
25 Lament
28 Persian Gulf nation
30 Media watchdog agcy.
33 Muscat native
34 Particle studied in physics
35 "The Martian" actress Kate
36 Portable music player
39 Moose relatives
40 Top of a rotunda, often
41 Feed false information
42 ___ Plaines, Illinois
43 Widespread
44 Glittery strands
45 Shelter rescue
46 Watches the kids
47 Taker of minutes on a student council
54 Place for a belt
55 Mystical light field
56 Succulent plant
57 Act hammily, perhaps
58 Alum
59 Cry of distress
60 ___ it down (got quieter)
61 A handful of
62 Part of a plan

**DOWN**

1 Grab with a toothpick
2 Oyster ___ (Chinese takeout container)
3 Rights org. since 1920
4 Rocket sections
5 Regular customer
6 View from a porthole
7 Historical periods
8 Cluttered state
9 "Moonlight" actor Sanders
10 Flout the rules
11 Furnace output
12 Place for Christmas lights
13 No longer damp
21 Alternative to AOL
22 "Forever" post-office purchase
25 Acknowledged applause, perhaps
26 Novelist Zola
27 Blemishes and such
28 "Who's there?" response
29 Thorny flower
30 Forged works of art, e.g.
31 Greek island home to Knossos
32 Burnett with a namesake Golden Globe

**USA TODAY**

**34** Beginning on
**35** Old standbys
**37** Revises for publication
**38** Upper-echelon
**43** Took a break
**44** Angry outburst
**45** Computer command after "copy"
**46** "Get lost!"
**47** ___ pants
**48** Predatory feline
**49** Gets less firm
**50** Currency in Milan

**51** Much of the time
**52** Sportscaster Holly
**53** Cry of distress
**54** Damp

# 40
## PHOTO FINISH
By Claire Rimkus

**ACROSS**

1 TV puppy who leaves clues
5 Petty clash
9 Surfer's ride
14 ___ light (round photography tool)
15 Ballet bend
16 Wide assortment
17 Prefix meaning "eight"
18 Unicorn projection
19 Coffeehouse order
20 Scotch-making device
23 Catch a glimpse of
24 Hospital depts.
25 "Drive Sober or Get Pulled Over" ad, e.g.
26 Director DuVernay
29 Ultimate purpose
31 Sudden period of chilly weather
33 Acidity-measuring system
35 Firefighter's tube
36 Letter after gamma
39 Valuable underground find
40 Cousins' parents
41 Too
42 Students take them
44 Hockey move following a windup
46 Bit of wearable merch
50 Bit of wearable merch
51 Faux ___
52 Pixar short about a steamed bun

53 ___ process
54 Persian-derived clothing feature
57 Slip-up
60 Snakelike sea creatures
61 Deeply admired person
62 Mall booth
63 Fruit named for its unsightliness
64 Tree with cones
65 Fencing blades
66 ___ and groan
67 Online crafts marketplace

**DOWN**

1 Casually look through
2 Rock growth
3 "Your shoelaces are ___"
4 Senses of self-importance
5 Round solids
6 Strategic schemes
7 Is shown on TV
8 Film studio's cash cows
9 Power ___ (type of song)
10 Like some histories
11 Subject of many a coffee table book
12 Remy or Rizzo
13 Indigo, for one
21 "Praying" singer
22 Cruise ship's destination
26 Unidentified, for short
27 Very large
28 Bonobos and chimpanzees

**30** "Gimme five!"
**31** Jeweler's measure
**32** "Zip it!"
**34** Ancient Roman amphitheater
**36** Track event
**37** Fitzgerald, First Lady of Song
**38** 180 is the highest score on it
**40** "The Ant and the Grasshopper" fabulist
**42** Spiced tea
**43** Spends the night at home
**45** Ogwumike sisters' WNBA team

**47** "Yay me!"
**48** Sentences that need editing
**49** Lipton competitor
**52** Actress Thorne
**54** Show starring Mj Rodriguez as a house mother
**55** Toy brick brand
**56** Ready to be plucked
**57** ___ out (barely get)
**58** Jeans feature
**59** ___ v. Wade

# 41
# YEAR OF THE RAT

By Zhouqin Burnikel

**ACROSS**

1 Like Death Valley's climate
5 Snapshots, for short
9 Song at a 50-year reunion, probably
14 Party, from the French
15 Teensy amount of liquid
16 Intoxicating
17 At the end of the line
18 Genealogical diagram
20 Did a monologue, say
22 Lake between Ontario and Ohio
23 Prof's aides
24 Zuma in "Paw Patrol," for one
28 Playful river mammal
29 "One of ___ days . . ."
32 Afflict
34 Bull's sound
37 Really impresses
39 Use a QR code reader on
41 Smug grin
43 Place to get a pastrami sandwich
44 Low-carb diet
45 "___, but Better" (Christine Riccio novel)
47 Clairvoyance, e.g.
48 College officials
51 All thumbs
53 Seeming valid
58 Twelfth graders (Abbr.)
61 In the not-so-distant future
62 Instant replay option
63 Really dark
67 Weaving device
68 Beyonce song about emotional investment
69 "Frozen Fever" queen
70 Jazz great ___ James
71 Audra McDonald has won six
72 Narrow cut
73 "After that . . ."

**DOWN**

1 Company with a duck in its logo
2 Within ___ (close by)
3 "Train's left the station!"
4 Sniff out
5 File type developed by Adobe
6 Name that's another name backward
7 Tailed celestial body
8 Tapering structure on a church
9 "That so?"
10 "___ me know"
11 It's thrown at a bull's-eye
12 Creative spark
13 They blink and wink
19 Jaunty tune
21 Polka ___ (fabric pattern)
25 Periscope glass
26 Fragrance
27 Part of a rosary
30 Someone frequently returning to a cobbler might have one

**31** Long fishes
**32** Inquire
**33** Like some tea
**35** Fix illegally
**36** The Polar Express, e.g.
**38** Drink slowly
**40** Biblical ark builder
**42** Piece that gets checkmated
**46** Norah O'Donnell delivers it
**49** Snacks
**50** Messy person
**52** Forklift's burden
**54** ___ out (allots)
**55** As a whole
**56** Overplay the scene
**57** From Italy's capital
**58** Skewer for roasting
**59** Puerto ___
**60** Suffix for seven country names
**64** Show joy or sorrow
**65** CBS forensics franchise
**66** Kit ___ (candy bar)

# 42
## CASH DISTRIBUTION
By Mark McClain

**ACROSS**

1 Triangle's sound
5 Neatnik's opposite
9 "___ legit"
14 Tech support client
15 Fruit cocktail staple
16 Radio host Martinez
17 Not inclined to be in a lot of photos
19 Created a novel
20 Nintendo's home city
21 Not yet proofread
23 Devices in some drive-thrus
26 Jean-___ Picard
27 Fall behind
30 Sneakers made from sturdy fabric
36 Not feeling great
37 Before long
38 ___ firma
39 Plundered stuff
41 Dare alternative
43 "Rats!"
44 Nautical greetings
46 What comes after Delta in the NATO phonetic alphabet
47 Palindromic youth
48 Cover for a pickup truck's bed
51 Noted period
52 "Let Me Blow Ya Mind" rapper
53 Honey-based beverage
55 Like a prima ballerina
60 Fruit peel scrapings
64 Aired again
65 Seller of sweets
68 Inner turmoil
69 In ___ of (rather than)
70 Unit of weight, for short
71 Vendor's spot at an expo
72 Upping the ___
73 Stuff in a shaker

**DOWN**

1 "Get down!"
2 "Do as ___ . . ."
3 "Finding Dory" character
4 Activist Thunberg
5 Pampering place
6 ___ Twins (French dance duo)
7 Hawaiian island
8 ___ Mawr College
9 Woodworker's waste
10 Added nutrients to, perhaps
11 Awards foursome (Abbr.)
12 Relative of a tick
13 Bit inside a pumpkin
18 Military grp. on campus
22 Golfer hidden in "Mickelson"
24 Sailboat post
25 Takes a noisy nap
27 Shrub with fragrant pink flowers
28 Hawaiian expression
29 Doom's partner
31 "I can ___ for her"
32 National song
33 Preach, e.g.
34 Miscue

## Crossword Grid

|   1 |   2 |   3 |   4 |     |   5 |   6 |   7 |   8 |     |   9 |  10 |  11 |  12 |  13 |
|-----|-----|-----|-----|-----|-----|-----|-----|-----|-----|-----|-----|-----|-----|-----|
|  14 |     |     |     |     |  15 |     |     |     |     |  16 |     |     |     |     |
|  17 |     |     |     |  18 |     |     |     |     |     |  19 |     |     |     |     |
|  20 |     |     |     |     |     |     |  21 |     |  22 |     |     |     |     |     |
|     |     |     |  23 |     |  24 |  25 |     |     |  26 |     |     |     |     |     |
|  27 |  28 |  29 |     |  30 |     |     |  31 |  32 |     |     |     |  33 |  34 |  35 |
|  36 |     |     |     |  37 |     |     |     |     |  38 |     |     |     |     |     |
|  39 |     |     |  40 |     |  41 |     |     |  42 |     |  43 |     |     |     |     |
|  44 |     |     |  45 |     |  46 |     |     |     |     |     |     |  47 |     |     |
|  48 |     |     |     |  49 |     |     |     |     |  50 |     |  51 |     |     |     |
|     |     |  52 |     |     |     |     |  53 |     |     |  54 |     |     |     |     |
|  55 |  56 |  57 |     |     |  58 |  59 |     |     |  60 |     |  61 |  62 |  63 |     |
|  64 |     |     |     |     |  65 |     |  66 |  67 |     |     |     |     |     |     |
|  68 |     |     |     |     |  69 |     |     |     |     |  70 |     |     |     |     |
|  71 |     |     |     |     |  72 |     |     |     |     |  73 |     |     |     |     |

**35** Yuletide home invader
**40** Stuck getting the same kinds of roles
**42** Result of digging
**45** Middle school grade
**49** Hoops official
**50** Not effortful
**54** Office furniture
**55** Seize
**56** Nevada city on the Truckee River
**57** Big name in cornstarch or tea
**58** Campus slated to host 2028's Olympic Village
**59** Past participle of "lie"
**61** Branch of Islam
**62** Highway payment
**63** Catch a glimpse of
**66** Mosquito stopper
**67** Scheduled to be born

# 43
## O CAPTAIN! MY CAPTAIN!
By Rachel Fabi

**ACROSS**

1 Chickens coming home to ___
6 Fertile area of a desert
11 Result of addition
14 "Exile in Guyville" rocker Liz
15 Fingerprint pattern
16 Transmissions on Slack, for short
17 Sorceress in Arthurian legend
19 Color similar to beige
20 Bad atmosphere
21 An arm or a leg
22 Not on target
25 Devilish
28 August zodiac sign
29 Match composition
32 Corn on the ___
33 Small-scale
35 Deliveries via parachute or smartphone
39 Sham trial
42 Well-known for negative reasons
43 Hoot
45 Home plate worker
46 Warrior princess of TV
49 West who wrote plays under the pen name Jane Mast
50 Nearest
54 Word before "tax" or "sale"
56 Visibility obstacle
57 Nemeses
60 A long time ___

61 Nature series narrated by Sigourney Weaver
66 "White ___ Can't Jump"
67 Burlap bags
68 Muppet with a rubber duckie
69 Lead-in to "fix"
70 Latin phrase abbreviated to two letters
71 Silent-letter hymn

**DOWN**

1 Vinyl stat
2 Surprised interjection
3 Its blade gets wet
4 Letter before tau
5 Gets ready to compete
6 Nocturnal hunters
7 Polite cough sound
8 Living room furniture
9 Rollover ___
10 Cunning
11 Protest type
12 Savory taste
13 Rachel Maddow network
18 Name that's 47-Down rearranged
21 U.K. political party
22 Slippery ___ (tree)
23 Japanese energy healing
24 "Catch and Kill" author Farrow
26 Band with a slash in its name
27 Landscaping brand with a bull-related name
30 Starchy root vegetable

31 People involved with the #NoDAPL movement
34 Imbue
36 Washington Spirit star Lavelle
37 ___ donna
38 Short-tailed weasel
40 ___ the system
41 Sound-boosting gear
44 Golf peg
47 Tidy
48 Snoozing
50 Winner, for short
51 Oktoberfest drink

52 ___ layer (stratosphere part)
53 "Hustlers" actress Lysette
55 Russian monarchs of old
58 Calligraphy supplies
59 Sleeveless garment
61 Letter before omega
62 Boy
63 Messenger molecules
64 ___ Tuesday (Aimee Mann band)
65 Sewing border

# 44
## ROOM DIVIDERS
By Gail Grabowski

**ACROSS**

1 Elaborate heist
6 Web address part
9 Did nothing
14 Cream-of-the-crop
15 Altar affirmation
16 Not well-off
17 Stew-cooking kettle
19 Developmental phase
20 Stretcher carrier (Abbr.)
21 Notable periods of time
22 Made sounds like a shorthair
23 Some homework helpers
24 Jeans go-with, perhaps
25 Make certain
28 Now and then
32 Org. opposed to fur farms
33 Wrapping paper unit
36 Middle of a peach
37 Order to Rover
38 Jouster's ride
40 Vein of ore
41 Apple desktop computers
43 Shoreline phenomenon
44 Responsibility-claiming statement
45 Choreographer Agnes
47 Tops with icing
49 Cake layer
50 End of a hammer
51 Like the people photographed for Project 562
54 "Stormy Weather" singer Horne

55 Org. encouraging flossing
58 Knock the socks off
59 One of a religious septet
61 Dog breed from Germany
62 Play it by ___
63 Path of ___ resistance
64 Potato coverings
65 Org. in the film "Concussion"
66 Pulls suddenly

**DOWN**

1 Relinquish legally
2 Grad
3 Pennsylvania university's nickname
4 And so forth, for short
5 Try again in court
6 Some aria singers
7 Homages in verse
8 Significant amount
9 Remarks that sting
10 Ford Field footballer
11 Shakespearean king played by Glenda Jackson
12 Good place to start on a jigsaw puzzle
13 Like pink hair
18 Selects from the menu
22 Greenhouse container
23 Legal resident of two countries
24 Lost color
25 Ladybug's snack

**USA TODAY**

**26** Words next to a bad grade, perhaps
**27** Sauna stuff
**29** Inspirations for some boards
**30** Break up
**31** They're sown
**34** Mink relative
**35** Floral necklace
**39** Stand up for
**42** Thin wood fragments
**46** "Hulk" director Ang
**48** "And you believe that?"
**50** Necklace part

**51** Seizes
**52** Run ___ (go wild)
**53** Metered vehicle
**54** Bit of kale
**55** "___ aside . . ."
**56** Floppy ___
**57** Industrious insects
**59** Room divided in this puzzle's four longest entries
**60** Supporting vote

# 45
## THIS IS SO META
By Zhouqin Burnikel

**ACROSS**

1 Fess up to
6 Fell in the standings
10 ___ like a glove
13 Largest city in the Middle East
14 Bodega, for one
15 Get 100% on
16 They're collected in April
18 Big name in jeans
19 University bigwig
20 Pony up
21 Airballs, e.g.
23 Verb in a guac recipe
25 Like some coincidences
26 Not quite shut
28 "Stop interrupting!"
32 Midday meal
34 Flash ___
35 Fashion designer Saab
36 "___ Miz"
37 Silly
39 Electric guitar attachment
40 Gracing the small screen
42 Mai ___ (tropical drink)
43 Feel contrite about
46 Piece of rec room furniture
49 Jamaican liquors
50 Tales that are "spun"
51 Copy paper unit
53 Herding dog
55 "Let You Love Me" singer Rita
56 Lairs for bears
60 "The World of ___" (Satyajit Ray film)

61 One most likely to be singled out
64 Baked ___ and cheese
65 Shaped like kumquats
66 Principles you're not supposed to question
67 Species whose males have antlers
68 Bit of car damage
69 Utensil for yogurt

**DOWN**

1 Etching fluid
2 University of Copenhagen student, typically
3 Flaky mineral
4 Participant in a grueling triathlon
5 Guitarist Morello
6 Hang around
7 Brined salmon
8 "Time was . . ."
9 Yearn for
10 Instance of crying wolf
11 Sister brand of Slush Puppie
12 Rock concert souvenirs
14 Lesley of "60 Minutes"
17 Installments of a show, for short
22 DuckDuckGo.com result
24 Curved path
25 English boarding school
26 Rock concert venue
27 "Ugh, figures!"

**USA TODAY**

**29** Text alternative
**30** Green grove growths
**31** Didn't throw out
**32** Page with posts
**33** Touch on a sore subject
**38** Snatches up
**41** Osso buco meat
**44** Age
**45** Piece on a gingerbread house's roof
**47** Photographer's stand
**48** Got it wrong
**52** Enjoy some risotto, say

**53** Showed up
**54** Iridescent Australian gem
**55** Leave out
**57** Brand of frozen waffles
**58** Pixar's lost clownfish
**59** Member of the Rihanna Navy, e.g.
**62** Lithium-___ battery
**63** Pop-up annoyances

# 46
## SOUNDS UNFORTUNATE
By Evan Kalish

**ACROSS**

1 Buckwheat bowlful
6 Does sum work
10 Cajole
14 Bovine glue mascot
15 Round shape
16 "... and what ___ you"
17 Frigidly dismiss
20 French for "head"
21 Twelve people have walked on it
22 Like some questions
23 Stick-to-itiveness
25 Nine-___ battery
27 Financially solvent
30 Closely examine
34 Hung on a clothesline
35 Negative sort
36 "You da ___" (Rihanna song)
37 Goes bad
38 Is visibly dejected
39 Amusement park attraction
40 Optometrist's specialty
41 Makes sharper
42 Power line supporters
43 "Please" translation
45 False front
46 At any time
47 Went to the bottom of the ocean
48 K-pop group with a cosmic name
51 Italian wine region
53 Hit the ___ (go to bed)

57 Blood flow concern
60 Part of a thesis
61 Old name for Thailand
62 Contents of a jetliner's underside
63 Tiff
64 Alice Coltrane played it
65 Secretive meeting

**DOWN**

1 Declined to discard
2 Its best-known species is "vera"
3 Raunchy material
4 "Trying it now ..."
5 Tee shot's path
6 Distribute
7 Extinct bird
8 Negative feedback on some online posts
9 Business with soothing music
10 Orange puff
11 Whitewater rafting tools
12 Mary Kay competitor
13 Prefix meaning "foreign"
18 Fail to include
19 "Holding Out for a Hero" singer Bonnie
24 Super cool
26 Unearthed deposits
27 Person selling spots, for short
28 Swirled dessert
29 Seltzer bottle size
30 Contents of a ream

**USA TODAY**

31 "Check it out!"
32 Expired
33 Hello Sunshine founder Witherspoon
35 Payments to guest speakers
38 "C'mon already!"
39 Celeb with an ax, perhaps
41 Wreak ___
42 Cooking vessel
44 Pet that's illegal in California and Hawaii
45 Pass-___ (course type)
47 Remnant of a chopped tree

48 Girls Who Code alums might create them
49 Bar in the bathroom
50 Ancient Roman garment
52 Remnant of a wound
54 Conducive to breezes
55 Gear parts
56 Tie choice
58 "... more or less"
59 "___ your age!"

# 47
# OPENING NUMBERS
By Gabrielle Friedman

**ACROSS**
1 Grown-up
6 "___ fair in love and war"
10 Pop group whose music inspired "Mamma Mia!"
14 Host's handouts
15 Extend a membership, say
16 Grouch
17 "The Princess Bride" character Montoya
18 Very positive review
20 State of matter
21 Donkey, in biblical speak
22 ___ Gatos, California
23 Soccer fan's refrain
26 Internet addresses
28 Word before "stop" or "viper"
31 High income
34 Beeps or boops
35 "Now!"
36 Cuaron who directed "Harry Potter and the Prisoner of Azkaban"
39 Words for making a bakery selection
42 Place to take a load off
43 "Por favor" translation
45 Sloth, etc.
51 Org. in airports
52 Ages
53 Set free
54 Letter seen on frat row
55 They might hold office hours, for short

57 "The Karate Kid" (2010) protagonist
58 Pool game
62 Come about
64 Real estate measurement unit
65 Whoppers
66 Conference feature
67 Part of a settlement agreement
68 Therefore
69 Alternative to 39-Across, if you're hungry

**DOWN**
1 Friends
2 National park with a caribou herd
3 Like some bathrooms
4 Haul
5 General on a Chinese menu
6 Shelter sounds
7 Time to relax
8 <3 alternative
9 Sorcerer's repertoire
10 Parts of plays
11 Victoria's Secret purchase
12 Restaurant seating area
13 Workout goal, perhaps
19 Baseball's "Slammin' Sammy"
21 Mythological word that can mean "backing"
24 Memorable
25 "The ___, the Witch and the Wardrobe"
27 Took a load off

## Crossword Grid

Grid with numbered cells: 1, 2, 3, 4, 5, 6, 7, 8, 9, 10, 11, 12, 13 (top row); 14, 15, 16; 17, 18, 19; 20, 21, 22; 23, 24, 25, 26, 27, 28, 29, 30; 31, 32, 33; 34, 35; 36, 37, 38, 39, 40, 41; 42, 43, 44; 45, 46, 47, 48, 49, 50; 51, 52, 53; 54, 55, 56, 57; 58, 59, 60, 61, 62, 63; 64, 65, 66; 67, 68, 69.

**28** El ___, Texas
**29** Tehran's country
**30** Feel some ___ of way
**32** Arthur Ashe Stadium tournament
**33** Most recent
**36** No. 2 (Abbr.)
**37** Journalist Paris
**38** Bean variety
**40** Places for monitors in grade school
**41** "___ sow, so shall . . ."
**44** What the anchor runs, in a relay

**46** Not messy
**47** Increase by 100%
**48** First-aid antiseptic
**49** "Grey's Anatomy" extras
**50** "Remington ___"
**54** Not us
**56** Furthermore
**58** Put away
**59** Wintry road hazard
**60** "I'm so angry!"
**61** Broadcast
**62** Suitable
**63** Cheer word

**USA TODAY**

# 48
## MERLOT
By Mark McClain

**ACROSS**

1 Particle with a nucleus
5 "We ___ Overcome"
10 Highest point
14 Prefix meaning "large"
15 Workplace roster addition
16 Tiny cut
17 Container ships, for example
20 Tip jar bill
21 Fidgety
22 Like some fries and hair
23 Modest dwellings
24 Old German coins
25 In the past few days, say
28 Pointy architectural feature
30 Composer Stravinsky
31 "In the Country We Love" author Guerrero
32 "Mr. Holmes" star McKellen
35 It's not part of some grand conspiracy
39 "Without further ___ . . ."
40 Door piece
41 Al who received a Nobel Peace Prize in 2007
42 Stirs up
43 Gave a call
45 List entries
47 "Unspeakable giant bugs," per Calvin of "Calvin and Hobbes"
48 Singer with the album "25"
49 Bit of turbulent weather
51 Boat in Genesis

54 "The Music Man" composer
57 Become entitled to
58 Rings forth
59 Senate staffer
60 Part of a Venetian blind
61 Religious group with Swiss roots
62 First layer of makeup

**DOWN**

1 Water balloons, e.g.
2 Many a driver's ed student
3 Creature that might have green skin
4 Scottish surname prefix
5 Modest dwelling
6 Helpful clues
7 ___ and crafts
8 TV star Dan
9 Name that's a sea creature backward
10 Instill confidence in
11 Courtroom figure
12 Sources of paper or pepper
13 Website for homemades
18 Transport
19 Struck fear into
23 "Take this"
24 Prefix meaning "small"
25 Bean variety
26 Like sharp cheese
27 Spanish bull
28 Performs in a chorus
29 Change of ___

**31** Have a sit-down meal
**32** Get ___ the ground floor
**33** Equivalent of 4,840 square yards
**34** Must have
**36** Rang forth
**37** Essential ___
**38** They might be easily bruised
**42** Yield
**43** Priest's domain
**44** Web design language
**45** Standard of perfection
**46** Sci-fi name for Earth

**47** Soup kitchen stack
**48** Iowa campus town
**49** Cherry discard
**50** Bangkok language
**51** Bangkok continent
**52** Cones' counterparts
**53** On bended ___
**55** Hoppy pint, briefly
**56** Scientist's workplace

# 49

## IT'S A SNAP!

By Zhouqin Burnikel

**ACROSS**

1 Pizza party beverages
6 Competitor of Enterprise
11 Word before "lion" or "serpent"
14 Letter-shaped skirt style
15 Pale purple
16 Cucumber water dispenser
17 Geri Halliwell's stage name
19 Variant of rummy
20 "___ Bayou" (1997 film)
21 Memoji platform
22 Capital of Cuba
24 ___ floss
26 Range above bass
27 Website with an alien mascot
30 "That's terrible!"
33 Implicitly understood
37 Far from common
38 Ran out of battery
39 K-pop stars
40 "A Wrinkle in Time" director DuVernay
41 Cube or sphere
42 Herb often paired with lemon
43 In the thick of
44 Turnpike payments
45 Comes to a close
46 Got by
48 Is invested
50 Device used to treat an allergic reaction
55 Dua, e.g.
57 Have a negative balance

59 "Out of my way!"
60 Slippery as an ___
61 Upstate New York travel destination
64 Equivalent of four qts.
65 Greeting sent online
66 Deal negotiator for authors
67 Soon-to-be grads (Abbr.)
68 Hits the roof
69 Outperforms

**DOWN**

1 "I Know Why the ___ Bird Sings"
2 Black or green pizza topping
3 Tea towel fabric
4 Emotion in emo music
5 "Catch my drift?"
6 "One more thing . . ."
7 Carmex recipients
8 "Float like a butterfly" boxer
9 Cane-cutting tool
10 Pirates' domain
11 Harlem district in the name of an early rap group
12 "___ Brockovich"
13 "True Blood" star Paquin
18 Aggravate
23 ___ doll
25 Film and theater, for two
26 Long-winded rant
28 Some plays
29 "___ Makes Man" (OWN series)

**31** Astronaut Armstrong
**32** Bookie's numbers
**33** Coastal erosion cause
**34** Point after deuce
**35** Long shots in sales
**36** "That's so true!"
**41** "Cut that out!"
**43** Country with the most billionaires
**47** "In the headlights" critter
**49** Send to a different doctor
**51** Mental picture
**52** ___ around (snoops)

**53** Heptathlon component
**54** Alligators' homes
**55** Wooden fasteners
**56** Front's opposite
**57** Shrek is one
**58** Ties the knot
**62** Constantly find fault
**63** Chocolate dog

# 50

## AVIAN ANATOMY

By Kate Hawkins

**ACROSS**

1 Muppet whose birthday is Feb. 3
5 Truth alternative
9 Holey cheese
14 "A Visit From the ___ Squad"
15 Roundish nail shape
16 Cringe
17 Shape for pipes and lamps
19 Anagram of "runic"
20 One taking it all in
21 Rabbit breed that requires regular grooming
22 Move quickly
23 "THIS ___ UP"
24 Award in pro sports
25 Horses for knights
28 Keen power of observation
30 Conscious
31 Prefix for "fish" or "fly"
32 Seaweed for sushi
33 Under attack
34 Fictional journalist Lois
38 Uses a chisel
40 Penny-pincher
41 Slicked-back style
44 Penny metal
45 "It's ___ from me"
46 "___ We Meet Again"
47 Surplus
48 Messy obstacle course contest
50 Like sea otters, among all animals
54 Like pad thai and nasi lemak
55 One of the houses of Hogwarts
56 Literary classification
57 Kiln, e.g.
58 "Search Party" star Shawkat
59 Barely defeated
60 Orion's has three stars
61 Young chaps

**DOWN**

1 Waffle cereal brand name
2 Be imminent
3 Earth orbiter
4 Long-shot option for a losing football team
5 Givers of blood or money
6 Ward off
7 5K, for one
8 National ___ Refuge (Wyoming wildlife area)
9 Con
10 One of two on a biplane
11 It's not taxed by Texas or Alaska
12 Ailment treated with citrus
13 Brightly colored shawl
18 Get away from
21 Unfocused dread
23 "Powers of Ten" creators Charles and Ray ___
25 Francisco's title
26 Only even prime number
27 Lobe locale
28 Painter's prop

**Across**

29 Treadmill alternative
31 "The ___ is in the details"
33 Lobe locale
35 Venomous caterpillar
36 French word before a former name
37 Mess up
39 In harmony
40 Show sorrow
41 "What's your ___?" ("Heathers" catchphrase)
42 Still in its packaging
43 Web development work

44 Attorney-___ privilege
47 Judge's mallet
49 Not very common
50 Possess
51 Fitzgerald known as the Queen of Jazz
52 Uttered
53 Past-tense 'tis
55 Steal from

# 51
## TOYMAKING
By Karl Ni

**ACROSS**

1 Sign of things to come
5 Relaxing soaks with rubber duckies
10 Signature item for Superman or Doctor Strange
14 "If I had wings like this ___ . . ."
15 Beginning
16 Lotion ingredient
17 Artist's tablet
19 Quiet period
20 Transmits
21 American currency (Abbr.)
22 Awards show that went hostless in 2019
23 Some alert broadcasts (Abbr.)
25 Small sled
27 "See?"
30 Drake's Cakes makes it
34 Some light-colored beers, for short
35 Booths
37 Scat syllable
38 "To ___ is human"
39 Life ___ (mint)
40 GPS fig.
41 Spare piece of cloth
42 Split from a country
43 Lizard part
44 2,000-pound unit
46 Extracts the metal from
48 Jabba the ___
49 Ruler of old Russia
50 Kitchen garment
53 "u serious?"
55 Canada's national tree
59 ___ and slayed (rhyming description for hair)
60 What you can do by combining the last words of 17-, 30-, and 44-Across
62 Fries, e.g.
63 Peaks
64 "Insecure" star Rae
65 Singles
66 Tennis garment
67 Tater ___

**DOWN**

1 Betting statistics
2 "Another!"
3 "Dear ___ Hansen"
4 Recent adopters, perhaps
5 ___ Appetit
6 Cattle breed
7 Recipe amts.
8 Was the star of
9 Regulation (Abbr.)
10 Quieted down
11 College donation drive target, for short
12 Roly-___
13 Fish in unadon
18 Kid's guessing game
22 They're sold in dozens
24 Angela who played Rosa Parks
26 Lose the threads

**27** Levels
**28** TV mogul Winfrey
**29** Key ___, Florida
**30** Bird in a Poe poem
**31** Best possible
**32** Tag phrase
**33** Aspirations
**36** Mobile source of al pastor
**42** Surprise
**43** Large unit of data
**45** Apt-sounding surname for a driver
**47** Family nickname

**49** "Whose Line" host Aisha
**50** As well
**51** Total hassle
**52** Merry-go-round, for example
**54** Long vehicle, for short
**56** Coin in Mexico
**57** Show stamina
**58** Stretches of history
**60** Univ. degrees
**61** Something the Navajo Nation observes that the Hopi Reservation doesn't (Abbr.)

# 52
## LEAN IN
By Zhouqin Burnikel

**ACROSS**

1 Corrosive chemical compound
5 Office sub
9 Vaping device, for short
13 ". . . ___ speak"
14 Lake that drains via the Niagara River
15 Contemporary of Monet
17 Frenzied activity
20 Fill the tank
21 "___ as directed"
22 Sign of sorrow
23 Rotten to the core
24 Comedy bits
26 Actors hire them
28 Smeltery material
29 Part of a prof's email address
30 Initials aptly found in "Obamacare"
31 Podiatrist's focus, perhaps
32 "Make it fast!"
34 "No more for me, thanks"
37 Well-behaved kid
41 Animal tracking device
42 Trickster in Norse myth
45 Spaceship's escape vehicle
48 Take care of the bill
49 Do something wrong
52 Do something wrong
53 ___ bars (Olympic event)
55 "Makes sense now"
56 "Naughty, naughty!"
57 TV host Kelly
58 Seltzer container
60 Story lines
62 Web traffic tracking tool
66 Happen next
67 "I'm a Survivor" singer McEntire
68 Apple desktop computer
69 Pomegranate bit
70 "Birds of ___"
71 Prefix for "final" or "circle"

**DOWN**

1 Fireplace residue
2 Mountain lions
3 Statement accompanying a handshake
4 Morse code symbols
5 Disc golf starting point
6 Historical time span
7 Negative quality
8 "YIELD TO ___" (street sign)
9 Bird with green eggs
10 Social stratum
11 Counterpart of impact
12 Frozen Italian treat
16 Far from talkative
18 Olympic sled
19 Guiding light
23 Fluffy fashion accessory
25 "Yup, that's me"
27 "Our ___"
30 Proverbs
33 Thrown dessert
35 "___ culpa"

**36** Long, slithery fish
**38** Word after "duct" or "gaffer"
**39** Hypnotic state
**40** Old friends sometimes make up for it
**43** Source of awkward moments on jumbotrons
**44** Octopus's defense
**45** Rid
**46** Bermuda and Vidalia are varieties of them
**47** Take testimony from
**50** Sportscast's second look

**51** Depend
**54** Clear as mud
**55** ___ circle (closest friends)
**59** Group for those 50 and older
**61** "Respect" songwriter Redding
**63** Headed the pack
**64** Midge Maisel's dad
**65** ___-fi conventions

# 53

# PARTY LEADERS

By Mark McClain

**ACROSS**

1 "Rate the Bars" guests judge them
5 "Middlemarch" novelist George
10 Research facility
13 Mucho, in English
14 Rolls with wasabi
15 "Welcome to Night ___" (podcast)
16 Footwear item for Ingrid Silva
18 Aware of, as a plot
19 Letters accompanying a hot take
20 "___ America Be America Again" (Langston Hughes poem)
21 Did some arithmetic
22 Prescription info
24 More pleasant
26 Stir-fry staple
31 Fury
34 At the crack of dawn, say
35 By way of
36 Lopsided game
37 Comic book installment
38 Possessive pronoun
39 Tony winner Stroker
40 Chips in for a hand
41 Horse farm moms
42 Financial summary
45 ___ lightly
46 "We're on!"
50 Word in a very cold forecast

52 Narcissist's baggage
53 Gen ___
54 Greek god of war
55 Poor performance
59 Sage
60 Land of the Pharaohs
61 Hour, in Spanish
62 French article
63 The Ninja Turtles, e.g.
64 Sign for the superstitious

**DOWN**

1 Overly enthusiastic
2 Rental car brand
3 Short-sleeved shirts with collars
4 Gateway Arch city, for short
5 High regard
6 Intense desire
7 Estimator's suffix
8 Cry akin to "aha!"
9 Ascot, for one
10 British car brand
11 Soothing succulent
12 Curve in a river
15 TikTok posting
17 Composer whose name is an anagram of "regal"
21 Sore
23 Aid and ___
24 "Take your time!"
25 "___ of Capri"
27 Outperformed

**28** Pleasant areas within unpleasant areas
**29** Tucker out
**30** Backtalk
**31** The "A" in UAE
**32** Acronymic nickname for Bourbon Street's city
**33** Innocent
**37** Ancient Peruvian
**38** Some church wear
**40** All over again
**41** Movement founded by Tarana Burke
**43** Came to light
**44** Skating figures
**47** Basic principle
**48** Movie category
**49** Heart or kidney, for example
**50** Sob loudly
**51** Fourth-largest city in Pennsylvania
**52** "SportsCenter" channel
**55** Roulette table action
**56** "Iron" or "Stone" period
**57** Color changer
**58** "Name's not ringing any bells"

# 54
## RIGHT-HAND MEN
By Gail Grabowski

**ACROSS**

1 Range below soprano
5 Salsa singer Cruz
10 Swelter
14 Underlying cause
15 Informal term for the head
16 Is in the hole financially
17 Support for a window treatment
19 ___ dish pizza
20 "The ___" (2019 film about a boy and his horse)
21 Mole from another country, perhaps
23 Staircase feature
26 Burden
27 Walgreens competitor
30 Hamburger meat
35 Weeding tool
36 Make as a salary
37 Biker's invitation
38 Covered with frosting
40 Chairs and benches
43 Game with mallets
44 West Point student
46 Paid athletes
48 "Immediately!"
49 Hilma af Klint paintings, e.g.
52 Medical drama locales, for short
53 Mystical glow
54 Salon treatment
56 Keeps under wraps
60 Point toward
64 "___, I'm Falling in Love Again"
65 Disgustingly wealthy
68 Construction location
69 Car that's 53-Across with an added letter
70 Beige shade
71 Reinforced parts of work boots
72 Bar mitzvah scroll
73 Palindromic document

**DOWN**

1 Hammer throw trajectories
2 Violent troublemaker
3 Zoomed along
4 Animal in the weasel family
5 Some 3D graphics
6 Geologic time period
7 Entice
8 Like some patches
9 Part of a sum, in math
10 Fender-bender repair place
11 Leaves speechless
12 "Just ___ swimming"
13 Best Female Athlete, for one
18 Old saying
22 "That Don't Impress Me ___"
24 Some tax-deferred investments
25 Handed-down tales
27 Spanish for "girl"
28 SAT fare
29 Watermelon discards
31 Not appropriate

**32** Ahead by a point
**33** Crayola choice
**34** Is aware of
**39** Takes off
**41** Spiderweb, essentially
**42** ___ loser
**45** "Can't argue with that"
**47** Wander off course
**50** Former Palestinian leader
**51** Colorful cat
**55** Bogged down
**56** Price to pay
**57** Kent State's state

**58** Margin jotting
**59** Pronounce indistinctly
**61** Computer clickers
**62** Vineyard measure
**63** Sound of impact
**66** Singing syllable followed by "la"
**67** "A likely story!"

# 55
## EXPANSION TEAM
By Patrick Jordan

**ACROSS**

1 Leave too little room for
6 Beanies, berets, etc.
10 Opinion-gathering tool
14 Milk & ___ ("Watchmen" bakery)
15 Name that becomes a grain if you move its first letter to the end
16 Continent with 10-Downs
17 Bakery appliances
18 Grandmother's nickname
19 Make like a firefly
20 Meteorological floater
23 Aidy Bryant's show
24 Be too inquisitive
25 Pea holder
26 ___ for the course
27 Stages, as a historical event
32 Wave phenomenon
36 Stuck in a ___
37 Bird's beak
38 Radon-regulating org.
39 PlayStation maker
40 "___ never too late!"
41 Document-closing substance
44 Pleasing visuals
47 Director's workspace
48 A tenth of diez
49 Domino marking
50 School grp.
53 It might be sliced for risotto
58 Fingers-crossed feeling
59 Boundless enthusiasm

60 Course that's hard to fail
61 Granola bar bits
62 Momentous time periods
63 ___ up (becomes aware)
64 Gabriella's "High School Musical" love interest
65 Rounded ceiling
66 They hurtle down hills

**DOWN**

1 Dark-tongued dogs
2 Black bird
3 Country singer Jamie
4 "Can't stop, ___ stop"
5 Kitchen basin
6 Folk hero John
7 Word before "Spring" or "League"
8 Singer Turner
9 Surgical tool
10 Religious tower
11 Norwegian Nobel Institute location
12 Stalker on the savanna
13 Attorney's field
21 Goes off the mark
22 Horror actor Chaney
26 "Arthur" dog
27 "How can I ever ___ you?"
28 Israeli airline
29 Black bird
30 Fish in melts
31 Mythical Greek river
32 "Book of Addis" author Brooke

**33** The "C" in KCMO
**34** Aside from that
**35** Unwanted plant in a garden
**39** Rank above cpl.
**41** Grabbed some shut-eye
**42** Egyptian goddess
**43** Nieces' brothers
**45** Excessively adorable
**46** Industrious crawler
**49** Beat felt at the wrist
**50** Squad
**51** ___ with (pondered)
**52** Collect a pile of

**53** Piglet's papa
**54** Engaging in
**55** Roman emperor after Claudius
**56** Palindromic term of address
**57** Transit option
**58** In great demand

# 56
## UP FOR SALE
By Zhouqin Burnikel

**ACROSS**
- **1** Big brass instrument
- **5** Tony ___ (Iron Man's alter ego)
- **10** Roadside rescue
- **13** Warms up the crowd
- **15** "Aw, shucks!"
- **16** "Now I see!"
- **17** Pithy expression
- **18** Exhilarating
- **19** "Skrrt" source
- **20** "I could use some help"
- **22** Dove or hawk, for example
- **23** "Geaux Tigers!" sch.
- **24** Brings to life
- **26** Bandmate of Jisoo, Jennie and Rose
- **29** "___ Dalloway"
- **31** Bit of ink, for short
- **32** "My mistake!"
- **33** Warms the bench
- **35** Places to play catch
- **39** Helmet fastener
- **41** Org. that Katie Sowers coaches in
- **42** Pasta sauce tidbit
- **43** Final authority
- **44** Cap toss participant, for short
- **46** "Charlie's Angels" star Balinska
- **47** "___ boy!" ("Whew!")
- **49** Be in debt
- **50** High-pitched exclamation
- **51** Boy who refused to grow up

- **55** Enjoyed a blueberry muffin, say
- **57** Country west of Vietnam
- **58** Lacked accomplices
- **63** Ages ___
- **64** Calamari source
- **65** "I Still Believe" singer Mariah
- **66** Not the picture of health
- **67** Blend into a thick liquid
- **68** Hollywood statuette
- **69** The ___ Moines Register
- **70** Have a longing
- **71** Jackrabbit, e.g.

**DOWN**
- **1** Fly-catching amphibian
- **2** Bouffant, for example
- **3** Smile from ear to ear
- **4** 1996 Frank McCourt book
- **5** Manhattan neighborhood north of TriBeCa
- **6** Nickname for Alaska
- **7** Once more
- **8** Website with "Ask Me Anything" interviews
- **9** Door opener
- **10** Unspoken
- **11** Busy Midwestern airport
- **12** Hospital parts
- **14** Blue areas in an atlas
- **21** Bottom-line numbers
- **22** React
- **25** Cinco de ___
- **26** Defeat

27 Greek I
28 Like someone still polkaing at 90
30 Sumo wrestler's workplace
34 Tangy side dish
36 Tick off
37 American Girl product
38 Flip out
40 "___ Unfortunate Souls"
45 "___ to Me" (Christina Applegate show)
48 Hard to see through
51 Kilt pattern

52 Walking ___ News (satire site)
53 Items in a shed
54 Honda's upscale line
56 Enchilada alternative
59 Genesis garden
60 Whale with a large dorsal fin
61 Close at hand
62 Filmmaker Chris
64 Undercover agent

# 57
## LOOKING THE PART
By Gabrielle Friedman

**ACROSS**

1 "I hear that!"
5 Unsolid rock
10 Exam type
14 ___ sale
15 Spanish coins
16 Sandy feature of the National Park in Indiana
17 Testimony source, perhaps
19 Partner to odds
20 Flips out
21 List-ending abbreviation
23 E.R. workers
24 Director Lynne
26 Star-cross'd lover in Shakespeare
28 "Yes, captain"
31 Method for locating a fracture
33 Smith who had their first number one album in 2017
34 Flatbread eaten in Armenia
35 Seoul-based automaker
39 Will subjects
43 Target
45 "Golden" or "Gilded" period
46 ___ mirror
49 Echo
52 Disability activist Wong
53 Like mares
55 Apt rhyme for "pursue"
56 2016 Olympics locale
58 Out of control
62 Rip off
64 Accessory with a face

66 Georgia's continent
67 Take place
68 Ingredient in some chips
69 Musical pause
70 "Valley of the Dolls" character
71 Anna's sister in "Frozen"

**DOWN**

1 Biblical brother
2 Deli spread
3 ___ out (barely gets)
4 A regime change might usher one in
5 Introvert's need
6 Mothers' sisters
7 LSAT alternative
8 Arrive in no hurry
9 No. 2 (Abbr.)
10 "___ to the Hexagon" (Chen Chen poem)
11 Rap trio with the hit single "Walk This Way"
12 NBC News correspondent Mitchell
13 Something learned
18 "What more can ___?"
22 Competitor of Colgate
25 Org. for lawyers
27 Workplace inspection org.
28 Far-reaching volcanic output
29 "Huzzah!"
30 Flightless bird
32 "Old Town Road" singer Lil ___ X

 **USA TODAY**

**34** One translation of "qi"
**36** Drug sniffer, for short
**37** Deep-sea explorer
**38** French for "friend"
**40** Pit gunk
**41** "Saturday Night Live" star Nwodim
**42** Part of a tennis match
**44** Be behind on rent, say
**46** Place to eat oysters
**47** Plaza Hotel girl
**48** Sauces made from garlic and olive oil

**49** Food storage room
**50** "There ought to be ___!"
**51** Try again, as a test
**54** City in northern Iraq
**57** Triumphant boast
**59** List-ending abbreviation
**60** Knee parts, for short
**61** Flightless bird
**63** Kit ___ bar
**65** Bar supply

# 58
## HOLD MY BEER
By Caitlin Reid

**ACROSS**

1 Try to sell
6 Sound like a snake
10 Disney snowman
14 Allergic outburst
15 Not mention
16 Vatican leader
17 Dwelling-selling biz
19 Swimming site
20 ___ bar (serve drinks)
21 ". . . woo wop da bam" (Abbr.)
22 Right on time
24 Partner of fortune
26 Female deer
27 Features of many big-budget features
33 Increments that good things are said to come in
34 Clumsy people, unkindly
35 What some people do through their teeth
36 Trot or gallop, for example
37 Dad ___
38 Bring to tears, maybe
39 Rage
40 Grievance of the organic movement (Abbr.)
42 Heeded
44 Former name of a UPS competitor
47 Murdock aka Daredevil
48 Harvest
49 Movies
52 Site of a small canal
53 Letter after alpha
57 Reason to use an air freshener
58 Checkup on choppers
61 "Soul Food" star Nia
62 Minor injury
63 Invigorate
64 Sunburn soother
65 Colorful-sounding surname
66 Leopard's print

**DOWN**

1 Hair line
2 Frozen drink brand
3 Word of comparison
4 Second thoughts
5 Soil-scraping tool
6 Soothing brew
7 Desktop computer since 1998
8 Use a chair
9 "Leave me alone!"
10 Be against
11 Tapestry machine
12 Each
13 Fuzzy fabric
18 Round before the finals, for short
23 Rec league officials
25 Expert
26 Out of batteries
27 Post on social media
28 Snooped around
29 Baggy
30 Is sickly sweet

**31** Bikes have them
**32** Part of a gardener's supply
**33** "Friyay!"
**37** Lightning ___
**38** Road Runner's catchphrase
**40** Nutrition Facts unit
**41** Bullfighter
**42** "Carmen," for one
**43** Supporting undergarment
**45** Appear
**46** Far from G
**49** Some soda pop
**50** Adored one

**51** Prohibited thing
**52** "Ghost World" protagonist
**54** Convention center event
**55** Having no slack
**56** Rock concert gear
**59** She-sheep
**60** Some records

# 59
## FANTASY SERIES
By Zhouqin Burnikel

**ACROSS**

1 "Oh, shucks!"
6 Hydrotherapy offerer
9 Left-hand side of a ship
13 From that time
14 Parka feature
15 Geometry calculation
16 "Y'all know each other?!"
18 Color similar to cyan
19 Sch. fundraiser sponsor
20 Opposed to
21 Online attention-seeker
22 "Othello" villain
24 "Get out of here!"
26 Immensely impressive
32 "On the ___ of Morning" (Angelou poem)
33 Road groove
34 Sulky state
35 Swelled head
36 Some minor injuries
40 Vet's patient, often
41 Camera attachment
43 Young bloke
44 Two-time WNBA MVP Delle Donne
46 Adventure novel by Robert Louis Stevenson
50 Hightail it
51 Highly skilled
52 "Downton ___"
55 Jessica of "Hitchcock"
57 Midwest ___ (rock subgenre)
60 Thick slice

61 Manuscript ready to submit
64 Pricey Japanese beef
65 Bothers greatly
66 "I swear!"
67 Sing "tweedle do dah doe doop boop," perhaps
68 Six-pt. plays
69 Rita's role in "West Side Story"

**DOWN**

1 Equine with long ears
2 Fraidy-cat
3 Silent-letter pest
4 Log-shaped pastries
5 Slippery fish used in hitsumabushi
6 Put in alphabetical order, e.g.
7 Improve
8 Throw in
9 Groups of Girl Scouts
10 Cookie that some people eat with mustard
11 "Got to Be ___" (Cheryl Lynn hit)
12 Like many supermodels
14 Roll out the red carpet for, say
17 Hourly salary
21 Amount of bricks
23 Gets on in years
25 Absolutely detest
26 Olympic sled racer
27 Flying solo
28 Wall Street transaction

29 How some contracts are signed
30 Evil spirit
31 "At Last" singer James
32 Clobber with snowballs, say
37 Hint
38 Florida scrub jay, for one
39 ___-care
42 Low-risk wager
45 After a while
47 Shrewdly tricky
48 Creative flashes
49 Fly off the shelves

52 Queries
53 Group of like-minded voters
54 Ali ___ ("Open sesame!" speaker)
56 Tattooing fluids
58 Country east of Mauritania
59 "Come to think ___ . . ."
61 Tailor's concern
62 Molecule researched by Rosalind Franklin
63 Brewed beverage

# 60
## IT'S RUINED
By Gail Grabowski

**ACROSS**

1 Apprehensive feeling
6 Complete collections
10 "Hidden Figures" org.
14 Bed on a boat
15 Runner-up in a fable
16 Carries a negative balance
17 Part of a flight between floors
18 One of the Great Lakes
19 Position in an ordered list
20 Evidence of unreliability
23 ___ and don'ts
25 Sound booster
26 "This Film Is Not Yet ___"
27 Copes with change
29 Group of plotters
32 Zero
33 Watercolor prop
34 Sadness
37 Got ready for exams
41 Paranormal skill, for short
42 Upper crust
43 Zoo ditch
44 Star count on the U.S. flag
45 Colorful Easter dip
47 Teapot part
50 Wreath of blooms
51 U-turn from NNW
52 Soft, lustrous fabric
57 Participates in a marathon
58 Minnesota's state bird
59 Avoid wedding expenses
62 On a single occasion
63 Auctioneer's call
64 Akwaeke Emezi creation
65 Property owner's document
66 Some first responders, for short
67 Move on tiptoe, say

**DOWN**

1 Parts of a six-pack
2 ___ worth
3 Takes some snooze time
4 Pudding recipe instruction
5 A turtleneck partially covers it
6 Wool-bearing animal
7 Be worthy of
8 Ballroom blunder
9 Visionary
10 Usual
11 Look forward to
12 Touch or smell, for example
13 FAQ part
21 Canada hwy. distances
22 Dental care brand
23 Move to the music
24 Baking soda can neutralize them
28 Upper-bod muscle
29 Subtly spiteful
30 Tennis stadium namesake Arthur
31 Nectar collector
33 Make revisions to
34 Log cabin heater
35 Gives approval to
36 Lauder of cosmetics

**Down (partial clues shown)**

36 Artist Haring
39 Keebler sprite
40 "I'm shocked!" letters
44 Fretted
45 Sushi fish
46 They're assumed to be true
47 New England seafood
48 Wrinkled snack
49 Fraction of a pound
50 Provides temporarily
53 "You're something ___!"
54 Gloom's companion
55 Electric unit

56 School located in North Carolina's Piedmont Triad
60 Potpie morsel
61 Caribou relative

# 61
## V-DAY
By Kate Hawkins

**ACROSS**

1 Sums
5 Swedish Music Hall of Fame group
9 Actress Midthunder
14 Climactic part of a dance song
15 Defeat decisively
16 Workplace benefit for a new parent
17 The other way around
19 Glove material
20 Supper time
21 Skirt feature
23 Lets
24 "Little Miss Sunshine" Oscar winner Alan
26 Recede
29 Sandwich initials
30 One might be shared millions of times
32 Tegan and Sara, e.g.
34 Borg who advocated for gender parity in technology
35 Accidents
38 Animal
40 Form option accompanied by a text box
41 Liquid-Plumr alternative
42 Revving sounds
45 ___-ray disc
48 Feature of a needle or a potato
49 Deep Blue's game
50 Shade that Amadeus Cho turns, in the comics

52 Be defeated
53 Import/export taxes
55 Run ___ of
58 Simple Congressional procedure
60 "Cool!"
61 "___ kleine Nachtmusik"
62 Diva's highlight
63 Dissuade
64 Traversed a hardwood floor in socks, perhaps
65 Observance before Easter

**DOWN**

1 "Always" or "never," grammatically
2 Nonsense
3 Museum tour guide
4 Very weary
5 "Hear, hear!"
6 Steals
7 Do a table-clearing job
8 Largest U.S. state by area
9 Totally ineffectual
10 Food group sometimes avoided on Mondays
11 Vampire in disguise
12 12/31, e.g.
13 Tyrannosaurus ___
18 French word before and after "a"
22 Rapper ___ Kim
25 Monopoly board quartet (Abbr.)
26 Turn from rough draft to final draft

 **USA TODAY**

**27** ___ noire
**28** Wild swine
**30** A-lister
**31** Digging
**32** Actor Germaine
**33** Red, orange, or yellow
**35** Relocate
**36** Humble response to a compliment
**37** Wedge or mule, for example
**38** Italian bread-and-toppings appetizer
**39** Male sheep
**41** Uno x 2

**43** "Be Kind Rewind" medium
**44** 19th-century lawman Bass ___
**45** Prior to
**46** Didn't take out
**47** Depose
**50** Standardized test for a future Ph.D., often
**51** Nemesis
**52** String instrument
**54** Got every question correct on
**55** "Go on . . .?"
**56** Finder's reward
**57** Nondairy milk source
**59** Stir-fry need

# 62
## ALL-INCLUSIVE
By Mark McClain

**ACROSS**

1 Olympic award
6 "Black Girls ___!" (BET award show)
10 Sharp flavor
14 Entertain
15 Bubble tea add-in
16 Do the bidding of
17 All night
19 Cat's rumble
20 Numerical guess (Abbr.)
21 ___/neuter
22 Bit of body art
24 Cook over high heat
25 Popular sport in Japan
26 Altogether
28 Sound intensity unit
31 Painter Claude or singer Victoria
32 Brood silently
33 Chilling sign, perhaps
35 Seriously gloomy
36 Nemesis
37 Early DVR service
38 "It's a ___ point"
39 "Power" star ___ Anthony
40 Scatter around
41 Loud sleepers
43 Not far
44 Sock away
45 Phony
46 Solo diner's response to "How many?"
49 Marine mammal

50 Back muscle, for short
53 First word of some fairy tales
54 All day, in some offices
57 Sirius, e.g.
58 Swiped
59 Imitate
60 Rhino's protrusion
61 O'Hare and DFW, for two
62 Secret supply

**DOWN**

1 Created
2 Birds that can outrun humans
3 Airborne soil
4 Make inquiries
5 "Dig in!"
6 Navigation aid
7 Skin care brand
8 Dairy farm asset
9 Berea College's state
10 All the way down
11 Share a border
12 The one Roman emperor hidden in this clue
13 Pita sandwich
18 October birthstone
23 "___ missing something?"
24 All over the ship
25 Seat of Dallas County, Alabama
26 Spanish for "bulls"
27 Bulbous veggie
28 Swashbuckler movie showdowns

**29** Leaders of Kuwait
**30** Flood protection
**31** "Doctor Zhivago" studio
**32** Trap
**34** "Right this instant!"
**36** Month, day, and hour of the 1918 armistice
**40** Zigzag ski races
**42** Male in a flock
**43** Casual conversation
**45** Looks for
**46** Rogan ___ (curry dish)
**47** Golden Rule preposition

**48** Surgery souvenir
**49** Holier-than-thou type
**50** Peruvian capital
**51** Hertz competitor
**52** Word in some college names
**55** "Good for it" note
**56** Temper tantrum

● **USA TODAY**

# 63
## ON THE LINKS
By Zhouqin Burnikel

**ACROSS**

1 ___-rate (decidedly inferior)
6 Home office fixture
10 Dot on an ocean map
14 "Judy" star Zellweger
15 Sportscaster Andrews
16 Potato's exterior
17 Take in or let out
18 Lithuania currency
19 Like games that go into overtime
20 Singer's knack
23 ___-Caps (movie candy)
24 In need of a map
25 Prepares for a trip
29 Tiny amount
30 Drink that might be dirty
32 Voting alliance
34 Nowhere to be found
36 Small-screen spot
37 Feature of many cars
40 British bathrooms
41 Enjoys some fried tofu, say
42 Game guideline
43 "You're on!"
45 Favorable vote
46 "A League of ___ Own"
47 Get an F
49 CD predecessors
52 Triangular scooper
56 Take the lead
59 "Excuse me . . ."
60 Eucalyptus-loving marsupial
61 Marathoner's rate

62 Mama's mama
63 ___ salt (foot bath additive)
64 Poker stake
65 Neat as a pin
66 Spots for parking it

**DOWN**

1 They might be sprung
2 "Twister" star Hunt
3 Emcee's opener
4 Snorkeling site
5 Dilapidated
6 Specifics, in slang
7 Explode volcanically
8 iPad voice
9 Shoelace formation
10 "For real?"
11 Slide down slopes
12 Tell a whopper
13 Final part
21 Basic bed
22 EMT's procedure
26 ___ rights
27 Another name for a jack, in cards
28 Entree accompaniment
29 Small ornamental plant
30 ___ Southwest Grill
31 Every part
32 Soup base
33 Untethered
34 At the drop of ___ (instantly)
35 Like some burritos
37 Dart like a dragonfly

**USA TODAY**

**Down (continued)**

**38** Minuscule
**39** Salt flats, e.g.
**44** Frat cat
**45** Feel poorly
**47** Fanatic
**48** Maybelline alternative
**49** Capital city where yak butter tea is popular
**50** Cockpit worker
**51** Floods with junk email
**53** Long-winded complaint
**54** Khao Sod language
**55** Deal
**56** Place to be covered in mud
**57** Fashion expert France
**58** Play segment

# 64

## ACK UP

By Evan Kalish

**ACROSS**

1 Struck down, in biblical language
6 Collide with
9 Ruler in old Moscow
13 "Sure, you can have a ride"
14 E pluribus ___
16 Arm bone
17 Foreboding signs
18 "The Real" host Love
19 "Big" student of Mrs. Godfrey, in the comics
20 Get out of Dodge
23 TV's Remini
24 Hefty stack of paper
25 "Wish you ___ here!"
28 Discipline practiced on mats
30 Bicycle parts
34 Enjoyed some sashimi, say
35 Pigeon's murmur
36 "Yeah, su-u-ure"
37 Start cohabiting
41 Tall accessory
42 "Mulan" invader
43 Latin for "eggs"
44 Doreen St. Felix work
45 Regarding
46 Rowing team
47 Wheelchair incline
49 Cafeteria food holder
51 Give someone a lot of money
57 Food that might be made with frybread
58 Plum relative that gets paired with gin
59 Sierra Nevada lake
60 Actress Akana
61 German for "mister"
62 "Don't put all your eggs ___ basket"
63 Banana protector
64 Witness
65 Singer Leonard

**DOWN**

1 Bodega or boutique, for example
2 NYC home of Romare Bearden's "Patchwork Quilt"
3 Grp. influencing oil prices
4 Chimelike sound
5 Come as a direct result
6 Round dancing accessory
7 Privy to
8 Arctic landscape
9 Hot fish sandwich
10 Person from Croatia or Serbia, perhaps
11 Prefix for "penultimate"
12 "The Photograph" star Issa
15 One of 13.1 in a half marathon
21 Salary reduction
22 "Bald" bird
25 Garbage scow's haul
26 Cultural value system
27 ___ the benefits (gets rewarded)

**29** People who dye their hair black, often
**31** Detest
**32** Christopher who played Superman
**33** Tube near a soda fountain
**36** Pay no mind
**38** Grilling fuel
**39** River rental
**40** Really bizarre
**45** Pandowdy fruits
**46** "___ de Bergerac"
**48** Semisolid substance

**50** Room below a roof
**51** Scourge
**52** Condition treated by retinoids
**53** Ripped
**54** "That didn't sound good . . ."
**55** Orange road marker
**56** Peachy ___
**57** Faucet

# 65
## SAVE IT!
By Gail Grabowski

**ACROSS**

1 Ritzy
5 "Miracle on 34th Street" store
10 Performs a part
14 "Ocean's 8" actress Hathaway
15 Edgar ___ Poe
16 Fireplace buildup
17 Friendly emoticon
19 "Fine by me"
20 Lukewarm
21 Arthur who won the 1968 US Open
22 From the top
23 Skillet or wok, for example
25 Narrow body of water
27 Slumber party garments
31 Bonnie's partner in crime
34 Small earring
35 Thermometer unit
39 "Chandelier" singer
40 Mule's sire
41 Enclosures for sows
42 Sci-fi crew members, for short
43 "I ___ a Song Go Out of My Heart"
44 Rubbed off the page
45 Fence entryway
46 State home to many Wolastoqiyik
48 Triangular snacks
50 At that
54 Edwin Starr asked, "What is it good for?"
55 Prefix meaning "against"
57 Sluggish-sounding fruit
59 Courtroom hammer
63 Aromatic necklaces
64 Like some lines
66 Sao ___ and Principe
67 Friend
68 A light blue, pink, and white one represents the trans community
69 Tip jar fillers
70 Ingredient that causes dough to rise
71 Snakelike swimmers

**DOWN**

1 "The ___ is never dead . . ." (start of a Faulkner quote)
2 "My turn to treat"
3 Scissors sound
4 Rooftop landing area
5 ALS Awareness Month
6 First letter of the NATO phonetic alphabet
7 Reunion group
8 Fancy boat
9 Scornful look
10 Attack
11 Local government center
12 Pulled apart
13 Concoction from a slow cooker
18 Dutch cheese
24 Low point that's an anagram of "drain"

Crossword grid (14×14 with numbered cells):

Row 1: 1 2 3 4 ■ 5 6 7 8 9 ■ 10 11 12 13
Row 2: 14 ■ 15 ■ 16
Row 3: 17 18 ■ 19
Row 4: 20 ■ 21 ■ 22
Row 5: ■ 23 24 ■ 25 ■ 26 ■
Row 6: 27 28 29 ■ 30 ■ 31 ■ 32 33
Row 7: 34 ■ 35 36 37 38 ■ 39
Row 8: 40 ■ 41 ■ 42
Row 9: 43 ■ 44 ■ 45
Row 10: 46 47 ■ 48 49
Row 11: ■ 50 ■ 51 52 53 ■ 54 ■
Row 12: 55 56 ■ 57 ■ 58 ■ 59 60 61 62
Row 13: 63 ■ 64 ■ 65
Row 14: 66 ■ 67 ■ 68
Row 15: 69 ■ 70 ■ 71

**26** Gets 100% on
**27** Old Testament song
**28** Sailing
**29** Without a minute to spare
**30** Producer of many arcade games
**32** "Same here"
**33** Makes less stressful
**36** Navigational aid
**37** Marsh stalk
**38** Provide funding for
**41** Spa skin treatment
**45** Tall mammal

**47** Creaks and squeaks and such
**49** Anger
**51** Writing assignment
**52** Stuff that oozes
**53** Supreme Court justice Sotomayor
**55** Palo ___, California
**56** Store sign filler
**58** Omelet ingredients
**60** Despicable
**61** Airline that serves Tel Aviv
**62** Chair parts
**65** Place to park a car

# 66
## OUTER SPACE
By Zhouqin Burnikel

**ACROSS**

1 Fashion house founded in Milan in 1913
6 Waterproof sheet
10 Sports ___
13 '60s lunch counter protest
14 Tappable tablet images
16 Place for a bud
17 Obstacle course event
19 Convenience store convenience
20 Athletic trainer's roll
21 Kept in the email loop
22 Airport areas
24 ___ rug (dance energetically)
26 "Breaking Bad" lawyer Goodman
28 Leading by example
34 Wood for model airplanes
35 "To Kill a Mockingbird" author Harper
36 "You ___ Live Once"
37 Have debts
38 "Just give it a try!"
42 Wingtip tip
43 Omega-3-rich fish
45 Mermaid's habitat
46 Monsoon season events
48 Marinara, for one
52 Civil rights activist Parks
53 ___ out (deduce)
54 Elephant in children's books
57 ___ on (shower with affection)
59 Pizza crust option
63 Bighorn's mother
64 Side dish similar to pilaf
67 Dim sum beverage
68 All gone from the plate
69 Coal digger
70 Pose a question
71 Item on a chore list
72 Defeated in chess

**DOWN**

1 "Over here!" whisper
2 Kelly on TV
3 Give ___ on the shoulder
4 Heads up a movie set
5 Crumb-carrying insect
6 Part of a very simple telephone
7 Orchard measurement
8 Open two-seat car
9 PA-based bank
10 Defeated
11 Review on Thumbtack, say
12 "A Farewell to ___"
15 Transition between topics
18 First part of a play
23 Dog food brand
25 Sundance state
27 "Beg pardon . . ."
28 Cut into pieces
29 Kagan on the Supreme Court
30 Dance in the end zone, maybe
31 Bit of tomfoolery
32 Sci-fi duplicate

 **USA TODAY**

**33** Private ___ (detectives)
**34** Automated programs
**39** Takes advantage of
**40** Website info
**41** Chapters of history
**44** Taj Mahal city
**47** Mozart's homeland
**49** Lady Godiva's ride
**50** Self-critical remark
**51** Takes legal action
**54** ___ carotene
**55** Blows away
**56** Woodpecker's feature

**58** Small bills
**60** Indicate indirectly
**61** Beverage brand with a polar bear mascot
**62** Crossword fanatic, perhaps
**65** Touch gently
**66** "Very interesting . . ."

# 67
# LEADING LADIES

By Caitlin Reid

## ACROSS

1 "My bad!"
5 Mary had a little one
9 Poems that praise
13 Little fight
14 Brownish photo filter
15 Testing phase
16 ___ to the throne
17 Some are checkered
18 Lie adjacent to
19 Yearly credit card charges
21 Earned
22 Part of a dining hall stack
23 Delivers an address
25 "Understood"
28 Opt for
30 Wandered
31 "No justice, no peace," e.g.
32 Letters rebuking oversharing
35 Got older
36 "The Lion King" sounds
37 Sympathize with
38 "Young man . . ."
39 Big name in fables
40 Upright or grand, for example
41 "Hey, respect the line!"
43 AMC drama set in the '60s
44 "Aw, ___!"
46 Trig ratio
47 Mild, not wild
48 Like experimental art
54 "Dancing Queen" band
55 Suit
56 Snoozefest

57 Narrow valley
58 ___ and bounds
59 Idyllic place in the Bible
60 Listeners lend them
61 Goofs
62 Descriptor for grass or skin

## DOWN

1 Work watchdog grp.
2 Unlocked
3 Pest
4 Walked with confidence
5 ___ greens
6 Architectural feature that's an anagram of "peas"
7 Tiny pest
8 They might be played with low A extensions
9 2010s first family
10 Argumentative school squad
11 Musician's practice piece
12 Makes full
14 Spilling sound
20 Desert-dry
24 Decay
25 Some savings plans
26 Rare Essence genre
27 One is not one
28 Utter confusion
29 Dorothy Ashby instrument
31 Doing business has one
33 Long hair
34 Element name that can also be a verb

**36** Eco-friendly, perhaps
**37** Convertible couch
**39** "Yipes!"
**40** Hungry ache
**42** Atlantic and Pacific, for two
**43** Oven gloves
**44** Place for actors
**45** "Se ___ espanol"
**46** Salon sounds
**49** Swerve suddenly
**50** Worshipped from ___
**51** Went by camel
**52** Physician Charles R. ___
**53** Start of a counting rhyme

# 68
## GARDENER'S GRIND
By Patrick Jordan

**ACROSS**

1 Southern accent feature
6 Casino transactions
10 Karate student's accessory
14 Poppins portrayer Andrews
15 Word above an emergency door
16 "Garfield" dog
17 Had an odour
18 City that rhymes with "casino"
19 Religious offenses
20 Alternate version of a film
23 It's slung during some campaigns
26 King ___
27 Nutritional plans
28 Coat completely
30 Doesn't show up
32 Simmered fruit
34 Part of IOU
37 Aries or Aquarius, e.g.
38 Matter-Eater ___ (superhero)
39 Raw material for linen
40 Victorious shout
41 Forefront
45 Shrewd
46 More seepy
47 Leg up
49 Dog trainer's command
50 Clock setting for Jacksonville in Jan.
51 Boxer's ideal condition
55 Sports anchor Duncan
56 Soda fountain option
57 Seedless orange type
61 Prefix akin to "super"
62 "My longest yeah boy ___" (hit YouTube video)
63 Jeweled headpiece
64 Medication portion
65 Went down in the ocean
66 Available

**DOWN**

1 Mix makers
2 Cuba libre liquor
3 Pub drink
4 Word before "card" or "rice"
5 "You don't have to control everything"
6 Hat associated with France
7 CFO, for one
8 Subtle coloration
9 Served as a proxy
10 Supervisors
11 Decree from the throne
12 Blanket carrier in "Peanuts"
13 Student's stressor
21 Felt remorse about
22 Make mad
23 Far from organized
24 Free from a bind
25 Drink remnants
29 Have
30 Sitcom bunch surname
31 Volkswagen Group subsidiary
33 Architect's rendering
34 Nostalgic song

35 Laborers' income
36 Make use of
39 Cylindrical hat
41 Worst place in a race
42 Tempts
43 Film ___
44 Became a fan of
45 Stick together
47 "The Hobbit" hobbit Baggins
48 Gazes rudely at
49 ___ contrast
51 Conflict between families, say
52 Bright astronomical event
53 ___ Burnie, Maryland
54 Major water pipe
58 Large tub
59 Swath of history
60 Spot for a mall Santa's visitor

# 69
## FAIRY-TALE ENDINGS
By Gabrielle Friedman

**ACROSS**

1 Disney's "___ Rock"
5 Like phat si-io
9 Cause to curl
14 Cookie in some crusts
15 Have over
16 Very, in slang
17 Wednesday evening, e.g.
19 Perfect
20 Bedsheet fabric
21 One way to see
23 Big name in pasta sauce
25 Holy Trinity part
26 ER test
29 Dimmer, for one
35 Rookie gamer
37 Designer Saab
38 Earl or baron, for example
39 Palindromic pop group
40 "___ Marner" (George Eliot novel)
42 Actress Wells
43 They can be "fiddlers" or "ghosts"
45 ". . . or ___"
46 Purse fastener
47 Prompt accompanying some pictures on social media
50 Aliens (Abbr.)
51 Grad students, often
52 Store away
54 "Wake Me Up When September Ends" band
59 "Scooby-Doo" exclamation

63 Moved like molasses
64 Sugary breakfast option
66 St. ___ (Caribbean island, for short)
67 Electronics company hidden in "face recognition"
68 Olympic blade
69 State home to the Sawtooth Range
70 Homies
71 Everything bagel bit

**DOWN**

1 Major sources of methane
2 ___ rug
3 Swim event
4 Texas Hold 'em, e.g.
5 Whatchamacallits
6 Blanket ___ (person who steals the covers)
7 Queens tennis stadium
8 ___-bitty
9 Nickname for the Windy City
10 Guacamole ingredient
11 Gas station drink brand
12 "Get me?"
13 Deficient in color
18 Oscar winner Patricia
22 Suffix for "lion"
24 More of an eyesore
26 Make into law
27 Snake that might spit
28 Portable survival kit
30 Places for tobogganing

USA TODAY

**31** Rags on
**32** Butcher shop offering
**33** Shoe spike
**34** Lends a hand
**36** They're often put under pillows
**41** Fizzy drinks
**44** Name placeholder
**48** Currency exchange letters
**49** One of three in a yard
**53** It's confusing when they get crossed

**54** Asian desert home to some jerboas
**55** "Let's get this show on the ___!"
**56** Scribe in the Hebrew Bible
**57** "Right away!"
**58** Anti-racist women's org.
**60** "I'm not going near that"
**61** Swiss artist Paul
**62** Toboggan, for one
**65** Elongated fish

# 70
## FOREMOTHERS
By Zhouqin Burnikel

**ACROSS**

1 On the subject of
5 Great Lake fed by the Detroit River
9 Garment for messy meals
12 Bosom buddy
13 Rest period
14 Striped candy shape
15 Piercing inside the mouth
17 "Pitch Perfect" star Kendrick
18 Place for a seaweed wrap
19 Skilled person
20 Pot starters
21 Where an appeal may be heard
26 Cups, saucers, etc.
28 Picked out
29 Sat at a red light
30 Animals in pens
31 Tony winner Ramirez
35 Meadow hidden in "pleasant"
36 Sneaker strings
37 Dejected
38 Puts a stop to
40 Landmass that sounds like part of a supermarket
41 Speedy
43 Hopping mad
45 Des Moines Register readers, often
46 Miranda Lambert, for one
50 Quadriceps-strengthening exercise

51 Name that's alphabetically consecutive
52 Smidgen
55 End in ___ (come out even)
56 Outdoor stroll
60 Queens-based baseball team
61 Hill on CNN
62 "I couldn't agree more!"
63 ___-K (program for toddlers)
64 Watch sound
65 Appealing

**DOWN**

1 Talent show segments
2 Hit the mall, say
3 Deli offering
4 "holy [cow emoji]!"
5 Faux pas
6 Camping gear retailer
7 "Cats" actor McKellen
8 Heart test, for short
9 Language group that includes Swahili and Zulu
10 Word before "child" or "circle"
11 Centaur, for one
13 Round hat
14 Summer camp boats
16 Escalated
20 Cooling appliances, for short
22 Put into practice
23 Winter roof hangers-on
24 "Well, golly!"
25 "Upside Down" singer Diana
26 Scrabble piece

**27** Garden with forbidden fruit
**30** Pale-looking
**32** Sugar substitute
**33** Delay cause
**34** Throws into the mix
**36** Pants-on-fire person
**39** Slightly burns
**41** Go ___ (ignore orders)
**42** More than impress
**44** Map app path (Abbr.)
**45** Prefix for "net" or "mural"
**46** Workbench gripper

**47** ___ Banks (North Carolina coast area)
**48** Bring together
**49** Defeatist's lament
**53** Soccer star Morgan
**54** Big Apple-based fashion house
**56** Badminton barrier
**57** Name that's another name backward
**58** ___ Tacs
**59** "That ___ a close one!"

# 71
## SPIES
By Gail Grabowski

**ACROSS**

1 Fruits poached in red wine
6 Carpentry tools
10 Went down a chute
14 Palindromic principle
15 Injured
16 Folktales and such
17 Church structure
18 Inventor's starting point
19 Ready for customers
20 Product that removes dirt
23 In addition
25 Tailless simians
26 Lingering looks
27 Self-confidence
29 Garbanzo ___
31 Lowly worker
32 British noblemen
34 Green veggie
37 Living decoration
41 Opposing vote
42 Bygone
43 DVR pioneer
44 Runs smoothly
45 "Excuse me!"
47 Regarding
50 Unit of lettuce
52 Ingredient in drain openers
53 Small mammal with a
   distinctive snout
57 Was a tattletale
58 Big gulp
59 Make fun of
62 Got up

63 Take cover
64 Toymakers in Santa's
   workshop
65 Poetic tributes
66 During
67 Smooth and glossy

**DOWN**

1 School support org.
2 Fish for which a California
   river is named
3 Home to millions of workers,
   perhaps
4 Legit
5 Small waterway
6 Glisten
7 Upscale German cars
8 Little brown bird
9 Deer dad
10 Campaign catchphrase
11 2020 Super Bowl halftime
   performer Jennifer
12 "Fame" star Cara
13 Damage that might be
   hammered out
21 Alert akin to a BOLO
22 Let out ___ (express shock)
23 Strike lightly
24 Musical drama
28 Out ___ limb
29 High-fiber stuff
30 Country singer Lindsay
32 Circle's lack
33 Had a meal

**34** Time off for jury duty, say
**35** Diplomatic agent
**36** Make amends
**38** Lament over a loss
**39** National Mall tree
**40** Dating abbr. hidden in "altruism"
**44** Massive crowds
**45** "Coffy" star Grier
**46** Is very fond of
**47** Prefix for "physics"
**48** Got up
**49** Word before "start" or "alarm"
**50** Swiss miss in kid-lit
**51** Double-___ sword
**54** Fed. workplace monitor
**55** Enjoy the pool
**56** Recline lazily
**60** "Told you so!"
**61** Scolding sound

# 72
## SLEEP ON IT
By Kate Hawkins

**ACROSS**

1 Flexible
6 Armor-___
10 Cried
14 ___-faced (pale)
15 "Zero to ___" (song from "Hercules")
16 Jai ___
17 Note paper, of a sort
19 Pinball no-no
20 Needle-nose tool
21 Car decoration
22 Poker hand asset
24 Pantry item
25 Jodie's role in "The Silence of the Lambs"
27 Placed loosely
29 Yearned
30 Word before "straits" or "consequences"
31 Like a latte
32 It covers various things
38 Roof edges
39 Spill a secret
41 Struck heavily
45 Food in a corn husk
47 Not yet in stock
48 Dallas NBAer
49 Go out with
50 Likely to hold a grudge
51 Chocolaty winter drinks
53 Bubble tea flavor
54 Intimate chatter
58 Home to Bahrain and Bhutan
59 ___ hygiene
60 Live show host
61 Curve
62 Declare untrue
63 Nickname for Dorothy

**DOWN**

1 Article for Vegas
2 Suffix meaning "sorta"
3 Steinbeck novel inspired by a Mexican folk tale
4 Part of the foot
5 Draw in
6 Butter-making device
7 Word akin to "fewer"
8 Ms. Grande, fondly
9 Nonfiction movie, for short
10 Muddy the ___
11 Draw forth
12 Royal residence
13 Like books and nobles
18 Cultural anthropologist Margaret
21 Actress ___ Hannah
22 Sum up
23 Baby's bed
25 Cowboy's garment
26 Prom queen's ride
28 Edible green orb
29 Lugged around
31 High-temperature condition
33 Impoverished
34 Leafy green with a "dinosaur" variety

**35** Tech co. nicknamed "Big Blue"
**36** Stand-up human
**37** College home to the Beinecke Library
**40** "Full Frontal" host Samantha
**41** Aluminum piece on a soda can
**42** Discomfort
**43** Ibuprofen brand name
**44** Amphibian with a Wild Ride at Disneyland
**45** Food in a hard or soft shell
**46** Stated openly

**48** "The Unsinkable ___ Brown"
**51** Family
**52** Prefix for "sphere"
**54** 28-Down case
**55** Anger
**56** Cause for a redo in pickleball
**57** Crucial

# 73
## REIN IN
By Zhouqin Burnikel

### ACROSS
1 Restaurant bills
5 Twinkler at night
9 Menzel who won a Tony for "Wicked"
14 Farm area unit
15 ___-Cola
16 Farm storage towers
17 Genuine
18 Not in favor of
19 Togetherness
20 Rate hike for commuters
23 Aspirin's target
25 Opponent
26 Upper part of a semicolon
27 Removes from the computer
30 Back in the day
32 Wrath
33 Suffix for "movie" or "concert"
35 Common storage site
39 Lawyer's salary, often
43 Santa ___ (city near San Jose)
44 Glaswegian girl
45 Roll of cash
46 They might be even, ironically
48 Dangerous skating surface
51 Baggage attachment
54 French for "me"
55 Tiny quibbles
56 Uncommon event
61 Standing upright
62 ___ truck
63 Symbol on a staff
67 2014 Winter Games host city

68 Way out
69 "Goodbye ___" (The Chicks song)
70 Haughty sort
71 Trip on a train
72 Like an octogenarian yoga practitioner

### DOWN
1 Viscous black liquid
2 Blackjack half
3 Garment under a blouse, perhaps
4 Pic that might be taken with a stick
5 Swordfight remnant
6 Voicemail signal
7 Play's opening segment
8 The Amazon, e.g.
9 "No prob!"
10 Eat
11 Epic poem about the Trojan War
12 "That's false!"
13 Until now
21 Pest at a picnic
22 Debate side
23 Danger
24 Actress Demie
27 Hockey puck shape
28 Salade nicoise ingredient
29 Rare groove DJ with an apt name
31 "And so forth," for short

**34** History book section
**36** "Specifically . . ."
**37** Apple computers
**38** Hand over
**40** To and ___
**41** "You caught me!"
**42** ". . . kinda"
**47** Mafia boss
**49** "Monsters, ___" (Pixar movie)
**50** Flower girls, frequently
**51** Lock of hair
**52** Alphabetically early name
**53** ___-Roman wrestling

**57** Tunnel sound effect
**58** Curbside call
**59** Corrosive chemical
**60** One might be left on a fridge
**64** Trip around the track
**65** Make the wrong choice
**66** House buzzer

# 74
## CHANNEL THREE
By Mark McClain

**ACROSS**

1 Mortgage update, for short
5 Out of harm's way
9 Actor's double's assignment
14 Country where Nowruz is celebrated
15 Object of worship
16 Capital of Vietnam
17 Very rare
20 Concert seating sections
21 Garage ___ opener
22 "Thanks for coming to my ___ Talk"
23 Concluded without a trial
26 Bathroom fixtures
28 Sign word in red
30 Suppose
34 Angry commentary
38 Nights before
40 Big name in little trucks
41 It's studied in U.S. schools
44 Very harmful
45 Palindromic time
46 "___ the night before Christmas . . ."
47 Respect
49 Court officials
51 Gush forth
53 Most imminent
58 Appropriate
61 Dry as a bone
63 More achy
64 Something stumbled upon
68 Performed decently
69 Group of three
70 Does something
71 Feline weapons
72 One who saves the day
73 "Hurry up," in hospitals

**DOWN**

1 Disorganized demonstrations
2 Orange Muppet
3 Aspect
4 Not chemically reactive
5 Serious offense
6 Org. for periodontists
7 Toss in your cards
8 "Silas Marner" novelist George
9 Fruity desserts
10 Bit of body art, for short
11 The "U" in "SVU"
12 Alaskan city also known as Siqnazuaq
13 Secured with rope
18 Presque ___, Maine
19 English number that's a noun in French
24 Corporate higher-up, for short
25 Backless couch
27 "Star" star Amiyah
29 Operatic voice type
31 Be aware of
32 Pods that might be pickled
33 "No" votes
34 Pay figure
35 Singer Tori

**36** Postal clerk's cry
**37** Makes an effort
**39** Sneakers, e.g.
**42** They're applied to sprains
**43** Deets
**48** ___ mortals
**50** "Meh"-worthy
**52** Length counterpart
**54** Sudden brightenings of stars
**55** Put up
**56** Sealy alternative
**57** Secret rendezvous

**58** Band whose name refers to electric currents
**59** "The Fresh Prince of Bel-Air" uncle
**60** Triumphant cry
**62** ___ straits
**65** At this moment
**66** "To ___, With Love"
**67** Dove's call

# 75
## FADE TO BLACK
By Caitlin Reid

**ACROSS**

1 "Mind blown!"
5 Elected position
9 Moo's source
12 Bracelet trinket
13 Name that becomes another name if you put it between C and S
14 No longer here
15 Figurative gateway to a long series of distractions
17 Give off
18 "Always Be My Maybe" star Wong
19 Out of charge
20 Frozen rains
22 Sister in "Little Women"
24 Opera piece
26 68-Across alum Gasteyer
27 Florida NBA team
32 Having the wherewithal
34 Clothing
35 "It just doesn't ___ up"
36 Emphatic refusal
39 Bullying types
41 Little criticism
42 "Is ___ so?"
44 Movie critic Stevens
45 Occasion to dress down at work
49 Little rascal
50 Father
51 Droops
55 Sty

58 Another name for bubble tea
60 ___ fitting
61 Benzoyl peroxide target
62 Try to fall asleep, perhaps
65 "Frog and ___ Together"
66 Keen on
67 Greek vowels
68 Long-running sketch show, briefly
69 Noticed
70 Suffix for "Oktober"

**DOWN**

1 Marine mammal
2 It might be hard to break
3 Sphere
4 Amongst
5 Desert traveled by Ibn Battuta
6 Wearing away
7 Not just some
8 Pedicurists work on them
9 "Say what now?"
10 "Way ahead of you!"
11 Sprays, say
12 Sideways-walking crustacean
14 The ___ Davis Institute on Gender in Media
16 Bluish-green color
21 Brazilian dance that's a Greek letter with an extra A inserted
23 Spring festival
25 Biblical garden dweller
28 Bureaucratic headache
29 Mining target

**USA TODAY**

**30** Brainstorming breakthrough
**31** Some music holders
**32** Japan's continent
**33** Searchlight in Gotham
**36** Abbr. in a company name
**37** Willie O'Ree played in it (Abbr.)
**38** People prone to clumsiness
**40** Ayes' counterpart
**43** Homage
**46** Called a softball game
**47** Patch applied using heat
**48** Ower's onus

**52** Helps with something illegal
**53** "That's what's up!"
**54** Exhausts
**55** Positive feedback on the back
**56** App symbol
**57** Long-running CBS drama
**59** Skeptical retort
**63** Word before "blastoff!"
**64** Tool in a shed

USA TODAY

# 76
## LEAP DAY
By Sara Nies

**ACROSS**
1 Sweet stuff
6 Included on an email
10 Bros, e.g.
14 Not these
15 Distinctive air
16 The band Haim, for one
17 Leap with glee
19 Messes up
20 Unrefined metal
21 Famous ___ (rhyming cookie brand)
22 Guiding principle
23 Result of wax buildup, perhaps
26 Pieces in the board game Mastermind
27 Leap from place to place
32 "___ you were going to say that"
35 Pooh's feathered friend
36 Gift in 18-Down
37 Pork, beef, or lamb
38 Pin place
40 Density times volume
41 "___ my last email . . ."
42 Choose
43 Soil
44 Leap into consciousness
49 Pop, by another name
50 Possible purchase from a lot
54 "Namely . . ."
55 Syrup sources
57 Un, translated

58 Newspaper essay
59 Leap ahead in school
62 "___ of the d'Urbervilles"
63 Heap
64 Paid to play a hand
65 Aware of
66 Job title abbr.
67 Smart-mouthed cat in "Homeward Bound"

**DOWN**
1 City near K.C.
2 "Star Trek" role for Nichols and Saldana
3 Pyle of '60s TV
4 Reptile that becomes an insect if you add a W
5 Pro whistleblower
6 Model Carrera
7 Killer dog in a Stephen King novel
8 Love god who's an anagram of "rose"
9 ___ and night
10 Not mono
11 Like some verbs
12 Expensive soup ingredient
13 Not great, not terrible
18 Honolulu's home
22 Lifesaving letters
24 Drive the getaway car for, say
25 Sacred bovine
28 Admit, slangily
29 Female sheep

**30** "Clarissa Explains It ___"
**31** Gossip
**32** Little devils
**33** Doesn't close
**34** Least wide
**38** Enter in a journal
**39** On point
**40** Grp. opposed to intoxicated motoring
**43** Direction opposite WSW
**45** Rebuttal to "You never . . ."
**46** Turner who led a rebellion
**47** Kermit or Ernie, for example
**48** Rae who voiced the mom in "Hair Love"
**51** Layers of paint
**52** South American mountain range
**53** High and thin
**54** Four-legged friend of Dorothy
**55** Goes downhill (or cross-country) fast
**56** Is sick
**59** Relaxing spot
**60** Neon is an inert one
**61** Genetic messenger

# 77
# BIRDWATCHING
By Zhouqin Burnikel

## ACROSS

1 Do some sketching
5 Range
10 Part of a checkout aisle count
14 Letter that precedes kappa
15 "What a surprise to run into you here!"
16 Prego competitor
17 Cartoonist Lubchansky
18 "War and ___"
19 Glasgow resident
20 Royal proclamation
22 Mesozoic, e.g.
23 Place for a fanny pack
24 Loses one's nerve
27 Luau garland
28 Baseball great Radcliffe
29 Skirt past the knee
32 Around, in date ranges
36 "___ hardly wait!"
40 Post-op places, often
41 "Doe, ___ . . ." ("Do-Re-Mi" lyric)
42 "You're right"
43 Religious offshoot
44 Vision
45 Carbonated drink
46 "Shame on you!"
47 Criticizes severely
49 Joke writer's specialty
50 From Zurich, say
52 Long poems about heroes
54 Gradually lost color
56 Fantasy creature
58 Indigenous New Zealanders

61 Fe, on the periodic table
62 Thrash around
64 Reindeer in "Frozen"
65 Vulgar
66 Call off
67 Hardwood used in furniture
68 Tons of
69 Headquartered
70 Gets it wrong

## DOWN

1 Thinnest U.S. coin
2 Pothole site
3 High room
4 Queue to view
5 ___ up (absorb)
6 Place to apply blush
7 Airport on the CTA's Blue Line
8 Butter ___ (ice cream flavor)
9 Contact lens location
10 Nightmares for tax dodgers
11 Anagram of "attic"
12 They might be checked at the door
13 Jeff's partner in the comics
21 Suit accessory
23 Misery
25 Noisy bugs
26 Diagram showing constellations
29 Spray in the produce section
30 Frosts
31 Gets low

**33** People's 2018 Sexiest Man Alive

**34** Rod and ___

**35** Break in hostilities

**37** Boasts loudly about

**38** German car with a four-ring logo

**39** "How cool!"

**47** Get ___ of

**48** "Friday Night Lights" fullback Riggins

**51** Talk show host Williams

**53** Social class

**54** Sundance entry

**55** 86,943 square miles, for Minnesota

**57** Country with a large Hmong population

**59** Hindmost

**60** Tattoo artist's supplies

**62** "How cool!"

**63** "(Every Time I Turn Around) Back in Love Again" band

# 78
## JIBBER JABBER
By Rachel Fabi

**ACROSS**

1 Conspiratorial group
6 Possesses
9 "Hey, you!" but quieter
13 Greeting that may be accompanied by a 36-Across
14 Choose
15 Jazz singer Fitzgerald
16 Not decisive
18 Sign on again
19 Green prefix
20 Itty-bitty
21 Persistent offensive
22 Reserved
24 Each
25 Candy-coated popcorn brand
31 Name that rearranges to spell "Robyn"
34 Lion's sound
35 Long fish
36 Hawaiian welcome gift
37 Small caves
40 Undergrad degrees
41 "Who am ___ say?"
42 Greek letter I
43 Form of yoga
45 Sound of little feet
49 Model Hadid
50 Religious manifestos
54 Anatomical trunk
56 Baby deer of film
59 "___ me tell you . . ."
60 Makes a mistake
61 Dawdle
63 Color hidden in "pie crust"
64 "Fine!"
65 Motrin alternative
66 Word before "gaze" or "bonding"
67 "Gosh!"
68 Dressed to the ___

**DOWN**

1 Made a crow's sound
2 "The Color Purple" author Walker
3 ___ buddies
4 Sound of relaxation
5 Putting on multiple jackets, say
6 Angry cat noise
7 Sore
8 The limit, to an optimist
9 "___. End of Sentence." (2018 documentary)
10 It's often accumulated by medical residents
11 Slimy garden denizen
12 Adhesive material
14 Saute vessel
17 Marijuana
21 Place to get pampered
23 Mystery in the sky, for short
24 Prefix for "futurism"
26 Wilt
27 Ton of, informally
28 Bother
29 Biblical sister of Rachel

## Down

30 "Frozen" queen
31 Radar dot
32 Creature of Himalayan legend
33 Feminist punk movement
38 Nickname for Rihanna
39 "Desperate Housewives" actress Nicollette
44 "___ We There" (Sharon Van Etten album)
46 Kleenex product
47 Prefix for "centric" or "mania"
48 Frozen dessert chain
51 Ripley's first name in "Alien"
52 ___ into (investigate)
53 Eye afflictions
54 Abound
55 Aquatic apex predator
56 Vehicle with pedals
57 Genus with "vera" and "ferox" species
58 "I've Been to the Mountaintop" orator, for short
61 Hound
62 Boxer and conscientious objector Muhammad

# 79
## WHAT A FLOP!
By Gail Grabowski

**ACROSS**

1 Double-jawed eel
6 Agile
10 Serving of ribs
14 "Hello" singer
15 Part of the mnemonic device HOMES
16 Saintly aura
17 Car confiscations, for short
18 Tiny quantity
19 Appliance on a board
20 Pie variety with a fluffy topping
23 "___ Maria"
25 Nabisco brand
26 Monopoly cards
27 Change the title of
29 Broadway backgrounds
31 Kilogram, for one
32 Alabama city in civil rights history
34 Sound from a Holstein
37 Crack up
41 Shade of gray
42 Biblical hymn
43 Person downloading an app
44 Unreliable narrator, at times
45 "Patience is a ___"
47 Neighbor of Portugal
50 Provide a fake alibi for, say
52 Vinyl records
53 Hissing scavenger bird
57 Eye creepily
58 Capitol Hill helper
59 Quick messages
62 Hose storage device
63 Reflex hammer target
64 Magazine celebrating its 75th anniversary in 2020
65 Crafts website
66 Texting button
67 Bird feeder fill

**DOWN**

1 Women's History Month (Abbr.)
2 "___ to the Loom" (Monica Sok poem)
3 Equip with new supplies
4 Ingredient in some lip balms
5 Obedient child's reply, perhaps
6 River near the Louvre
7 Teaser ad
8 Religious ceremony
9 Timeline part
10 Glistens
11 Pizza size
12 Not silently
13 Osteologists study them
21 Smeltery input
22 Dog collar attachment
23 Island whose flag bears a red star
24 Tennis legend Williams
28 Sports stat that counts tries (Abbr.)
29 Criticize severely

**USA TODAY**

**USA TODAY**

# 80
## FORECAST
By Zhouqin Burnikel

**ACROSS**

1 Go toward the summit
6 Sleep under the stars, perhaps
10 Overly curious
14 Daytona 500 entrant
15 Spanish for "love"
16 Whale with powerful teeth
17 Style used for emphasis
19 League member
20 Big ___ (London attraction)
21 "How silly of me!"
22 Descendants
24 Nickname for Ignatius
25 Closest landmass to the Marianas Trench
26 Highway divisions
28 Marine Corps motto, for short
32 Milestones for new pilots
33 Reasonable
34 Unable to decide
35 Back ___ again
36 Goads
37 Norse god of war
38 Salt Lake Tribune's state
39 "Well played!"
40 Essay alterations
41 Suffer humiliation
43 Essential ___ acids
44 Leaf-collecting tool
45 High point
46 Fair hair color
49 Beam of sunlight
50 ___-mo

53 125, to 5
54 Well-matched pair
58 People also known as the Apsaalooke
59 Enthusiastic about
60 Like a lamb or a ram
61 Gets the point
62 Adolescent
63 Bumble meetups

**DOWN**

1 Nursery bed
2 Past the deadline
3 "___ only imagine . . ."
4 Actor Rodriguez
5 Ways across rivers
6 Comics character who says "Ack!"
7 "Little Women" role for Florence Pugh
8 Floor-washing tool
9 Takes as a given
10 2021 Bond film
11 Brand of creme-filled cookies
12 Look over quickly
13 They might be candied
18 Gear components
23 Toothpaste tube closer
24 "Also . . ."
25 Pop or folk, for example
26 Game with bouncing balls
27 Pseudonym
28 Hoisin, e.g.

USA TODAY

**29** Sculptor whose name is a letter + 37-Across

**30** ___-Lay

**31** Quaint stopovers

**32** "Better Call ___"

**33** Ingredient from a rack

**36** Dangerous environment

**40** TV star's recognition

**42** Fleeting trend

**43** Purple smoothie ingredient

**45** Fire felony

**46** Discreetly keeps in the email loop

**47** Temptation

**48** Double-reed instrument

**50** Rotisserie rod

**51** Texas, the ___ Star State

**52** Poems with dedicatees

**55** Dir. that's to the right and a little up on a map

**56** Scarfed down

**57** DuVernay who founded the film distribution company ARRAY

USA TODAY

# 81
## IT'S IN THE CARDS
By Patrick Blindauer

**ACROSS**

1 Ready, willing, and ___
5 Pasta sauce brand
9 Jump from a board above a pool
13 Detonation sound
14 Movie excerpts
16 Environmental activist Brockovich
17 Place to catch catchers and pitchers
20 "The Jetsons" dog
21 Sandals might leave them
22 Sticky stuff
25 Luggage-inspecting org.
26 Big name in handbags
30 Make it through to
35 Wedding phrase
36 "___ Colors" (Cyndi Lauper hit)
37 Aviator Earhart
38 Ripped up
40 Grant permission
42 Some pretzels, shape-wise
43 Feeder on the farm
45 Clothing labels
47 Female pheasant
48 Like some two-option questions
49 Don't get discouraged
51 "Blerg"
53 Sea creature that might bark
54 Invited on a date
59 One side of the "Cola Wars"

63 Razor company that owns MEL Magazine
66 School graduate, for short
67 Go get married in secret
68 "Leave it ___!" ("I got this!")
69 Workplace note
70 Mongolian tent
71 "X marks the ___"

**DOWN**

1 Swedish pop quartet
2 Big snakes
3 Got checkmated, e.g.
4 Come out of hiding
5 Electronics brand
6 "I'm ___ ears"
7 Gold in a thin layer
8 Bit of news
9 "Sorry Not Sorry" singer Lovato
10 Base metal of steel
11 Climbing plant
12 Comes to a close
15 Does bad things
18 Give a leg up to
19 Bedside awakener
23 Winfrey who starred in "Beloved"
24 Rwandan hero Rusesabagina
26 Li'l cat
27 Love to pieces
28 Spanish bulls
29 Triangular Greek letter
31 Suffix for "profit" or "puppet"

**32** Hawaiian word of peace and love
**33** Fall beverage
**34** "It ___ been easy"
**37** "Well, golly!"
**39** Convent member
**41** Sources of acorns
**44** Cheese from the Netherlands
**46** Hexagon, for one
**49** Like so
**50** Puts into office
**52** Feature of some horror films

**54** Savage who co-hosted "MythBusters"
**55** Foot bottom
**56** Fashion star Heidi
**57** Red "Sesame Street" character
**58** Ten Commandments pronoun
**60** Dropping-into-water sound
**61** Japanese wrestling form
**62** "That tracks"
**64** Fourth pg. of a calendar
**65** Pet checker

# 82
## BREAKING BAD
By Caitlin Reid

**ACROSS**

1 It might be unfolded into a bed
5 Sharp comment
9 Having the capacity
13 See 58-Down
14 A long ways away
15 Acquire
16 Fields of expertise
17 Not "for here"
18 YouTube star Chamberlain
19 Long-eared dog
22 Telly network
23 Top of a wave
24 In addition
26 C-3PO and R2-D2, for example
29 Prefix for "grade" or "virus"
30 Alias letters
31 Save for later
34 XS and XL, for two
37 Adorers
39 Sneakerheads buy them
41 9-Across in reverse
42 Tots
44 Mainstream ___
46 Nosh on
47 Team race
49 Brightly colored shirt style
51 Thingamabob
53 Spiral pattern
55 Unwell
56 Sign in a car's back window
61 African waterway

63 Sound from a cat or an engine
64 Sleep malady
65 At any point
66 Cut down
67 "Are You Gonna Go My Way" singer Kravitz
68 Ruby and maroon, e.g.
69 Places to get peels
70 Exam for a future "Esq."

**DOWN**

1 Indie pop duo Tegan and ___
2 Minecart fillers
3 Utter disaster
4 Declares
5 They might involve bubbles
6 Get ___ in the door
7 Italian sauce
8 Emily who wrote "Wuthering Heights"
9 Get on in years
10 Hoodwinked
11 "How low can you go?" dance
12 Establish legislatively
13 Great, for short
20 Tries out
21 Connect the ___
25 "Captain Marvel" star Larson
26 River floater
27 "That's fine"
28 Funded
29 Woodwind piece
32 "Egad!"

**33** Caviar and such
**35** Bidding site
**36** Satisfy
**38** Flower-to-be
**40** A&T Four protest
**43** Big piece of concrete
**45** Point guard's big miss
**48** Evolves
**50** Has a small wedding
**51** Purveyor of hash browns
**52** "___, the Other Reindeer"
**53** Neighbor of Lebanon
**54** Sidewalk wrigglers

**57** Possible result of a pat on the back
**58** With 13-Across, star of TV's "Mom"
**59** Pad payment
**60** Calendar unit
**62** Workplaces for some RNs

# 83
## TIEBREAKERS
By Zhouqin Burnikel

**ACROSS**

1 Unwanted stuff in a fish tank
6 Hummus and salsa, for two
10 Spam source
13 "Beauty and the ___"
14 "Same here!"
15 Futbol fan's cheer
16 Youthful aesthetic
18 Poem that pays homage
19 Aide for an exec (Abbr.)
20 Oceanographer Sylvia
21 Comparable
22 Was in attendance
24 Trees tapped for sap
26 Doesn't defy
28 "Immediately!"
30 Where driftwood washes up
31 Like unseasoned food
32 Appliance that sucks, for short
35 "The ___" (Chloe Zhao rodeo film)
36 Competed like Allyson Felix
37 Go viral on Twitter
39 Vegan protein source
40 Having debts
42 Band section
43 Fragrant spring blooms
45 Dealership document
46 At a leisurely pace
48 Grow closer
49 "The Wizard of Oz" dog
50 Pandemonium
53 Dog's tail movements
57 R&B star Lennox

58 Shopped at the farmer's market, say
60 Response following ". . . and nothing but the truth?"
61 Juliet's flame
62 Speak formally
63 Bear hibernation spot
64 Tour de France mountains
65 Raced down slopes

**DOWN**

1 "Gimme! Gimme! Gimme!" band
2 Early August births
3 ___ Against Guns (LGBTQ activist group)
4 So to speak
5 Alleged aviators of UFOs
6 Place for a peephole
7 Person with a fan club
8 Pikachu or Gengar, for example
9 Soror, e.g.
10 Bibliophiles
11 Song that might bring back memories
12 Low temps
14 Window blind part
17 Egg farm residents
21 Fitting
23 "Oh, puh-leeze!" expression
25 "What happened next?"
26 Wilberforce University's state
27 Skin soother

**28** Prepares for the future
**29** Vibrated, perhaps
**30** Many campus tourers (Abbr.)
**31** ___-a-brac
**33** "The Vampire Chronicles" author Rice
**34** Contents of jewel cases
**38** Cause of a traffic delay
**41** "Awesome!"
**44** ___ Jima
**45** Completely confused
**46** Straitlaced
**47** "Royals" singer

**48** ___-chic (fashion style)
**51** A dromedary camel has one
**52** Quite some time
**54** Bowl berry
**55** Airport area
**56** Slider on a snow day
**58** Chantelle purchase
**59** ___ Alamos, New Mexico

# 84
## STRETCH PANTS
By Claire Rimkus

**ACROSS**

1 Performs a role
5 Big jump
9 Papa ___ (blue cartoon character)
14 Trunk, to a Brit
15 Therefore
16 Haircut similar to a fade
17 Sectional, for one
18 Spanish for "aunts"
19 Low-cost, in product names
20 Government employees
23 Comic's routine
24 Poked one's nose where it didn't belong
25 "No way!"
28 Shirley Ann Jackson's alma mater
30 Chewed like a hamster
34 Straw headwear
38 Suga ___ ("The Proud Family" character)
39 Clear off the whiteboard
40 Environmentalist's prefix
41 Plains stampeder
42 Dallas Mavericks great Nowitzki
43 Federal subsidies for college students
45 Comfort
47 Chloe x Halle, for example
48 Simple shirt
49 Assigned stars to, say
52 ". . . you get the picture" (Abbr.)

54 Some Grand Canyon photos
60 As prompted
61 Undergarments with clasps, often
62 Spam, e.g.
64 Obsessive fans
65 "To be," to Colette
66 Create
67 Coin flip call
68 Like hot pink hair
69 Word before "code" or "rug"

**DOWN**

1 Stomach muscles
2 Hen's home
3 Kimchi-jjigae ingredient
4 Tries
5 "Black Panther" actress Wright
6 Ncuti Gatwa's "Sex Education" role
7 Let out ___ (show surprise)
8 Wannabe
9 "___ Universe"
10 Hawaiian nut
11 Atop
12 Monthly payment
13 Picked hairstyles, for short
21 "___ see!"
22 Dishonestly fixes
25 Opinion columns
26 Nintendo plumber
27 Knot on a tree trunk
29 Archaic pronoun

31 "That ___ Me" (Brandi Carlile song)
32 Show feelings
33 Ballet, for example, in French
35 Do an informal poll
36 Knee part, for short
37 Broke the news to
41 Chicken soup ingredient
43 Anti-leather grp.
44 Made an estimate
46 Lover's touch
50 Firmly fix
51 In need of washing

53 List punctuation
54 Swanky
55 It might be upped at the poker table
56 Org. impacted by the Fair Pay to Play Act
57 Nurses provide it
58 Pantyhose mishap
59 "For goodness' ___!"
63 What "chai" means

# 85
## COLORFUL CELEBRATIONS
By Erik Agard

**ACROSS**

1 "___ hai!"
5 Fountain drinks
10 Antlered animal
14 Like some letters
15 Japanese dog breed
16 People of southern Africa
17 Reach a high point
18 Environmentalist bloc
20 Blew it
22 Carne ___
23 Rejections
24 Power tool that smooths
26 A ___ Called Red ("Stadium Pow Wow" group)
28 Afro pick, e.g.
31 Regardless of the date
34 Threat in a Ralph Ellison short story
39 Thing you oughtn't do
40 Shoestrings
41 Prefix meaning "new"
42 Like a lamb
43 Racetrack shape
44 Rare brew
46 Day of work for a TV host
49 Perform in a band
50 June birthstone
52 Blah
57 "Why ___ you booing me? I'm right"
59 Sends postally
62 Thoroughly enjoy

63 Event at which Hicham El Guerrouj set the mile world record
66 Short-sleeved shirt with a collar
67 Baker who said "Strong people don't need strong leaders"
68 Judo technique
69 Apt name for an eye doctor
70 ___ dunk
71 Victoria or Tasmania, for Australia
72 Colorful substances

**DOWN**

1 ___ and dreams
2 Show with arias
3 Take lessons
4 Tattooed
5 Lose firmness
6 Bhindi masala ingredient
7 Stops functioning
8 Went to for dinner, say
9 "Killing Eve" star Oh
10 "Love Galore" singer
11 Ended up
12 Voice above tenor
13 Fellas
19 Nuisance
21 Packs of cards
25 Unfairly deprive
27 At this point
29 A lot of

**30** Censoring sound

**32** "Coming of Age in Mississippi" author Moody

**33** "Skill in action," per the Bhagavad Gita

**34** Bit of spatter

**35** Volcanic output

**36** Without instruments

**37** "The Color Purple" protagonist

**38** Hang loosely

**42** Toys on strings

**45** Science setting

**47** Top line on a form, often

**48** Bestows

**51** ___ sleeper

**53** Fast

**54** Word before "Coast" or "tower"

**55** "For real!"

**56** Icky

**57** Gets older

**58** Bubble wrap comes in one

**60** Fictional archaeologist Croft

**61** Schedule opening

**64** Water barrier

**65** Reverence

# 86
## SMART SET
By Zhouqin Burnikel

**ACROSS**

1 World's longest above-water mountain range
6 Name that sounds like a food
9 Govt. broadcast monitor
12 Crack up
13 Singer ___ Del Rey
15 Not a sham
16 View a whole season of in one day, say
18 Prefix for "space"
19 Microbrewery brew
20 Wrestler's feat
21 End of a long trip
23 Offer as an enticement
25 Laundry batch
26 Searches high and low
29 Give the green light
31 Screwed up
32 "Because I ___ so!"
33 "To All the Boys I've Loved Before" author Jenny
36 French for "Christmas"
37 Rays from lasers
39 Fictional explorer Marquez
40 Lowest prime number
41 Tha ___ Pound (hip-hop duo)
42 Spice in curry powder
43 The sixth element
45 Got by
46 Comic actress Imogene
47 Grow up
49 Savannah's state
51 ___ carte

52 Place for a mineral scrub
55 Tool for a zen garden
56 Exactly right
59 Flea market stipulation
60 Spanish for "boy"
61 Wear away
62 Garden buzzer
63 Enjoyed a gyro, e.g.
64 "The Mother of Black Hollywood" memoirist Jenifer

**DOWN**

1 "Dark Angel" actress Jessica
2 Place for polish
3 Windswept hill
4 Bibimbap topper
5 Alan who was the first American in space
6 Lexicographer's study
7 Parlor creation, for short
8 Finger-pointer on a poster
9 Fit in
10 Was concerned
11 Plumbing problem
14 "Gotcha!"
15 Betray, in a way
17 Emerges victorious
22 "Calvin and Hobbes" vehicle
23 "Hamilton" climax
24 Layered pasta entree
26 Shipped out
27 Cornfield intruder
28 Snack that's sometimes deep-fried

**30** Term of address that's a palindrome

**34** Low on rainfall

**35** Prefix that means "very small"

**37** Short haircut

**38** Self-obsession

**39** "Bro!"

**41** Big bore

**42** Apple coating

**44** "Green ___" (farm sitcom)

**45** Backless shoe

**46** ___-and-desist letter

**48** Tourist destination near Carson City

**49** Seize suddenly

**50** Particle in an electrolyte

**52** Blizzard component

**53** Mani's partner

**54** Favorable votes

**57** Demolitionist's stock

**58** Rock in a mine

# 87
## MAGAZINE STAND
By Gail Grabowski

**ACROSS**

1 Winter outerwear
6 Words on a spine
11 A treater picks it up
14 Media mogul with a Presidential Medal of Freedom
15 It might be sent with a click
16 "Right you ___!"
17 Fun-loving types
19 WNBA All-Star Nurse
20 Opening for a keycard
21 Calligrapher's stock
22 Athletic shoe feature
24 Used a broom
26 Hwys. with numbers
27 Stat for an emergency service
33 Initial stage
36 Push rudely
37 "Gossip Girl" character Humphrey
38 Clarinet or oboe, for example
39 Short basketball shot
40 ___ to (take care of)
41 Timeline division
42 Baptism and confirmation, for two
43 Red gift
44 Vitally important
47 Investor's purchase
48 Bother incessantly
51 Thin pancake
53 Roofing support

56 Sign it's time to clean out the fridge
58 Verizon subsidiary
59 Luck
62 Large vessel for liquid
63 Senior
64 Influence of musica nortena
65 Hospital show settings, for short
66 Refuse
67 Music genre with "death" and "speed" varieties

**DOWN**

1 Buys, in slang
2 Gems from Australia
3 Symbol on a freeway exit sign
4 Ragged
5 Unready to mingle
6 Many a "Riverdale" character
7 "Don't worry about me"
8 Phone spying devices
9 Rapper ___ Mama
10 Winning candidate
11 Forgo neutrality
12 Operatic solo
13 In need of a nap
18 Auto racing service areas
23 ___ down (disappoint)
25 ___ peeve
26 Answer an invite
28 Exams for H.S. juniors
29 "But of course!"
30 Pointless

 **USA TODAY**

31 Giraffe's hair
32 Brings to a halt
33 Hydrox cookie lookalike
34 Foam ball brand
35 "Click It or Ticket" devices
39 Wasn't forthright
40 In direct confrontation
42 Backs out of a deal
43 Color TV pioneer
45 Short jump
46 "Finding Dory" fish
49 Chaperone, typically
50 Toy truck company

51 Give in
52 Loud engine sound
53 Word before "pillow" or "politic"
54 Garden depicted on the ceiling of the Sistine Chapel
55 ___ puffs (hairstyle)
57 Honest-to-goodness
60 Suffix for "pay"
61 Tach reading

# 88
## WHAT'S YOUR ASSESSMENT?

By Mark McClain

**ACROSS**

1 ___ Christian Andersen
5 Meatless, for short
8 Mine passage
13 "No problem here!"
14 Cost of a bus ride
15 Capital of Egypt
16 Court proceeding with a panel of peers
18 With 49-Down, personal struggle
19 Donkey
20 Competitive successes
21 Attended
22 Contacted via pager
24 Palindromic first name
25 Wake-up call
32 Novelist's framework
34 Utterly silly
35 Card game with unspoken rules
36 Sound of a magical disappearance
37 Not warranted
38 Goals
39 Descendant of hardcore punk
40 "Tender Buttons" author Gertrude
41 "Do ___ others . . ."
42 Uncoverer of abilities
45 Word that often accompanies "neither"
46 Decisively defeated
50 "Jumping the Broom" star Paula

53 Lady on the charts
55 Ginger ___
56 Throw away
57 End-of-semester challenge
59 Tremble
60 Even once
61 Legislation stopper
62 Used a keyboard
63 Moisture on grass
64 ___ Prairie, Minnesota

**DOWN**

1 Ibtihaj Muhammad won an Olympic medal while wearing one
2 Cause laughter
3 Like Odin
4 Cranes' place
5 "You're So ___"
6 Historical times
7 Hair goop
8 Biology or geology, e.g.
9 Oscar winner Beachler
10 "___ Too Proud to Beg"
11 Guitar part
12 Spanish for "bull"
14 "The Wounded Deer" painter Kahlo
17 Short social media post
21 "Batman" surname
23 T.A.'s boss
26 Like legal pad pages
27 Not from a big studio
28 Tease

**Down**

29 Send forth
30 Green-and-brown pattern, for short
31 Ends of many boxing bouts (Abbr.)
32 Partner of circumstance
33 Heist haul
36 Mattar paneer morsel
37 180
38 Six-legged kitchen pests
40 Bent down
41 The ___ (regular customer's order)

43 Outflow's opposite
44 Mystery Writers of America award
47 Placed a tariff on
48 Bring joy to
49 See 18-Across
50 "Hey, over here!"
51 Feeling the flu, say
52 Lint catcher
53 Donate
54 From the start
57 Made a meal for
58 Day before a holiday

# 89
## TOPFLIGHT
By Zhouqin Burnikel

**ACROSS**

1 Rodent pet
4 Untidy states
10 ___ to (admits)
14 Three, for Kentucky Derby horses
15 Chevy named for an antelope
16 Instrument associated with angels
17 Chilled potluck dish
19 Hong Kong's continent
20 Backsplash piece
21 Portable bed
22 Bracelet's place
23 Glenn Research Center org.
25 One-eighty from WSW
26 Words after the title line of Adele's "Hello"
27 Womb's rhyming counterpart
29 Out of danger
31 Large quantity
35 Inner ___ (closest advisors)
39 Structure featured on Missouri's state quarter
40 "The Luck of the ___"
42 Ditch around a castle
43 Heads off
45 Nice people
47 Senses
49 Rug-making machine
50 Crow after a rout
53 Stock market debut (Abbr.)
55 Auction site
58 Foamy pick-me-up

59 "The Bernie ___ Show"
60 Consequential time periods
62 Arthur ___ Stadium
63 Fast-cook side dish brand
66 Animals silhouetted on road signs
67 Longtime buddy
68 "Mystery solved!"
69 Misses an easy catch, say
70 Creatures
71 Mo. city

**DOWN**

1 Totally spellbound
2 "You can say that ___!"
3 Inventor Nikola
4 Soccer legend Hamm
5 Letters on an ambulance
6 Longest keyboard key
7 Hairstylist's workplace
8 Delights
9 Melancholy
10 Co-founder, perhaps
11 Desert water site
12 Refractor of light
13 Sudden outpouring
18 Send up a trial balloon
22 Cafe convenience
24 Acquirer of TechCrunch in 2010
28 Like a good muffin
30 Sound of a sneeze
31 No longer edible
32 Portland's st.

**33** Take the stage, perhaps
**34** Use a shovel
**36** Tooth on a gearwheel
**37** Online gamer's frustration
**38** They're not of this world (Abbr.)
**41** Party supplies that are often red
**44** Bar mitzvah, for one
**46** Anonymous Jane
**48** "Cold as ice," for example
**50** Febreze alternative

**51** Word before "pointer" or "printer"
**52** Catchall category
**54** China's national animal
**56** Songs for prima donnas
**57** Watercraft for the uber-rich
**61** Make watertight
**63** Angry crowd
**64** Tit for ___
**65** Golfer Ernie

# 90
## KNOCK KNOCK
By Olivia Mitra Framke

**ACROSS**
1 Tag beam
6 Delight
11 Avocados are high in it
14 "Au revoir!"
15 ___ chord
16 Regret
17 Taking a turn for the worse
19 Magazine higher-ups, for short
20 Texting letters
21 Centers of solar systems
22 Peeved mood
23 "This is your captain speaking" speakers
25 Fake duck, e.g.
26 ___ networking
29 One of the senses
31 "Chestnuts roasting ___ open fire . . ."
32 Site of a year-round winter wonderland
36 Land area unit
37 Revealed
38 Second word of a fairy tale, often
39 Places you probably wouldn't want to sleep, despite the name
41 Turn down
42 Wipe away
43 Meeting itinerary
45 "Righty tighty, lefty loosey" subject
47 Baked yesterday

50 Adore
51 Actress Headey
52 Designer's advanced deg.
55 Comedian Wong
56 Some entrances, and a hint to 17-Across, 11-Down, and 28-Down
60 Apple product
61 Give a tattoo to
62 Purchase on a Kindle
63 Direction opposite NNW
64 Works by Keats and Yeats
65 "Lady ___ the Blues"

**DOWN**
1 Many service dogs, briefly
2 Companion of Eve
3 Incites to attack
4 Scared sound
5 "Crime and Punishment" country
6 ___ acids
7 Center
8 Prefix for "verse" or "cycle"
9 Family member
10 Indoor rowing machine, for short
11 Paris tennis tournament
12 Sound transmission
13 Irritable
18 Break in the action
22 Off the beaten path
23 Cone dropper
24 Tucks away

**25** Enjoyed
**26** Fly like an eagle
**27** First word of a fairy tale, often
**28** Provider of wheels
**30** Part of BYO
**32** Furnished with footwear
**33** Eating sound
**34** "Skyfall" protagonist
**35** One-named Celtic singer
**37** Distress signal
**40** How sashimi is served
**43** Top-notch
**44** Forest clearings

**45** Shuts with a bang
**46** Some sodas
**48** "Rumours" or "The Fame Monster"
**49** Squeals
**52** "Goodnight ___" (children's book)
**53** Former tadpole
**54** Requests
**56** Word after "bean" or "skinny"
**57** Hawaiian food fish
**58** Hawaiian instrument, for short
**59** ___-Wan Kenobi

# 91
## DIGGING UP DIRT
By Evan Kalish

**ACROSS**

1 Smartphone download
4 Big Apple NBA team
10 ___ rain
14 Female deer
15 Compassionate
16 Nothing
17 Braille bit
18 Like some clocks
19 Man created from clay in the Quran
20 Movie ogre
22 Nick Fury's original rank (Abbr.)
23 Well into the evening, say
24 Sugary coat on a cake
27 Emulated a hummingbird or a helicopter
29 Change the decor of
31 Country home to Vienna and Salzburg
33 "Me? Definitely up for it!"
34 French fashion house
35 Fancy neck accessory
39 Family nickname
40 Get sick
42 "I get it now!"
43 Disappear into the ___
45 All neatened up
46 ___ and proper
47 Made-___ breakfast
49 Resting at the summit of
50 College major dealing with governments, for short

53 Broadcast again
55 "The Little Mermaid" prince
56 Football scores (Abbr.)
58 Menzel who voices Elsa
61 Quick kiss
62 Deviates from a script
65 Spanish for "two"
66 Jab with a finger
67 Anagram of "Lauren"
68 Earth prefix
69 Pt. of T.A.
70 "Don't ___" ("Just ignore it!")
71 Christmas creature

**DOWN**

1 Totals up
2 Rhyming friend of Roo
3 Scientific container with its own emoji
4 Pants color
5 Pistachio, for one
6 "If you ask me," in a text
7 Pic capturers
8 1980s TV series with a self-aware car
9 Zone
10 Springtime shrubs
11 Moth-repelling wood
12 Enraged
13 Like most U.S. statehouses
21 Class that covers inflation, for short
25 Nothing
26 Filled with remorse

28 Holder of a blood sample
29 Increase in altitude
30 Give off
32 Like a rock
36 Printer insert
37 Neighbor of Indiana
38 ___ down (compress)
40 Natural hairstyles, for short
41 Old harp relative
44 Digitally delivered pass
46 Financially compensated
48 87 or 89, at a gas station
50 "___ Pig" (children's TV series)

51 Nabisco cookies
52 Dog greetings
54 Beverage cart's path
57 Snail relative
59 Actress Sydelle
60 Starting from
63 Investment option with a Roth variety
64 Word after "swag" or "grab"

# 92
## LAWBREAKERS
By Zhouqin Burnikel

**ACROSS**

1 Fast, tawny felines
6 "Right away!"
9 In separate places
14 Pro wrestler Bliss
15 Shout of realization
16 Oceangoing ship
17 Birthplace of the espresso machine
18 Freight weight
19 Many a karaoke song
20 You might stay up to watch it
23 Prime number factor
24 Cross ___ (meet by chance)
26 Past the expiration date, perhaps
29 Unjustified teachings
32 Enjoyed a bowl of beef udon, say
34 It's measured in karats
36 Fahsa, for one
39 Princess voiced by Aimee Carrero
40 Not forthcoming
41 Celebrity photographer Leibovitz
42 Mandible
44 Labor organizations
45 Genesis matriarch
46 Shocking victory
48 WNBA scoreboard stat (Abbr.)
49 Be a cast member of
52 Down in the dumps
54 Sheer chance
61 "Thelma & Louise" star Davis
63 Brewpub selection
64 Use the pink end of a pencil
65 Radio studio sign
66 Accompaniment for skinny jeans, often
67 Nail ___ (manicure providers)
68 Like one-word replies
69 ___ and haw
70 "Nice!"

**DOWN**

1 Beach bucket
2 Sephora competitor
3 Pork or turkey, e.g.
4 Bar between wheels
5 Reject an offer
6 Magazine since 1888, for short
7 "I know! Pick me!"
8 Long for
9 Word of affection in Waikiki
10 Plane worker
11 "Et cetera"
12 Outdoor gear chain
13 Italian for "three"
21 ___ 500 (Memorial Day weekend event)
22 Filtered email
25 Oktoberfest mugs
26 Luxury watch brand
27 "Understood?"
28 Wine and ___
30 Beams with pride

**USA TODAY**

# 93
## ON THE MARKET
By Gail Grabowski

**ACROSS**

1 Wood that rhymes with a dance
6 Wear a long face
10 Hardly thrilling
14 From India, say
15 ___ testimony
16 Bit of dialogue
17 Worker who shelves merchandise
19 Prefix for "virus" or "toxin"
20 Archie, to Meghan
21 "None of that is true!"
22 High-tech intruder
24 Wagers
25 Utensil for spaghetti
26 Second in command
29 Teatime treats
33 Lesser of two ___
34 Profit
35 Name hidden in "unbelievable"
36 Telemarketer's convo
37 Took a wrong turn, e.g.
38 "Juno" star Elliot
39 Tributes in verse
40 Be sorely lacking in
41 ___ out of (withdrew from)
42 Felt offended by
44 Snide smiles
45 Arrange into stacks, say
46 Word after "ginger" or "root"
47 Reliable
50 Sonia Sanchez creation
51 Mythical being with pointy ears
54 Rice-A-___
55 Application for an itchy pet
58 Choral range
59 Right on a map
60 Series of mountains
61 Lowly laborer
62 Obstacles to teamwork
63 Remove all traces of

**DOWN**

1 Barbershop quartet member
2 In the matter of
3 Safari sighting
4 Cul-de-___
5 Lower-body jewelry
6 Lawn-wrecking mammals
7 Mine extractions
8 Number on a golf course
9 Norwegian dog
10 Seasoning in a mill
11 It's clicked to open a website
12 Draw poker bet
13 Future throne occupant
18 Dot on a map
23 Starfish's regenerable feature
24 Informal discussion
25 Like alcapurrias
26 HGTV topic
27 Give the slip
28 Stacks of stuff
29 Gave a darn
30 Tickle pink

**31** ___ Balm (ointment)
**32** Gardener's plantings
**34** Say "Hi!" to
**37** Price to participate
**41** "Almost done"
**43** "___ my problem"
**44** Leak slowly
**46** Marina occupants
**47** Hidden hazard
**48** Coretta Scott King or Harriet Tubman, for Cicely Tyson
**49** Golden rule preposition
**50** Cuban currency

**51** "The Incredibles" character Mode
**52** Stages of a journey
**53** On the house
**56** Fall behind
**57** Two-player card game

# 94
## PR BLITZ
By Stella Zawistowski

**ACROSS**

1 Partner of doom
6 Verb in a legal drama or "The Great British Baking Show"
11 ___ Championship (annual golf major)
14 Insurer named for a volcano
15 Oscar winner Sophia
16 Coffee holder
17 Beatrix Potter bunny
19 Snug as a bug in a ___
20 Gradual destruction
21 House shoe
23 Arm of the sea
25 Comeback
26 What to do after a bad ruling
29 Words upon arrival
32 Earth's outermost layer
33 "Now I'm in It" trio
34 Make a boo-boo
36 Ballerina's support
37 Slice of time
39 Note above fa
41 Lend a hand to
43 Use a crowbar
45 Canadian shoe brand
47 "If only!"
49 Switch
51 Moves stealthily
52 Clean with steel wool, say
54 Persuades
56 Outdoor space in some apartments
59 Totally chill

63 "I'm so mean, I make medicine sick" boxer
64 Fortuneteller's offering
66 Short moment
67 Come after
68 Disney elephant
69 Where to watch "Watchmen"
70 Spit-out parts of a watermelon
71 Glasses, for short

**DOWN**

1 Have one's jaw on the floor
2 Creepy look
3 Palindromic name
4 Baby garments
5 Soak in something savory
6 Amelia Earhart vehicle
7 Burglarize
8 Round things
9 Mantilla or hijab, e.g.
10 Whole
11 Title hit in a 1984 Prince movie
12 Unappetizing food in "Oliver Twist"
13 Hopping mad
18 Take a turn in Yahtzee
22 Remove the skin from
24 Spanish for "aunt"
26 Perform in a play
27 Item for a play
28 Home to San Juan
30 ___ soup (sushi accompaniment)

**31** Medical insurance grp.

**33** Corridor

**35** Actuary's specialty

**38** An old T-shirt might be used as one

**40** Perches for frogs

**42** Baseball players who don't field (Abbr.)

**44** Second-person possessive

**46** ___ Moines

**48** Got a clue

**50** Fruit with Moon Drop and Witch Finger varieties

**51** Make full

**52** Squirrel's acorn hoard, for one

**53** Cardi B or Kim K, e.g.

**55** Merchant's offerings

**57** Christmas candy shape

**58** "What ___ you got?"

**60** "Je t'___"

**61** Network with financial news

**62** Psyche parts

**65** Dirt plus water

# 95
## I'M IMPRESSED
By Zhouqin Burnikel

**ACROSS**

1 Member of an ancient Andean empire
5 Distort
9 Defensive wear
14 In a bit
15 Where cold cuts are cut
16 Lacy mat
17 Santa checks it
18 Contact by phone
19 "The 21st century's author of adolescent evolution," per Cyrena Touros
20 Scheduling stat
23 Plankton's place
24 Free File org.
25 Aloo ___
26 Line on a map
28 Source of solar power
29 Blues singer ___ James
33 Drug extracted from poppies
35 Beat a hasty retreat
36 "___-Seed" (Atwood novel)
37 Illegal act that doesn't hurt anyone
41 Words before "mode" or "carte"
42 "How clumsy of me!"
43 Watering tubes
44 Pre-Easter period
46 Tiny speck
47 "___ help you?"
48 Prefix meaning "very"
50 Angry dog's sound
51 Member of the fam
54 Aircraft emissions have a big one
57 Way up or down
59 "Phooey!"
60 Chunk of drift ice
61 Use bait on
62 "Troy" star Bana
63 Person from Helsinki, say
64 "Good gracious!"
65 Regarding
66 Classroom challenge

**DOWN**

1 New York hockey team, for short
2 Bing or bang, e.g.
3 San Jose resident
4 Dead set against
5 Digital camera insert
6 "Ode to a Nightingale" poet John
7 Palindromic magazine
8 Bit of idle speculation
9 Speak off the cuff
10 Dorm bud
11 Deep mud
12 For ___ times' sake
13 High-fiber bread
21 Home to the Heat
22 Shades of color
27 So last year
28 Took a nap
30 Statement that's a paradox

 **USA TODAY**

31 Bring under control
32 Matures
33 Skating rink shape
34 Large amount of money
35 Carpet installer's measurement
38 Computer device with blinking lights
39 Bracelet ornament
40 Howard with two stars on the Hollywood Walk of Fame
45 Bulbiferous blooms
47 Big name in cooking oil

49 Maternity ward event
50 "Does that make sense?"
52 Touchscreen images
53 Interventional cardiologist's insertion
54 ___ clean (confessed)
55 Besmirches
56 Sound of a spit take
57 Muddy enclosure
58 Peg for a drive

# 96
## OFF CENTER
By Brooke Husic

**ACROSS**
1 Continent that awards seven bonus armies in Risk
5 NASA countdown term
11 Knight's title
14 Where all roads lead, in a saying
15 Sister of Beezus
16 Mine stuff
17 "Too bad," old-style
18 How 14-Across wasn't built
19 Use oars
20 Place to get tickets
22 Japanese noodles
23 Birth control form
24 Opposites of intros
26 Penultimate Greek letter
29 Action requiring trust
32 Instruction on a shampoo bottle
34 Comeback
35 It's sworn
36 Set of peas or whales
37 General feeling
40 They're classified I-VI for rafters
43 Prophets
44 Felt attacked
48 Deplete
49 Crow relatives
50 "___ Enchanted"
52 They might be yoked
53 Employment invitations
58 Glass product from Ball

59 Generate
61 Style of hip-hop music
62 Bit of legislation
63 Transaction at a vintage store
64 "Stranger Things" waffle brand
65 Lil ___ X
66 Background actors
67 Defeat handily

**DOWN**
1 The "A" in UAE
2 Ben and Han's surname
3 3D film option
4 Creator of many fables
5 Thing of little importance
6 Envelope option
7 Apple desktop computer
8 Lymph ___
9 Spanish article
10 Put into words
11 Line sisters' groups
12 Will Smith sci-fi movie
13 Clean again
21 Something to open or save
22 Deprive
24 ___-quoted
25 Flying saucer, for short
26 Big-league player
27 Wig-wearing singer
28 People who might take alone time to recharge
30 Poetry's counterpart

**31** Its 2019 Word of the Year was "climate emergency" (Abbr.)
**33** Alternative to stirred
**36** E-ticket format
**38** Clothing item with a sister size
**39** Mind power, for short
**41** "___ de Replay" (Rihanna song)
**42** Hypotheticals
**43** Lead-in to "care" or "love"
**44** Like a mythical wooden horse
**45** State bordered by Chiapas
**46** Space cloud

**47** They're "slippery" in some arguments
**51** Following
**53** Righteous
**54** Mathematician Khayyam
**55** Therefore, to Descartes
**56** Brand of pasta sauce
**57** "That hit the ___!"
**59** Football star Greenlaw
**60** "Oedipus ___"

# 97
# FIRST DOGS
By Mark McClain

## ACROSS

1 Luggage attachments
5 Embraces
9 Animated duck
14 Spend carelessly
15 Aid and ___
16 Like an acrobat
17 Liquid at the end of the names of a Central American country and its capital
18 In this exact location
19 Restaurant stack
20 Labelle hit covered on the "Moulin Rouge!" soundtrack
23 Rental agreement
24 Powder holder
25 "Finding Your Roots" channel
28 ___ Pueblo, New Mexico
32 Escort through the exit
34 Mouse batteries, often
37 Trial's partner
39 Travel document
40 Committee of experts
44 "Didn't mean to do that"
45 Cut off
46 Disdainful cluck
47 Some sweaters
50 Second try
51 Suffix for "mountain" or "musket"
52 Brief snooze
54 Roughs up
59 Sticky situation
64 Storage floor, often

66 New Zealand bird
67 "Let's get this show on the ___"
68 Hut
69 Diabolical
70 ___ mater
71 Special privileges
72 Movie star Russo
73 Member of a "hive"

## DOWN

1 Sport for young batters
2 Pond growth
3 Dutch cheese
4 Moves back and forth
5 "Very funny!"
6 "Mega" relative
7 Microbe
8 Portobello entree
9 Result of vandalism
10 Up in years
11 Feature of some pens
12 Seasonal malady
13 Affirmative answer
21 Taxi fare calculator
22 "___ Miserables"
26 Freedom Riders rode them
27 Corn supporter
29 Actress Graynor
30 Globular objects
31 Serious
33 Model Marcille
34 On top of
35 Without company
36 Exceptional performer

**38** Wander around
**41** Corner keyboard key
**42** "The Normal Heart" protagonist
**43** ___ code (online retailer's offering)
**48** Raps on the door
**49** Plopped down
**53** Game with flushes
**55** Paranormal energy fields
**56** Fastener shaped like the 21st letter of the alphabet
**57** Andean animal

**58** Car type named for a chair
**60** Choice
**61** End of the workday, often
**62** Bed size
**63** Irritate
**64** Venomous viper
**65** Not just any

# 98
## COUNTER CULTURE
By Zhouqin Burnikel

**ACROSS**

1 Food court's place
5 Spa hot spot
10 Recipient of a special pass
13 Brownstone's front
15 "Citizen Kane" director Welles
16 Tennis champ Ivanovic
17 It might say "Feel better soon!"
19 Sister Helen Prejean, for one
20 Veggies in samosas
21 Big theft
23 Station with salsa
27 World's most visited website
29 Attach using heat
30 Disappear
31 Fraught with risk
32 Trajectory
33 Drains of energy
36 Spanish for "that"
37 Fenway Park, e.g.
40 Part of a comedy routine
41 Email folder
43 Hilarious person
44 Author Ferrante
46 Requiring immediate action
48 Peace agreement
49 Looks without blinking
50 Pizza Hut competitor
51 Florida city nicknamed "The Big Guava"
52 "Carol" star Rooney
53 Prez on pennies
54 Ideal pair of candidates

61 Lily of France item
62 Creepy
63 Heretic's bane
64 Solidify
65 Diagnostic procedures
66 Microsoft game console

**DOWN**

1 Fast-food additive
2 Enjoyed some jiaozi, say
3 "Thanks a ___!"
4 Like bass voices
5 Renewable energy type
6 Characters' journeys
7 "Party in the ___"
8 Negative conjunction
9 "Very much so!"
10 Creme brulee ingredient
11 Occupied
12 Breathe heavily
14 Car repair chain
18 Low in fat content
22 They might cause stars to explode
23 Motions of oceans
24 Originate
25 Tropical food often dried and shredded
26 "___ moment, please . . ."
27 "I understand!"
28 Waikiki Beach island
30 "Justice League" star Gal
32 Aches and ___
34 Horse with white patches

**USA TODAY**

**35** Hangs around
**38** Genealogy chart
**39** "The Little ___"
**42** Ensnare
**45** Flowery accessory with a muumuu
**47** Exam marks
**48** Wrongful act
**49** Buffalo NHL player
**50** Magdalene Odundo and Helen Mirren, for two
**51** Keep ___ on (monitor)
**52** Principal water line

**55** ___ room
**56** Part of an eon
**57** Courteney of "Cougar Town"
**58** Soviet espionage org.
**59** Music hidden in "demo tape"
**60** Word before "shelter" or "haven"

# 99
## TAKE THE WHEEL
By Gail Grabowski

**ACROSS**

1 Captain in "Twenty Thousand Leagues Under the Sea"
5 Comprehend
10 Says as an afterthought
14 League of ___ States
15 Without a service charge
16 Gait faster than a walk
17 Meet a standard
19 Pitchfork point
20 Cosmetics businesswoman Lauder
21 "Half" prefix
22 Admit openly
23 Lead-in to "way" or "well"
25 Vail visitors, often
27 Expired
30 Forbidden City's country
31 "Rosemary's Baby" novelist Levin
32 Part of SATB
35 Swimming pool measurement
38 Cone-dropping trees
40 Wall painting
42 Have the nerve
43 Like a saved seat
45 Glitzy affair
46 Pina colada ingredient
47 Molecule parts
49 Arched part of the foot
52 Not sweet
54 Thatching material
56 Actress Espinosa
57 Gin flavoring

59 City near Phoenix
63 Fully cooked
64 Disintegrate
66 Make ___ for it (flee)
67 "No it ain't!" retort
68 Character who sings "Let It Go"
69 Can't do without
70 Bit of data viz
71 Lacrosse stick features

**DOWN**

1 Neck part
2 Timeline segments
3 Sail holder
4 Think about something a lot
5 African antelope
6 Portia de ___
7 Chasing
8 Come off as
9 "___ the thought!"
10 Achieved
11 Pit against one another
12 Blood drive participant
13 Slow-cooked dishes
18 ___ out (allocate)
24 Headmaster's son in "Sex Education"
26 Baby goat
27 Hitchhiker's desire
28 Song in Italian, often
29 Big Apple boulevard
30 Fuel from a mine
33 Drags along

**USA TODAY**

**34** ___ la la (singing syllables)
**36** Factual
**37** Rope fiber
**39** Place upright, say
**41** Hideaway
**44** Hide-hair connector
**48** Member of the WNBA's 2019 championship team
**50** Brussels-based mil. alliance since 1949
**51** Neighbor of Norway
**52** Car rental choice
**53** Be extremely fond of

**54** Not exactly, informally
**55** Part of SATB
**58** Brand of bath bombs
**60** Proverbially stubborn creature
**61** Furtive "Hey!"
**62** LAX listings
**65** Nanny's charge

# 100
## CHIEF JOINTS
By Kate Hawkins

**ACROSS**

**1** Green iguanas have three
**5** What tons measure
**9** Prima donna's performance
**14** Shade of green
**15** For each one
**16** Shops with cold cuts and hot bars
**17** Painful "food"
**20** Flotsam or Jetsam in "The Little Mermaid"
**21** Taken by mouth
**22** Guerrilla Guevara
**23** Green ___ (salad dressing)
**27** Impedes
**29** Shut-eye
**30** "In ___ of gifts . . ."
**32** Non-earthlings (Abbr.)
**33** Name that's a palindrome
**34** Patrick's surname on "SpongeBob SquarePants"
**36** Stat for a vinyl record
**38** Pasta salad base
**43** Game with Reverse cards
**44** Story
**45** One of eight on an octopus
**47** Vessel for hot chocolate
**49** Rank
**51** Apia's country
**53** Income for a retiree
**55** Income for a grad student
**57** NBC talent show, for short
**58** Heron's home
**60** "Much ___ About Nothing"

**61** Bear a burden
**67** Dip that may be verde or roja
**68** "Adios," in Italy
**69** Legends and such
**70** Provide with funds
**71** Ripped
**72** Emotionally unguarded

**DOWN**

**1** Member of the deer family
**2** Yang's complement
**3** Australian bird
**4** Formally withdraw
**5** Shopping centers
**6** Donkey Kong, for one
**7** Meh
**8** Not dense
**9** Bizarrely
**10** Church bench
**11** Bring out
**12** Wealth
**13** What a phoenix rises from
**18** Doesn't fire
**19** Like some hair
**23** Org. that might sponsor a Pride Month assembly
**24** Ye ___
**25** Business agreement
**26** Hit hard
**28** Note that might start "Re:"
**31** Incensed
**35** Like some sloths
**37** Act as chairperson
**39** Bunny voiced by Mel Blanc

**40** Garage occupants
**41** "The ___ of the Rose"
**42** Metal in red blood cells
**46** Incensed
**47** Markle who wrote the foreword for "Together: Our Community Cookbook"
**48** Countless
**50** Butterfly or wasp, for example
**52** Harlem theater
**53** No longer in fashion
**54** Relative by marriage

**56** Lake on the California/Nevada border
**59** The Chicks or Destiny's Child
**62** Troop-entertaining grp.
**63** Coal liquid
**64** Alley-___
**65** "___ You My Mother?"
**66** Lair

# 101
## INSTANT CONNECTION
By Zhouqin Burnikel

**ACROSS**

1 Synagogue scroll
6 Lavish parties
11 Person with a fake passport, maybe
14 Pro wrestling venue
15 "This is so frustrating!"
16 Dessert with a crust
17 Possible cause of a vibration
19 On the ___ (at large)
20 In bad condition
21 River through Cologne
23 Pieces of asparagus
26 Precisely correct
27 Reprimands
28 Keith Haring movement
30 Tennis star Osaka
31 Stuff to the gills
32 Religious branch for most Iranians
35 With 18-Down, listening closely
36 Biggest bird in the world
39 Key for exits
40 Courteous chap
42 Honey Bunches of ___
43 Honeycrisp, for one
45 "The Gift of the Magi" author
47 Hasbro action figures
48 Sewing kit items
50 Groundbreaking accomplishments
51 Anagram of "cedar"
52 Sacred song

54 "___ be right back"
55 "The Big Lebowski" is one
61 Service charge
62 Good dog's reward
63 Reject with disdain
64 Platform for Siri
65 Leaves in stitches
66 Gillan in "Jumanji" films

**DOWN**

1 Rat-a-___
2 Valuable underground material
3 "Toy Story" dinosaur
4 Six-legged tunnel-digger
5 Hobby involving transmissions
6 Goes without food
7 Utah-to-Colorado direction
8 Bit of bakeware
9 Fried rice ingredient
10 Ethnic group of Nepal
11 What co-winners might do
12 Baby grand, e.g.
13 Arabian Peninsula country
18 See 35-Across
22 ___ d'oeuvres
23 Bathroom device
24 Tubular floating toys
25 Wood with interlocking grain
26 Builder's guideline, for short
27 Unexpected problem
28 Whoop it up
29 Elevator company

**USA TODAY**

**31** Michelin rating unit
**33** Dots on a sea map
**34** Good serves
**37** Some kids
**38** Treatment for tresses
**41** God with a hammer
**44** Nightwear, for short
**46** Votes into office
**47** Fish's breathing organ
**48** "Fast Color" genre
**49** Diet that avoids dairy
**50** Indisputable info
**52** Heartfelt appeal

**53** Hotel visit
**56** Web address
**57** Place to get a facial peel
**58** Big ___, California
**59** Fury
**60** Channel whose letters appear nonconsecutively in "channel"

# 102
## BODYBUILDER
By Debbie Ellerin

**ACROSS**

1 Nukes in the microwave
5 Pre-K subject
9 Sulk
13 Jazz icon Fitzgerald
14 Achy
15 Underworld king in Greek myth
16 Digitized document
17 Weaver's device
18 Makeup of a layer in the stratosphere
19 "She sells seashells . . ." for example
22 Himalayan beast
23 Loch known for a mythical monster
24 Traveling the ocean
26 Place for gloss
27 "Why Women Kill" star Lucy
28 "Without further ___ . . ."
30 Bio in a newspaper
32 Close contest
35 That person
36 Does a Hawaiian dance
37 Brazilian with lots of goals
38 Wake-up call
40 Extremely uncommon
41 Lion's home
42 Contains
43 Angry
44 "The Hate U Give" protagonist
46 Part of a dance lesson

48 One of the five W's for a journalist
51 Puzzling situation
54 Swimming contests
56 Picked up the tab
57 Chill
58 Jules who created Captain Nemo
59 A cappella group member
60 Bone near the radius
61 "Don't leave me this way," for one
62 Spout forth
63 "___ Girls"

**DOWN**

1 Full of spice
2 Metals company hidden in "metal coating"
3 One-minute exercise, perhaps
4 Performed in a choir
5 Out for the night, in a sense
6 "These ___ Are Made for Walkin'"
7 Brags
8 Prefix for "colon"
9 Cornfield challenges
10 Sneaker insert
11 It's said to be mightier than the sword
12 Suffix in many language names
15 Place for a soak
20 Textbook section

**USA TODAY**

**21** Mast attachments
**25** "Rolling in the Deep" singer
**26** Vehicle with a chauffeur
**27** Deceiver
**29** Mine output
**30** "For sure!"
**31** "Done that" preceder
**32** Sisters
**33** Pub pour
**34** Apple tablet
**35** ___ Talks (lecture series)
**36** Found out
**39** Part of a sentence

**40** Engrossed
**43** Grassy area
**45** Cigna competitor
**46** Resell for a profit
**47** Hardly original
**48** Moby Dick, for one
**49** Dye also known as mehndi
**50** ___ donor
**52** Mani-pedi spots
**53** Good buddy
**54** WNBA award
**55** Electric ___

# 103
## THREE PER ELEVEN
By Erik Agard

**ACROSS**

1 Receive a ___ welcome
6 Mouth-related
10 2020 zodiac animal
13 2009 blockbuster with blue aliens
15 Prefix for "biography"
16 Bird that can't fly
17 "Theydies and ___ . . ." (gender-neutral address)
19 Sports judge
20 Impulse
21 French for "water"
22 Totally drained
24 Reaction to a corny line
26 Unicycle part
28 Pride
32 Fall out of a hot streak
36 Place horizontally
37 ___ Alto, California
38 Neighbor of Montana
39 Gulp's opposite
40 Money in Mexico
41 Last word in some business names
42 Money in Japan
43 Floppy hats
44 Fashion icon, say
47 Ship equipment
48 "If I pay $40 for a ___ house I better die" (@hodgesboi15 tweet)
53 Political takeovers
55 Big car

56 "This is bad!"
57 URL ending
58 Standard in feminist film criticism
62 "Literally Show ___ Healthy Person" (Darcie Wilder book)
63 Dull pain
64 Save
65 Word before "favor" or "que"
66 GPS line
67 Brought to the impound lot

**DOWN**

1 The ___ (Dutch city)
2 Each's partner
3 Actor's versatility
4 Badger relative
5 Common Italian nickname
6 Third-largest Hawaiian island
7 Feel regret over
8 Cash source
9 Competitive disappointments
10 Anniversary edition, for example
11 "Ain't that the truth!"
12 Clump of hair
14 Showed surprise
18 Like skyscrapers
23 Chile relleno ingredient
25 Capital of Norway
26 Stop filming
27 "'Sup"
29 Water crisis city
30 Form a solidified mass

**31** Light throw
**32** Basic idea
**33** Smell
**34** Sweetener from a mill
**35** "Daaang!"
**39** Dates
**40** Neighbor of Ecuador
**42** Fashion initials
**43** Dam-building animal
**45** Legal anagram of "braids"
**46** Sound of something landing
**49** "That's inaccurate"
**50** "Nancy Drew" channel

**51** Happen afterward
**52** Was very loving
**53** Provide for free
**54** Great Value's Twist & Shout cookie looks like one
**55** Leave fur everywhere
**59** Nature-friendly prefix
**60** "___-ching!"
**61** Allow

# 104
## GO FOR A DRIVE
By Zhouqin Burnikel

**ACROSS**

1 Off the beaten ___
5 Worked with a scene partner
10 Mad scientist's workplace
13 Beagle-biting bug
14 Lying facedown
15 "Gone Girl" star Rosamund
16 Memorization aids
18 Foot or yard, e.g.
19 Turkey farm resident
20 "It can't be!"
21 Tennis great Williams
23 Comb-over alternative
25 Bossip subject, for short
26 Virtual person in a video game franchise
27 Ingredient in 25-Down
30 The Devil
33 Civil wrong
34 Meeting, informally
35 Polished off some paella, say
36 Serengeti sounds
37 "Dear Girls" author Wong
38 Perfect season spoiler
40 Cornell grad in "The Office"
41 Arcade coin
43 Gives the right
45 Trash holder
46 ___ on Wheels
47 Marie Curie won two
50 Like some dogs' coats
52 Dirt in a window box
53 Platform for Apple devices
55 Can't stand

56 Open audition
59 Javelin trajectories
60 Peak performance
61 "Stuf"-stuffed cookie
62 "Not really a fan"
63 Dressed like Judge Judy
64 Discreet "Hey, you!"

**DOWN**

1 Scornful sound
2 Parcel out
3 "I love you," in a telenovela
4 "Where ___ the time gone?"
5 H.S. science class
6 Construction site hoist
7 Deere competitor
8 Wrap up
9 Cobbler and pie, for two
10 Poet's device
11 Similar
12 Letter after alpha
15 Creamy pastes
17 "I'll give you a ride"
22 Wood that's difficult to split
24 NOR's runner-up in the all-time Winter Games medal count
25 Many a Thai dish
27 Warty amphibians
28 Cruise ship destination
29 Goatee's place
30 Inventory-clearing event
31 Oodles
32 Cricket competition

**USA TODAY**

**33** Mandarin Chinese has four main ones

**36** Road-racing vehicle

**39** Protracted attacks

**41** Dining room fixture

**42** Number of K tiles in Scrabble

**44** Gift attachment

**45** Arranged in rings

**47** "Who would've thought?" response

**48** Untrustworthy people

**49** Shoe bottoms

**50** Fake

**51** Also-ran in an Aesop fable

**52** Attempt

**54** Mailbox opening

**57** "Long ___, the four nations lived together in harmony . . ."

**58** "That's a ___-out!"

# 105
## COME APART
By Gail Grabowski

**ACROSS**

1 Low-voiced singer
5 Sound of a high-five
9 Pokes fun at
14 Radiate
15 Drag along
16 How solitaire is usually played
17 "Rage to Survive: The ___ James Story"
18 "Breaking Bad" star Gunn
19 Flood-preventing barrier
20 Recipe guideline
23 Exclamation not likely to be heard from the intrepid
24 Truthful
25 Interior designer's concern
27 Quantity of ice cream
30 Bronzed
33 Curved lines
37 "Downton Abbey" title
39 Pageant headpiece
40 Italy's shape
41 Slow-moving creature
43 "Monsieur Ibrahim" star Sharif
44 Farm bundles
46 Berry with a Branco cultivar
47 Source of many tweets
48 Intensely enthusiastic
50 Stepped
52 Moves smoothly
54 Regular
59 Sedan, e.g.
61 Interior designer's concern
64 59-Across rental company

66 Apple music player
67 Cassini who designed for Jackie Kennedy
68 Like the Colosseum
69 "___ the Great"
70 Forbidden activity
71 Farm equipment brand
72 "Galveston" singer Campbell
73 Burn the candle at both ___

**DOWN**

1 Tree with a homophone
2 Rebuttal to "Are not!"
3 Suppress
4 Pointed piece of wood
5 Songs for sailors
6 Singer k.d.
7 Family member
8 Flannel shirt pattern
9 Tom
10 58-Down inventor ___ Kirk Christiansen
11 Identity used for clandestine purposes
12 Body part with menisci
13 Hunt for
21 Co. affected by net neutrality
22 Crossed paths
26 Pizza topping
28 "Peter Pan" dog
29 Area of land
31 Historians' focuses
32 Pub projectile

**33** Pop quartet named for its members' first initials
**34** Laugh good and loud
**35** Transparent enclosure for garden plants
**36** Iron alloy
**38** Person who isn't 24-Across
**42** Pride's quarters
**45** Shaved ice concoction
**49** A couple
**51** Physician, informally
**53** Support for an injured arm
**55** French wine valley
**56** Fruit served in balls
**57** Modify
**58** Plastic bricks
**59** Swiped item
**60** Plant with therapeutic properties
**62** Gem with "boulder" and "fire" varieties
**63** Repetitive learning method
**65** Spoil

# 106
## INQUIRE WITHIN
By Caitlin Reid

**ACROSS**

1 Brave
5 Meetup from Scruff, perhaps
9 Word after "gift" or "chop"
13 Southernmost Great Lake
14 Shinbone
15 Buzzing sounds
16 Totally nails
17 Getting older
18 Beer garden offerings
19 Marx treatise
21 Screen ___ (film website)
22 San ___ County, New Mexico
23 Lead-ins to holidays
25 College paths
28 Beer garden offerings
32 Island near Venezuela
33 Brings down the house
34 Savings plan initials
35 Not hit the target
36 Old ___ (ex)
37 Gloat
38 "Aight, cool"
39 Florida city home to Calle Ocho
40 Landform similar to a mesa
41 Restaurant ordering option
43 Come to your ___
44 Bit of ballet gear
45 Rushed
46 Construct
48 Gets in a tizzy
54 Soothing gel ingredient
55 Type of belly button

56 Urgent request
57 Hot ___ (disaster)
58 Microphone holder
59 "Quickly, please!"
60 Tooth ailment
61 Seemingly forever
62 D.C. baseball team, for short

**DOWN**

1 Bracelet bit
2 Dolphin relative
3 "Big Little ___"
4 Careers in cubicles, say
5 "Let's eat!"
6 Slightly
7 "Queen Sugar" star Lifford
8 Asset for a "spot the difference" player
9 Stock units
10 Some dancewear
11 Warning sign
12 Sibilant summoning sound
14 Spanish bites
20 Vibe
24 Some German cars, for short
25 Fast snake
26 Animated mermaid
27 Not very much
28 Hold liable
29 Name that becomes another name if you move the first letter to the end
30 Beyond mad
31 Wise ones

**33** Wooden strip
**36** Equipment on a red truck
**37** Baking tin with a central tube
**39** Figure skater Asada
**40** Its juice might help lower blood pressure
**42** Nachos need
**43** Did intelligence work
**45** Potato ___ (appetizer)
**46** Mother's nickname
**47** "Shadowhunters" character who falls for Magnus
**49** Prefix for "pilot"
**50** Obsessive fan
**51** Role for Ciara Renee in Broadway's "Frozen"
**52** All tidied up
**53** Liquids from maples

# 107
## AHA MOMENT
By Evan Kalish

**ACROSS**

1 Animals with pincers
6 Sports officials in black
10 Diner order
13 Part of a drum kit
14 Suggest
16 Garland of flowers
17 Home Depot competitor
19 Dominate
20 Electronics brand hidden in "power cable"
21 Ridicule
22 Rambunctious
24 Iowa's region
26 School reunion attendee, for short
27 Community meeting space
32 "Next in Fashion" host Chung
35 "___ you for real?"
36 Encourage
37 Recycling receptacle
38 Walks sneakily
42 "Conan" network
43 Boxers' contest
45 ___ and cheese
46 Play lists
48 Oscar winner for "Les Miserables"
52 Study in a hurry
53 Forms a row
57 Does some laps, perhaps
59 Burn with liquid
61 Number in Spanish or Italian
62 "Mamma ___!"

63 Georgia baller
66 Decide
67 Supermodel Campbell
68 Riverside structure
69 "Gosh . . ."
70 Bills between ones and fives
71 Places for tools

**DOWN**

1 "Third time's a ___!"
2 Christina who played Zelda Fitzgerald and Nellie Bly
3 In the lead
4 Word of contempt
5 Observes unflinchingly
6 Revise with new information
7 Does some lawn work
8 Exam for a H.S. junior
9 "Dude . . ."
10 Projectiles propelled by exhalation
11 Smutty
12 Pint-sized
15 "Waiting to Exhale" author McMillan
18 Supremes singer Diana
23 Mount Ka'ala's island
25 Candle stuff
26 ___ club (musical group)
28 Detachable stick in a book
29 "Dude . . ."
30 Letters before QIA+
31 "I couldn't care ___!"
32 "Dancing Queen" group

Crossword grid with numbered cells:

Row 1: 1, 2, 3, 4, 5, ■, 6, 7, 8, 9, ■, 10, 11, 12
Row 2: 13, 14, 15, 16
Row 3: 17, 18, 19
Row 4: 20, 21, 22, 23
Row 5: 24, 25, 26
Row 6: 27, 28, 29, 30, 31
Row 7: 32, 33, 34, 35, 36
Row 8: 37, 38, 39, 40, 41, 42
Row 9: 43, 44, 45, 46, 47
Row 10: 48, 49, 50, 51
Row 11: 52, 53, 54, 55, 56
Row 12: 57, 58, 59, 60, 61
Row 13: 62, 63, 64, 65
Row 14: 66, 67, 68
Row 15: 69, 70, 71

**33** Animal that the phrase "main clause" might make you think of

**34** Speak clearly

**39** Taraweeh leader

**40** Touch that's another touch backwards

**41** "-gate" events

**44** Semester, e.g.

**47** "Sure thing, cap'n!"

**49** "Patriot Act" host Minhaj

**50** "Jagged Little Pill" singer Morissette

**51** Droop

**54** Charming and confident

**55** Not married

**56** Jabs

**57** Consequence of traffic emissions

**58** Rub clean

**59** Pump the brakes

**60** Blending-in garb, for short

**64** "Black Ink Crew" creation, for short

**65** Chuckle sound

# 108

## FIRST STEPS

By Zhouqin Burnikel

**ACROSS**

1 Tidal recession
4 Easily duped person
9 Hobby shop wood
14 Deep-___ exploration
15 Like a howl at midnight, perhaps
16 To no ___ (unsuccessfully)
17 72, for most golf courses
18 Not directly deal with
20 Piece of chicken
22 Google Play download
23 Creative flash
24 Personal assistant
25 Tater
27 Like devoted fans
29 Loud sound
32 English racecourse town
35 Godiva competitor
37 Roman-inspired partywear
39 Still in original condition
41 Debut single by Britney Spears
44 "Moonlight" actor Mahershala
45 "Make it stop," in Spanish
46 Boy Scout group
47 Derisive look
49 March-to-Nov. letters
51 Research center (Abbr.)
52 Partner of "culture" or "crafts"
54 Stadium sound
56 Karaoke selection
59 Like non-Rx drugs (Abbr.)
61 More unsightly
64 1 or 2, but not 1/2
67 Confidentiality document, for short
68 Fjord, for instance
69 Library no-no
70 Job for a musician
71 Eggs on
72 Bantu ___ (hairstyle)
73 "Is this not exactly what I said would happen?"

**DOWN**

1 "High Noon" channel
2 Steady
3 Place for clearance items
4 Relinquished
5 Like an intense argument
6 Banquet coffee dispenser
7 Mineral that splits into sheets
8 Easter candies
9 Limbo need
10 Shies away from
11 Give props to
12 ___ wave (math curve)
13 "Rhapsody in Blue" star Robert
19 Come into view
21 Euphoric
26 Unexpected win
27 Jessica who played Sue Storm
28 Lab tubes
30 Checkout unit
31 Wanderer

**USA TODAY**

**33** Deep-fried side dish
**34** Office notes
**36** Step in a beauty routine
**38** Hot ___ (titillating rumors, for short)
**40** Reacted to a tearjerker
**42** Big name in antivirus software
**43** Courtroom proceeding
**48** Scored two under 17-Across
**50** Most faithful
**53** Performed badly
**55** Folklore meanies
**56** Gulp from a bottle

**57** "We're in trouble now"
**58** Another nickname for the Big Easy
**60** "Hurry up!"
**62** "Nurse Jackie" Emmy winner Falco
**63** Extreme anger
**65** UFO mechanics, perhaps
**66** Book jacket bit

# 109
## DIGITS
By Kate Hawkins

**ACROSS**

1 Freestyle or crawl, for example
5 Savory jelly
10 Dexterous
14 Give in
15 Mapo doufu's country of origin
16 Shallowest of the Great Lakes
17 Amway competitor
18 Portable storage device
20 Got together
22 It's golden, they say
23 Food eaten on March 14
24 Translation of "estoy"
27 Still in the wrapper
28 Items in recipe boxes
31 Material for modern "miners"
35 Chutzpah
36 Neighbor of India
37 Sixth-graders, often
42 Some April births
43 ___ to (should)
44 Require
45 Heist planner, perhaps
50 Do something immoral
51 The slender giant moray is the longest one
52 Lyric poem
53 Tien len's country of origin
57 Host of the 2024 Olympics
59 Binding oath
62 Shout out in a bibliography
63 Penny ___

64 Inviting words on a cake in "Alice in Wonderland"
65 English prep school for boys
66 Some July births
67 Vacuum brand
68 Categorize

**DOWN**

1 Shrimp ___
2 Silently allow entry
3 Election Day sticker phrase
4 Diner list
5 Play a part
6 Test proctor's interjection
7 Apt name for 12 popes
8 Not forgotten
9 Half Dome handholds
10 "Little Women" actress Laura
11 "The Very Hungry Caterpillar" author Carle
12 Number of digits that some hands have
13 Shirt named for its shape
19 Morning droplets
21 Parts of a digital image
25 Unit smaller than a hectare
26 Dallas NBA squad
29 Concluded
30 Scouting mission, for short
31 ___ State (Mississippi university)
32 Large primate
33 Word after "coal" or "pine"
34 Critic Hilton

**Down (continued)**

36 Totally useless
37 Artist Chella
38 Wrath
39 Item in Trouble's Pop-O-Matic
40 Ginormous
41 Leer at
45 De-sudsed
46 Of sorts
47 Triangular snack chip
48 Who approved this clue
49 Take offense to
50 Pig's digs
53 Predecessor of TikTok

54 Really digging
55 ___ out a living (gets by)
56 New York MLB squad
58 Blackjack assets
59 Bud
60 "Te ___"
61 Stimpy's Chihuahua compadre

# 110
## TEMP JOB
By Patrick Jordan

**ACROSS**

1 Get rid of
5 Off in the distance
9 Caesar ___
14 Stat for a carpet installer
15 Septum's place
16 Among the best
17 Mimic the Tower of Pisa
18 Crisscross pattern
19 Drink that might come with art
20 Insufficient consolation
23 That fellow over there
24 Rust-colored planet
25 They spoke Nahuatl
27 Desert home to the Tibesti Mountains
30 They seek secrets
32 Stalkers seen on safaris
33 Doritos flavor
37 Spelman email address ending
38 Fills a teacup
39 Yes, en francais
40 Friendly quality
43 Conspiracies
45 Unpopular creatures
46 Trembles
47 Bull's-eye, for one
50 Chandelier insert
51 Name contained by 16-Across
52 Something sought after
58 Medieval Japanese spy
60 Frequently

61 "Always and Forever, ___ Jean"
62 Supply funding for
63 Rhyming counterpart of "break"
64 "Have I ___ lied to you?"
65 Some are standardized
66 Peelers take them off potatoes
67 Do a good ___

**DOWN**

1 Powdered mineral
2 Cookie bearing the Nabisco logo
3 Tight closure
4 "Mr. ___, bring me a dream . . ."
5 Mohair-producing goat
6 Application documents
7 "Dream on!"
8 Have another go at
9 Carbonated water
10 Pie ___ mode
11 Gracefully flexible
12 Room beneath a roof
13 Regards as
21 Pixar film set in Radiator Springs
22 Complains
26 Grp. that screens carry-ons
27 Large quantity
28 Tony-winning lead role for Heather Headley
29 Lunch break length, sometimes

## Crossword Grid

| 1 | 2 | 3 | 4 | | 5 | 6 | 7 | 8 | | 9 | 10 | 11 | 12 | 13 |
|---|---|---|---|---|---|---|---|---|---|---|---|---|---|---|
| 14 | | | | | 15 | | | | | 16 | | | | |
| 17 | | | | | 18 | | | | | 19 | | | | |
| 20 | | | | 21 | | | | 22 | | | | 23 | | |
| | | | 24 | | | | | 25 | | 26 | | | | |
| 27 | 28 | 29 | | | | 30 | 31 | | | | | | | |
| 32 | | | | | 33 | | | | | | 34 | 35 | 36 | |
| 37 | | | | 38 | | | | | | 39 | | | | |
| 40 | | | 41 | 42 | | | | | 43 | 44 | | | | |
| | | 45 | | | | | | 46 | | | | | | |
| 47 | 48 | 49 | | | | | 50 | | | | | | | |
| 51 | | | 52 | | 53 | 54 | | | | 55 | 56 | 57 | | |
| 58 | | | 59 | | 60 | | | | 61 | | | | | |
| 62 | | | | | 63 | | | | 64 | | | | | |
| 65 | | | | | 66 | | | | 67 | | | | | |

**30** Turns unpleasant
**31** ___ of Spain, Trinidad and Tobago
**33** Word after "lab" or "trench"
**34** Cozy breakfast spot
**35** Adorable
**36** Leaky tire's sound
**38** Sauce for gnocchi
**41** Fuel economy stat
**42** Donkey sounds
**43** Orange juice stuff
**44** Wrote identifying information on

**46** Interview excerpts
**47** Palindromic belief
**48** Skirt style
**49** Cantaloupe parts
**50** Stopped functioning
**53** Not wild
**54** Remote button
**55** Wildly positive review
**56** Producer of pears or peaches
**57** One of 1,760 in a mile
**59** Scribble

**USA TODAY**

# 111
## GO TIME
By Zhouqin Burnikel

**ACROSS**

1 Fried rice veggie
4 Bit of birthday mail that doesn't require postage
9 Desktop computer brand
13 Body parts that might ring
15 Subject of a Manohla Dargis review
16 ___ beans
17 Fried rice veggie
19 Winter shovelful
20 Drum kit part
21 Leopard or lion
22 Motherless calf
23 "That's a ___ order"
25 ___ Lilly (pharmaceutical company)
27 Like 7 and 11
28 Place for hiking or camping, reverently
33 Minister's title, for short
34 Neruda's "___ to My Socks"
35 Many "EastEnders" watchers
37 One-eyed Norse god
39 Plane assignments
41 Determiner of heredity
43 Sledding spot
45 Dojo floor covering
46 End a fast
47 Ribbon-cutting events
51 Gibbon, e.g.
53 "___ ta Be My Girl"
54 Eighth of a fluid ounce
55 Championship game

57 Styled after
59 The ones here
63 Travel method
64 Read quickly
66 Heavy burden
67 Hajj destination
68 Rip
69 Unexceptional
70 Move furtively
71 End-of-school-year pranksters (Abbr.)

**DOWN**

1 Coats and hats can be hung on them
2 Work hard for
3 What square footage measures
4 Paramore genre
5 Bring to an end
6 Running shoe brand since 1979
7 Expressed dissent, perhaps
8 Dragon's home
9 "Assuming that's true . . ."
10 Tropical fruit with a purple rind
11 Keep clear of
12 Imitated a crow
14 Mattress brand
18 Tidy
22 YSL competitor
24 Makes less tight
26 Crayfish relative

**USA TODAY**

**28** Miracle-___ (plant food brand)

**29** Many lipstick shades

**30** Villainous scientist character, maybe

**31** Declaration of love

**32** Oil drilling structure

**36** Unforeseen obstacle

**38** Neither's partner

**40** Nicholas Brothers specialty

**42** Aliens (Abbr.)

**44** Folklore figure Bunyan

**48** Casino employee

**49** Love interest for Blair and Serena in "Gossip Girl"

**50** "Can we turn on a fan?"

**51** Natural hairstyles

**52** Aretha Franklin played it

**56** As well

**58** Negligee material

**60** Anticipatory times

**61** Cook with high heat

**62** Makes a mistake

**64** Acadia automaker

**65** Salary ceiling

# 112

## OVERSHOES

By Gail Grabowski

**ACROSS**

1 Tater ___
4 Holders of valuables
9 Queen Latifah's "Set It Off" role
13 Each, informally
15 Reference book containing insets
16 Buyer's financing
17 Neighbor of Bolivia
18 Tenant's contract
19 Belonging to us
20 Ill will
22 Nimble
23 Manufacturing facility
24 Process food
25 Adds fuel to
28 Avoid capture by
30 Arc de Triomphe city
31 Golf instructors
32 Dull-colored
36 Neighbor of Pakistan
37 Tailor's measurement
38 Like many slasher movies
39 Softest of minerals
40 ___ up (confesses)
41 Evaluate
42 ". . . was the friends we made ___ the way"
44 Part of a celestial shower
45 "All I Wanna Do" singer Crow
48 Royal emblem
50 Cut in two
51 Assessments for drivers

55 Prefix for "biotic"
56 Not flimsy
57 Ginseng or ginger, for example
58 Midday
59 Coral formation
60 Long-running Vaughan/Staples comic book series
61 Mattress size
62 Short-winded
63 ___ for the course

**DOWN**

1 Spanish appetizer
2 Ready for business
3 "A Sorta Fairytale" singer Amos
4 Taco bar options
5 Had leftovers, perhaps
6 Hue that looks good on you
7 "Calm down!"
8 U-turn from NNW
9 Reason for using a ladder at home
10 Cartoon brother of Huey and Dewey Duck
11 Some British nobles
12 Starting phase
14 Halloween activity
21 Soccer stadium cheers
22 Assistance
24 Bookshelf buildup
25 Cooking skewer
26 Strong who voiced Bubbles

**27** Like some exams
**29** Figure in red ink
**31** Unwitting tool
**33** Went by bike
**34** 2012 film that becomes a 1996 film if you add an F at the beginning
**35** "Why Won't You Date Me?" host Nicole
**37** Sweater material
**41** "Surely you ___!"
**43** Corrosive substance
**44** Be a buttinsky

**45** Leg part
**46** Capital on the Red River
**47** "Emma" surname
**49** Shower fixtures
**51** Memorization method
**52** Hotel freebie
**53** Garment in ancient Rome
**54** Word after "gold" or "guest"
**56** Pulled up a chair

# 113
## YOU ARE WHAT YOU EAT

By Gabrielle Friedman

**ACROSS**

1 Totes dreamy
5 Prefix for "pub"
11 Language at Gallaudet
14 Length times width, for a rectangle
15 "The Wind in the Willows" amphibian
16 Word that Ohio State University tried to trademark in 2019
17 Person who's sharp as a tack
19 Vietnamese holiday
20 Stable occupant
21 Ignored some road signs
22 Busy buzzers
23 "___ the season . . ."
24 Selections on tap
26 Frolics
27 Fire up
29 Not-so-good member of an otherwise good group
32 Millennials' successors, for short
33 Invests
35 Piece of softball practice equipment
36 Yours and mine
38 Shakespearean villain
40 Mercedes competitor
43 Lower-body exercise
45 Hard precipitation
49 "Magic Mike" selling point
51 Small mammal that determinedly hides
53 /

54 100%
56 Alternatives to tents
57 ___-A-Whirl
58 Smile
60 Partners of manis
62 Wager
63 Frequent channel surfer
65 Disgusted utterance
66 Rip into
67 "I wouldn't touch that with ___-foot pole"
68 "L.A. Law" actress Susan
69 Olympic swimmer Michael
70 Celebrated Holliday

**DOWN**

1 #
2 Wardrobe
3 Irritates
4 Applies a viscous substance to
5 Maker of the Yukon SUV
6 Got out of bed
7 Comes for a visit
8 Puff
9 Midnight visit to the pantry, maybe
10 "___ to Gold Teeth" (Danez Smith poem)
11 Try
12 "Wake up, ___!"
13 Words of deliberation
18 Drinks made from leaves
22 Punch lightly
25 NBA star James

**26** Sounded like a bell
**28** "Orange Is the New Black" actress Aduba
**30** Tian Shan's continent
**31** Baby's garment
**34** Like consignment shop items
**37** Bryce Canyon's state
**39** Unit of electrical resistance
**40** Close confidant
**41** Lordly address
**42** Like the Park family in "Parasite"
**44** Hardly surprising
**46** Bit of TV Guide info

**47** Asks to the party
**48** Teachers plan them
**50** Chicago clock setting (Abbr.)
**52** Result of a car loan default, briefly
**55** Not cool
**58** "Holy cow!"
**59** Trick
**61** Coup d'___
**63** Item of headwear
**64** "Thx" counterpart

# 114
## TREE PART HARMONY
By Mark McClain

**ACROSS**

1 Publisher of the video game Alien: Isolation
5 Fastener with a ridge
10 Foot part
14 Rowboat pair
15 Device with apps
16 Puerto ___
17 Hinged sections on some dining tables
19 Vegas WNBA team
20 Off-road four-wheeler
21 Condition treated by a dermatologist
22 Dwelling
23 Small herding dog
25 Distrustful person
27 Some satellite offices
31 Org. with Bruins and Red Wings
32 Metallic fabric
33 They're not from 2-Down (Abbr.)
34 Guitar relative
37 Boxer's move
38 With 34-Down, co-creator of Scarlet Witch
39 Drop the ball
40 In this manner
42 Ignore a request to MYOB
44 Cosmic formation named for part of an animal
48 Hydro ___
49 Soccer ejection sign

52 Parade creation
54 Artist's inspiration
55 Hive dweller
56 Thoroughly spoil
57 Metaphor for bottom-up activism
60 Up to the task
61 Lipstick option
62 Place setting item
63 Model McMillan
64 Phiona Mutesi's game
65 Wally with a "Famous" cookie brand

**DOWN**

1 Soft drinks
2 Starfleet HQ's planet
3 Humble yourself
4 Venomous snake
5 Listing on a restaurant chalkboard
6 "Know My Name" author Miller
7 Wander
8 U-turn from WSW
9 "Older Than America" star Studi
10 Official language of Egypt
11 Rebound at an angle
12 Looped in via email
13 Gardener's tool
18 Door securer
22 "The Last Thing He Wanted" star Hathaway
24 Sole

**25** Zodiac animal
**26** Starchy staple
**28** Good time
**29** Greek letter that looks like an H when capitalized
**30** ID on IRS forms
**34** See 38-Across
**35** Internet address
**36** Shortbread Girl Scout cookies
**37** Worthless stuff
**38** Bring into alignment
**40** "I love ___ for you!"
**41** "That ship ___ sailed"

**42** Printing machines
**43** More likely to butt in, say
**45** They take off
**46** Puts faith in
**47** Explosion sound
**50** Old-style
**51** Classroom stations
**52** Omega Psi Phi, e.g.
**53** Auto service center job
**54** Suffix for "class" or "room"
**57** Sierra automaker
**58** Cheerleader's word
**59** Birds ___ feather

# 115
## TOTALLY
By Zhouqin Burnikel

**ACROSS**

1 "Look what I just did!"
5 Features of distressed jeans
9 "Didn't expect to see you here!"
13 Vacuum brand
15 From scratch
16 Backside
17 Lovestruck teen from Verona
18 Sushi burrito wrapper
19 Word after "raw" or "big"
20 Musical finale
23 Egg producer
24 Lemon meringue ___
25 Many a Utahn
28 Polka ___
29 Told a whopper
31 Milk source
32 Interpol city
34 Wall-climbing plant
35 Most bears have five per paw
36 Dismissive response to an irrelevant example
39 Contest of speed
40 Docs for dogs
41 Uninvited picnic guests
42 Firepit residue
43 Mushroom tops
44 Hang on a clothesline
45 Security assignment
47 Be the right size
48 Heat in the microwave
51 Principal character
55 Partner of willing
57 Greek vowel
58 Bull on a glue stick
59 Like belly laughs
60 Barnes & Noble e-reader
61 Capital near Casablanca
62 Research places
63 Small-screen honor
64 Recipe guesstimate

**DOWN**

1 Liberty Island symbol
2 Play ___ in (influence)
3 Exorcism target
4 Golf rarities
5 Kitchen appliance
6 Privy to
7 Country north of Chile
8 Pool event
9 Request to a waiter
10 "I can explain"
11 Fez or fedora
12 Rollover ___
14 Habitat for ornamental carp
21 Little quibble
22 Dad ___
26 Olympic track legend Jesse
27 Kite's home
28 Be adoring
29 To-do documents
30 Places where travelers stay
32 Capital on the northern slope of the Himalayas
33 Group for boating enthusiasts
34 Julia Louis-Dreyfus comedy

**35** Broadway award
**36** Spiderweb, for one
**37** Chocolate drink since 1904
**38** Luxury watch brand
**43** Take for a ride
**44** "What's the ___?" ("Who cares?")
**46** Clarinets and saxophones, e.g.
**47** Unreliable
**48** Exercise program founded by three Albertos
**49** Zones
**50** Capital of Western Australia
**52** Motel offering
**53** Molecular unit
**54** Happy
**55** Synonym for "totally" hidden in this clue
**56** Constricting snake

# 116
## EARLY BIRDS
By Brooke Husic

**ACROSS**

1 Soup paste
5 ___ milk
8 Opponent of "us"
12 Fan's opposite
13 Christmas tree type
14 Malek who played Freddie Mercury
15 Escape from a grasp, perhaps
18 ___ mater
19 Piano brand
20 Enthusiastically
22 Bit of body ink, for short
23 Word after "cast" or "step"
24 Yellow Muppet
25 How you might feel after reading the third letter of every clue in this puzzle for a secret message
29 Clean Air Act org.
31 Postpone
33 "Have fun!"
34 Actress Doris
35 Made mad
37 State next to Ida.
38 Rub it in
41 Episode that's not new
43 Color of some first date "flags"
44 Tries to be like
46 Danger
48 Wolverine's weapons
49 Hail makeup
50 Twin of Artemis
52 Supply with oxygen

56 One whose surname may end in -ic
57 Highlight of a collection
60 Optimist's feeling
61 Seoul-based automaker
62 Closing time for some bars
63 Guesses from GPSes
64 Crafty
65 ___ clef

**DOWN**

1 "Where Am I Now?" author Wilson
2 Object
3 Congress part
4 Place for apple picking
5 Not on
6 Something to come up for
7 Handler of funds
8 Exchange
9 Only four-letter room in Clue
10 TV award
11 "Mamma ___! Here We Go Again"
12 Major rd.
16 "Alice in Wonderland" character
17 Wicked
21 "___ hands are the devil's workshop"
23 Seemingly eternally youthful
24 Louisiana body
26 First woman to headline Coachella
27 Mythology, e.g.

**28** Follower of "brown-" or "starry-"
**29** Advantage
**30** Body part read by a chiromancer
**32** Parts of some pyrotechnic displays
**36** Fruit banned on some public transport
**39** Nooks
**40** Like some orders, metaphorically or coffee-wise
**42** "Good work!"
**45** Soft mineral

**47** Clothing line created by a tennis star
**50** Tons
**51** Nickname for dad's partner, perhaps
**53** Amazes
**54** Earl Grey and such
**55** Oak's Johto counterpart in "Pokemon"
**56** "___ Works Hard for the Money" (Donna Summer hit)
**58** Vinegar accompaniment
**59** Very

# 117
## TAG IN
By Evan Kalish

**ACROSS**

1 Muscular
5 By means of
8 Brass = copper + ___
12 Valuable mushroom
13 Button that fires off an email
14 Berry big in Brazil
15 "Bald" bird
16 Blue-green shade
17 Obnoxious person
18 Director of 2019's "Little Women"
21 "Need I ___ more?"
22 Put in
23 Prohibit
24 Modern library offering
26 Drug agents, for short
28 "Strong Black Legends" host Clayton
31 "Ugh, we just dealt with this!"
34 Detest
35 Give off
36 Nasty look
38 "The Day the Earth Stood Still" star Patricia
39 Figure of speech such as "happy as a clam"
41 "You have to calm down!"
43 Rogers aka Captain America
44 Masonry material
45 Citrusy ingredients
48 Dull routine
49 Pecan or pumpkin delight
52 "___ asked you?"

54 Undercover operative
57 Charged particles
59 Solo for Renee Fleming
60 Is emotionally invested
61 Run away
62 Enthralled
63 Tower color
64 ___ St. Louis, Illinois
65 Relaxing destination
66 Bumper blemish

**DOWN**

1 ___ of directors
2 Pushed for
3 Timpani mallet cloth
4 Phoebe Waller-Bridge series
5 Swerve
6 Absolutely amazed
7 Make up lines as you go
8 Strike with electricity
9 Rink performer
10 Space shuttle org.
11 Metropolis, e.g.
12 Prefix for "byte" or "mall"
13 Aid for painting big letters
19 Place to park
20 Attend
25 Valencia or mandarin, for example
26 The "N" in NAJA
27 Hitches in plans
29 Drink that might be served in a kulhar
30 Cry of pain

**31** Scotland's Loch ___
**32** Fail to mention
**33** Central and Mountain, for Texas
**34** Release
**37** Relaxing destination
**40** Not as much
**42** Heartburn reliever
**46** Droplets from a duct
**47** Fight
**49** "Evita" surname
**50** Like an unreactive gas

**51** Website with handmade items
**52** Ali Krieger, to Ashlyn Harris
**53** "Howdy" alternative
**55** Morning TV host Kelly
**56** Donated
**58** Collection

# 118

## A.P. COURSE

By Zhouqin Burnikel

### ACROSS

1 Terminus of Chicago's Blue Line
6 Chicago soccer team
10 Part of LGBTQIA, for short
13 Strait-___
14 More approachable
15 Truck brand with a horned logo
16 Dust-filtering appliance
18 Possible alternative to a CT scan
19 Liberate
20 Pentathlon swords
21 Canoe or ferry
22 Some band releases
24 Shows up
26 #TransCrowdFund, for one
30 Hog food
31 WNBA official
32 Obnoxious people
34 Book of maps
37 Provide banquet food
39 Ooh and ___
40 Title holder
41 Fashion designer Chung
42 June celebration
44 Actress Mowry
45 "___ Baby" (Tochi Onyebuchi novel)
47 Given the cold shoulder
49 "See if you can do better!"
52 Eggs in ikura don
53 Significant time periods
54 Country north of Jordan
57 Kansas-to-Missouri direction
61 Mr. ___ (counselor in "Holes")
62 Seller's figure
64 Auction unit
65 Has a bawl
66 Capital of Jordan
67 "___ day now!"
68 Besides that
69 Crows' homes

### DOWN

1 Snowman in "Frozen"
2 Makeup of some beehives
3 Corn maze measure
4 Drives away
5 www.wesley.___
6 Instrument similar to the piccolo
7 Less approachable
8 Brand of peanut butter cups
9 Slip up
10 Protective covering
11 Gemstone measure
12 Radiates
14 Playful bite
17 Takes a break
21 Diner seating choice
23 Ancient Egyptian ruler
25 Sugar pill, e.g.
26 Get better
27 Celebration following the main event
28 "Make it snappy!"

USA TODAY

29 Transmission components
31 Record label for Alicia Keys
33 Spot covered by a knee sock
35 In the thick of
36 Place to get a deep tissue massage
38 Leaves the stage
43 Garment with a cape
46 Mortarboard attachment
48 "Another cold one, please"
49 Inventor Nikola with a namesake scientific unit
50 Constellation with a belt
51 Little ones
55 Yielding slightly to a gentle squeeze, as a peach
56 Shoo-___ (obvious winners)
58 Objectives
59 Improvised jazz style
60 Bills featuring Hamilton
62 Thunderstruck feeling
63 Sweeping camera shot

# 119

## SNAKEHEADS/BELTED UP

By Erik Agard and Aaron Shoemaker

### ACROSS

1 Raring to go
6 ___ shui
10 Golf ball holders
14 ___ Haute, Indiana
15 Continent home to every country ending in "stan"
16 Wrath
17 Demolish in competition
18 Do some boxing training
19 Strongly encourage
20 Agricultural tools
21 Hoodwink
22 Person making alterations
24 "Finding ___" (2003 film)
26 App's clientele
28 Light show beams
30 Shiver
34 Cul-de-___
35 Garden figurines
37 Denounce
38 Basketball filler
39 Character-limited communication
40 Intention
41 Parasitic insect
43 Drilling platform
45 Not just tear up
46 Maryland time zone
48 Investment portfolio parts
50 Stop clinging to something
52 Paper fastener
53 Mogadishu citizen
56 "Well, ___-di-dah!"
58 City where muffulettas are popular, for short
61 Penultimate word in some fairy tales
62 Meat cut
64 Made dresses, say
65 Made a resonant sound
66 Zero, in tennis
67 Make improvements to
68 Color that's "azul" in Spanish
69 More than none, less than many
70 Cookout locations

### DOWN

1 Draw using acid
2 Prefix for "dynamic"
3 Sitcom whose first episode was "Oliver Buys a Farm"
4 Removes from the whiteboard
5 Sleep phase letters
6 Burkina ___
7 Channel covering college athletics
8 "Love Jones" actress Long
9 Knitting technique
10 Obvious sayings
11 Grey's title
12 Frozen waffle brand
13 Prophet
21 Taco option
23 "These Boots ___ Made for Walkin'"
25 "Avalon High" author Cabot

**USA TODAY**

**27** Directs the vehicle
**28** Boxer Ali
**29** Scattering seeds
**31** Subject of a 1968 Olympics salute
**32** Hideouts
**33** Part of EGOT
**34** Out of harm's way
**36** Name shared by two Spice Girls
**42** On the loose
**44** Futbol commentator's exclamation
**47** Elongated fish
**49** Movies
**51** Morsel in a Greek salad
**53** Belgrade citizen
**54** Shape whose name comes from the Latin for "egg"
**55** List of options
**57** Over again
**59** Give temporarily
**60** Introduces
**63** "This is hard to watch"
**64** Express in words

# 120
## KEEP AN EYE ON THINGS
By Gail Grabowski

**ACROSS**

1 Sets loose
6 Hidden stockpile
11 Letters of distress at sea
14 Head out the door
15 Knee-ankle connector
16 Website address
17 Give something up, perhaps
19 "In Too Deep" actress Long
20 Fork over
21 By way of
22 Camera brand that sounds like a weapon
24 Ceiling fixture
29 Like the remnants of a volcanic eruption
31 "If ___ falls in the forest . . ."
32 Doesn't play fairly
34 Connections
35 Part of a play
38 Challenging
39 "We hold ___ truths to be self-evident . . ."
41 Small jazz group
42 Flock mother
43 Wheel with teeth
44 Daytona 500 org.
46 "Brown Girls" star ___ Denis
47 Emerald Bay lake
48 Large reptile
53 Island near Curacao
54 $1,000,000, for short
55 "___ your head!"
58 Car washer's challenge

59 Pouch for a timepiece
64 Sci-fi characters, often (Abbr.)
65 Accused's excuse
66 Gushes forth
67 Take notice of
68 Leavening agent
69 Full of attitude

**DOWN**

1 Total failure
2 Country star McEntire
3 "Calm down!"
4 "1919" author Ewing
5 Word after "public" or "civil"
6 A vegan might make it from tofu or cauliflower
7 Up to, informally
8 He's next to Teddy on Mount Rushmore
9 Topic in a sermon
10 Emerges from an egg
11 Branch of Islam
12 Hunter constellation
13 Topic in some cultural appropriation discourse
18 Name comprised of Roman numerals
23 Enjoyed some french fries, say
25 Enjoy some flash fiction, say
26 Sideways
27 "You know how ___"
28 Eco-friendly
29 Tiger Balm target
30 Irish actress Fiona

**USA TODAY**

**33** Person taking dictation, for short
**35** Former Austrian rulers
**36** "Ta-ta!"
**37** Moved really fast
**40** Salon sweepings
**41** Former Russian ruler
**43** Eluded capture
**45** Totally puzzled
**46** Bro or sis, for short
**48** Friends, in Australia
**49** Give a keynote, say
**50** Physician's colleague

**51** Paintball cry
**52** Move really fast
**56** Wields a needle
**57** Site with homemade jewelry
**60** Ginger ___
**61** Aunt, in Spanish
**62** "All Rise" channel
**63** Tax prep pro

# 121
## WRENCH IN THE WORKS
By Patrick Jordan

**ACROSS**

1 They're like fogs but thinner
6 Bringing up the rear
10 Fat for frying
14 As graceful as ___
15 Sound effect in a cave
16 Software customer
17 2004 or 2016
20 Totally prepared
21 Enclosed
22 Underpaid employee's desire
23 Pungent taste
24 "The Assistant" star Julia
25 Bulb holder
30 Waiting for the next task, say
31 One of a limerick's five
32 Golfers try to stay under it
35 Appear outwardly
36 Pastry at a tea party
38 Prefix akin to "self-"
39 Brown shade
40 Singer Marlena
41 Counterparts of cons
42 Item in Frosty the Snowman's mouth
46 To whom the Fresh Prince yelled "Smell ya later"
50 Fills with wonder
51 Emotionally unengaged
52 Journalist Shriver
54 Used to be
57 Middle East region often called "the cradle of civilization"
60 Business leader, for short
61 Deeply engaged with
62 Rich cake
63 Waist accessory
64 Vacant shelf's accumulation
65 Having a sharp incline

**DOWN**

1 Baseball Hall of Famer Willie
2 "Oh, OK"
3 Hit with a sharp blow
4 Road surfacing goop
5 Winter vehicle brand
6 "We need to leave"
7 Feel sore
8 "Nobody burned down your she ___, Cheryl"
9 Male cat
10 ___ eclipse
11 Invite to enter
12 "Little Fires Everywhere" star Witherspoon
13 Laundromat appliance
18 People in stadium seats
19 Speak from a lectern, perhaps
23 They/___
24 ___ pool
25 It might be written before shopping
26 Innovative thought
27 Narrow valley
28 Performer who might be found funny or scary

**USA TODAY**

**29** Family
**32** Fried bread
**33** Opposite of beneath
**34** Part of a romantic bouquet
**36** Sandal or sneaker
**37** Game show prize
**38** Tablet downloads
**40** N.K. Jemisin's genre
**43** Snack for Bugs Bunny
**44** Toddler's minor injury
**45** Animals
**46** Some eateries
**47** Actress PenaVega

**48** Causes to yawn, say
**49** Make a mess of
**52** Card with entrees
**53** Random ___ of kindness
**54** Used to be
**55** Upped the ___
**56** Stairway segment
**58** Carryout coffee cover
**59** Simple bed

# 122

## D.M. ME
By Zhouqin Burnikel

**ACROSS**

1 Bull's-eye hitter
5 Voice role for Idina Menzel and Gam Wichayanee
9 Staff supervisor
13 The "A" in UAE
14 Turn sharply
15 Dame Judi
16 "G.I. Jane" star
18 Opening words
19 A lot of pranks happen on its first day
20 Foot or pound
22 Chop with an ax
23 "Gravedigger" singer
26 Value of D or G in Scrabble
29 Tex-___
30 Flower bed filler
31 Capital northeast of Vientiane
33 "I'm ___ hurry" ("Take your time")
36 Go-ahead signals
39 "Oh, really?"
40 Gather bit by bit
41 Perform adequately
42 Opportunity
43 Gas used in lighting
44 Nori-wrapped rolls, e.g.
45 Pixar clownfish
47 Pseudonym lead-in
49 Enjoy some 44-Across
50 "Will & Grace" star
55 Obamacare, for short
56 Tenant's payment
57 Points along routes
60 "Got it"
62 Dolphins quarterback in the Pro Football Hall of Fame
65 Lamenting poem
66 Great Lake that touches four states
67 Swarming pest
68 Rural storage structure
69 Shoulder muscle, for short
70 They might be soaked in tea

**DOWN**

1 Palindromic relative
2 Region
3 Skate park slope
4 Ford car, for short
5 Develop over time
6 Late-July zodiac sign
7 Skin care product
8 Barclays Center, for one
9 "Stand by Me" singer ___ E. King
10 Running free
11 Carpenter's fastener
12 Theater productions
15 "You and me both!"
17 Florida's second-largest city
21 "Challenge accepted!"
24 The Dalai Lama went into it in 1959
25 Like Diwali
26 "___ too shall pass"
27 ___ the dishes

**28** Food item similar to a bialy
**32** Hand-holding sea animal
**34** Opposite of "paleo-"
**35** Grannies
**37** The Pearl-Qatar city
**38** Improv piece
**40** Garden ornament that's often bearded
**44** Year-end mall temp
**46** Tie the knot
**48** Fate
**50** Has the guts
**51** Cause for a lettuce recall

**52** Drew to a close
**53** Unblinking look
**54** Qutang, Wu or Xiling, along the Yangtze River
**58** ___-Pong
**59** Unforeseen glitch
**61** Cause of bragging
**63** Zero bid, in spades
**64** NBA tiebreakers

# 123
## PIECE OF CAKE
By Debbie Ellerin

**ACROSS**

1 Slight advantage
5 One of the senses
10 Quite a distance
14 "What ___ it matter?"
15 Betting everything
16 Japanese sport
17 Former currency in Dublin
19 Had been informed of
20 Roastmaster, for one
21 "Leggo my ___!"
22 Nine-digit ID
23 Hedgehog who collects gold rings
25 Closes with needle and thread
27 Word after "cash" or "bumper"
29 Apple music players
32 Judge's garment
35 Programmer's activity
39 Zero
40 "What ___ supposed to do now?"
41 Game with battling trainers
42 Student's stat
43 Joke
44 Luxury sunglasses brand
45 Gnat or brat, for example
46 Family member
48 Discipline with asanas
50 Source of danger
54 Fabrics for aerial performers
57 Bear's place

58 Small songbird
60 Do a double take, e.g.
62 Pay close attention to
63 Atmospheric area with a "hole"
65 Move carefully
66 Many a book club selection
67 Bowling alley assignment
68 Wintertime transport
69 Like spanakopita
70 ___ out (barely gets)

**DOWN**

1 "What I Am" singer Brickell
2 College residences
3 Company repped by a gecko
4 Magazine with an annual music festival
5 Bug on a phone line
6 Soothing gel source
7 Snail's relatives
8 Hint of hue
9 Fund
10 Invites in from downstairs
11 Killjoy
12 "You got that right!"
13 One of 15 in this puzzle
18 Next in line
24 Hot drink that may come with marshmallows
26 Use ASL, say
28 "The ___ Little Puppy"
30 They go with chips
31 Part of a blind

**32** Big name in pasta sauce
**33** Country whose capital is Muscat
**34** VIP
**36** Politician Haaland
**37** Noncommittal response
**38** Taboos
**41** Veep's boss
**45** Brew with a rhyming name
**47** Came down to earth
**49** "The ___ With the Dragon Tattoo"
**51** ___ for the ride

**52** Shaving tool
**53** Competed in a NASCAR race
**55** Canoe's cousin
**56** Embarrassing public display
**57** "I agree to your terms"
**59** Leg part
**61** Number after dos
**62** "For ___ a Jolly Good Fellow"
**64** Big deer

# 124
## WATCH OUT!
By Mark McClain

**ACROSS**

1 Cream cheese option
6 Butterfly relative
10 Tree part
14 Long-handled tools
15 Bouncing sound
16 Cricket field shape
17 Six-ball sets, in cricket
18 Lima's state
19 Spanish for "bull"
20 Evasive language
23 Brazilian city, for short
24 "It's ___-win situation!"
25 Not departing on time
27 Sound-boosting device
30 Stage signals
33 Tapered fold in a skirt
34 Pick up on
36 Model Jordyn
39 Fruit cocktail ingredient
40 Sown things
43 Make a trade
44 They may be cloudy or sunny
46 Source of aggravation
48 Russo who played Frigga in "Thor"
50 Crystal ball user
51 Alert color
52 Some sunglasses
55 Kanga's son in "Christopher Robin"
57 Bread for a reuben
58 The Funk Brothers, e.g.
64 Electrically flexible
66 "Downton Abbey" worker
67 Numerical comparison
68 "No ___!" ("Don't mention it!")
69 "What ___ is new?"
70 ___ acids
71 Gives in to gravity
72 Not as frequently
73 Alma ___

**DOWN**

1 Canuck, the knife-stealing icon of Vancouver, for one
2 Possess
3 Furniture chain that sells mustard
4 Vice ___
5 Fundamental nature
6 "My bowl is empty," perhaps
7 Cuatro doubled
8 Place for bronze medalists
9 Like a parka
10 Parking place
11 "Building" disconnected from the real world
12 "Now That the Buffalo's Gone" singer Buffy Sainte-___
13 It's drawn for lab tests
21 Jazz legend Armstrong
22 Barbecue joint side
26 Came up
27 Meal starters, for short
28 Not bold
29 Burrowing critter of the plains
31 Night before

**32** Moves slowly
**35** Move slowly
**37** Buster's partner
**38** Moved quickly
**41** "The Bold Type" star Aisha
**42** Severe
**45** Person who acts superior
**47** Handout at a school play
**49** Tooth covering
**52** Casino game
**53** Tights material
**54** Numerical range
**56** "Becoming" author Michelle

**59** Meaning of X, sometimes
**60** Midmonth day, in ancient Rome
**61** "Look ___ this way..."
**62** Three squared
**63** Word after "stage" or "screen"
**65** Network with an eye logo

# 125
## GRAND OPENING
By Zhouqin Burnikel

**ACROSS**
1 Disinfectant spray's target
5 Low-___ diet
9 Trudge
13 Solo for Cecilia Bartoli
14 Someone who's doomed
15 Passed-down tales
16 Guitarist's tool
17 Sister brand of Miracle-Gro
18 Carpet layer's measurement
19 Where you might be greeted with "Siyo!"
22 Between sm. and lg.
23 Wheel bar
24 Have a fistfight
29 Doorstep coverings
32 What two halves make
33 Tzatziki herb
34 Painter Holloman
36 Evil character in a soap opera, often
38 Paris transit system
40 Heroic tale
41 Colorful wrap
43 Overhasty
45 Cow's chew
46 Title for Emma Thompson
47 Building super's item
49 "No sweat!"
51 Proverbially 49-Across dessert
52 El Salvador's region
59 Footwear brand
60 "Specifically . . ."
61 Circus safety items

63 Show off some pipes
64 Pizzeria fixtures
65 Much-worshipped celebrity
66 "Sad to say . . ."
67 Wasps' abode
68 Fish in "Finding Dory"

**DOWN**
1 Gender pay ___
2 "Here for It" author R. ___ Thomas
3 Rolling in dough
4 Defiant phrase
5 Bottle stopper
6 Toss in chips before the deal
7 Put in the microwave, say
8 Birthplace of hip-hop
9 Levels off
10 Model Harvey
11 Sister brand of Nilla
12 Lucy Diggs Slowe served as one at Howard University
14 Blast
20 Actress Tara
21 ___ mater
24 Connect the ___
25 Not married
26 "Atonement" star Knightley
27 Flamenco shout
28 Prefix for "sound" or "marathon"
30 Racing venue
31 "In other news," for one

**34** Reward poster subjects, perhaps
**35** "Portrait of a ___ on Fire"
**37** Handouts at sign-in desks
**39** Dorm supervisors
**42** One translation of the Hungarian word "korte" (another being "lightbulb")
**44** Successor
**47** "Mi amor," in English
**48** Bring under control
**50** Tried to suppress
**52** "House," in Spanish

**53** Rotten to the core
**54** "What Happened, Miss Simone?" name
**55** Bowls over
**56** Tzatziki herb
**57** Surrender
**58** Smallest unit of matter
**62** ___-mo

# 126
## (S)EATING ARRANGEMENTS
By Erik Agard & Alex Trevino

**ACROSS**

1 Inspiration for a spotted print
8 Emotional turmoil
13 Consumer of both plant and animal matter
15 Sang forcefully
17 *Surveillance session
18 *Move quickly
19 Lure in
21 Make fun of
22 Tax org.
25 Resume initials
26 Resume initials
28 "Check ___ Juliet" (We the Kings song)
29 Like some highway lanes
31 Knitting project
33 *Intelligence gatherers
34 Tailless primates
35 "I need it urgently!"
39 Message to employees
40 *Like smooth, glossy hair
41 Golf org.
42 Biblical garden
43 Counterpart of the Grammys, for short
44 *Contempt
45 What a malfunctioning robot might say
47 Seasides
48 Burning Man rentals
51 Common batteries
52 Payment for legal services
53 "Locke & ___"

54 Hawkeye State resident
56 Headwear for "Toddlers" in a TLC reality show
59 *Playground fixtures
61 *Draw a draft of
65 Place for a dog
66 Place for a chicken
67 Suspicious
68 "Look!"

**DOWN**

1 ___ Angeles
2 Person in an ambulance, for short
3 Based ___ true story
4 Actress Rosamund
5 Exacts retribution for
6 Firmly embedded
7 Ancient Celtic priest
8 Six-pack muscles
9 Sweet liquid
10 Adhesive sold in sticks
11 Go off course
12 Not wordy
14 And so on, for short
16 Substances that may be semipermanent
20 Onstage hosts
22 "Are You There God? ___, Margaret"
23 ___ off (separated with a cord)
24 *Green goo at the Kids' Choice Awards

**27** Enjoy the sun
**30** Bon Appetit chef Brad
**31** *Long weapon
**32** "The Sopranos" star Edie
**34** "So close!"
**36** *Hybrid utensil
**37** See eye to eye
**38** Flower whose name comes from the French for "thought"
**40** Actress Gilbert
**44** Put in a protective cover
**46** Word after "park" or "Power"
**47** Peaceful

**48** Hazard
**49** Consonant's opposite
**50** Pigs
**52** Ungenuine "friends"
**55** Fictional orphan on Prince Edward Island
**57** Suffix for an estimate
**58** "Nae" sayer
**60** As ___ as a fox
**62** "Come again?"
**63** Rapinoe's team, on scoreboards
**64** Friend with soft fur, often

# 127
## TAKING A NAP
By Stella Zawistowski

**ACROSS**

1 Draped garment
5 Baecation destination
10 Make less difficult
14 Newspaper tribute, for short
15 Huge city in India
16 Hospital procedure
17 California wine tour hub
19 Part with
20 Having fun
21 Got up
23 Ignited again
24 Tech for "Cats" or "Cars"
25 Ensnare
28 Part of a min.
29 Jolly Rancher flavor
32 "___ Not There" (Zombies song)
33 Performing in a series of locations
34 It might be uncut
37 Amount of cash or gum
38 Train sched. listing
39 Golf org.
40 Welcomes through the door
42 Hospital procedures
43 "The Piano" actress
45 Lamb's sound
48 Season associated with a log
49 Alma mater of Shonda Rhimes
50 Bach composition
52 Reward for sitting and speaking
54 Slot in prime time
55 Indonesian island, or a bra brand
58 Crunchy cookie
60 Forbidden fruit's place
61 Word after "morning" or "crowning"
62 Revise
63 Stat on a medicine label
64 Bone-related prefix
65 ___ a one (none)

**DOWN**

1 Shipwreck-finding tech
2 Lets up
3 Metaphor for an aftereffect
4 Like slanted type
5 Beyonce album released when she turned 25
6 Fish with poisonous blood
7 Family-friendly
8 "My ___ Amour"
9 "Ba-dum-tss!"
10 Selected passage
11 "Roses ___ red . . ."
12 Like this: :(
13 Side-___
18 Dyeing vessel
22 Fan seating
24 Believability, for short
26 Each
27 Publicize
29 Nkrumah's country
30 Out

## Crossword Grid

|   |   |   |   |   |   |   |   |   |   |   |   |   |
|---|---|---|---|---|---|---|---|---|---|---|---|---|
| 1 | 2 | 3 | 4 | ■ | 5 | 6 | 7 | 8 | 9 | ■ | 10 | 11 | 12 | 13 |
| 14 |   |   |   | ■ | 15 |   |   |   |   | ■ | 16 |   |   |   |
| 17 |   |   |   | 18 |   |   |   |   |   | ■ | 19 |   |   |   |
| 20 |   |   |   |   | ■ | 21 |   |   | 22 |   |   | ■ |   |   |
| 23 |   |   |   | ■ | 24 |   |   | 25 |   |   | 26 | 27 |   |   |
| ■ | 28 |   |   | 29 |   |   | 30 |   |   |   |   |   | ■ | 31 |
|   |   |   | 32 |   |   | 33 |   |   |   |   |   |   |   |   |
| 34 | 35 | 36 | ■ | 37 |   |   | 38 |   |   | ■ | 39 |   |   |   |
| 40 |   |   | 41 |   |   | 42 |   |   |   |   |   |   |   |   |
| 43 |   |   |   | 44 |   |   |   | ■ | 45 | 46 | 47 |   |   |   |
| ■ | 48 |   |   | 49 |   |   | 50 |   |   |   |   | 51 |   |   |
| ■ |   | 52 |   | 53 |   |   | 54 |   |   |   |   |   |   |   |
| 55 | 56 | 57 |   | 58 |   | 59 |   |   |   |   |   |   |   |   |
| 60 |   |   |   | 61 |   |   |   | ■ | 62 |   |   |   |   |   |
| 63 |   |   |   | 64 |   |   |   | ■ | 65 |   |   |   |   |   |

### Clues

**31** Proposal ratified by Va. in 2020

**32** Thieving fox on "Dora the Explorer"

**34** School org. that might observe Day of Silence

**35** Start of a counting rhyme

**36** Restaurant handout

**38** Big brother on "Boy Meets World"

**41** Thin cracker

**42** Prohibitive phrase

**44** Producers of tiny spotted eggs

**45** Lab burner namesake

**46** List of topics

**47** Host family's helper

**50** Tree with needles

**51** E, on a fuel gauge

**53** Waffle brand

**54** Singer who judges "World of Dance"

**55** Place for a nap

**56** "Much ___ About Nothing"

**57** Guitar maker ___ Paul

**59** Test hidden in "degree"

**USA TODAY**

# 128
## SUB DIVISION

By Evan Kalish

**ACROSS**

1 Modify
5 Marshy spot
8 Slog through a 5-Across, say
12 Chef's special, e.g.
13 Single-stranded molecule
14 Sporting venues
17 Escort through the exit
19 ___ Nevada mountains
20 Do a palms-up dance move
22 "Fiddler on the Roof" is set in one
25 Karate kid who said "I hate it here"
26 Otherwise
27 Golf course number
28 Upper-left key
30 Commotion
32 "___ Miz"
33 Opera highlight
35 Roll out
38 Button material
43 Lilongwe's country
44 Apt rhyme for "float"
46 Nickname for the singer of "Umbrella"
49 Got together
50 Bottle topper
53 Exploit
54 Famous ___ cookies
56 Floor washer
58 Provide pain relief
60 Storm's shorefront effect, perhaps

63 Like a lifeless landscape
64 "One, the other . . . it's all good"
68 Newspaper ad supplement
69 Scan in a tube
70 "Shrill" star Bryant
71 Some sheep
72 Palindromic sib
73 Mine vein

**DOWN**

1 Grad student's email ending
2 Prefix for "respect"
3 ". . . more or less"
4 "Whoomp! (___ It Is)"
5 Cooks with radiant heat
6 Burden
7 Like some communities
8 Past one's prime
9 Singer India.___
10 Big name in farm equipment
11 Sign up for classes
15 Popped up
16 Strongboxes
18 Give five stars to, say
21 Rush hour issue
22 Pedicure place
23 "No ___ done"
24 Quartet minus one
29 Museum worker
31 73-Across material
34 Banking convenience
36 "Right this second!"
37 Research location

● **USA TODAY**

**39** Pineapple's pizza partner
**40** Gold and silver, but not bronze
**41** Very lopsided ballgame
**42** Hair on a lid
**45** Casual shirt
**46** Bar mitzvah figure
**47** "That is to say . . ."
**48** Croaky
**51** The way things are now
**52** Fictional honey-loving bear
**55** Fastener tightened by rotating

**57** Angelou compositions
**59** "Basketball Wives" star Shaunie
**61** "Present!"
**62** Voice in Apple products
**65** ___ Grande
**66** Like 911, and each of its digits
**67** Deli bread choice

# 129
## BACKWARD LAWS
By Zhouqin Burnikel

**ACROSS**

1 Feature in the funny pages
6 Lightbulb, in cartoons
10 "Go Set a Watchman" author Harper
13 University of Baghdad student, typically
14 First name that's a verb in reverse
15 Support with funds
16 Restaurant category
18 Big Apple tennis venue
19 Enter via keyboard
20 Throws in a high arc
21 "For here ___ go?"
22 Gulp
24 Down-to-___ (unpretentious)
26 Bread with a pocket
28 Hopeless endeavor
32 Bowling pin count
33 Canned meat
35 Tiny maze runner
36 QVC sister station
37 "Wicked" star Menzel
39 Dirt road problem
40 Relaxed
43 "Crimes of the Heart" actress Harper
45 "One step ___ time"
46 Opposite of ideal
48 Possible result of doing power yoga
50 This puzzle has 78
51 Analyst fodder
53 "ETA?"
54 Let the cat out of the bag
56 Frozen Four org.
60 Southernmost Great Lake
61 Vacation spot that might allow clothing
63 Site with restaurant reviews
64 Lots and lots
65 "The Tortoise and the Hare" storyteller
66 Pull the plug on
67 Floating ice hazard
68 It might be broken or stained

**DOWN**

1 ___ through (search)
2 Cafeteria carrier
3 Sore throat sound
4 Assessment with a median score of 100
5 Snap story upload
6 "That's great to hear!"
7 Smear
8 Removes all evidence of
9 Knee part, for short
10 Final performance, say
11 Canyon sound effect
12 ___ out (barely manage)
15 Bill for drinks
17 Mahershala or Muhammad
21 Whale that preys on sharks
23 "I ___ Made to Love Her"
25 Book with insets
26 Sauce for linguine

**USA TODAY**

**27** What might make an adult swing on a swing set
**29** Skips over
**30** Cook in a small amount of fat
**31** Jazz legend James
**32** Defrost
**34** Fragment
**38** Teasing
**41** In dreamland
**42** Leave speechless
**44** Used a chair
**47** Sharp as a tack
**49** Call off

**52** YouTuber's income source
**53** Little warbling bird
**55** Scent
**57** Place with un garaje, perhaps
**58** Singer Tori
**59** Headspace and Calm, e.g.
**60** Contact lens site
**61** Seize
**62** Playground game

# 130
## WASTELAND
By Allison Uttaro

**ACROSS**

1 Pack animal in Peru
6 Annoying person
10 Hosp. section
13 ___ and aahed
14 Bit of 2-Down
15 Con artist's plan
16 Another name for a raccoon
18 Video game protagonist Croft
19 Decide when the wedding will be
20 Liquefies
21 Pecan or cashew
22 Tons and tons
23 End of a blowout game
29 Cookies with creme
30 Historical period
31 Take back due to default
35 Lake near Jordan
38 "Do you have a guess?"
40 Sentimental types
41 Sra. counterpart
43 At an angle
44 Four-legged siblings
47 Computer user who might say "I'm in"
51 Dec. 24 or 31, e.g.
52 "The game is ___!"
53 5K or half marathon, for example
59 Large chunk

60 Spot for paper clips and rubber bands and screwdrivers and pencils and takeout menus and . . .
62 British 37-Down institution
63 "Ah, makes sense"
64 Make amends
65 Aliens (Abbr.)
66 Home planet of many fictional aliens
67 Martial arts goals

**DOWN**

1 Parking areas
2 Body of traditions
3 At the drop of ___
4 Flat-topped landform
5 Adderall is prescribed for it
6 Stone figure in a park
7 Hannah Gadsby stand-up special
8 Not recent
9 Drink that might be full of bubbles
10 Bet-matching phrase in poker
11 A la ___
12 New England college, for short
15 Vehicle such as the qamutiik
17 Hunger pain
20 One of the Three Stooges
22 Neighbor of Yemen
23 Deities
24 Trig calculation
25 "You ___ what you sow"

Crossword grid with numbered cells: 1, 2, 3, 4, 5, 6, 7, 8, 9, 10, 11, 12, 13, 14, 15, 16, 17, 18, 19, 20, 21, 22, 23, 24, 25, 26, 27, 28, 29, 30, 31, 32, 33, 34, 35, 36, 37, 38, 39, 40, 41, 42, 43, 44, 45, 46, 47, 48, 49, 50, 51, 52, 53, 54, 55, 56, 57, 58, 59, 60, 61, 62, 63, 64, 65, 66, 67.

**26** Physiques, for short
**27** Donkey
**28** Savings letters
**31** Acting legend Moreno
**32** Get from rough to final
**33** Brazilian soccer star
**34** Breakfast sometimes prepared overnight
**36** Qatar leader
**37** Murals and such
**39** Staple of Nigerian cuisine
**42** More dour
**44** Allow

**45** Calls to mind
**46** Peruse a book
**47** "___ makes waste"
**48** G sharp equivalent
**49** Layers of paint
**50** Japan's sixth-largest city
**54** Dull
**55** "At any ___ . . ."
**56** Missing, for short
**57** Penny's worth
**58** Spanish for "you are"
**60** Muppets creator Henson
**61** "Briarpatch" network

# 131
## TUTEES
By Caitlin Reid

**ACROSS**

1 Puts to work
5 ___ godmother
10 Religious branch
14 List header
15 An ___ but a goodie
16 Rake's creation
17 "Yeah, right!"
18 Very funny people
19 Rio Grande contents
20 Chewy cinnamon candies
22 "Mamma Mia! Here We Go Again" star
23 Partiality
24 "Must be"
26 Bestow, as wisdom
29 Wooded areas
32 Dentist's trayful
33 Audibly disagreed with a ref's call
34 Humdrum routine
36 Hardly angelic
37 Roll in a first-aid kit
38 Mascara wearer
39 Of Monsters and ___
40 ___ asada
41 Coffee option
42 Super mad
44 Finally dawned
45 "The Office" star Catherine
46 Playlist component
47 "Dagnabbit!"
49 Mardi Gras, literally

55 One might start with "Knock knock"
56 X-ray protection garment
57 Camouflage
58 ". . . said no one ___"
59 Had the capability
60 King cake's shape
61 Say it ain't so
62 Fencing blades
63 Short-term worker

**DOWN**

1 Neighbor of Nevada
2 Just average
3 Fine-tune, perhaps
4 Dot Richardson's sport
5 The "F" of PDF
6 "aka" name
7 Object of worship
8 Sacred ceremony
9 "Absolutely!"
10 Completely forgets
11 Obsolete tape type
12 Murder mystery board game
13 Cheek wetter
21 Runs on the radio
25 Sleep on it
26 Big-ticket ___
27 Gets a new address
28 "I hear you"
29 Establish
30 Move like slime
31 Food served with gari
33 Nekkid

**35** "Strangor ___ Fiction"
**37** Something "put on" before a competition
**38** Major underdog
**40** Feline
**41** Feature of a 40-Down, maybe
**43** Place to get some grub
**44** Word before "good" or "legit"
**46** Plagiarized
**47** Spun tunes at a party
**48** Be a vagabond
**50** For each one
**51** Not false

**52** Explore a roof, say
**53** "Parenthood" parent
**54** Business-reviewing app

# 132
## CAPITAL IDEA
By Susan Smolinsky & Zhouqin Burnikel

**ACROSS**
1 Milk qty.
4 Place of worship
9 Spots for couch potatoes
14 With 17-Across, quantity for a small omelet
15 $$$
16 In the loop
17 See 14-Across
18 Socialite (France)
20 Animal in Genesis
22 Lawn material
23 What ruminant animals chew
24 "I ___ the Fifth"
25 Twiddle one's thumbs
27 Alleviate
28 Like a positive outlook
29 Run for it
30 Playful mammalian swimmer
31 Published
32 ___ monster
33 Horse feed bit
34 Actress (Yemen)
38 "On the other hand . . ."
39 Desmond who said "There is nothing more difficult than waking someone who is only pretending to be asleep"
40 Pose a question
43 Giza pyramids, e.g.
46 Jazz musician Puente
47 Part of a Sherlock Holmes costume
48 Apex predator of the sea

49 "That's not good!"
50 Travel annoyance
51 One-named Australian pop singer
52 St. Patrick's Day mo.
53 2015 Bond film
55 Model (Bulgaria)
58 Carpet hue
59 Vote into office
60 Lend
61 "As I see it," for short
62 Tries to find
63 Uses a keyboard
64 Boyz II ___

**DOWN**
1 Gives up amateur status
2 "I Know Why the Caged Bird Sings" author
3 Wheelchair parts
4 Fired up
5 Lend
6 Taquito exterior
7 "Love Story" star MacGraw
8 Compete in a ring, colloquially
9 Put into words
10 Nocturnal bird
11 Wealthy political donor, e.g.
12 Awaken
13 Return to ___
19 Low-tech weed whacker
21 Settle a debt

**USA TODAY**

Crossword grid (numbered cells): 1, 2, 3, 4, 5, 6, 7, 8, 9, 10, 11, 12, 13 across top row; 14, 15, 16; 17, 18, 19; 20, 21, 22, 23; 24, 25, 26, 27; 28, 29, 30; 31, 32, 33; 34, 35, 36, 37; 38, 39, 40, 41, 42; 43, 44, 45, 46, 47; 48, 49, 50; 51, 52, 53, 54; 55, 56, 57, 58; 59, 60, 61; 62, 63, 64.

**26** Gave a hand, at the poker table

**27** Blues singer ___ James

**29** Italian automaker

**30** Honolulu's island

**32** Wildebeests

**33** Name that's a palindrome

**35** Pop group that's a palindrome

**36** Place for dent repair

**37** Part of a dog's grooming appointment

**41** "Enough already!"

**42** Targeted

**43** Hurls

**44** Baltimore bird

**45** Computer security brand

**46** Frugality

**47** Torso muscle, for short

**49** Rowing tool

**50** Specifics, in slang

**52** Yoga accessories

**54** Tree with needles

**56** "Gross!"

**57** Shed tears

# 133
## BREAD STARTERS
By Erik Agard & Jackson Ingram

**ACROSS**

1 River's movement
5 Musical phrase
9 Sit-___ (protests)
12 Norwegian capital
13 Anticipate
15 Became acquainted with
16 Sauce hidden in "asparagus"
17 Sign that's three before Gemini
19 Flattery
22 ___ Dame
23 Yiddish lament
24 502, in Roman numerals
26 Financial planning initials
27 Scallion relative
28 Vessel for Union, Wade, Paul, and James in an infamous vacation photo
32 Levy on TV
33 Traveled
34 Silent-letter bird
35 Reigning over
37 Colorful parrots
39 Food that's a mineral backward
40 Fourth planet from the sun
41 40-Across hue
43 Rat race, say
46 Eat
47 MLK's title, for short
48 "Pushing Daisies" pie-maker
49 Complete
50 Bedard who voiced Pocahontas
53 Latte alternative
56 Sparrow, for one
58 Statement of comprehension
59 "Just kidding!"
60 English major's assignment
61 Acceptable
62 College senior's test, perhaps
63 Opposite of difficulty
64 Dorothy's first victim hails from this direction

**DOWN**

1 Number of winks in a nap
2 College senior's test, perhaps
3 Author Tokarczuk
4 "___ that be nice!"
5 Genre with freestyles
6 Triumphant shout
7 Burkina ___
8 Short story author's field
9 "Sounds good to me!"
10 Time to switch calendars
11 He . . . is a Crystal Gem
14 Lead-in to "firma" or "cotta"
18 Spot at the table
20 "Get it away from me!"
21 Hyundai competitor
25 Away from the outside
28 Not harmful
29 Director Lee
30 Curving paths

**31** "How to ___ Human Being" (Glass Animals album)

**33** Lean but strong

**36** "ur hilarious"

**37** "Jeez!"

**38** Politician with a six-year term

**40** Time when some crises take place

**42** Rhyme of 49-Down, and what you might do to one

**43** ___ coffee

**44** Bird of prey's nest

**45** Official with a whistle

**46** "I goofed!"

**49** Receiver of likes

**51** Rocket-launching org.

**52** GPS calculations

**54** Vietnam's continent

**55** Some bills

**57** Anatomical palindrome

# 134
## THE FIVE W'S
By Brooke Husic

**ACROSS**

1 Practical joke
4 "A Lady" for Jane Austen, e.g.
9 Train units
13 "... like ___ got diamonds / at the meeting of my thighs?" (Angelou)
14 Sticky note brand
16 Clarifying phrase when spelling
17 Early lookout shift
19 ___-chic
20 Makes easier to control
21 Furniture store that sells meatballs
23 Crow sound
24 Asterisk
25 Renewed energy
28 Geologic time unit
29 Prefix for "issue"
30 Basketball great Taurasi
31 Put in effort
32 Iron-deficient, maybe
36 Frequent verb in Beyonce's "Formation"
37 '90s-'00s era of feminism
39 Gorillas are "great" ones
42 Trig ratio
43 Trident-shaped letter
46 Pale purple
48 Permissive
49 First Asian-American NBA champion Jeremy
50 Ferris Bueller breaks it
54 Small amount of salt
55 "Furthermore..."
56 Be shocked
57 "Get ___ My Way" (Kylie Minogue song)
58 Parent of Ben Solo
60 One who might pull up a chair to a booth
63 ___ off (repel)
64 Inter ___ Council of Arizona (nonprofit advocacy group)
65 Linking verb
66 Ship Athena helped design
67 University higher-ups
68 An American might exchange them for JPY

**DOWN**

1 Multipart present
2 Pilot
3 Deutschland
4 Some vacation rentals, for short
5 Lead-in to "key" or "profile"
6 "God ___ Woman" (Ariana Grande hit)
7 Room below a roof
8 "___ MODE" (Travis Scott single)
9 Taxi
10 Preferring solitude
11 Bajan pop star and beauty mogul
12 Procrastinating student's wish
15 Now's partner
18 Spanish 101 verb
22 Contribute

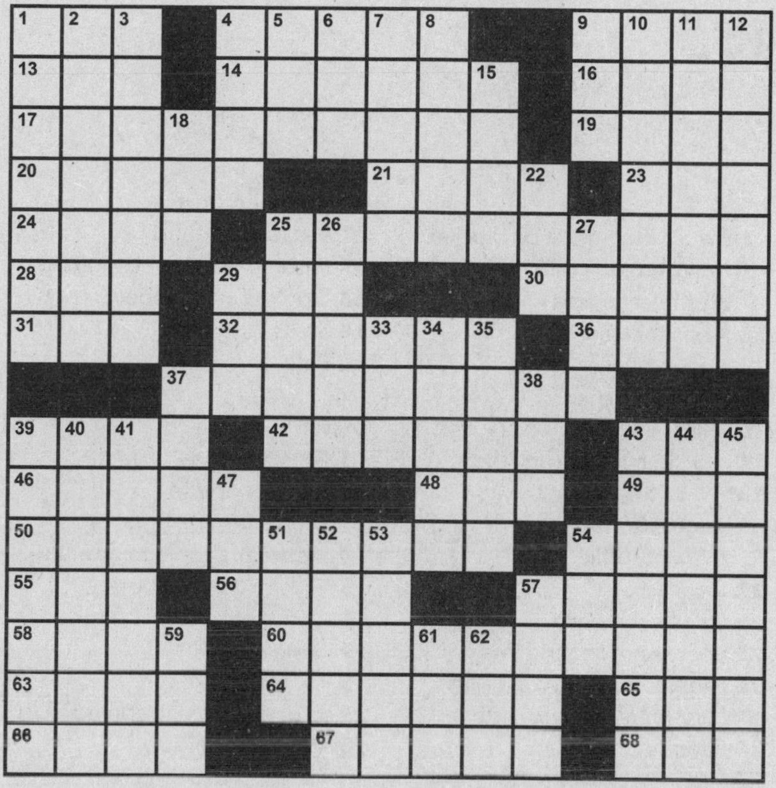

**25** Chain with carhops
**26** Month numero uno
**27** Sage
**29** Curt dismissal
**33** Some residents' degs.
**34** Reassuring response to "Be careful!"
**35** Ear passage
**37** Former Russian title
**38** Annoy
**39** Rabbit food
**40** Trailblaze
**41** Avoiding

**43** Stop improving, say
**44** Venus and Serena, e.g.
**45** Got air
**47** Middle, geometrically (Abbr.)
**51** Weight
**52** Unusual
**53** Lily Allen's actor brother
**54** "Obviously!"
**57** Barn birds
**59** Fuss
**61** Sched. placeholder
**62** Parent of Ben Solo

# 135
## APPLE ANATOMY
By Patrick Jordan

**ACROSS**
1 Emails that might be blocked
5 Holiday highlight, often
9 Bramble, for one
14 Prefix for "renewal"
15 Andes dweller of old
16 Numerical goal
17 Spinal cord connector
19 Having a lower rank than
20 Fish of the order Anguilliformes
21 Ailment suffix
22 Most wise
23 Salon substance
25 Sport with long mallets
26 Workouts that aid stability
31 "Didn't we just deal with this?"
34 Sentence segment
35 High-ranking exec, for short
36 Word before "record" or "leaf"
37 Motif in Hew Locke's work
39 Participate electorally
40 Telepathy, e.g.
41 Take it ___ yourself
42 Jockey alternative
43 Wear a revealing garment
47 "Take this"
48 Temporal delay
52 Obedient
55 1962 Bond film
56 French recipe phrase
57 Coax a laugh from
58 Startup capital

60 Commemorates
61 Bell tower sound
62 Fashion designer Lagerfeld
63 Garlic-crushing tool
64 Swiss ___ knife
65 Refer to

**DOWN**
1 Fencing blade
2 Blender option
3 Even a bit
4 French first-person pronoun
5 Sister from another ___
6 Complete
7 Superb serves
8 On the ___
9 In dire need of cleaning
10 Wouldn't give up
11 Gave a hard time
12 Colorado Natives
13 Oakland subway letters
18 "Sex and the City" star Cynthia
22 Heads for the clouds
24 Etching liquid
25 Bit of set dressing
27 Package-binding cord
28 Total legend
29 "And that's why you always leave a ___"
30 Doesn't stick around
31 They increase on birthdays
32 "Gee!"
33 Dog food brand

**37** Reproductive cell
**38** Morrison novel
**39** Device rotated by the wind
**41** Of zero help
**42** Greeting often heard on the second Sunday in May
**44** Meringue-making tools
**45** Watch online
**46** Warmhearted
**49** Hawaii's sixth-largest island
**50** Urgent notification
**51** King of television
**52** Not quite dry

**53** Actor Sharif
**54** Objective of some medical research
**55** Members of Brother Nature's squad
**58** Seaweed wrap offerer
**59** Capital city near Shawnee, for short

# 136
## IN CONCLUSION
By Zhouqin Burnikel

**ACROSS**

1 Exercise that might be done with crossed arms
6 Driver's aid
9 Bites
13 Pinterest upload
14 Manhattan area west of Little Italy
15 European capital lauded by Vision Zero proponents in 2019
16 Place for discounted merchandise
18 Rod and ___
19 Strikebreaker
20 Mattress spring
21 Soft jacket material
22 Air freshener target
24 Embellishes, say
26 The Himalayas, e.g.
31 Sudden flurry
33 Post-Mardi Gras period
34 Pigeon's sound
35 Converse competitor
36 "No bid from me"
38 Summer camp beds
39 Savings plan that might be "traditional"
40 Tend to polenta
41 Impressive selection
42 Fall pastry
46 Go upward
47 Winter road sprinkle
48 "Well done!"

51 Warm spell that causes melting
53 Falsetto-voiced Muppet
57 List entry
58 Rhyming emigration
60 ___ down (pack tightly)
61 Patch up
62 Target walkway
63 Golf stroke
64 Tie the knot
65 Foundations

**DOWN**

1 Some relatives, for short
2 Apple product
3 Actress Reid
4 Australian footwear
5 Veggie in mame gohan
6 Desert along the Silk Road
7 MLB team with a Phanatic mascot
8 "Like father, like ___"
9 "Take your time!"
10 "Gotcha"
11 Appealed earnestly
12 Dover fish
14 Sound of disdain
17 Tappable picture
21 Religious offshoot
23 Scheduled to arrive
25 Rustic stopovers
26 "___ Secretary"
27 Clock radio feature
28 Squirrel's treat

**29** Letter before kappa
**30** Like a busybody
**31** Not attend
**32** Cuzco's country
**36** Tell it like ___
**37** Maine's flag features a moose under one
**38** Yardsticks
**40** Biathlete's pair
**41** ___-CIO
**43** Right on time
**44** Foreign relief org. whose motto is "From the American people"
**45** Baby deer
**48** Meal prep boxes
**49** State home to the world's largest Mormon temple
**50** Trade show presentation
**52** Word after "second" or "helping"
**54** Lad's counterpart
**55** Frequent flyer's unit
**56** Most tip jar bills
**58** Munich-based automaker
**59** Bit of eye gel

# 137
## HANG AROUND
By Gail Grabowski

**ACROSS**

1 Bearers of corn
5 "Now That's What ___ Music!"
10 Prefix for "connect"
13 Zagreb citizen
14 Finnish phone brand
15 Take advantage of
16 Jarring touchdown
18 Red, Yellow, Black, or White, e.g.
19 Italian sparkling wine
20 "This I Promise You" band
21 Mushroom part
22 Motive
24 ___ pole (carving on which the most important figures are often toward the bottom)
26 Salon service
31 Programming glitch
34 Not fictitious
35 Spay/___
36 Sleep like ___
38 Wet dirt
40 City near Phoenix
41 Uses the wheel
44 Currency in Montenegro
47 Farm dwelling
48 Dish similar to polenta
51 Tripped and fell, perhaps
52 Bit of pasta
56 Bright object that's the title of a Beyonce hit
58 ___ and crannies
61 Noisy
62 Under the weather
63 Per Orson Welles, it "depends, of course, on where you stop your story"
65 Letter before omega
66 Sans-serif font
67 Bumble alternative
68 Singer Trinh Cong ___
69 No longer fresh
70 Staying power

**DOWN**

1 Rub off of the page
2 Major blood vessel
3 Salad veggie
4 Toasted ravioli city, for short
5 Places to stay
6 "Juno" screenwriter Diablo
7 Comparable with
8 Capital of Nebraska
9 Online gaming annoyance
10 Microscopic pests
11 "Got it"
12 Jeans line
13 Burn slightly
17 "Tomorrow" musical
21 Truth ___
23 Rowboat implement
25 "Little piggy"
27 Male sheep
28 Like crosswords
29 Hatchling's home
30 Like gloomy skies
31 Big celebration

**32** Beauty chain

**33** Risks everything at the poker table

**37** Arrive at

**39** Total flop

**42** Dense bread

**43** Paintings on rotating canvases

**45** Wash off

**46** Palindromic fish

**49** Paradise

**50** "The First Wives Club" star Hawn

**53** Performing

**54** Chest organs

**55** Margin

**56** Body parts involved in the macarena

**57** Part of aka

**59** Fall birthstone

**60** Catwoman's surname

**63** Possesses

**64** Org. with defenders on skates

# 138
## PARTY ANIMAL
By Rachel Fabi

**ACROSS**

1 Word before "pool" or "splicing"
5 Partner of every
9 Esport with the map Summoner's Rift, for short
12 Margot Robbie figure skating biopic
15 Third-largest Hawaiian island
16 Parisian assent
17 Source of a slime trail
19 Bill dispenser
20 Tardy
21 "Bodak Yellow" rapper
23 Religious dissenter
26 Applications
27 "Mila 18" author Leon
29 Upset with
32 Grew taut
35 Consumer protection group, maybe
39 Throw in
40 Venue for a small concert
42 Wall St. debut
43 Big-eyed buzzer
45 Tilted
47 Walking
49 Scarlet and crimson, for two
50 ___ seeds
53 Axes
56 Went on and on
59 Molten rock
60 "Mrs. America" actress Aduba
61 2019 hit by Tones and I

67 Lead-in to X, Y, or Z
68 Arrangement of squares
69 Hold the attention of
70 Sneaky
71 ___ and Escalators (board game in "SpongeBob SquarePants")
72 School on the Thames

**DOWN**

1 ___ economy
2 Airport approximation (Abbr.)
3 Partner of neither
4 Without cease
5 Long unit of time
6 Roadside assistance grp.
7 Fashionable
8 Polynesian dance
9 Units of laundry
10 Protruding belly button
11 Large tree branches
13 Long unit of time
14 Poker payment
18 Tennis match components
22 "Loving" star Negga
23 With 38-Down, Brahma and Vishnu, e.g.
24 Words of indebtedness
25 Bad-tempered person
27 Arches National Park state
28 Subsequent try
30 Shortened Latin phrase at the end of a list
31 Farmland unit

**33** Garden in Genesis

**34** "What's the ___?" ("Isn't it all the same?")

**36** Chows down

**37** Column with a view

**38** See 23-Down

**41** Many a YouTube upload

**44** "Days of Our Lives," for one

**46** Organize

**48** Scrabble piece

**50** Downs quickly

**51** Greenish-brown eye color

**52** Ungenuine tone

**54** Not wild

**55** Multilevel marketing beauty company

**57** Living on the ___

**58** Truth or ___

**62** Nada

**63** Music holders in cases

**64** Kit ___ bar

**65** Sense of self-importance

**66** Japanese currency

# 139
## ALARM SYSTEM
By Zhouqin Burnikel

**ACROSS**

1 "Great ___ think alike"
6 The "A" in UAE
10 Evergreen trees with toxic seeds
14 "Gotta go"
15 PBS science show
16 Aloha Tower's island
17 Stealthy stealer
19 Brought into play
20 Top poker card
21 ___ straits
22 Some shopping sessions
24 Like a room post-Kondoing
25 Skin opening
26 Ballet handrails
29 Silly Putty maker
32 For all to hear
33 Word before "coffee" or "irrigation"
34 Boy, in Spanish
36 Hint
37 Black-white-black snacks
38 Dart like a butterfly
39 Ugandan activist David
40 In close proximity to
41 City close to Fort Lauderdale
42 "This is me"
44 People working together join them
45 "20 Feet ___ Stardom"
46 Increase
47 "Aw, dang it!"
50 Sports journalist Kimes

51 "New Rules" singer Lipa
54 Legit
55 Totally quiet
58 Up in ___ (incensed)
59 Not busy
60 Apartment alternative
61 Easy gait
62 Places
63 Watch secretly

**DOWN**

1 Flaky mineral
2 Device that's an anagram of 1-Down
3 Brief message
4 Provide with a soundtrack in a different language
5 Cracked the books
6 Incensed
7 Clarice Starling, for Jodie Foster
8 "13th" director DuVernay
9 Bathroom dish occupants
10 Compliment regarding a hot streak
11 Ill at ___
12 "This ride is fun!"
13 Foam from 9-Down
18 Disabuses
23 Poke one's nose into others' business
24 Question format
25 Previous
26 Spine's place

**27** Part of iA
**28** Bus map line
**29** Shade named for a dairy product
**30** Shade named for a flower
**31** Hayao Miyazaki works
**33** Aspiration
**35** Moving walkway maker
**37** Potato chip accompaniment
**41** Umayyad Mosque designs
**43** Get the time wrong, say
**44** Dolphins have them
**46** Bus journeys

**47** ___ history
**48** Dr. Li Wenliang, to many
**49** Like towel-dried hair
**50** Barley product
**51** Declare untrue
**52** Reverse the effects of
**53** Plenty
**56** College URL ending
**57** ___-eared

# 140
## SALES LEADS
By Brooke Husic & Evan Kalish

**ACROSS**

1 Not new
5 "I did NOT need to know that"
8 Wilts
12 Ifill in the NABJ Hall of Fame
13 Penobscot state
15 Unadulterated
16 The Pleasure Seekers, for one
18 Citation-shortening abbreviation
19 Tried to hurt
20 Emma Watson's "Little Women" role
21 IUD, by another name
22 Spotted
23 Passionate types, in astrology
25 Wax stamp
27 Instruction in some tofu recipes
28 High-ceiling apartment, often
31 Like a clammy cave
34 "Como se ___?"
37 Bike shop amenity
38 Competition involving ovens
40 Escape vehicle
41 Spherical map
43 "Don't Go to Strangers" singer Jones
44 The thing right here
45 Largest loch by volume
47 Smallest Great Lake by volume
49 Inheritor's payment
53 Prefix for "physical"
56 Pole on a ship
57 Sugarcane-derived spirit
58 St. Louis Bread Co., by another name
60 Some brews
61 Studying set
63 Religious leader
64 ___ up (assessed)
65 Understand
66 Delayed
67 Bench with a kneeler
68 Units of maize

**DOWN**

1 Aussie boots
2 Exchanges
3 Spooky
4 Bit of forensic evidence
5 Helpful key for Python coding
6 City aka the 305
7 Word before "circle" or "peace"
8 Featured dish
9 A celebrity might be asked for one
10 Silo stuff
11 Gets money in return for
13 ___ school (destination for some bio majors)
14 Hair that might be laid
17 Chromosome part
23 Bit of snow
24 "We hold these truths to be ___-evident . . ."
26 Lovelace considered the first computer programmer
28 Fall behind

**USA TODAY**

## Crossword Grid

A crossword grid with numbered cells: 1-11 across top row; 12, 13, 14, 15; 16, 17, 18; 19, 20, 21; 22, 23, 24; 25, 26, 27; 28, 29, 30, 31, 32, 33, 34, 35, 36; 37, 38, 39, 40; 41, 42, 43, 44; 45, 46, 47, 48; 49, 50, 51, 52, 53, 54, 55; 56, 57, 58, 59; 60, 61, 62; 63, 64, 65; 66, 67, 68.

**29** Flaxseed product
**30** Car DJ's place, often
**32** Tennis divider
**33** Pad brand
**35** French for "me"
**36** Commercials
**38** Finest
**39** "Near, ___, wherever you are . . ."
**42** "I've got no clue"
**44** ___ Mutant Ninja Turtles
**46** Feudal laborers
**48** Apple desktop computer

**49** Many a meeting could have been one
**50** Hayek who played Kahlo
**51** Floral symbol of the Netherlands
**52** Really impress
**54** ___ firma
**55** Zeal
**58** Degree involving a defense
**59** Queries
**62** Stitch

# 141
## MORNING PEOPLE
By Stella Zawistowski

**ACROSS**

1 Bunch of bees
6 Cake in the bathroom
10 "Style ___" (1983 documentary)
14 Hot drink
15 Bicep exercise
16 Wrinkle remover
17 Co-founder of Sony
19 Cheese on a Greek salad
20 Metaphor for bureaucracy
21 Key related to B-flat major
23 Dine at a restaurant
26 Biblical transport
27 Actor who played Doc Ock
33 Hawaiian feasts
34 Observed
35 Ran away
39 Coat that goes on before paint
41 Rich cake
43 Novi Sad local
44 Beyond amazing
48 Car dealer's deal, often
49 Former world leader with a doctorate in quantum chemistry
52 Baby seal or mouse
55 Ornate part of a belt, perhaps
56 26-Across passenger
58 Do an impression of
64 Number of Supreme Court seats

**65** Nobel-winning Canadian author
68 "Pamela" band
69 Casino city near Tahoe
70 Extra feature
71 "You know nothing, Jon ___"
72 Some offspring
73 Homes in an aviary

**DOWN**

1 Evidence of an old injury
2 Roused from sleep
3 Base's opposite
4 Thing a plant puts down
5 One of the Three Bears
6 Reacts in horror
7 French agreement
8 Word after "concept" or "conceptual"
9 Bedeviling
10 Alternative to mobile data
11 Venue for a big concert
12 Helicopter blade
13 Snide comments
18 Slanted article
22 Part of a range (Abbr.)
24 Support for a ballerina en pointe
25 Word in a futbol chant
27 Brenner Pass range
28 Attract
29 Equitable
30 Afro-Cuban dance
31 Suffix for "Japan"

**USA TODAY**

32 "___ the Love Has Gone"
36 Problem with plumbing or security
37 Lack of problems
38 Battle head-to-head
40 They might order "the usual"
42 India pale ___
45 Chest muscle, for short
46 Kind
47 Tricolor cats
50 Antetokounmpo's league
51 Image saved on your phone, perhaps
52 Skirt alternative
53 Worker's group
54 Bean variety
57 "Feed me, human!"
59 Model Chanel
60 Sassiness, for short
61 No ifs, ___, or buts
62 Moderately fast gait
63 Long, long times
66 "War and Peace" author Tolstoy
67 Lorelai managed one on "Gilmore Girls"

# 142
## T.V. JONES
By Erik Agard

**ACROSS**

1 Capital of Peru
5 Income for waiters
9 Grew older
13 Spoken
14 Bit of creativity
15 Neighbor of Ghana
16 TV show whose protagonist wears a red hat
19 Elite squad
20 Phone plan subject
21 French article
22 English, in Spanish
26 Brief quarrel
30 Cleared of snow, perhaps
31 Japan's seventh-largest city
32 Letter after upsilon
34 "___ culpa"
35 Rainbow color
36 TV show starring Jane Fonda and Lily Tomlin
39 Made a sound like a pig
40 ___ Tome and Principe
41 "Wow!"
42 Reek
43 Not yet here
45 Yard tube
46 The field of film
47 Actor-director Longoria
50 Starting point
52 Titled
54 TV show that's the eighth series in its franchise
59 Tropical tree
60 Opponent of good
61 It might be turned or stemmed
62 Is under the weather
63 Not acknowledge
64 Sliding vehicle

**DOWN**

1 In the area
2 Infuriated
3 Female horses
4 ___ mater
5 Only three-letter element
6 DMVs issue them
7 Fried rice ingredient
8 Smoothed down
9 Back ___ again
10 "Remember, I'm new at this"
11 Fried rice ingredient
12 "Scooby-___, Where Are You!"
17 Name that's 47-Down minus a letter
18 German article
23 Wandering type
24 Singer Stefani
25 Deceives, in a way
27 Dance style with a Hall of Fame in Euclid, Ohio
28 Had a meal at home
29 Bag with handles
30 Sport with paddles
31 "___ ora!" (Maori greeting)
32 Real good
33 Fruit of the Loom competitor

**35** Engine sound
**36** "My word!"
**37** Sushi fish
**38** Watch part
**43** Like some cakes
**44** Pedi's partner
**46** IA time zone
**47** Contact online
**48** Salsa color
**49** Extra
**51** Kept at ___ length
**53** Behaves
**54** Weekend getaway spot

**55** ___ chi ch'uan
**56** Pre-holiday observance
**57** Folks
**58** Toilet paper unit

# 143
## HIDDEN INGREDIENT
By Zhouqin Burnikel

**ACROSS**

1 Gem associated with good luck in Chinese culture
5 Sahara animal
10 Jerry's partner
13 Unaccounted for, for short
14 Studio Ghibli specialty
15 Bring on board
16 Stay-at-home's spouse, perhaps
18 Toaster waffle brand
19 Glide down a snowy slope
20 Ikebana vessel
21 Like the LDS Church
23 Accompany
25 Spanish for "I love you"
26 Ask nosy questions
27 Vaccine pioneer Louis
29 Brand name that's pig Latin for a band name
32 "Chicago" star Richard
33 Small earring
35 Negative conjunction
36 Fit to be tied
37 She/___ pronouns
38 Destine for failure
40 Bumper ___
41 Cheeky
43 Places for genetic testing
45 Every last bit
46 Smiles widely
47 Insurance filings
50 Org. that makes a lot of cents
52 ___ splints (runner's woe)

53 "Gotcha!"
55 Common lunchtime
56 It's no longer full and not yet new
59 Plunge
60 "You got me"
61 Gait slower than a canter
62 Grand ___ Opry
63 Students might take them
64 Workbench gripper

**DOWN**

1 Face parts
2 Stopped sleeping
3 Burke hailed by the New Yorker as "basketball's best TV analyst"
4 Relative of the caribou
5 Yellow songbird
6 Apprehensive feeling
7 Silent performer
8 Music genre associated with 6-Down
9 "I wanna look!"
10 Windbags
11 Consequently
12 Ultra-bright
15 Big name in luxury bags
17 Off-white shade
22 Granola tidbit
24 Letters for some tax experts
25 Small desserts
27 Homophonous fruits
28 Has regrets about

**29** "In addition . . ."
**30** Miffed state
**31** Regrettable action
**32** Seizes
**34** Deadpan
**36** Exasperated exclamation
**39** ___ biology
**41** Interpreter's challenge
**42** Kentucky-born boxing legend
**44** "F9" director Justin
**45** Dresses with flares
**47** Baked potato bit
**48** New Zealand people

**49** Waves away
**50** Revert
**51** Garden center bagful
**52** Miffed state
**54** Part of a.m.
**57** "That was years ___"
**58** "The Challenge" network

# 144
## GLASS CEILINGS
By Kate Hawkins

### ACROSS

1 Item in a shed
5 Ziti or farfalle
10 Open ___ night
13 Money in Marseille
15 Fixer-___
16 Gorilla, for one
17 Garment worn by Fred in "Scooby-Doo"
18 "Tearin' Up My Heart" boy band
19 Fishing pole
20 "Buffy the Vampire Slayer" weapon
21 Couch
22 ___ your time
23 Global finance org.
25 Blow away
27 Hall of Famer, say
30 Oil grp.
33 Green New Deal legislator from the Bronx, for short
34 Nickelodeon title character who's friends with Skeeter
35 Touched down
36 Move sneakily
39 Chows down
40 Card game subtitled "The Gathering"
42 One of the Great Lakes
43 The ___ State (Hawaii)
45 Marvel god who faces Ragnarok
46 One more than 32-Down

47 Enthusiast
48 Active Italian volcano
49 19-Across attachment
50 State home to Heat and Rays
53 "Peace!"
55 Group for people 50 and up
56 Exam type
59 Pacific or Atlantic
63 Cause of some trips
64 Dance with a guaguanco style
65 Avoid
66 "Look here . . ."
67 How bedtime stories are read
68 Debate
69 Mess up
70 Word after "third" or "toga"
71 Out of juice

### DOWN

1 Drinks from pots
2 Remove from office
3 Black-and-white whale
4 "Sweet outfit!"
5 Many pub quiz team names
6 Lhasa ___
7 "Code Name Verity" genre
8 Coffee break time, perhaps
9 Rainbow shape
10 Only person to win the Nobel Prize in two different scientific fields
11 Apple music devices
12 Gives up
14 Place for a thorn

**22** Repetitive person
**24** Froth
**26** Faux ___
**27** Concept
**28** Undesired stocking stuffer
**29** Sign on a broken machine
**31** Protection for a knight
**32** Factor of this clue number
**37** It might be dotted
**38** Structure on a ship's bottom
**41** Grumpy sort
**44** Righteous Babe Records founder DiFranco

**50** Like some lashes
**51** Metaphor for intense focus
**52** Birthing companion
**54** "The greatest teacher, failure is" speaker
**57** Be adjacent
**58** "___ Marmalade" (No. 1 hit in 1974 and 2001)
**60** Boundary
**61** Spanish for "water"
**62** Require
**64** Genre for HAWA

USA TODAY

# 145
## BREAK TIME
By Patrick Jordan

**ACROSS**

1 Gold medalist's place
6 Easy win
10 Dances like Bill Robinson
14 French actress Haenel
15 Canceled
16 Plaintive reed instrument
17 Fresh start
19 The Christmas season
20 Fail to keep a secret
21 Not in good health
22 Gave an owl call
24 Feared creature in folklore
26 Colorado-to-California direction
27 Images seen in ads
32 French painter Claude
33 Not deceived by
34 Ungraceful sort
36 Verb that sounds like a type of poem
37 Has yet to be settled
39 "The Farewell" director Wang
40 ___-ray disc
41 Skirt type
42 Refrain from revealing
43 Young person
47 Listener's phrase
48 Garfield's slobbering housemate
49 Takes home from a shelter, say
52 Obeyed a growling stomach
53 Equipment for bassists

57 Contribute
58 Slumbering deeply
61 Perfectly balanced
62 Toddler's injury
63 Fancy cake
64 Places for illicit activity
65 Back area
66 Horse, old-style

**DOWN**

1 See 35-Down
2 Not active
3 Short video compilation
4 Skied through gates
5 "Listen up fives, a ___ is speaking"
6 ___ derby
7 Slightly stretched circle
8 Began an acquaintance
9 Warms up ahead of time
10 Japanese automaker
11 Share a border with
12 Word after "telephone" or "totem"
13 Bit of bird food
18 "Your majesty" alternative, perhaps
23 City home to Norway's royal family
25 UTC equivalent
26 Kite-flying need
27 Monks' hoods
28 Top

**USA TODAY**

29 ___ sections (ellipses, parabolas, and hyperbolas)
30 Letter carrier's assignment
31 Eagle's claw
32 Out-of-control crowd
35 With 1-Down, cool bit of trivia
37 Desires intensely
38 Part of a sword
39 Appreciate greatly
41 Atomizer's output
42 ___-fi
44 Matures
45 More popular

46 "What gives you that ___?"
49 Matured
50 Jump into a pool
51 Kitchen fixture
52 Largest of seven
54 ___ mortals
55 Plop's other name on "The Office"
56 Went too fast
59 Deeply impress
60 Beale and such (Abbr.)

USA TODAY

# 146
## M.R.I. SCAN
By Zhouqin Burnikel

**ACROSS**
1 ___ likely to succeed
5 Highly proficient
10 Feng shui life force
13 False name
15 Undercover spies
16 Aries symbol
17 Like sardines and tofu
19 Clairvoyant's claim, for short
20 Jetsam's partner
21 Extremely angry
23 Hotel room freebie
24 Popcorn coating
26 Place for oysters on the half shell
30 Waver
31 Cancel
32 Esprit de ___
33 Hockey rink surface
36 Movie star Farmiga
37 Rains really hard
38 Apt rhyme for "fit"
39 Street near Chestnut, perhaps
40 Adjective in a forecast
41 Green sauce
42 Raised to maturity
44 Glossy cotton fabric
45 Cook in a wok
47 Barbie's boyfriend
48 Miembro de la familia
49 Phrase of desperation
53 Bring to a halt
54 Southeast corner of a map

58 Number on someone's Wiki page
59 Royal decree
60 Birdbath buildup
61 Swanson who said "Give me all the bacon and eggs you have"
62 Lab workers, for short
63 Minnesota WNBA team

**DOWN**
1 Cheese's partner
2 St. ___, Minnesota (Rose Nylund's birthplace)
3 Window part
4 Al pastor serving
5 Capital where Arab Bank is based
6 College building
7 Valerie's son on "Days of Our Lives"
8 Muscle used for benching
9 Some are screen-printed
10 Another name for hair conditioner
11 It's said to make waste
12 Urge on
14 Make no changes
18 Live chat participant
22 "The Misadventures of Awkward Black Girl" author Issa
24 Have in stock
25 Jungfrau's range

🔴 **USA TODAY**

26 Stellar review
27 Brother of Cain
28 Like some bad apples
29 Lingerie item with a band size
30 Came across
32 ___ Island, Brooklyn
34 Quote as a source
35 British boarding school
37 Sound of a happy cat
38 Movie backdrop
40 Pretty sure thing
41 Chain with bread
43 Forget an appointment, e.g.
44 Appear
45 Asparagus piece
46 Dance to "La cumparsita"
47 Bad thing for a stomach to be in
49 Result of a bug bite
50 Gravlax herb
51 "New Amsterdam" psychiatrist
52 As compared to
55 Sappho's "___ to Aphrodite"
56 ___ Tacs
57 ___-Mex

# 147
## LEAD TIME
By Gail Grabowski

**ACROSS**

1 Variety show lineup
5 "Back in Black" band
9 Points on a fork
14 Folktales and such
15 "Movies (And Other Things)" author Serrano
16 Let your feelings show
17 Not just ajar
18 Swindles
19 Swindle
20 Flee
23 Calculate a total
24 "You should have just sat there and ___ your food" (Pollard)
25 Peevish mood
26 Field trip vehicle
27 Suffix for a scandal
28 Place to luxuriate
31 Canvas holder
34 Source of a footprint
35 Hunt for bargains
36 Be feverish
39 Like ___ of bricks
40 Pickle containers
41 OkCupid linkups
42 Female pig
43 Long sandwich
44 "If I Were a ___" (Beyonce hit)
45 International treaty
46 Play it by ___
47 Twosome
50 Texts to customers, e.g.
55 Via pen or stamp
56 Shrek's species
57 Damaging precipitation
58 Teatime snack
59 Zig or zag
60 Initial poker stake
61 Supply the food
62 "Electric Avenue" singer Grant
63 Victim of a gardener's hoe

**DOWN**

1 Word of great significance in Hawaiian culture
2 Dealt with adversity
3 34-Across pattern
4 Put in the mail
5 Fancy neckties
6 Taking out the trash, for one
7 Bit of progress, metaphorically
8 Some real estate transactions
9 Computer whiz
10 Paintballer's shout
11 Word sung at Christmas
12 Two-word phrase hidden in "double-talk"
13 Complete collections
21 Shortcoming
22 Cross the threshold
26 Red ___ paste
27 Hit the big leagues
28 Not even ajar
29 ___ over (read carefully)
30 Big primates

31 Geologic units of time
32 Computer-controlled mode
33 Chilly powder
34 "That was a wise decision"
35 Don't take off
37 DVD player button
38 Absolutely love
43 Computer whiz
44 Place to buy bear claws
45 Cylindrical pasta
46 Slipped up
47 "So You Want to Be a Wizard" author ___ Duane

48 Form an alliance
49 Stared rudely at
50 Hockey puck shape
51 Person in old Cuzco
52 "The language of the unheard," per MLK
53 Like some cheeses
54 Become less frozen

# 148
## BUTTONDOWNS
By Rachel Fabi

**ACROSS**

1 Jar tops
5 Profession
8 It returns a result from 0 to 14
14 Norse namesake of Wednesday
15 Prefix for "lateral"
16 More sizable
17 In addition
18 Enter into a record
19 "Bueller?"
20 Translate
22 Arctic explorer Louise Arner ___
24 Pigpen
25 Five-digit postal code
26 Capital aka "The Crossroads of America," for short
27 Equine pack animals
30 Like some sleep
35 Since
36 ___ XING
37 Alter to fit
38 Country where Wolof is spoken
40 "Moonlight" writer-director Barry
41 Yanks at
42 Clear away dishes
43 List-ending Latin abbreviation
44 Hot-tempered individuals
46 Nail file material
47 Dull pain
48 Comedian Wong

49 Decompose
52 Asthma trigger
53 Communicate with via eyelid
57 Not totally against
59 Tonight Alive genre
61 Dungeons & Dragons necessities
62 Remained
63 "Yikes!"
64 Stately shade trees
65 Guarantee
66 Gendered pronoun
67 "The limit ___ not exist"

**DOWN**

1 "That's a ___ off my mind"
2 "The devil finds work for ___ hands"
3 Frisbee, for one
4 Boring event
5 Minty cocktail
6 Makeup artist Priscilla
7 Friend of Snuffleupagus
8 Entries in a toddler's social calendar
9 Guy to see "if your broken heart needs repair," in a song
10 Attempt
11 They might clash
12 Status of an email that has left the outbox
13 Card higher than a deuce
21 Prefix for "assemble"
23 Gender-neutral pronoun

**USA TODAY**

**27** Nautical poles
**28** Deplete
**29** Vowel sound in "time"
**30** Lana ___ Rey
**31** Of a similar opinion
**32** Top-tier
**33** Sound-based detection method
**34** "r u for real?"
**36** Uncalm mindset
**39** "Speed it up!"
**40** French dip cupful
**42** "How Deep Is Your Love" band

**45** Letter after pi
**46** Love interest of Clare on "Degrassi"
**48** Came to
**49** TikTok character who said "Let me find out you like me dude"
**50** Chooses
**51** Oolong and rooibos, for two
**54** Unit of mass, for short
**55** Highest point
**56** "___ of the d'Urbervilles"
**58** Tisch School of the Arts college
**60** Neither great nor terrible

**USA TODAY**

# 149
## STATION BREAK
By Patrick Blindauer

**ACROSS**

1 Group resulting from a religious schism
5 Suffix meaning "somewhat"
8 Goliath's foe
13 Great Salt Lake state
14 Armstrong who took "one small step"
16 "Rolling in the Deep" singer
17 Arrive
18 Wise
19 Things to avoid doing
20 Be totally ignorant (OWN)
23 Shaming sound
24 Jeans edge
25 Opposite of WNW
26 First aid boxes
27 Teems
30 Thermometer type
32 Ad in an awareness campaign
33 Funny person
34 Make really happy
37 Chemist's garment (ABC)
39 Midriff-baring garment (BET)
41 Secretly monitor
42 List of dishes
43 "La-la" lead-in
44 Nothing to write home about
46 Make more entertaining
48 "Journey to the Center of the Earth" star Arlene
50 "Panini" singer Lil ___ X
52 Quarterback Manning
53 Altar response
54 Purse thief (GSN)
59 More recent
61 Even, scorewise
62 "Voila!"
63 Jessye Norman performance
64 Rescue
65 "The Great British Bake Off" appliance
66 Wander off
67 "I Guess ___ Rather Be in Colorado"
68 Monthly expense

**DOWN**

1 Use a straw
2 School that's part of Princeton, in a sense
3 ___ pants
4 "I Can See for Miles" band
5 Sleepless condition
6 Plane reservation
7 Like soprano, among voice types
8 Cousin of "darn"
9 "Much ___ About Nothing"
10 Drink that becomes a word meaning "air out" if you remove a T
11 Phrase from a runner-up
12 Office workstations
15 Floral neckwear
21 Impulse-transmitting cells
22 Prefix for "cortex"

**USA TODAY**

26 Leafy green
27 "Pronto!"
28 Party at which a pacifier might be given as a gift
29 Pointillism mark
31 Put back together
32 Counterpart of "thx"
35 Unable to decide
36 Office of Air and Radiation org.
38 Calm and controlled
39 Midmorning hour
40 Gas option
42 Savior
45 Stop ___ dime
47 Winner
48 Ancient reptiles, for short
49 Very skilled
51 Real estate workers (Abbr.)
54 Donkey sound
55 "Scream" star Campbell
56 Include
57 Paradise
58 ___ and rave
60 Part of an eon

# 150
## HOLY ONES
By Zhouqin Burnikel

**ACROSS**

1 Currency of Colombia
5 Office honcho
9 Schooner pole
13 Place to tie the knot
15 Activewear brand
16 Prefix meaning "all"
17 Home safety device
19 Like tamarind
20 Tank or tee
21 Pack to the brim
22 Come to light
24 Rolaids alternative
25 "Don't try ___ at home"
26 Bricklaying workers
29 Get ready for a cocktail party
32 Physique
33 Tea leaves reader
34 Sports team apparel, informally
36 Up the ___
37 First odd prime
38 "Bad Moms" actress Kunis
39 Upright support in a wall
40 Lung protectors
41 Nosy person
42 Pandora competitor
44 Air freshener choices
45 Like silken tofu
46 ___ Sinise Foundation
47 "I need a hand"
50 Distinctive atmosphere
51 "Don't Start Now" singer Lipa
54 Operatic solo

55 Purported pasture prank
58 ___ Field (home of the Mets)
59 "Terrible" stage for tots
60 Causing goose bumps
61 Sharp
62 Partner in battle
63 Companion animals

**DOWN**

1 Blast from the ___
2 Muppet with a "Tickle Me" doll
3 "Hold it!"
4 Tree in the genus Quercus
5 Bouncing toys
6 Shape of some bar soaps
7 Title for a knight
8 "Likewise!"
9 "grae" singer-songwriter
10 Telenovela theme
11 Close-fitting
12 Pit stop replacement
14 Give money back
18 Goals
23 Prefix for "fit" or "fire"
24 Museo del Greco location
25 Arboretum growths
26 Degrees for some CEOs
27 Mom's sisters
28 Straighten in a chair
29 Demolition ___
30 Labor group
31 Test episode
33 Work stretch
35 Maple extracts

**37** Combination of 37-Across
**41** ___ the bottom of the barrel
**43** Male turkey
**44** Wedding garment
**46** Full of courage
**47** Programmer's workaround
**48** Only Great Lake that borders Pennsylvania
**49** Lo-cal
**50** Missing
**51** Really serious
**52** Meter or yard, for example
**53** Seemingly forever
**56** Temple has a great horned one for a mascot
**57** Oomph

# 151
## BEAR LEFT
By Katja Brinck

**ACROSS**
1 Geographic collection
6 Frozen waffle brand
10 Waikiki's island
14 Poem with 17 morae
15 Algebra and such
16 Tourist ___
17 Best players on the squad
18 Cosmic object first photographed in 2019
20 Rotten
21 Land measure
23 ___ band
24 Stick around
25 Green gem
26 Air mass that affects winter weather
30 Beauty brand owned by Estee Lauder
31 "Who am ___ judge?"
32 Leaning Tower locale
36 Travel by ship
37 Car type
39 Related
40 Kill it
41 Playground game
42 "Things ___ looking good . . ."
43 Comforting bit of mail
46 Looks after Fluffy, say
50 Machu Picchu dweller of old
51 Traffic cone hue
52 Choir member
53 Alter ___

56 Blue cartoon character whose French name is Le Grand Schtrou
58 "What's ___?"
60 Instagrammer, e.g.
61 "It suits you to ___"
62 San Francisco athlete, for short
63 Job benefit
64 Fall farmer's market find
65 Mock

**DOWN**
1 "Moby-Dick" captain
2 "Cheerio!"
3 Told a falsehood
4 Letters before an alias
5 Island near Java
6 Early stage of life
7 Strong wind
8 Car-stealing video game series (Abbr.)
9 "You can't be serious!"
10 None of the above
11 Bakery emanation
12 Like all Iran Air meals
13 Flip on its head
19 Construction toy brand
22 Cleveland athlete, for short
24 Unfortunately
25 "At Last" singer James
26 "No thanks, I'm good"
27 Track shape
28 "Star Wars" princess

**USA TODAY**

**29** Range of hills
**32** Winter coat
**33** Retailer associated with a coat-wearing monkey
**34** Perform "Happy Birthday," say
**35** Payment in poker
**37** Page in a U.S. 1-Across
**38** Minnie Mouse headband features
**42** Bank holding
**43** Tobacco products, for short
**44** Swipe
**45** Powerlifting insect

**46** Ad in its own window
**47** Wipe away
**48** Get progressively narrower
**49** Sarcastic attitude
**52** Side times side, for a square
**53** "The Incredibles" fashion designer Mode
**54** Doesn't stick around
**55** Species in fairy tales
**57** Native of Colorado
**59** Diner dessert

# 152
## HAPPY BIRTHDAY
By Erik Agard

**ACROSS**
1 Rift
7 Flowers grow from them
11 Furious Styles, to Tre
14 Something a broad outline lacks
15 Singapore's region
16 Green prefix
17 "___ learned!"
18 Trail mix ingredients
19 Rhyming amount of fun
20 Like someone who embraces their inner child
23 Breathe hard
25 Capital of Norway
26 Shortened word after "PED" or "DEER"
27 High-to-low movement
29 "Another point to consider . . ."
30 Words from the brides
31 Tomato variety
33 Org. playing on ice
35 Enriched learning programs, e.g.
41 Poem type with a Pindaric form
42 Attention ___
43 Pencil number
44 Visa competitor, for short
47 Cut with a beam of light
49 With 23-Down, combo beauty treatment
50 Feng ___
53 Small bodies of water

54 Killmonger's foe
57 Translation of "je suis"
58 "The Little Mermaid" prince
59 Bad-tempered
63 Female sheep
64 Country where Quechua is spoken
65 Program for a future doc
66 Nothing
67 Try out
68 They're poured on pancakes

**DOWN**
1 Ego Nwodim's show, for short
2 Signal
3 "Rumor ___ it . . ."
4 Coordinated
5 Traveled on two wheels, perhaps
6 Server's handout
7 Forehead-covering style
8 Ordinary
9 "Same here"
10 Shoulder-to-hip band
11 Something a broad outline lacks
12 Oaks grow from them
13 "Stay!"
21 Blame-deflecting phrase
22 Glorify
23 See 49-Across
24 Starting from
27 Like
28 Lymph ___

**32** They might be blocked
**33** Org. that coined the term "student-athlete"
**34** "A Raisin in the Sun" playwright born 5/19/1930
**36** Very unhealthy
**37** Illuminated from below
**38** Modest response to a compliment
**39** Is indebted to
**40** Wordless greeting
**44** Drug for insomnia
**45** Neighbor of Tanzania

**46** Tooth material
**48** Person bringing in money
**50** Shopping ___
**51** Baby ___
**52** Not edited
**55** Maintained
**56** Quick jumps
**60** Bird that's a primate minus its first and last letters
**61** Workout unit
**62** Three-ft. units

# 153
## IN THAT CASE
By Zhouqin Burnikel

**ACROSS**
1 Optics nightmare
6 "Broad City" actress Jacobson
10 Tai ___
13 Make a speech
14 Prizes for early birds
16 Bathroom, to Brits
17 Bird with a long black neck
19 Cozy honeymoon destination
20 Civil War prez
21 Causes of overtime
22 Shed some tears
24 Bundle of hay
25 Museo de la Revolucion city
26 Not lowercase
29 L'Oreal, to Maybelline
30 ___ and desist
31 Empress or queen
32 Bit of softball equipment
35 Piercing places
36 Fathered
37 Punk rocker Laura ___ Grace
38 Goof up pretty good
39 Flower of the genus Viola
40 Cut and ___
41 Citrus fruit
43 Collapse
44 Periods of work
45 "Rugrats" voice actress Strong
46 Lucknow's country
47 Gets broadcast
48 Feeling down
51 "On the Floor" singer's
   nickname

52 Request to a 15-Down
55 Approves
56 Greet someone
57 Water brand that forms a
   word in reverse
58 "Later!"
59 Tops at merch tables
60 Shrill barks

**DOWN**
1 ___ Raton, Florida
2 Part of UAE
3 Hans Christian Andersen,
   for one
4 School fundraising org.
5 Bureaucratic holdup
6 "What a shame"
7 Jeers from hecklers
8 Frat dude
9 Fearful comment
10 Regular customers
11 Pilot automaker
12 Electrolyte particle
15 Restaurant employee
18 Is sick
23 "At Seventeen" singer Janis
24 Low singing voice
25 "The Autobiography of
   Malcolm X" collaborator Alex
26 Beverage with a spoon straw
27 Within easy reach
28 Snowperson's facial feature
29 Evening bag, e.g.
31 Wedding bands

33 ___-inflammatory diet
34 Adolescent
36 Christmas accessory
37 Island between Sumatra and Bali
39 Freaks out
40 Herb in chimichurri
42 "Get ___ of it!"
43 Complain
44 Soft and lustrous
45 Polynesian carvings
47 Reason for percussive therapy
48 Go yachting, perhaps

49 "On the double!"
50 Homes to hibernate in
51 Jopwell listing
53 Word after "good" or "evil"
54 Night before a holiday

# 154
## IT'S COLD OUTSIDE
By Evan Kalish

**ACROSS**

1 Column counterparts
5 Makeshift boat
9 Home to some Buddhists
14 Swedish furniture giant
15 Brainstorming success
16 Colorful rock
17 Storage place on a boat
19 Kidney-related
20 Celebrity chef Curry
21 ___ Cruces, New Mexico
23 Like most WNBA players
24 Networking assets
26 Annoyance
28 Military man in the game Clue
35 The "C" of TLC
36 "thank u, next" singer Grande
37 Pony up
38 Stashes out of sight
40 Finale
41 Annoyance
43 Angry feeling
44 Arctic landscape
47 Marsh plant
48 Realm of office politics
51 Young deer
52 Bowen Yang's show, for short
53 12 p.m.
55 Took a seat
58 "We're on the same page"
63 Winfrey who played Deborah Lacks
65 Common agricultural sight in Nebraska
67 ___ cum laude
68 Ladder step
69 8 on the Beaufort wind force scale
70 Susan Sontag piece
71 Time traveler's destinations
72 Bridge stat

**DOWN**

1 Costa ___
2 "Fine by me"
3 "Wish you ___ here!"
4 Droops
5 "Disturbia" singer
6 "Without further ___ . . ."
7 Collapsed
8 Self-satisfied exclamation
9 Black goop
10 "Ohh, that joke makes sense now!"
11 It might go from green to yellow to black
12 Abbreviated list ending
13 Inform
18 The Buckeye State
22 Like dreidels and roulette wheels
25 ___ Slam (alliterative tennis feat)
27 High-priority acronym
28 Capital on the Nile
29 Catalog pages meant to be filled out and returned
30 Model Precious

## Crossword Grid

A crossword grid with numbered cells: 1, 2, 3, 4, 5, 6, 7, 8, 9, 10, 11, 12, 13, 14, 15, 16, 17, 18, 19, 20, 21, 22, 23, 24, 25, 26, 27, 28, 29, 30, 31, 32, 33, 34, 35, 36, 37, 38, 39, 40, 41, 42, 43, 44, 45, 46, 47, 48, 49, 50, 51, 52, 53, 54, 55, 56, 57, 58, 59, 60, 61, 62, 63, 64, 65, 66, 67, 68, 69, 70, 71, 72.

**31** Brand of chocolate truffles
**32** Spanish for "mothers"
**33** Gave an enthusiastic review
**34** Like ombre hair
**35** Stylish
**39** Put in the overhead bin, say
**42** To do this is human, it's said
**45** Coffee vessels
**46** Storefront coverings
**49** Canal locale
**50** "Frozen II" snowman
**53** Keep your ___ clean
**54** Numbered musical work

**56** 43,560-square-foot unit
**57** Museum's virtual offering
**59** Jobs
**60** Harvest
**61** Jazz singer Fitzgerald
**62** Genesis setting
**64** Horse food
**66** Molecule hidden in "fingernails"

# 155
## EASY AS 1-2-3
By Brooke Husic

**ACROSS**

1 Grad
5 Cricket ground shape
9 Plummet
13 Maggie ___ Walker
14 Olympian Ledecky
16 Close by
17 Medieval storyteller
18 Fancy-schmancy
19 Prefix for "penultimate"
20 All over the place, perhaps
23 Device at a concert
24 Pop star Cyrus
25 Musical conclusion
26 Soccer great Hamm
27 NBC sketch show, for short
28 Glass's lip
31 ___ Double (special "Jeopardy!" clue)
33 Holds together
37 Printer purchases
38 "Don't just stand there!"
40 Whirl
42 Rectangular toaster pastry
43 Wave's highest point
45 "A long time ___ in a galaxy far, far away . . ."
46 Most-nominated female artist of the 2018 Grammys
49 Decay
50 Outer limit
54 Jots down
56 Connections
57 Unwelcome visitors
60 Place to do laps
62 Up through
63 Sunburn soother
64 Sass, colloquially
65 Director Gerwig
66 "You go, ___ Coco!"
67 Hiccup
68 Notable periods
69 Sunrise direction

**DOWN**

1 "19," "21," and "25," for Adele
2 Shift one's weight forward
3 Straighten out from a coil
4 Sierra ___ (literally, "mother mountain range")
5 Vegetable in kurkuri bhindi
6 Conceited
7 Room with cobwebs, maybe
8 "Cuz I Love You" singer
9 Double-helix molecule
10 Giving a new designation
11 Vegan hot chocolate option
12 Settles ahead of time
15 Follower of "eagle-" or "wild-"
21 Greek wraps
22 Robbie Rogers or Greg Berlanti, to Caleb and Mia
29 Breakfast chain
30 Office communication
32 "If I ___ Got You" (Alicia Keys single)
33 Pros' opposites
34 Congressional title (Abbr.)

**35** R&B singer ___ James
**36** Rug with a coarse texture
**38** Sugar-free drink
**39** Some golf clubs
**40** Playwriting contest submissions
**41** Bit of bio info
**44** Vietnamese Lunar New Year
**46** Name that's the Latin word for "star"
**47** Binary digits
**48** Agreement
**51** Pharmaceutical product

**52** Literary category
**53** Title role for Rowin Amone in a 2019 web series
**55** Oklahoma people
**58** Hummus accompaniment
**59** Mournful word
**61** Trip segment

# 156
## PIANO PARTS
By Stella Zawistowski

**ACROSS**
1 Likelihood
5 "Better safe than sorry" is one
10 Police broadcast, for short
13 Invisible emanation
14 Tear to shreds
15 Asset
17 Citrusy dessert
19 Not cautious
20 He got engaged to JLo in 2019
21 Served as an intro for
23 Soviet Union symbol
27 Singer Costello
28 Used to be
29 Caplets or capfuls
30 Where gloss goes
31 Use a napkin, perhaps
32 Explosive block in Minecraft
33 Parts of a range (Abbr.)
34 "___ is for horses!"
35 Sister magazine of Ebony
36 IRS form input
39 Something to sign with
40 Possessed
41 "Get outta here!"
42 Pig food
45 Pick up the check
46 Instrumental practice piece
47 As fast as possible
50 Strident-sounding
51 Song such as "Nessun dorma"
52 "___ Karenina"
53 Lower-body accessories
58 Camper's shelter

59 Is ungracious, in a way
60 Bad to the bone
61 Faline from "Bambi," for one
62 Got up
63 Saleswoman's presentation

**DOWN**
1 Source of acorns
2 "My Soul to Keep" author Tananarive
3 High and ___
4 Some Italian meats
5 Jouster's protection
6 Slowly faded
7 Snapchat or Super Mario Run
8 Some Hollywood associations
9 Fencing equipment
10 Fuzzy fruit
11 Ab-strengthening exercises
12 Dress puffer-outer
16 Pumps and platforms
18 Angers
22 "They ___ tell you?"
23 Wheel of a ship
24 Got to the ground
25 Admired team members
26 Snag
31 "Gossip Girl" guy
32 "Story of Your Life" author Chiang
34 Telephone greeting
35 University of Kansas nickname
36 Open-and-___

**37** Fountain liquid
**38** French for "Christmas"
**39** Appease
**40** Word after "high" or "top"
**41** Cooked like shumai
**42** Jack who could eat no fat, in a nursery rhyme
**43** No longer fed milk
**44** "Beats me!"
**45** One who puts on an act
**46** Ras Al Khaimah ruler
**48** Oklahoma city home to the Tower of Reconciliation

**49** Wipe clean
**54** Mop & ___ (floor cleaner brand)
**55** "Tambourine" rapper
**56** Canyon's edge
**57** ___-mo

# 157
## PLAY IT COOL
By Zhouqin Burnikel

**ACROSS**

1 Go for a stroll
5 Gemstone mostly mined in Australia
9 Something drawn in a tub
13 "Eugene" singer Parks
14 "___ a good one!"
15 Messing in "Searching"
16 Taunt for a timid person
18 Slugger's opportunity
19 ___ yum (Thai soup)
20 Jacuzzi nozzle
21 "Let's do this thing!"
23 Strolls in shallow water
25 Boat builder in Genesis
26 "Money talks," e.g.
29 Antsy
33 "Waterloo" band
36 "Broadchurch" protagonist
38 Plagiarizing an essay about integrity, for example
39 Look outwardly
40 Polite address
42 Nearly shut
43 Some glee club voices
45 41-Down quality
46 Post-it message
47 ___ vs. Zombies (video game series)
49 Mr. Spock's strong suit
51 Speaker's platform
53 Results of cheer practice, perhaps
56 Tax-sheltered nest egg
59 Big ___ (difficult request)
60 Hot beverage at a sukiyaki restaurant
62 Flying saucer's pilot
63 Senate authority
66 Fancy fundraisers
67 Heartfelt appeal
68 Visibility hindrance
69 Examined closely
70 Korean New ___
71 Small bills

**DOWN**

1 Float like a scent
2 Symbol on many road signs
3 Peruvian pack animal
4 Ornamental fish
5 "No you're not!" retort
6 Possible result of peace talks
7 "I Will Follow" director DuVernay
8 Permit access
9 Risk everything
10 "Disenchantment" star Jacobson
11 Disney World vehicle
12 Can't stand
15 Coca-Cola's answer to Aquafina
17 Spun records
22 Overly
24 Landmark aka Le'ahi
27 Snowman created by Elsa
28 Bronze, for one

**Crossword grid** (numbered cells): 1, 2, 3, 4, 5, 6, 7, 8, 9, 10, 11, 12, 13, 14, 15, 16, 17, 18, 19, 20, 21, 22, 23, 24, 25, 26, 27, 28, 29, 30, 31, 32, 33, 34, 35, 36, 37, 38, 39, 40, 41, 42, 43, 44, 45, 46, 47, 48, 49, 50, 51, 52, 53, 54, 55, 56, 57, 58, 59, 60, 61, 62, 63, 64, 65, 66, 67, 68, 69, 70, 71

**30** Where students wear gis
**31** Insect in a cloud
**32** Jane at Thornfield Hall
**33** "Make it quick!"
**34** Door ringer
**35** Phi ___ Kappa
**37** Clothes for concealment
**41** Prominent celebrity
**44** Spray 'n Wash targets
**48** Polite address
**50** Gross
**52** Overly sentimental
**54** ___ Allen (furniture chain)

**55** Take hold of
**56** Fly off the handle
**57** Skin care brand with a Total Effects line
**58** Floor piece
**59** Rectangle calculation
**61** Primatologist's subjects
**64** Frothy beverage
**65** You-know-___

# 158
## SMOOTH TALKING
By Gail Grabowski

**ACROSS**

1 Pace
6 Spreadsheet sections
10 Nimble
14 Emotionally distant
15 Device that's a garment backward
16 Supported by facts
17 Non-glossy paint option
19 Hot streak
20 Earth tone
21 Part of MVP
22 Glossy paint option
24 Bits of dialogue
25 "___ have to?"
26 Mvskoke people
29 One breaking and entering
33 Fling with force
34 Turnpike expense
36 Science fiction award
37 Vineyard measure
38 Bus driver's itinerary
39 Journey
40 Like a skyscraper
41 Industrious insects
42 Photographer's instruction
43 Computer security concern
45 Card game with possibles
46 Mike's partner in the candy aisle
47 Edgar ___ Poe
49 Not bring a plus-one
52 Keister
53 Stretcher carrier (Abbr.)

56 Part of a foot
57 More preferable yet
60 Paper quantity
61 Pay attention to
62 Game most people lose
63 Dog biscuit shape
64 Places for mud baths
65 Breadmaking ingredient

**DOWN**

1 President elected in 1908
2 Title role for Anne Hathaway in 2004
3 ___ and groan
4 Cactus holder
5 Like distant voices on a podcast, perhaps
6 Dentist's instruction
7 Doesn't mention
8 "What ___ I thinking?"
9 Add to the calendar
10 Half of a comedy duo, perhaps
11 Senior's year-end dance
12 "Do not open my dressing room door," e.g.
13 Shout
18 Charged atoms
23 Neither here ___ there
24 "Be honest . . ."
26 Makes small talk
27 Sportscast wrap-up
28 With time to spare

**29** Sandwiches that might be made with tempeh
**30** Like some tabloid headlines
**31** Nimble
**32** Gear for Double Dutch
**34** It can be hard to discern over email
**35** Sleeping soundly
**38** Red diamonds, e.g.
**42** In an economical way
**44** Letters between alternate names
**45** Big chunk

**47** Place for a bout
**48** Provides temporarily
**49** Apparel
**50** Topping on some dessert pizzas
**51** Inspect quickly
**53** James or Jones in jazz history
**54** Big Apple baseball team
**55** Leisurely run
**58** Bigwig
**59** Part of a foot

# 159
## THE IN CROWD
By Zhouqin Burnikel

**ACROSS**

1 Intrepid
5 Butcher shop scraps
10 Largemouth fish
14 Wrapped up
15 Skirt with a flare
16 Not doing much
17 Actress who played Snow White on "Once Upon a Time"
20 Supply with financing
21 Unagi Pie ingredient
22 Copier paper purchases
23 "That's right"
24 One-ups
27 Pastrami sandwich bread
28 Cozy lodging place
29 Rae, the deer in an Olive Brinker webcomic, e.g.
31 Swiss tennis great with five Grand Slam singles titles
38 Biggest city in Qatar
39 Go separate ways
40 Not fooled by
42 Pollo ___ plancha
43 Chips with a Cool Ranch flavor
45 Firecracker that doesn't go off
46 Diminish
48 Payment from the IRS
50 Sound of the surf
51 Mushroom top
54 Germinated grain
55 "Why Not Me?" author
58 "___ They See Us"
60 Chilling in a cooler
61 Cheese in tirokafteri
64 Meghan Markle, to Princess Charlotte
65 Credits as a source
66 Apple debuted in August 1998
67 Obtains
68 Battle reminders
69 Surrender

**DOWN**

1 Four on a par-three hole
2 Like ewes
3 Gives temporarily
4 First Bond movie
5 Bumbling sort
6 Group of ships
7 ___ up (really excited)
8 ___-Saxon
9 Lion of the zodiac
10 ___ your time (wait)
11 Series of competing commercials
12 Like natto
13 Taste or touch, e.g.
18 Defiant refusal
19 "Citizen Kane" star Welles
25 In ___ (all together)
26 Masthead figure
28 Savings plan with a rollover variety
30 Blowhard's display
31 Wisdom tooth, for one
32 Instant of insight

33 "Planet Money" network
34 ___ Baba
35 Huge success
36 "If you would be so kind . . ."
37 Daredevil's feat
38 Howard or Harold, to Clyde McBride
41 Peculiar
43 "Big Little Lies" actress Laura
44 Weigh station vehicle
47 Art class supplies
49 Stories that might involve shipping, for short

51 Person with a jaded outlook
52 Japanese spitz breed
53 Indiana baller
56 Physicians, for short
57 Not as expensive
58 Movement of a dog's tail
59 Palette selection
62 Little bit
63 Expert

# 160

## LOCATION, LOCATION, LOCATION

By Caitlin Reid

### ACROSS

1 Word after "candy" or "snack"
4 Made a decision
9 Little tiff
13 Big fuss
14 Wedding application
15 Salad green
16 Jump done in ice skates
17 Place to swap vows
18 Its southeast contains Laos
19 Symbol on a list
22 Road goo
23 Sandra Bullock movie set on a bus
24 Makes happy
26 Adrenaline ___
29 Dashboard letters
30 Point-of-view column
33 Important part of the table
36 Visit for a meal
40 Parting words
43 Bright road signal
44 List of options
45 Up to the ___
46 Nonkosher sandwich
48 Elapse
50 "Kudos!"
54 In a fitting way
58 "I'm Not the Only One" singer Smith
59 Geometric measurement
62 Drain insert
64 Mathematical proportion
65 Name that's another name backward
66 Additionally
67 Occurrence
68 Ran quickly
69 ___ in the middle
70 Some hail damage
71 Espionage agent

### DOWN

1 Pack into a takeout container, perhaps
2 "Someone Like You" singer
3 Rough-and-tumble skating sport
4 Informal convo
5 "SOS!"
6 Ahead of the pack
7 Slimy garden creature
8 Breadwinner, e.g.
9 Music genre of Jamaican origin
10 Gochujang, for one
11 Fake name
12 Salty sign of sadness
13 Manila folder protrusions
20 School URL ending
21 Recorded for later
25 Know-it-all
27 "Nevertheless, ___ persisted"
28 Take the ___ (assume control)
30 Switch position
31 Buddy
32 Chunk of history

**34** The "A" of IPA
**35** "Wow!"
**37** Brewed cupful
**38** Total buffoon
**39** Disapproving sound
**41** Skin marks
**42** Simon & Garfunkel, for one
**47** Visited college campuses, say
**49** Significant other
**50** Pixar robot
**51** Entertain
**52** Very serious
**53** Time after time

**55** Girl Scouts unit
**56** Wary
**57** Where Sylvia Ardyn Boone was tenured
**58** Meat popular in Hawaii
**60** "If it ___ broke . . ."
**61** Rudimentary beds
**63** "I ___ Rhythm"

# 161
## HEAD OF THE RIVER
By Brooke Husic

**ACROSS**

1 Win's opposite
5 Chimney residue
9 Drag accessory
12 Name for a pet octopus
13 Receded like the tide
15 Place for sledding
16 Leave
17 Quick-moving
18 Norway's capital
19 Produce as a result
21 Distinctively colored vehicle
23 Calls before a court
25 ___ grrrl (feminist punk movement)
26 Steamed bun
27 Sidney's love interest in "Brown Sugar"
29 Basketball hoop attachment
31 Hardworking
36 ___ Tome and Principe
37 Pairs
38 Dollars and ___
39 Unhappy cat noise
40 Architect Maya
41 Parts of some costume jewelry
43 Superlative suffix
44 Singer-songwriter Janis
45 Consume
46 Gorillas, e.g.
48 Barista's talent
53 Lowest roll of two dice
56 Fish tank gunk
57 Accutane target
58 "L'shanah ___" (Rosh Hashanah greeting)
60 Brownie recipe verb
61 Hawaiian garlands
62 Concert venue
63 Word repeated in Hozier's "Take Me to Church"
64 "Exit full screen" key
65 Significant periods
66 They may look like greens to people with deuteranomaly

**DOWN**

1 Country on the Mediterranean
2 Currently broadcasting
3 Winter Olympics athlete
4 Handout with course information
5 Large amount
6 Reproductive health specialist
7 Off-Broadway awards
8 Show's counterpart
9 Madison's state
10 Self-conscious, maybe
11 Dollop
14 Dover's st.
15 "___ Met Your Mother"
20 "Buenos ___"
22 Mine materials
24 "Yup, understood!"
27 Be effusive with affection
28 Color akin to auburn
30 Throw out

**31** Inactive
**32** Headaches
**33** Calming advice from "The Hitchhiker's Guide to the Galaxy"
**34** Strap for guiding a horse
**35** Place to book a room
**39** Alternative to raiding the mini-fridge
**41** What unleavened dough doesn't do
**42** "See ya!"
**47** ___ out a living (gets by)

**48** One of the six simple machines
**49** Yoga pose
**50** Competitor's best effort
**51** Scratched
**52** Chilly temps
**53** Market transaction
**54** Bit of info that may follow "omw"
**55** Olden times, quaintly
**59** Owns

# 162
## FORWARD PASSES
By Patrick Jordan

### ACROSS

1 Beneficial possession
6 Remark of realization
10 Not going beyond
14 Biological copy
15 Gem with a "fire" variety
16 Gas in glowing signs
17 Toiling
19 Rider's payment
20 Pentathlon weapon
21 Apple Jacks grain
22 Green Monopoly pieces
24 "Can I get an ___?"
26 "Spring forward, fall back" amount
27 "Big bucks! No Whammies!" show
32 Symbol above 6 on a keyboard
34 Possesses
35 Neither rhyme ___ reason
36 Etcher's liquid
37 Prodded
39 Assistant that's a part of the eye backward
40 Was in command of
41 "For heaven's ___!"
42 ___ out (gives in portions)
43 Economic area with tax exemptions
47 Obligatory assignment
48 Provide with sustenance
49 Smooth and shiny
52 Son of Beyonce
53 Espresso serving
57 Not just every now and then
58 Place where legends are honored
61 Actor Wilder
62 ___ vera
63 End credits list them
64 Canceled
65 Asparagus tidbits
66 Fabric-smoothing appliances

### DOWN

1 Overexertion result
2 Noise from a high-five
3 Word before "subject" or "loser"
4 Made admirable
5 Iroh's favorite drink
6 Des Moines dwellers
7 Help with bench presses
8 Elephant's flapper
9 Norwegian dog breed
10 Open from a rolled-up position
11 Veggies paired with carrots
12 Caused a rip in
13 Low digits
18 Low digits
23 Shared by you and me
25 Got introduced to
26 Surname that sounds like a question
27 Word before "flag" or "parade"

**USA TODAY**

28 Swole
29 Merge
30 Center of the Earth
31 "KUWTK" star Jenner
32 Newborn on a dairy farm
33 Taiwanese computer company
37 New Year's Eve accessory
38 "No objection from me"
39 Summons
41 Amaze
42 Partner of Larry and Curly
44 Prepped for publication

45 Submits tax forms online
46 Lowest score, often
49 Long tale
50 Ice dancer Shibutani
51 Voice quality
52 Pig's dinner
54 Heavenly circle of light
55 Sign of impending doom, say
56 "Crossword Mysteries" protagonist
59 Undefeated boxer Laila
60 "Casual" day (Abbr.)

# 163
## SIDE TRIP
By Zhouqin Burnikel

**ACROSS**

1 Design detail, for short
5 Courses of action
10 Blackjack assets
14 Portuguese currency
15 Transit station
16 Director Ethan or Joel
17 Bed with bars
18 Contamination result
20 Tire pattern
22 Crunchy ingredients in pad thai
23 In need of a GPS
26 Thumbs-up votes
27 "Mississippi Girl" singer
31 Totally out there
35 Dog's sound
36 Bavarian automaker
37 ___ panels
38 Twins or Vikings
40 Range below alto
43 Dog name that means "faithful"
44 Bug to no end
46 Runs out of juice
48 Feel out of sorts
49 Majnun's love
50 Undeserving object of worship
52 First part of a musical
54 Deer with antlers
55 Throw back some Malort, say
58 Grant entry to
62 "Let me start by saying . . ."
65 Domesticate
66 Slush Puppie alternative
67 City on the Arkansas River
68 Supplements to Social Security
69 Loch ___ monster
70 Coasters on snowy hills
71 Diplomat's asset

**DOWN**

1 Religious faction
2 Smooth engine sound
3 Great Lake fed by the Maumee River
4 Bright blue color
5 Document file type
6 Late-July sign
7 Each, colloquially
8 "I won't accept those terms!"
9 Shelter adoptee, perhaps
10 Charge with
11 Layer of nail polish
12 Long swimmers
13 Show produced in NBC's Studio 8H
19 TV show with celebrity gossip
21 Where Qatar Airways is headquartered
24 Closed tight
25 Beachcomber's concern
27 Like some flaws
28 38-Across building
29 ". . . though there may be none"

**USA TODAY**

**30** Supermodel Evangelista
**32** Epic poem in Homeric Greek
**33** Talk show medium
**34** Dryly humorous
**39** Gingerbread ingredient
**41** Bottlefuls for a massage therapist
**42** Take a break
**45** Party boat, often
**47** Mammal that might clap
**50** Like some bad sleep
**51** "No need to explain further"
**53** ___ and the Maytals

**55** Board game rollers
**56** Metals can be extracted from them
**57** Event with slashed prices
**59** Winemaker Gomez
**60** Apple desktop
**61** Hatchling's spot
**62** Dorsal ___
**63** Psychedelic drug
**64** ___ Vegas Strip

# 164

6/1

By Rachel Fabi

## ACROSS

1 ___ and crafts
5 Slow-moving mammal
10 Strike with an open palm
14 "The Last Jedi" general
15 Soooo many
16 Alliance headquartered in Brussels
17 Green feeling
18 Brand of mineral water
19 Winged god of love
20 Hairpieces
22 "There are more things in heaven and earth, Horatio, than are ___ of in your philosophy"
24 Bites playfully
25 Zip through the air
26 Lacking good taste
28 Like many spiral-patterned shirts
31 Move stealthily
32 Ida B. who edited the Memphis Free Speech and Headlight
33 "What's up, ___?"
35 Albany-to-Buffalo canal
36 Selfish desire
37 Dice dots
38 Golf ball holder
39 Criticizes
40 Side of an issue or a diamond
41 Places where Cardinals and Orioles perch
43 Ballerina Copeland

44 "Loving" actress Negga
45 Swear
46 Supernatural
49 Shy
52 Pull an all-nighter, maybe
53 Bad smells
55 For a triangle, it's .5 x base x height
57 Instrument that might have 47 strings
58 Gently prod
59 Hero
60 Listen to
61 Fluctuates
62 ___ for life

## DOWN

1 Bitter brew
2 Musical loosely based on "La Bohème"
3 DVR brand
4 Admit defeat
5 Nodding off
6 Adores
7 "Respect" songwriter Redding
8 Org. with a 3.4-ounce liquid limit
9 Portable, perhaps
10 Suffering from hay fever, say
11 "GMA" anchor Spencer
12 Molecule component
13 Put on the internet
21 Coming down the ___
23 Unburdens

**25** Cunning ways
**26** Worn out
**27** "Au revoir!"
**28** Swarms
**29** Official command
**30** Silly
**31** Gelled
**32** "The Grapes of ___"
**34** Clarksdale, MS time zone
**36** Overindulgence
**37** Two-option grading system
**39** 49-Down partner
**40** Salmon, for one

**42** Foul-tempered
**43** Tousles
**45** Word before "plane" or "shorts"
**46** Cinco + tres
**47** Hermit or fiddler
**48** "I couldn't ___ less"
**49** Physical form
**50** Language of Pakistan
**51** They're between Cancers and Virgos
**54** Pair of people
**56** Prefix for some musical genres

**USA TODAY**

# 165
## IT'S TEE TIME
By Gail Grabowski

**ACROSS**

1 Performed a role
6 Show flexibility
10 Bit of sports trivia
14 Well-prepared
15 Region
16 Bit of folklore
17 Poisonous substance
18 Sandpaper coating
19 Wheel connector
20 Vote held by one of 50
23 Praiseful poem
25 Jello shaper
26 Removes from power
27 Justification
29 "There's more where that ___ from"
31 "If all ___ fails . . ."
32 Port-au-Prince's nation
34 ___ toe boot
37 Long pastry
41 Family
42 Alison who wrote "Dining In" and "Nothing Fancy"
43 Not doing anything
44 Small bits of paint
45 Family member
47 Thing of value
50 Elaborate ruse
52 App interruptions
53 Thing of no value
57 Commuter's expense
58 Very uncommon
59 Don't disturb

62 Luau instruments, for short
63 Direct-selling cosmetics company
64 Pick up the tab
65 Period of sacrifice prior to Easter
66 Mouth off to
67 Out of ___ (somewhat unwell)

**DOWN**

1 Gallery stuff
2 Business VIP
3 Yearly form-filing period
4 Make revisions to
5 Anagram of "Monday"
6 Breakfast sandwich base
7 Made mistakes
8 Playwright Simon
9 Palm fruit
10 Liberty Island attraction
11 Metered vehicles
12 Divvy up
13 Many characters in "Chilling Adventures of Sabrina"
21 Huge amount
22 Janelle James, for one
23 Dyson alternative
24 Uttar Pradesh neighbor
28 Fraction of a min.
29 One hundred, in Spanish
30 Munched on
32 Smokehouse offerings
33 Take it one day ___ time

34 "Adventures in Wonderland" character
35 Lubricated, perhaps
36 Rowing teams
38 Speak formally
39 High-arcing tennis shot
40 Word before "service" or "reading"
44 Really dislike
45 "Nope"
46 Puts on a pedestal
47 Really bad
48 Tremble

49 Sound in a chase scene, perhaps
50 The ___ journey
51 Unseals
54 Historical periods
55 Volcanic outflow
56 Emperor associated with the expression "fiddling while Rome burns"
60 Flying mammal
61 Non-earthlings (Abbr.)

# 166
## ENTAILED
By Zhouqin Burnikel

**ACROSS**

1 In a state of shock
6 Desktop computer from Apple
10 Hold tight
14 Reason for a romaine recall
15 Tennis star Gauff
16 Synonym of "tear down" that sounds like a synonym of "build up"
17 Smashed for access
19 Swellheads have big ones
20 President pro ___
21 Coop residents
22 Swimsuit brand
24 Boaters, berets, etc.
25 Credit union transaction
26 ___ off (lessens gradually)
29 Pope's jurisdiction
32 "This hand is too terrible to play"
33 Construction area
34 Thunder sound
36 YouTube star Mills
37 Final golf shots, usually
38 At any ___
39 Drizzle, say
40 A chauffeur might drive one
41 "Understand?"
42 Try to win
44 Gets presentable
45 Golden-years plans
46 Wu-Tang ___
47 Houston baseball team

50 An adjective modifies one
51 Significant stretch of time
54 Really 39-Across
55 All square
58 Bit of greenhouse glass
59 Word before "end" or "ringer"
60 Calendar addition
61 Reach across
62 Fiona or Shrek
63 Pub pastime

**DOWN**

1 Something owed
2 Pumpkin patch measure
3 Lens for closeups
4 Utah's state animal
5 Steadfast person
6 Images often double-clicked
7 Spill-cleaning tools
8 Get 100% on
9 Panels with controls
10 Background for an on-camera meteorologist
11 Extreme anger
12 Polo shirt brand
13 Cozumel coin
18 Anti-mosquito measures
23 Salary
24 "The Queen" Oscar winner
25 Game of numbers
26 Seating level
27 Supplemental insurance brand

**28** Sabin developed a vaccine for it

**29** Words before the title line in ". . . Baby One More Time"

**30** Fill with joy

**31** Dine at home

**33** Business outfits

**35** Kennel visitors

**37** "Be my guest!"

**41** Take for ___ (assume)

**43** Debate side

**44** "Besides . . ."

**46** ___ Nast

**47** Some daters use them

**48** Bubble makeup

**49** Sashimi fish

**50** In the vicinity of

**51** At any point

**52** Apartment payment

**53** Pangolins eat them

**56** Meatless, for short

**57** Longoria who executive produced the documentary "Food Chains"

# 167
## I FOUND A C.D.!
By Evan Kalish

**ACROSS**

1 Sings jazzily
6 Each
10 People who agree are on the same one
14 Ann ___, Michigan
15 First word in a letter, often
16 Way out
17 Court-appointed lawyers
20 One of two rolled in a craps game
21 Types
22 "___ enough . . ."
23 Enthusiastic reviews
25 City home to Ted Drewes, for short
26 Early maker of video games
28 Most undiluted
31 Car trip with great views
34 Portion of land
36 Not face the issue
37 "Queer ___" (Netflix reboot)
38 Ambience
39 Topping for some lattes
40 Alternative to a name-brand pharmaceutical
44 Evaluate
46 The ADA requires them to be at least 36 inches wide
47 And so forth, for short
48 Savory taste sensation
50 Marsh-dwelling white bird
53 Bad mood
54 Competed in a 5K

57 ROYGBIV for rainbow colors and HOMES for Great Lakes, e.g.
61 Lion's locks
62 Fitzgerald, the Queen of Jazz
63 Type of belly button
64 Astonished
65 Troubles
66 Author's representative

**DOWN**

1 Liquid from a maple tree
2 Filthy substance
3 Ilana's "Broad City" co-star
4 Permissive
5 ___ Lanka
6 Confuse
7 Takes an early look
8 Clumsy sorts
9 Post's opposite
10 Try to sell
11 Eliminated
12 See 58-Down
13 Website for artisans
18 Word before "duty" or "center"
19 ___ Dame
24 Name that's another name backward
25 Alternative to a minivan
26 Honda's luxury brand
27 Campground collapsibles
28 Waterside attraction in Santa Monica

29 Loudly enjoy soup
30 Bagel's shape
31 Microdermabrasion offerer
32 Lions' lairs
33 Toast choice
35 "You're it!" game
38 Thinking highly of
40 Bother
41 Top-left key
42 Acutely angry
43 Video capturer, for short
45 Came across as
48 "OK! You win!"

49 King with a golden touch
50 Jane Austen heroine
51 Chew like a beaver
52 Actress Russo
53 Structure for storing grain
55 ___-prone skin
56 Nyet, in German
58 With 12-Down, Zooey
   Deschanel sitcom
59 By way of
60 Part of a tennis match

# 168
## BREAKFAST
By Brooke Husic

### ACROSS
1 Word after "wrist" or "slap" in hockey
5 Clothesline fastener
8 Two make eight
13 Title for a checklist
14 Poet Armantrout
15 Olympic champion Yamaguchi
16 ___ and Ani (jewelry brand)
17 Player near the boundary in cricket
19 Herb common in Thai food
21 Places to mow
22 Like the University of Notre Dame
25 Big tub
28 Uses a turntable, maybe
31 Wrapped garment
32 Successors
34 Instagram's most-followed cosmetics brand in 2019
35 Put in effort
36 Cap holder
38 Shortening product
40 Rambled, perhaps
41 Absolutely stun
44 Currency of Iran
45 Off-roading vehicle, for short
46 They might be braided for a flower crown
49 Passed-down symbol
52 Chana ___
53 Fe, on the periodic table

54 Have ___ of problems (be issue-ridden)
55 Bread eaten with baba ghanoush
56 Religious title, for short
57 Nursing ___
58 Restaurant offering
60 Title role for Denzel Washington
61 Picnic invader
62 Goal for an assistant professor
63 Henna, e.g.
64 PreCheck org.
65 Talked back to

### DOWN
1 Attempt
2 Greeting preceding "Que tal"
3 Dedicated poems
4 Like cyanide
5 Con's opposite
6 ___ de parfum
7 Go closer to the ground
8 Fried brunch order
9 Aromatherapy substances
10 Currency of America (Abbr.)
11 Suggestion from a transit app (Abbr.)
12 Knight's title
15 Fuzzy fruit
18 Time to reap what's been sown
20 Bar announcement
23 Palpitate
24 Dried grass

**25** Using
**26** Character journey
**27** Chiding syllable
**28** Run-___, first hip-hop group with a gold record
**29** Jam container
**30** Film that might feature UFOs
**33** Young's partner in accounting
**37** "Brokeback Mountain" director Lee
**39** "An ally has been ___" (bad news in League of Legends)
**40** Prefix for "active" or "grade"

**42** Dominican dance
**43** Mind-numbing
**44** Not very often
**47** Grow up
**48** Scheduled
**49** Baked in a kiln
**50** Knitting supplies
**51** Palindromic math class
**55** Calligraphy utensils
**57** Halloween animal
**59** Mauna ___

# 169
## LET'S GET TOGETHER
By Mark McClain

### ACROSS

1 "___ So Shy" (Pointer Sisters hit)
4 Nickname for the artist Josh Agle (it's hidden in his name)
8 Shoe part
13 Mountaineer's destination, perhaps
14 Important vegetable in Hawaiian cuisine
15 "Hafa adai" translation
16 Relatively simple
17 Like some board exams
18 Leg joint
19 Roastery offering
22 Remark after a long wait
23 Coordinate
24 Not close by
27 Urgent request
29 Explain, in a way
31 Cry loudly
34 ___ Lauder
37 Pancake batter ingredients
38 Website for some religious daters
42 Cracked a bit
43 Check in a changing room
44 To date
45 Artwork made from small pieces
48 From the beginning
50 The "S" in GPS (Abbr.)
51 "Still I Rise" poet Angelou
54 Country singer Yearwood
58 Different version of a song
60 Huge horned animal
63 Self-satisfied
64 Zero
65 Dad's sisters
66 One-syllable Alaskan city
67 Tests that measure beats
68 Fundamental principle
69 Spheres
70 Sandwich option

### DOWN

1 Artichoke's center
2 Meeting room stand
3 Star chart
4 Maximally resolute
5 Cause damage
6 "___ Got Talent" (show won by Mayyas in 2019)
7 Quaint expression of surprise
8 Opportunity
9 Loan out
10 Large deer
11 Every single one
12 Shoe part
13 Salt-N-___
20 Silent-letter landmasses
21 Terminate
24 "Oh, bring us some ___ pudding . . ."
25 Figure that might be obtuse
26 Go back to zero
28 "While we're ___ . . ."
30 Wet lowland

**Down**

31 Spam emails, often
32 Mock expression of delight
33 Metal in a tuba
35 Something to "play it by"
36 Vocalist from Gaoth Dobhair
39 Stage actor Aldridge
40 Training sequences in sports movies, often
41 Motionless
46 "This really confuses me!"
47 Calico, e.g.
49 Hot dog

52 Dichotomous descriptor for some questions
53 Protective gear
55 Great ___ Mountains
56 Bit of hardware for a cabinet
57 Firefighters' tools
58 Prefix meaning "before"
59 Unfeeling
60 Remy from "Ratatouille," for one
61 Color
62 Lodging option

# 170
## THE DEVIL IS IN DE TAILS
By Zhouqin Burnikel

**ACROSS**

1 Rod for cooking
5 Disc golf standard
8 Parent company of Russell Stover
13 Fine-tune
14 Diva's showcase
15 Unamused Face, e.g.
16 Ancient
18 Pasted
19 Screenwriter in "Why Women Kill"
20 "___ Bayou" (directorial debut for Kasi Lemmons)
21 Forecast adjective
22 Residents of Riyadh
24 "Ah, makes sense"
26 Major Maryland newspaper
31 Created using a loom
34 Slender
35 Enjoyed natto
36 Done with
37 Sound accompanying a toast
39 Velociraptor's weapon
40 Scuff up, say
41 Like most Azerbaijani Muslims
42 People with dark aesthetics
43 Bruise colors
47 Add to the payroll
48 ___ in (curbed)
51 ___ Duck (insurance spokesfowl)
54 Cribbage pieces
55 ___ off (cut away)

57 Luxury hotel amenity
58 What Tinker Bell sprinkles
60 Spot seller, for short
61 Pound or ton
62 Mental spark
63 Clementine discards
64 Darling
65 Chaotic situation

**DOWN**

1 Clog or pump
2 Public opinion barometers
3 Site of the Dalai Lama's exile
4 Drink with cha siu bao
5 Catholic cleric
6 Put on ___ (act hoity-toity)
7 Chinese zodiac animal before ox
8 Preparatory effort
9 Words before quoting oneself
10 Proper ___
11 Spun records at a party
12 In apple-pie order
14 Motrin alternative
17 Family car type
23 Extremely
24 Country with a sultan
25 Sound of road rage
27 Epic about the siege of Troy
28 Miso paste ingredient
29 Only state with a three-word capital
30 Info about current events
31 Uterus

**USA TODAY**

**32** Toy train track shape
**33** Wedding gown designer Wang
**37** Blacken on the grill
**38** Ticket booth hassle
**39** "Fargo" director Joel
**41** Winter Olympics hats
**42** False appearance
**44** Model Iman
**45** Portmanteau describing the U.K.'s withdrawal from the E.U.
**46** Genuine
**49** Shake off

**50** Amounts of antibiotics
**51** "Make it snappy!"
**52** Disappear gradually
**53** Entice
**54** Household cleaner scent
**56** Orgs. that hold school fundraisers
**58** Little pooch
**59** Poorly lit

# 171
## THE SIGNS ARE THERE
By Erik Agard

**ACROSS**

1 Get groceries, say
5 OB/___
8 Like this clue
13 Prefix for "legal"
14 "Yoo-___!"
15 Vietnamese garment
16 End weakly
18 Soothing substance
19 Black-and-white cookie
20 Territory
21 Orchard growths
22 Toothpaste type
23 Part of mpg, for short
24 Poetic homages
26 Instruction from a dentist
28 Keep from decomposing
32 Award for an actor
34 Church letters
35 Mutual ___
36 Pattern-discovering technique
41 Decompose
42 "What did I tell you?"
43 Move in a leisurely way
44 Tries
47 See 48-Across
48 With 47-Across, genuine
49 Lair
50 Degree for a dentist
53 One-person performances
56 Bit of innovation
58 Word before "pick" or "puff"
59 Spanish goodbye
60 School rooms
62 Philosopher Alain
63 Flightless bird
64 Clutter
65 Lock of hair
66 Reason to "spring forward" (Abbr.)
67 Gentle touches

**DOWN**

1 Tapering structure
2 Legendary pianist and TV host
3 Rice-shaped pasta
4 Amigo
5 Evil being
6 Part of BYO
7 "I'll pass"
8 Preferences
9 Raspy-voiced
10 Unbusy
11 Really positive review
12 Runs out of battery
16 Obstacle to visibility
17 Coup d'___
23 "___ Town" (Casey Nowak graphic novel)
25 Judge
27 Panther's foot
28 Newspaper parts
29 Symbol of solidarity
30 Place for leaves
31 Boundary-pushing
32 The ___ Project (food security initiative)

**USA TODAY**

**33** Unpleasant person
**37** Source of sports news
**38** In-depth
**39** "Let's do it!"
**40** Silent greeting
**45** Offerings from 60-Across
**46** Rock growths
**47** Terror
**49** First appearance
**51** ___ rehearsal
**52** "Help!"
**53** Shaker contents
**54** Smell

**55** Adult nits
**57** Gets less bright
**58** Neck of the woods
**61** Piece of equipment for a band

# 172
## BRAVING THE ELEMENTS
By Martha Kimes

**ACROSS**

1 ___ of faith
5 Spanish for "house"
9 Layered hairstyle
13 Part of a truck's underside
14 Word said with a sigh
15 Best of the best
16 Brazilian soccer legend
17 Scatters seeds
18 Threw a fit
19 Win-at-any-cost
22 Part of a process
23 Address in a social media bio, often
24 Relatives, colloquially
27 Disastrous situation
32 "Survivor" channel
35 Make a scene, in a way
36 Roof overhangs
37 '60s nonconformists
40 Some listicles
42 State known for spuds
43 ". . . two if by ___"
44 Articulate
45 Beverage from a tropical fruit
50 "___ if by land . . ."
51 "The Simpsons" bartender
52 Marries
55 Keyboard cleaner
61 Pulitzer Prize category
63 Play to ___ (draw)
64 Sicilian volcano
65 Like some needs
66 Clue
67 Part of a timeline
68 Network that Antonietta Collins appears on
69 Understands
70 "The Sopranos" actress Falco

**DOWN**

1 Spots for cats
2 Corporate honchos
3 Mete out
4 Looked searchingly
5 Dough
6 Balm ingredient
7 Woodcutting particles
8 Declare with confidence
9 Part of a picket fence
10 Celebrations akin to fist bumps
11 Had shakshuka, say
12 H.S. diploma alternative
15 Make a misstep
20 Key component in 29-Down, for short
21 Ginger ___
25 Place for sporting events
26 Unlike Marie Kondo's home, presumably
28 Sallie ___
29 Laptops, e.g.
30 Agent, in brief
31 ___ Tuesday (last day before Lent)
32 Home to a California State University campus

**33** Try to buy in an auction
**34** What a future astronaut might attend
**38** Vietnamese soup
**39** Na+ or Cl-
**40** It can be sipped or spilled
**41** Cheerios grain
**43** Dear
**46** Person calling strikes
**47** Shul's sacred scrolls
**48** Palindromic farm animal
**49** Night flight
**53** Went out with

**54** Egyptian peninsula
**56** A good one bodes well
**57** Doorstep item
**58** Trig ratio
**59** Theater backgrounds
**60** Extremely uncommon
**61** Word before "date" or "diligence"
**62** ER workers

# 173
## A MATTER OF DEGREE
By Zhouqin Burnikel

**ACROSS**

1 Arrange systematically
5 October gems
10 Misdeeds
14 "Moonstruck" star
15 On the up and up
16 Joint used for squatting
17 Like a team that loses in the first round
19 Image representing an app
20 Most populated city in the world
21 Dublin's country
23 Poetry showdown
26 Title fish in a 2003 animated movie
27 CPR performer, perhaps
30 "You can't handle the truth!" movie
35 Relative of "BAM!"
36 Org. that developed the space blanket
37 Colorado River tributary
38 Ella Fitzgerald singing style
40 Horned ungulate on safaris
43 Bible garden
44 State east of Indiana
45 "Long live" translation
47 Word after "Hampton" or "Holiday"
48 Like a brilliant-cut diamond
52 For instance
53 Route through woods
54 Give the cold shoulder

56 "I'd advise against it!"
59 Disinfectant brand
63 Continent where Buddhism originated
64 Totally ready
68 Timely blessing
69 Track contests
70 Messes up
71 "Foxy Brown" hairstyle
72 Strong and thick
73 Palindromic verb

**DOWN**

1 Glaswegian, e.g.
2 "Such awful news!"
3 Stink to high heaven
4 Copier's paper holders
5 Ancient
6 ___ XING
7 A long time ___
8 Inner layer of a coat
9 Multi-speaker system
10 Slopeside shelter
11 Ancient Cuzco dweller
12 Element after fluorine
13 Mail away
18 TV host Katie who set a donut-stacking world record
22 Rock genre
24 Worshipping from ___
25 Mosquito net material
27 ___ salt
28 Chocolaty coffee order

**USA TODAY**

# 174

## INDIVIDUAL MEDLEY

By Rachel Fabi

**ACROSS**

1 Nickname for a father
5 Restaurant postings
10 Singer Erykah
14 "Don't touch that ___!"
15 "The L Word" creator Chaiken
16 Once ___ a time
17 Untrustworthy
19 Grasp
20 Song for two
21 British restroom
22 Fizzy refreshment
23 Postage piece
25 Capital of South Korea
27 "Ms. ___-Man"
28 Singer Winehouse
29 "Break's over!"
31 Gift registry, e.g.
34 Prescribed amount
35 Apiece
36 Neighbor of Benin
38 Goofs
40 Side that might be mayo- or vinegar-based
44 Sternum
47 Safe Drinking Water Act org.
48 U.K.-published reference work (Abbr.)
49 Spoken exams
50 ___-a-thon (animal shelter event)
52 Middle Eastern strip
54 Opposite of online, for short
55 Hoof noise

56 Foul scent
57 Final words of MLK's "I Have a Dream" speech
61 Bit of camping gear
62 Interlocking plastic bricks
63 Bunibonibee ___ Nation
64 Greek war god
65 "My Brilliant Friend" narrator
66 Biblical paradise

**DOWN**

1 File that can be e-signed
2 Feel sick
3 Instances of being compensated
4 Collection of photos or songs
5 Toothpaste flavor
6 Biblical priest whose name can be found in "belief"
7 Ignore
8 Detach, in a way
9 Begin a journey
10 Irritates
11 "___ of nothing . . ."
12 Question of courage
13 Empty a suitcase
18 Informal affirmative
23 Toothy tool
24 "I wish I could unhear that!"
25 Accessory for a Girl Scout
26 Firmly embed
29 Maker of lighters and pens
30 Tries to win over
32 Mother of 64-Across

**33** Catch with a rope
**36** Loads
**37** Word before "Miss" or "Opry"
**38** Digital book device
**39** Scoring range in football
**40** Morehouse, for example
**41** Big cat
**42** Phone download
**43** Doro ___ (Ethiopian stew)
**44** Capital whose first inhabitants were the Muisca
**45** Item of little value

**46** Annie Edson Taylor's Niagara Falls vehicle
**50** Genre modifier
**51** Partner of Gabbana
**53** Partner of crafts
**55** Translation of "house"
**58** Long time period
**59** Get eyes on
**60** Diamond, on the Mohs hardness scale

# 175
## STONEWORK
By Gail Grabowski

**ACROSS**

1 Summer getaways for kids
6 Woodwind instrument
10 Spreadsheet contents
14 Home to humpback whales
15 Pillow stuff
16 Multivitamin component
17 Burning orb
19 Lowly one
20 "Pull up a chair!"
21 Garden hose holder
22 "I can ___ to that"
24 Transmission choice
25 Angelic ring
26 Vacation destination
29 Sandwich counter offering
33 Doctoral students' challenges found somewhere in this clue
34 Far from timid
35 "Another thing . . ."
36 You might put in a good one for someone
37 Nightstand lights
38 Elevated landform
39 Good place to start on a jigsaw puzzle
40 Gets mileage out of
41 Convenience store inconveniences
42 Performs a dramatization of
44 Have the final turn
45 Vehicle with a pannier, perhaps
46 Pull with effort

47 Without bias
50 "___ in East L.A."
51 Do a winter sport
54 "You are ___ much trouble!"
55 Wearisome routine
58 Dish from a slow cooker
59 "___ Enchanted" (2018 fantasy novel)
60 Spine-tingling
61 Word before "angst" or "Titans"
62 Titans, e.g.
63 Rotisserie rods

**DOWN**

1 Corn cores
2 Brazilian bowlful
3 Go from solid to liquid
4 Friend
5 Noisy sleepers
6 Part of OBO
7 "Bring to a ___" (recipe phrase)
8 Piece of crew equipment
9 May birthstones
10 Illegitimate source of degrees
11 Room size calculation
12 Palindromic sound
13 TV chef Burrell
18 Noteworthy accomplishment
23 Actor Wallach
24 Color of nicely toasted bread
25 Assists
26 Crew competitor

**27** Wear away
**28** Military officer, informally
**29** Hemispherical roofs
**30** "Little Fires Everywhere" Journalist
**31** Braying beasts
**32** Wedding reception highlight
**34** Sew loosely
**37** Fortunate person, so to speak
**41** Relaxes
**43** Be under the weather
**44** SpongeBob's pet snail
**46** Swiss cheese features

**47** Clenched hand
**48** Poker stake
**49** "Understood!"
**50** Creature studied by an ornithologist
**51** Apple voice
**52** Work on a scarf, say
**53** The ___ of March
**56** Many years ___
**57** Weightlifting unit

# 176
## SEEN IN D.C.

By Evan Kalish

### ACROSS

1 Yield to demands
5 Phys ed class sites
9 Not sink
14 Measurement in two dimensions
15 Far from ubiquitous
16 The first ordained female one was Regina Jonas in 1935
17 "Remain calm!"
19 Banish from the country
20 First responder, at times
21 "Yuck!"
22 Made chirping sounds
24 Taiwan's capital
26 Six-pack muscles
27 Play reviewer
33 Baby mooer
36 Jian dui ingredient
37 "Obviously"
39 Should the need ___
41 Poke fun at
42 Gooey campfire-cooked treat
44 Something a swish doesn't hit
45 Place
48 Comedian Borstein
49 Long-running TV newsmagazine
52 "Chambers" actress Thurman
53 Royal court entertainer
57 Mean-spirited glare
61 Early provider of dial-up internet
62 "___ been thinking . . ."
63 Broadcasted again
64 Make absolutely no sense
67 Monetary boon for a researcher
68 Unit of 14-Across
69 Greek cheese
70 Drinking spots for camels
71 Happiness or sadness
72 Capture

### DOWN

1 Military trainee
2 Wonderful odor
3 Starbucks size above grande
4 Enjoy some aloo tikki, say
5 "Danke," in Spanish
6 Harsh tug
7 Medical scan
8 Religious offshoot
9 Giveaway items
10 Least stringent
11 Any entry in the NYT's "Overlooked" series
12 Surname of Sable and Mabel in "Animal Crossing"
13 Like knots
18 Docking spot
23 Toasty
25 Email attachments, often
28 "Danke," in French
29 Appropriate rhyme for "Malaysian"
30 TV-watching option
31 Person you look up to

**32** Medical breakthrough
**33** Dealership purchase
**34** Really dry
**35** Peru's capital
**38** Curse
**40** Earth, wind, and fire, e.g.
**43** Apple computers
**46** Skin care brand
**47** Had fun at
**50** New Orleans university that sounds like a type of road
**51** "Doesn't ring a ___"
**54** Striped cat

**55** Musical about Eva Perón
**56** Postgame summary
**57** "Thus . . ."
**58** Aloe ___
**59** 401(k) alternatives
**60** Dutch cheese
**61** Hairstyle for Diana Ross, at times
**65** Earth-friendly prefix
**66** Frequently, before a hyphen

# 177
## IT'S HOT OUTSIDE
By Zhouqin Burnikel

**ACROSS**

1 "Last week on . . ." segment
6 Electric guitar accessory
9 Hall of ___
13 Filipino dish
14 Cow's utterance
15 Burrito bar options
16 Meeting that's likely to be awkward
18 Readily available
19 Q's value in Scrabble
20 "Keep quiet!"
21 Unusual thing
22 Nemeses
23 Destiny's Child, for one
24 Liquid mishap
26 Agreements in family law, briefly
29 Go after
30 Highly stylish
31 Get warmer
33 "Chosen Ones" author Veronica
34 Leave speechless, perhaps
35 Partner
36 Big name in coolers
37 Thick piece
38 "Fearless" actress Perez
39 Business buzzword related to cooperation
41 Firetruck warning
42 Antelopes that sound like news
43 What Retin-A treats
44 Bend on a golf course
47 "Pose" clothes
48 Use a chair
51 Poppy-derived drug
52 Nonnegotiable number from a seller
54 Baseball legend Doby
55 Numero ___
56 "I'm so flattered!"
57 "Ex's & Oh's" singer King
58 Freshly minted
59 Beaver habitats

**DOWN**

1 Vessel that might be inflatable
2 "Tommy" star Falco
3 Major Iowa crop
4 Muscles worked by Russian twists
5 Road repair target
6 Stockpile
7 Insect attracted to light
8 "Star Wars" character often shipped with Finn
9 Gather further info
10 Play's first part
11 Source of protein
12 Best WWE Moment, for one
15 Beauty entrepreneur Linda
17 "The Three Musketeers" fight
21 Vacuum brand
22 Artificial bait
23 Magician's feat

**24** Bowling alley rentals
**25** Burger part
**26** Insincere
**27** Full or waxing crescent, for the moon
**28** Glossy bonnet fabric
**29** Burst into tears
**30** Gulps down
**32** Itty-bitty
**34** "I don't care" gesture
**38** Wearable candy
**40** Nemesis
**41** Bogus deal

**43** Item in a quiver
**44** Name on some banana stickers
**45** Gem such as Olympic Australis
**46** "You go, ___"
**47** Have a meal
**48** Roadside posting
**49** Chilled with cubes
**50** Short-sleeved shirts
**52** Word after "chow" or "mei"
**53** Letter before sigma

# 178
## GO-BETWEENS
By Margit Christenson

**ACROSS**

1 Drool catcher
4 Grump
8 Path through the woods
13 Moody music genre
14 Bona fide
15 Act as a go-between
16 Chilled tomato soup
18 Orchard harvest
19 Ride a Vespa
20 University locations
22 Word before "freeze" or "fry"
25 Has-___
26 Commercials
28 The very beginning
33 Sound when it's 10 below
34 Basic element of knitting
35 Boot reinforcement
36 "Becoming" author Michelle
38 "It's just OK"
40 Not follow through
41 "Friends, ___, countrymen, lend me your ears" ("Julius Caesar" quote)
43 Coral formation
45 Ethiopian flag color
46 Instrument at a John Legend concert
48 Throw in
49 Narrow valley
50 Click of the fingers
52 Most tired
56 Crane constructions
60 ___ flour

61 Game in which a player might ask, "Is your person wearing a hat?"
64 Accessories for magicians or boxers
65 Ocean landmass
66 Scuba tank contents
67 Alleviates
68 Not succeed
69 Letters on cartoon dynamite

**DOWN**

1 Asks for food under the table
2 Apple desktop computer
3 Clown created in 1946
4 Delivery container
5 "Parks and ___" (Amy Poehler sitcom, for short)
6 Spa sigh
7 Voting group
8 Alerted
9 Long-haired character
10 Is laid up in bed, maybe
11 "Oh, OK"
12 Not as much
15 "Woe is me!" for example
17 Pea holders
21 ___ Dhabi
23 A compliment might give it a boost
24 End-of-high-school event
26 Arch in a garden
27 Theater production
29 Theater production

**30** Something clicked open on a birthday
**31** Used a long-handled yard tool on
**32** Newspaper column
**33** "Star Trek" collective
**34** Nonwireless phones
**37** Swamp tree
**39** Coop occupants
**42** Goes fast
**44** Long, long time
**47** ___ and outs

**48** Chimpanzees and orangutans
**51** Nature photographer Adams
**52** Living ___
**53** "First Lady of Song" Fitzgerald
**54** "Famous" cookie maker
**55** End-of-workweek expression
**57** Attack on a fly
**58** Like tissue paper
**59** Arrange by type
**62** 2019 FIFA Women's World Cup winners
**63** Quarterback Manning

# 179
## ENTRY FORMS
By Patrick Jordan

**ACROSS**

1 Go by
5 ___ League
9 Gently taps
13 Stomach woe
14 Wander around
15 Formerly ___ Chicks
16 Oblong dairy-based appetizer
18 Deposed leader's fate, perhaps
19 Pedicured digit
20 Turn over ___ leaf
21 Brought through childhood
22 Form of classical music
24 Not absent
25 Checkout counter machine
31 Butter-making device
34 Likely to cause goosebumps
35 46-Across spot
36 Optimistic feeling
37 Ransacks
38 Containers of baby food
39 Stock debut (Abbr.)
40 Chocolate confection
41 Icy astronomical object
42 Bun eaten with chili
45 Program-launching picture
46 Irish stew veggie
50 Sliding fastener
53 Fastens with a knot
55 "good one"
56 Modify accordingly
57 Musical success

59 Earth has two
60 Swedish furniture source
61 Poker payment
62 Glider on a snowy slope
63 Becomes less luminous
64 Social equal

**DOWN**

1 Treaties between countries
2 Sneeze sound
3 Luster
4 Have an appointment with
5 Sports venues
6 Mary Birchbark, for Tantoo Cardinal
7 Declare
8 "I ___ to differ"
9 Dust-sprinkling sprites
10 Graph line
11 Part of a shower wall
12 Tidbit for a parakeet
15 Sweetie pie
17 The Devil
21 Kingly name
23 Unit of farmland
24 One looking after livestock
26 Direct way to deal with something
27 Monarch's term
28 Squad
29 Bronte character Jane
30 Remaining amount
31 Elegantly fashionable
32 Like noqkwivi

**USA TODAY**

**33** "___ further review . . ."
**37** Bit of gossip
**38** Shock
**40** Sapphire's sides
**41** Not far off
**43** ___ in the bud (stopped early on)
**44** Shows featuring arias
**47** "I'm not lonely, I'm ___ / And I'm holy by my own" (Jamila Woods)
**48** Dessert with a German name
**49** Having been around longer

**50** Hits with electricity
**51** 2018 BTS hit
**52** Like Casper's complexion
**53** Polynesian carving
**54** Part of a list
**57** Ducked out of sight
**58** Salary limit

# 180
## WOLF PACK
By Zhouqin Burnikel

**ACROSS**

1 "Yes, I'm Hot in This" garment
6 Drink like a cat
9 Up in the air
13 Island whose capital is Oranjestad
14 Dog command
15 Country bordered by Niger
16 Character often said to have been based on Bass Reeves
18 Book jacket part
19 Point value of a free throw
20 ___ sentence
21 Tamal wrappers
22 "Better Luck Tomorrow" director Justin
23 Arthur Conan ___
25 Slid while seated
29 Grape juice brand
32 Sound bounce
33 Quinoa or spelt
35 Mary ___ Williams
36 One of 28 won by One Direction
40 "Devious Maids" star Ortiz
41 Stopwatch button
42 Lends support to
43 Minnesota State Capitol's home
45 "What was I thinking?"
48 Central idea
50 Apple mobile platform
51 National Siblings Day month
53 Company with a duck mascot

56 Moo ___ shrimp
59 Author Lowry
60 Brains
62 Number before doce
63 Otherwise
64 Come to know
65 Little kid
66 Got together
67 Outer boundaries

**DOWN**

1 Symbol of saintliness
2 Mineral that tofu is rich in
3 National Best Friends Day month
4 "Honest" prez
5 Spanish for "neighborhood"
6 Business card graphic
7 Change
8 ___ capita
9 "No more for me"
10 Assertion flagged by a fact-checker
11 Harsh criticism
12 Kennel sounds
14 Channel with a "magic wall"
17 Hilda or Zelda, to Sabrina Spellman
21 Giggling scavenger
22 Avian symbol of Minnesota
24 Playground scrape
25 Trail for a bloodhound
26 Underhanded move
27 Parts of psyches

**28** Hangs on a clothesline
**30** Large crowd
**31** Bubble bath stuff
**32** Figs. for incoming flights
**34** Starting segment of a musical
**37** Vicious
**38** Captain's spot
**39** Routes
**44** "Now it's clear!"
**46** Name that's an anagram of 15-Across
**47** Venue

**49** "The World Is Blue" author Sylvia
**51** Tons
**52** "My Little ___"
**54** Like a sprinter
**55** Compound in drain cleaners
**56** Fawn's dad
**57** "Take this one"
**58** Caterer's coffee holders
**60** Emerald or jade, e.g.
**61** ___ Talks

# 181
## JUST MY TYPE
By Evan Kalish

**ACROSS**

1 "Hey you!" whisper
5 Named, for short
9 Skedaddle
14 Island where Queen Liliuokalani was born
15 Unaccompanied
16 Catherine who played Moira Rose
17 Thick slice
18 Got defeated
19 Person who avoids company
20 "Let's get moving!"
23 "___ Maria"
24 Medical coverage grp.
25 City name in Texas and Ukraine
28 Rope at a rodeo
30 "Yeah, right!"
33 "Enough of this!"
34 Amazement
36 Places to park
38 Alley-___
39 Different ownership
43 Letters that begin the names of both a lap dog breed and a fruit
44 Timeline sections
45 Coquito liquor
46 Dianna Russini's network
48 Little one
50 "On Becoming a God in Central Florida" star Kirsten
54 Sound of rushing wind
56 Jet ___
58 Abu Dhabi's country, for short
59 Something popes and Super Bowls have in common
63 Tolerate
65 Upscale German car
66 "Doing that now!"
67 Comedian Poundstone
68 The middle of March, to Caesar
69 Case for a dermatologist
70 More domesticated
71 ___ than ideal
72 Proof of ownership

**DOWN**

1 The "P" of USPS
2 Spit
3 Makes feel bad
4 Toothpaste container
5 Zakat is one of its pillars
6 Genre of the song "Duke of Earl"
7 Olaf's creator in "Frozen"
8 They might be connected with a pencil
9 Water : liquid :: ice : ___
10 They ring
11 Hughes who wrote "I, Too"
12 Rage
13 Goo for a paving crew
21 "I would like to see it"
22 Walk unsteadily
26 Chimney substance

## Crossword Grid

| 1 | 2 | 3 | 4 | ■ | 5 | 6 | 7 | 8 | ■ | 9 | 10 | 11 | 12 | 13 |
|---|---|---|---|---|---|---|---|---|---|---|---|---|---|---|
| 14 | | | | ■ | 15 | | | | ■ | 16 | | | | |
| 17 | | | | ■ | 18 | | | | ■ | 19 | | | | |
| 20 | | | 21 | | | | | 22 | | | | | ■ | ■ |
| 23 | | | ■ | 24 | | | | 25 | | | | 26 | 27 | |
| 28 | | | 29 | | | 30 | 31 | 32 | | | 33 | | | |
| ■ | | | 34 | | 35 | | 36 | | | 37 | | 38 | | |
| ■ | 39 | 40 | | | | 41 | | | | | 42 | | | ■ |
| 43 | | | | 44 | | | | 45 | | | | | | |
| 46 | | | 47 | ■ | 48 | | | | 49 | | 50 | | 51 | 52 | 53 |
| 54 | | | | 55 | | | ■ | | 56 | 57 | | | 58 | | |
| ■ | | | 59 | | | | 60 | 61 | | | | 62 | | |
| 63 | 64 | | | | ■ | 65 | | | | ■ | 66 | | | |
| 67 | | | | ■ | 68 | | | | ■ | 69 | | | | |
| 70 | | | | ■ | 71 | | | | ■ | 72 | | | | |

**27** Coding project
**29** Cutting tool
**31** Vessel in a chemistry lab
**32** Visibility reducer
**35** Kitt who said, "A man comes into my life and I have to compromise? You must think about that one again"
**37** Mark made by rubbing
**39** Snack
**40** Big store
**41** Vote from the opposition
**42** Australian bird

**43** Seat facing an altar
**47** Piece of linguine or udon
**49** Avoids
**51** Blanket statement's lack
**52** Salt-based
**53** Evaluated
**55** Mark made by rubbing
**57** Not right
**60** Do perfectly
**61** Clothesless
**62** "Hit the ___, Jack!"
**63** Appropriate
**64** Lamb's bleat

# 182
## START A FOUR-DAY WEEKEND
By Gail Grabowski

**ACROSS**
1 Actress Miranda
5 Planetary path
10 Scratching post users
14 Fifty-and-older org.
15 Terra ___ (solid ground)
16 4-Down solo
17 Pakora and medu vada, e.g.
19 Sharp taste
20 Future fern
21 Auction house where the original Rosie the Riveter painting was sold in 2002
23 Food for an aardvark
26 Be dressed in
27 Word often ignored when alphabetizing
30 Luxurious bedding items
35 Helpful clue
37 La Brea ___ Pits
38 Grant entry
39 Forever ___ day
40 Work duration
43 "Toodle-oo!"
44 Objects of adoration
46 Place for merfolk
47 Greasy
48 Submerged wrecks
52 "___ Miz"
53 Part of a piggy bank
54 Swimmer's units
56 Amphibian on a branch
60 Painter's stand
64 It's sold in skeins

65 Bill holders
68 Korean cars
69 Like a wide-open mouth
70 Locality
71 "You're something ___!"
72 Allow access to
73 What you eat

**DOWN**
1 Clumsy people
2 Protective cover
3 Small jazz group
4 Leontyne Price performance
5 Taking a personal day, say
6 Spanish for "river"
7 Warner ___
8 "Sounds good"
9 Takes a bite of
10 Indulged
11 The "A" in UAE
12 Minuscule
13 Gets less firm
18 Bears' lairs
22 "Good one!"
24 Pics on ankles
25 Numerical factoid
27 Bangkok residents
28 Like the Bhagavad Gita
29 "Let's ___ a high note"
31 Belfast residents
32 Contact option
33 Championship
34 Doesn't go
36 Speak rationally

**USA TODAY**

**41** "One More River" filmmaker Diamond
**42** Spanish appetizer
**45** Prefix akin to "auto-"
**49** Usual
**50** Lackey
**51** Blueprint detail, for short
**55** Word after "fruit," "pasta," or "Snickers"
**56** Small child
**57** Staircase feature
**58** Periods of historical significance
**59** Small fly
**61** Apple assistant
**62** One-on-one Olympic event
**63** Future attorney's exam
**66** Fuel economy testing org.
**67** Nevertheless

# 183
## THAT'S A WRAP
By Erik Agard

**ACROSS**

1 Blowing-out-candles thought
5 Picture holder
10 Deceptive scheme
14 Express the same sentiment as
15 They might be read between
16 Pudding ingredient
17 Temperature device
19 Regular payment
20 Does some cheffing
21 Nutrition plans
22 God who wields Mjolnir
23 Grads
25 Have on
26 Win back-to-back-to-back titles
30 Defeats
31 Songs of praise
32 Hollywood budget item (Abbr.)
33 Cosmetics chain
34 Nest noises
35 San ___, Puerto Rico
36 Sound of disapproval
37 Islam denomination
38 Limbless animals
39 Warm garment
41 Whom Jekyll becomes
42 Attempted
43 ___ and aahs
44 Competed in NASCAR
46 Oklahoma birthplace of 35-Down

48 Feel sore
49 Cheetara or Lion-O
54 Get ready
55 Spanish direction
56 Island of Indonesia
57 Perfect scores, often
58 Range that's an anagram of 55-Across
59 Instruction from a dentist

**DOWN**

1 Damp
2 Pronoun in German
3 Pronoun in English
4 Rice drink
5 Word before "plan" or "routine"
6 Something you might be averse to
7 Bridge-forming insects
8 "Just Give ___ Cool Drink of Water 'fore I Diiie"
9 Approximation (Abbr.)
10 Be frugal
11 Poutine ingredient
12 "___ No Sunshine"
13 Yoga surfaces
18 Ties up at the dock
21 Regular payment
22 Place to experiment with recipes
23 Place for deodorant
24 With 51-Down, camera protector

**USA TODAY**

**25** Language in Cardiff
**26** Subtle act of recognition
**27** "The Lion King" creature
**28** Full competitive intensity
**29** Pie holders
**30** Rear end
**34** Brownish-purple color
**35** "An American Sunrise" poet
**37** Slide
**38** "___ Bed Have Your Boots Been Under?"
**40** Moves stealthily
**43** "___ Than America"

**44** Totally absorbed
**45** Unit of area
**46** Rotate
**47** "Do ___ others . . ."
**49** Palindromic TV channel
**50** Gardening tool
**51** See 24-Down
**52** Broad street (Abbr.)
**53** Shade similar to khaki

# 184
## PICK UP THE PACE
By Zhouqin Burnikel

**ACROSS**

1 Not on the mark
4 Opposite of sharp, in music
8 Young 45-Down
12 Recoils
14 "Dear Therapist" columnist Gottlieb
15 "Right away!"
16 ___-loading (pre-marathon tactic)
17 Yousafzai autobiography
19 "___ we clear?"
20 Like most thrift store goods
22 Mother of Abel
23 Takes it back
25 Ice cream portions
28 "M*A*S*H" actor Alan
29 Banking transaction
30 Decisive NBA periods
32 Share online
34 "You betcha!"
35 Pet parasite
36 Mailing label abbr.
37 Lesser of two ___
39 Carefree adventure
40 Thick carpet
41 Spray paint holder
42 About-faces
44 Luau dish
45 "Rats!"
46 Trickster in Norse myth
47 Noses around
49 Catches the scent of, say
52 Some movie effects

53 "La ___ de Guadalupe"
54 Have Hainanese chicken rice, say
55 Peter out
59 Dive skin fabric
61 Concept
62 Skin condition
63 All lathered up
64 College faculty head
65 Auction units
66 FedEx alternative

**DOWN**

1 Chicago airport
2 Station leader
3 Groundhog Day mo.
4 Snacks for spiders
5 Washer input
6 Elbow's place
7 Buried caches for future generations
8 "The caveman diet"
9 Country with the most FIBA Women's World Cup titles
10 Buddy
11 Place for facial treatments
12 C-section mark
13 Bleeps and buzzes, e.g.
18 Romance fiction publisher
21 Denver or Dover, e.g.
24 "Just play ___!"
25 Heart and ___
26 Frozen planetary region
27 Far from lenient

**Down**

29 Making stuff up
31 Nordstrom competitor
32 Scratchy voice
33 Community spirit
35 Stroke of luck
38 Boxy vehicles
43 Bottom line figures
45 Pekes and pugs, e.g.
48 Title role for Bullock in 2018
49 They protect ball fields against rain
50 They protect ball fields against rain

51 "Don't leave!"
53 Tirade
55 Jar top
56 Poem with a dedicatee
57 Shark's home
58 ___-friendly
60 Pronoun that can be shortened to its last letter

# 185
## WAY TO GO
By Mark McClain

**ACROSS**

1 Fully engrossed
5 Earl Grey, say
8 Cartoon creature in a mushroom-shaped house
13 "The Sun ___ Rises"
14 Not tricky
16 Pay respect to
17 Throw a fit
20 Touch-related
21 "What's new?" reply
22 "Quiet!"
23 Percussion instrument
25 Animal hospital worker
26 Amusement
27 Visit "Nevada," say
29 Bear foot
32 Burn on the outside
34 Grassy spot
35 "It's the ___ of my existence"
36 Really get the message across
39 Russo of cinema
40 "A Farewell to ___"
41 Car bar
42 Thus far
43 Nickname for a III
44 Use a crowbar
45 Advanced degree
46 South Asian wrap
48 "Finally, the truth comes out!"
51 Controlled the direction of
55 Gets comfy
57 Proceed so as not to offend
59 Dance legend Debbie
60 North African river
61 Shoe part
62 Poke fun at
63 Aquarium accessory
64 Small bills

**DOWN**

1 Grand Canyon boats
2 Bismillah subject
3 Behavioral science, informally
4 "Not to ___ my own horn . . ."
5 Nonstick surface
6 Consumed
7 ___ Wednesday
8 Made to feel guilty
9 Painter Claude
10 Reverse
11 Sushi order
12 "Finding ___" (2019 podcast about Mister Rogers)
15 "Can I help you?"
18 Number
19 Caribbean capital
24 Beyonce won 13 in the 2010s
26 Top pick, casually
28 Female sheep
29 Bucket
30 Hathaway who played Mia Thermopolis
31 36-Down opposite
32 "Peyak, niso, nisto . . ." language
33 "Give me a ___"

**USA TODAY**

**34** Passed-down knowledge
**35** Square-shaped
**36** 31-Down opposite
**37** Get firmer
**38** Place for a priest
**43** Seat of royalty
**44** Car radio selection
**45** Small dogs, for short
**47** Selfie choice
**48** Greenlight
**49** Nametag heading
**50** Burros, e.g.
**51** Hit

**52** Word after "tall" or "fairy"
**53** She, in Spanish
**54** Colorado airport code
**56** Midterm, for one
**58** Rummy variant

# 186
## IF I MAY . . .
By Kate Hawkins

**ACROSS**

1 Slender
5 Super ___ Bros. (Nintendo game)
10 Walk through water
14 Ripped
15 Word after "pizza" or "tea"
16 One of the Great Lakes
17 Style ___
18 Think the world of
19 Light gas
20 Crush competitor
22 Hygienic
24 One who hears and is not seen
27 Source of romantic petals
28 Model's gig
31 Dinghy propeller
34 Not just were
36 "You're Never Fully Dressed Without a Smile" musical
38 Stem discipline
43 Word before "pitch" or "dream"
44 Suggestion, for short
45 Attachment in a thrift store
46 Scorches
48 Spill the beans
51 Event with a high bar
57 Rude
60 Voice above bass
61 Mend with stitches
62 Swear
65 Home of India and Indonesia
66 Hideout for a villain
67 "Normal People" star Daisy ___-Jones
68 Fiasco
69 One of 16 won by "30 Rock"
70 "Ta-ta for now!"
71 Percussive dance style

**DOWN**

1 Inflexible
2 Close to home
3 Sarcastic tone
4 Personal adviser
5 Many a Budapest tourist attraction
6 Furious
7 Came into being
8 "This is the last ___!"
9 Animals voiced by Whoopi Goldberg and Cheech Marin in "The Lion King"
10 Ran over the allotted time
11 Region
12 Big name in couture
13 "___, meeny . . ."
21 "I'll take that as ___"
23 Minnesota representative Omar
25 Old Russian ruler
26 Queen in Greek myth
29 "Coming right up!"
30 Hoops legend Thompson
31 Having a bad day, perhaps
32 Pub offerings

**33** Travel constantly
**35** Make a mistake
**37** Frozen custard ingredient
**39** Armory contents
**40** Name that rhymes with Meryl
**41** Country singer McEntire
**42** Legal advocacy org.
**47** Apple pieces
**49** Not mainstream, for short
**50** Second-string squads
**52** Piano practice piece
**53** Edge
**54** Map within a map

**55** What some headphones cancel
**56** Grip
**57** Like some speculation
**58** Respectful (at times) term of address
**59** ___ and proper
**63** Put into words
**64** Notable time span

# 187
## SPLIT ENDS
By Zhouqin Burnikel

**ACROSS**

1 Put in a secret location
6 Name that's a type of nail
10 Defib pros
14 Farfalle or fusilli
15 City near Carson City
16 Clever remark
17 "The First Wives Club" villains
19 Josephine and Joe Bruin's school
20 Like some home repairs, for short
21 Goalie's success
22 Rises abruptly
24 "Who ___ have you told?"
25 Hilarious person
26 Dame and duke, e.g.
29 Innocent-looking
32 Many residents of South Paterson, New Jersey
33 Rain really hard
34 Turn with a spatula
36 Basketball analyst Rebecca
37 Schlep
38 Puts into service
39 "I ___, right?"
40 Waste no time
41 Agitated states
42 "Sorry, not sorry"
44 Far from boastful
45 "You've got a point"
46 Country where Pi Mai is celebrated every year
47 Crib dweller

50 Solange, to Blue Ivy
51 Sedona automaker
54 Haunted house sound
55 What a magician might show at the beginning of a trick
58 Like hardcore fans
59 Ready to harvest
60 Concern for a food inspector
61 Roller coaster parts
62 Impudent replies
63 "Battle of the ___" (Emma Stone movie)

**DOWN**

1 Traveled quickly
2 Metered vehicle
3 In need of lotion
4 Apt-sounding name for a cook
5 Big inconveniences
6 Intrepid
7 "Yours, Mine & Ours" actress Russo
8 "What's more . . ."
9 Detailed file
10 Stock-based investments
11 Yucky gunk
12 Scrabble piece
13 Workplaces for massage therapists
18 Low tones
23 "Star Wars" pilot

**24** Acrobatic feats in which the body is balanced on the forearms
**25** Like some drafts
**26** Hash things out
**27** A lot of ___ in the fire
**28** Social prohibition
**29** Extinguish
**30** "Eighth Grade" actress Fisher
**31** Paleo and keto, e.g.
**33** Feather
**35** Furtive "Hey, you!"
**40** News agency founded in 1851
**41** Placates
**43** Large container for coffee
**44** Numerous
**46** String instruments
**47** Apple desktop
**48** ___ Scotia
**49** "You've got a point"
**50** Tablet downloads
**51** Kentucky's Fort ___
**52** Not doing anything
**53** Flea market disclaimer
**56** Soccer legend Hamm
**57** Top-notch

# 188
## MADE UP
By Evan Kalish

**ACROSS**

1 Obstacle to seeking help, sometimes
7 Org. where Mary Jackson worked as an engineer
11 Format for an e-ticket
14 Spain's capital
15 Request from an orthodontist
17 Burning the midnight oil
18 Close race
19 Adolescent
20 "___ is more"
22 GPA-boosting class
23 Headed for overtime
25 A key might be hidden under one
26 Drove too fast
28 Sci-fi vessel
34 Mild cheese from the Netherlands
35 Apple products
36 Discard
37 Special vibe
38 "The Moment of Lift" author Melinda
39 Hawaiian dance
40 Support for a sunflower
41 Among
42 They determine eye color
43 Events of scientific interest
45 Tallies up
46 "Dispatches From Elsewhere" actress Lindley
47 Comedy star Rudolph

49 Get up
52 Velvety green growth
54 Office letter
58 Literary sensation
60 Climbed to the top of
62 Children's get-together
63 Got a great score in golf
64 Do some needlework
65 Mining targets
66 Bird sounds

**DOWN**

1 Inappropriate material
2 Word after "cassette" or "duct"
3 Awaiting orders, say
4 Given a pardon
5 School near Harvard
6 "Send My Love (To Your New Lover)" singer
7 Silently agrees
8 Tailless primates
9 Kraken's habitat
10 From a South American mountain range
11 Dishes with crusts
12 June 6, 1944
13 Crumbly cheese from Greece
16 "How much do I owe you?"
21 Sushi bar appetizer
24 Journalist ___ B. Wells
25 Neatnik's bane
26 Toward Antarctica
27 Liquefy using a blender

**29** Pig ___ (pseudo language)
**30** Wintry roof buildups
**31** Doggedly pursue
**32** Caribbean multitude
**33** Anti-vaping spots, e.g.
**34** Astonished sound
**38** Spades, for example
**42** Part of LGBTQIA+
**44** "Don't ___ it"
**48** Positive aspect
**49** Audio boosters
**50** Govern with complete power
**51** "Guess who ___ today?"

**52** "G'day, ___!"
**53** Poems expressing praise
**55** Magazine that's a palindrome
**56** "Nice to ___ you!"
**57** Betting ratios
**59** Unit of corn
**61** Crow's sound

# 189
## COME TO REST
By Gail Grabowski

### ACROSS

1 Elite group of guests
6 "Dancing Queen" pop group
10 Part of an orange
14 Supreme Court justice Sotomayor
15 Car financing option
16 Buffalo's Great Lake
17 Begin
18 Remove from power
19 Maya Angelou, e.g.
20 Avoid making a decision
23 "___ to the Women on Long Island" (Olivia Gatwood poem)
25 Stages of a journey
26 Wedding cake part
27 Went by bike
29 Flu season protection
31 Ingredient in some lip balms
32 Origami medium
34 Lingerie item
37 Ecological revival
41 Now ___ then
42 Improbable win
43 Kellogg's waffle brand
44 Handful for a nanny
45 Car financing options
47 Completely flummoxed
50 Period of prosperity
52 Wrath
53 Compromise on your expectations
57 Subscription period, often
58 "Desperate Housewives" actress Delany
59 Evaluates
62 James who sang "All I Could Do Was Cry"
63 Overabundance
64 Athens resident
65 "So ___ say"
66 Apart from this
67 In advance

### DOWN

1 Mule's sire
2 Subdivision division
3 Momentarily
4 Voice-activated assistant
5 Tell on someone
6 Word after "get" or "move"
7 Boxing matches
8 Criticize severely
9 Draw poker bet
10 Say again
11 It can be dramatic or situational
12 Family tree part
13 Discourage
21 British lexicon (Abbr.)
22 Regional plant life
23 City west of Daytona Beach
24 Birth name of Dil Pickles
28 Was winning
29 Catch sight of
30 That girl
32 Whispered attention-getter

**33** Grabbed a bite
**34** Little kid's role model, perhaps
**35** "___ that!"
**36** Have ___ for news
**38** Like farm life
**39** Org. that published the newsletter GoGreen!
**40** Brewed drink
**44** Be disloyal to
**45** Texting chuckle
**46** Come into view
**47** Up to now

**48** Comb components
**49** Missouri or Mississippi, for example
**50** Year-end reward
**51** Give a keynote, say
**54** Live on the ___
**55** Take a spill
**56** "Grey's Anatomy" actor Ramirez
**60** Fish that can swim backwards
**61** Place for clouds

# 190
## THIS IS THE BAD PLACE!
By Erik Agard

**ACROSS**

1 Impact sound
5 Cut in the kitchen
9 Payment to a finder
12 Nabisco brand
13 ___ Inu (dog breed)
14 Cherry variety
15 Blue-green color
16 Punctuation mark before a list
17 Computer command
18 Cobb salad ingredients
21 Half of a 16-Across
22 Bar between wheels
23 Impact sound
25 "___, bomaye!" (Rumble in the Jungle chant)
28 Earth, in Latin
31 Large bodies of water
32 Place to record
34 Word after "Civil" or "Infinity" in the MCU
35 "And finally, equally importantly . . ."
38 Piece of legislation
39 Serves as ruler
40 Sports honorees
41 Temporary state
43 KC time zone
44 Take orders from
45 Part of an autumn pile
47 Business VIP
48 Valuables from the ocean floor
55 Experts

56 Regal
57 Practice like 25-Across
58 Part of a calendar
59 Part of a calendar
60 "Jump Into My Fire" singer James
61 Expert
62 Tilt
63 Female deer

**DOWN**

1 "Why not ___?"
2 Vicinity
3 In the vicinity
4 Shiny particles
5 "Permanent Record" author Mary H. K. ___
6 Mound of earth
7 Woodwind instrument
8 Black-and-white animal
9 Beauty shop technique
10 Draws to a close
11 Beyonce hit with the lyric "Some call it arrogant/I call it confident"
13 Get off ___-free
14 Brass instrument
19 Physique, for short
20 Speak highly of
23 Instruct
24 "See you later!"
25 High floor
26 Respiratory organs
27 Part of idk

USA TODAY

**29** Hoarse
**30** Part of B.A.
**31** Sound of a high-five
**32** Hoops great Bird
**33** "___ now or never!"
**36** Stop working
**37** Like some business cards
**42** Rational thinking
**44** One ___ kind
**46** Wild
**47** Spreadsheet box
**48** Injury aftereffect
**49** "Yup" opposite
**50** "ANTM" creator Banks
**51** Drops in a forecast
**52** No more than
**53** Pay stat
**54** History class units
**55** Subject of a phone update

# 191
## AFTER A MINUTE
By Zhouqin Burnikel

**ACROSS**
1 Dull-colored
5 Honeycomb component
9 Communicates silently
14 Exude
15 Cookie brand with a Carrot Cake flavor
16 "The Planet Is Burning" comedian Glazer
17 Someone to tip
19 Long past the "use by" date, perhaps
20 Enjoyed an egg tart, say
21 "No ___, ands, or buts"
22 Winter accessories
24 Joe ___ (average guy)
26 Tenant's document
27 Creepy
29 Online purchase button
33 ___ and void
36 Old Roman wrap
38 "Likewise"
39 "Make it fast!"
40 Become larger
42 Newton or tesla
43 Fabric named for a French city
45 Get the pot going
46 Pilates roll-ups
47 Convention venues
49 Beliefs not easily abandoned
51 Electrical networks
53 "Shut up!"
56 Hummus ingredient
58 One might be steamed

59 Joke
61 Clear wrap brand
62 NFL wideout with 1,549 career receptions
65 Speak your mind
66 Cricket field shape
67 Amway competitor
68 Mardi Gras mementos
69 Bothers persistently
70 Blue jay's home

**DOWN**
1 Qatar's most populous city
2 Tree anchors
3 Tenochtitlan resident of old
4 Pollen collector
5 Consoles
6 Periods that might be associated with heads of state
7 Fragrant necklace
8 Place to stay
9 Drinks served in champagne flutes
10 Admiring words to a bro
11 ___ gaze
12 Wraps up
13 "... to ___ the least"
18 Citrus for pico de gallo
23 Once around the track
25 Bit of assistance
26 Larger-than-life people
28 Major corn-producing state
30 Nickname for Grandma

**Down**

**31** Fail to include
**32** Keep your ___ about you
**33** Zip
**34** ___ experience
**35** Bowling alley division
**37** Choir member
**41** Hamstring exercises
**44** Naval personnel
**48** Moral lapse
**50** Loads of
**52** Mustard named for a French city
**54** "Enough already!"

**55** Tuesday treats
**56** Gift wrapper's roll
**57** Opera showstopper
**58** Talk boastfully
**60** Well-mannered fellow
**61** Cry noisily
**63** "Total Divas" star Marie
**64** Competed in the Twin Cities Marathon, say

# 192
## MUMBO JUMBO
By Brooke Husic

**ACROSS**

1 Assist
5 Largest deer species
10 Boom's opposite
14 Dark purple berry
15 Mistake
16 "___ the Next One" (2009 rap song)
17 Skilled person
18 Magic words
20 Minestrone pasta
22 Most Unangax people
23 Lung contents
25 Waterproof sheets
26 Vibrant display
32 Selina Meyer, in some seasons of "Veep"
33 Cheese paired with watermelon
34 Exam for a future psychiatrist
37 Vernal equinox mo.
38 Awesome
39 Unruly crowd
41 Gondola or punt
44 Southernmost Great Lake
46 PlayStation maker
47 Tin can telephone upgrade
50 Stop
52 A gray one may be demisexual
53 The story of John Henry, e.g.
56 Literary analysis target
59 Cloyingly affectionate
62 Bear who's Piglet's BFF

64 Related
65 "Fame" actress Cara
66 Pre-marathon event, often
67 Name hidden in "quintessence"
68 Fruit-flavored candy in a box
69 Optimistic

**DOWN**

1 Hem and ___
2 Repeat
3 Refuge
4 Glamorous style
5 Verbal shrug
6 Spanish for "gold"
7 Largest dolphin species
8 Heart's partner in a piano duet
9 Fake
10 Bibliophile's suggestion, informally
11 Open, in a way
12 Shocks
13 Gently throw
19 Seder reading
21 Pore secretion
24 NWSL official
26 Phonograph record stat
27 ___ American National Museum (Dearborn attraction)
28 "Holes" character with a numerical nickname
29 McDreamy's first name

USA TODAY

**30** Developer of the video game Breakout
**31** "White Teeth" novelist Smith
**35** Run ___ (be frenzied)
**36** "Sula" author Morrison
**40** Guaranteed tournament advancement
**42** Gains consciousness
**43** Delish
**45** GPS stat
**46** Late ___ (night owl)
**48** Intro
**49** Perform in a play

**50** Cycling champion Nicole
**51** Name that's an anagram of "lives"
**53** Not fizzy anymore
**54** 53-Acrosses and such
**55** At any point
**57** "Gossip Girl" signoff
**58** Counterparts of bottoms
**60** Conclude
**61** Active consent word
**63** "___ todo va a salir bien"

# 193
## GETTING IN YOUR HAIR
By Patrick Jordan

**ACROSS**
1 Black Panther or Black Lightning
5 Checkout line annoyance
9 Media mogul Winfrey
14 Admit without shame
15 Opposition research goal
16 Place to sweat
17 Stradivarius player's stick
19 Like toothpaste, often
20 Title street in a 1984 slasher film
21 Lowest soccer score
22 Porous cleaning aid
24 Parkway parts
26 Tiny pantry invader
27 Wrapped garment
30 Franklins
35 InDesign company
36 Game-stopping shout
37 Plow-pulling animals
38 Fearlessness
39 Readies
40 Common cosmetic surgery, for short
41 Not just some
42 Swimmers shaped like snakes
43 Grant permission for
44 Placed emphasis on
46 44-Across backward, usually
47 Greek letter after pi
48 Push a toothpick through
50 "Fingers crossed"
53 Annoy

54 "Grow up, ___"
57 ___ State University (home of the Bulldogs)
58 Cinematic excerpt
61 Campaign sign verb
62 Sunburn-soothing gel ingredient
63 Vi or Viv, on TV
64 Cubicle furniture
65 Safety items
66 Tent-securing spikes

**DOWN**
1 Be equipped with
2 "Deception, disgrace, ___ as plain as the scar on his face"
3 Suite component
4 Hooting hunter
5 Losing intensity
6 Walk casually
7 Letters introducing a POV
8 Brings to a body shop, say
9 Figure skater Kaetlyn
10 Coat-applying tool
11 Ladder part
12 Part of a.m.
13 Baler input
18 Lacking sense
23 Window parts
24 Seafood restaurant implement
25 Sword blockers
27 Detailed tales
28 Grown-up

**29** Helicopter mechanism
**31** National Pro Fastpitch officials
**32** Order to leave the country
**33** Building for passengers
**34** Comes down in flakes
**36** Squirrel's home, perhaps
**39** Mexican legal tender
**43** No longer napping
**45** 57-Down coverings
**46** Succession of issues
**49** Turning maneuver
**50** Rabbit ___

**51** Must repay
**52** Persian Gulf country
**54** Word after "light" or "true"
**55** Word before "light" or "true"
**56** Stops waffling
**57** Cot, e.g.
**59** Grand ___ Opry
**60** Soda bottle top

# 194
## STUFFED SOLE
By Zhouqin Burnikel

**ACROSS**

1 Desktop computer brand
5 Like some cheddar
10 Period in office
14 Tale spanning centuries, perhaps
15 Potato, e.g.
16 What some buns are made of
17 It usually bursts after a few seconds
19 Jump shot trajectories
20 "Modern Family" actress Winter
21 Source of "shtick" and "schmooze"
23 Bit of advancement
26 Compete
27 Blocking of the sun's light by the moon
33 Crunches strengthen them
36 Pocket bread
37 Asset for a comedian
38 "Ain't happening"
40 Flow back
42 Bit of publicity
43 Film editor Schoonmaker
46 Prejudice
49 Blowhard's problem
50 Who you know
53 Adelaide-born pop singer
54 Muffle
57 Free-roaming horse
61 Change direction
63 Lion feature
64 Like some storage devices
67 Soprano's showcase
68 Slip away from
69 Appreciative verses
70 ___-door neighbor
71 Kept under wraps
72 Signals that become greens

**DOWN**

1 "The Lovebirds" star Rae
2 Like the haka
3 One more time
4 Silly pranks
5 Nickname that links R and V
6 Airport with many layovers
7 Soccer great Wambach
8 Experience 3-Down
9 Prognosticate
10 Som tam cuisine
11 Some are pierced
12 Like mooncakes
13 "___ Dalloway said she would buy the flowers herself"
18 Low-pitched electronic noise
22 Place to get a sandwich
24 Broadway star Stroker
25 Medjool ___ (sweet fruit)
28 Synagogue leader
29 Little devil
30 Heap
31 Like skinny jeans
32 Frozen waffle brand
33 Insects with a carpenter variety

**34** ___ chic
**35** Design detail, for short
**39** Olivia's father on "Scandal"
**41** Eagle or kite
**44** Pole on a ship
**45** Made-up names
**47** Bandage brand
**48** Is really good
**51** ___ oil
**52** Job title for Emmanuelle Alt
**55** Slip away from
**56** Prominent
**57** Mule's mother

**58** Operating system developed at Bell Labs
**59** Aisle ___
**60** Excess
**62** Poet Gallagher
**63** "Holy Toledo!"
**65** Wedding words
**66** Skunk's home

# 195
## IN A BIT
By Evan Kalish

**ACROSS**

1 Assist
4 Actress Jessica
8 Baby's bed
12 Be unhumble
14 Den denizen
15 Speaker's asset
16 Region with many churches
18 ___ closet
19 Guarantee
20 Proven to be false
22 Chief Justice Warren
24 Rescue pro in an ambulance
25 Many animated images
28 Fashionista's sense
31 NGOs, e.g.
35 "I've got it!"
36 Beach getup
38 Reduce, ___, recycle
40 Enjoy some shabu-shabu, say
41 Many a Claudia Rankine opus
42 Dessert in a boat
45 Show that starts at 11:29:30 p.m. ET
46 Spoken exam
47 Knight's ride
48 Reusable bag
49 "___ seeing things?"
51 Brother of Cain and Abel
53 Portrayer of Eve in "Killing Eve" and Ava in "Meditation Park"
58 Comes up
62 Couldn't-have-done-it reason
63 Bearded farm dweller

65 Teeny bits
66 October birthstone
67 Garden sprayer
68 Does, bucks, and fawns
69 Catch sight of
70 Just-introduced

**DOWN**

1 Palindromic Swedish band
2 State flower of Tennessee
3 Hair gel amounts
4 Province where Joni Mitchell was born
5 Be dishonest
6 Assertive
7 Poker pot starter
8 50-50 flip
9 Skaters' place
10 "Ah, gotcha"
11 Curve in the road
13 Affixes with an adhesive
15 Fruit such as the damson
17 Noteworthy time period
21 "How have you ___?"
23 Most recent
25 "Grand Hotel" star Greta
26 "Rumor has it . . ."
27 Counterpart of flora
29 Geometric figure
30 Book publisher's offerings
32 Waverly Place surname
33 Not just big
34 Fashionista's sense
36 Big ___ (London landmark)

**37** Comprehend
**39** Station with greens
**43** Tajikistan's continent
**44** "If everything goes right . . ."
**48** Femur's place
**50** Hospital scans
**52** Give it a go
**53** "Mama ___" (Shirelles classic)
**54** Succulent plant
**55** Late time, informally
**56** Jennifer Paull's instrument
**57** Fanny pack's place
**59** Before long

**60** Alleviate
**61** Feijoada, e.g.
**64** Single trip across a pool

# 196
## INNER EAR
By Caitlin Reid

**ACROSS**

1 Food in an edible shell
5 Basil-based sauce
10 Place for a bib
14 So many
15 Decided
16 ___ vera
17 Provide some comic relief
19 Road-tripping game
20 School in Philly
21 Concert merch
22 ___ clown
23 Like your nose right when you can't scratch it, perhaps
25 "___ sells seashells by the seashore . . ."
26 Sasha Obama's sister
28 ___ job
32 Little kiddo
33 "Oh, boohoo!"
36 Ways to escape
38 High points
39 Snack in Spain
40 Peripheral regions
43 Small amount of glue
44 Lacking manners
45 Store sticker
47 "What ___ that?!"
48 Line on a cover
50 Starting sound of "cup"
53 Prefix for "existent"
54 Male deer
57 Bluish-green hue
58 Who said "A photograph is a secret about a secret"
61 July birthstone
62 Bookstore that's not part of a chain, for short
63 Fit for the task
64 Long to be with
65 Painting holder
66 School in New Haven

**DOWN**

1 ___ Mahal
2 Resting on
3 Pepsi's rival
4 Low-scoring futbol result
5 ___ favor (Spanish "please")
6 Geologic time unit
7 Prepare for an exam
8 Hundreds column neighbor
9 Kooky
10 Did a perfect job
11 Disney ice queen
12 Acquires, informally
13 Piano parts
18 Playful caper
22 Overcook on the barbecue, perhaps
24 Floor coverings
25 Seasoning derived from ocean water
26 Lament a loss
27 Upper-story room
28 Fake from a Washington Capital

**29** Manage to sidestep
**30** Country where the Himalayan Times is published
**31** Humdrum
**32** What douhua is made with
**34** "Woo!"
**35** Damage
**37** Winter school closings
**41** Dip for chips, for short
**42** Dip for chips
**46** Double-cross
**48** Bumpy amphibians
**49** Type of belly button

**50** Damage
**51** Spanish "here"
**52** Cleans with a cloth, say
**53** Simone, the High Priestess of Soul
**55** Swedish supergroup
**56** Beach bird
**58** Casino item
**59** Sushi fish
**60** "I told you so!"

# 197
## SIDE OF RICE
By Zhouqin Burnikel

### ACROSS

1 People with very dark makeup, often
6 "I have no ___!"
10 Not mention
14 Feel the same
15 Poutine bit
16 Swarming collective
17 Kodiak and grizzly, e.g.
19 Like small chances
20 Movie backdrop
21 Sale offerings
22 Minty drink
23 Old mattress problem
24 Touch affectionately
25 Fragrant blossom used in some green teas
31 Actress Essence
32 Breakfast food that might be rolled
33 Throw high
36 Invalidate
37 Target for some beetles
38 In real time
39 Sound system component
40 Like a center in the WNBA
42 Followed an eating regimen
44 Tendency to steal
47 Potpourri container
49 Bumbling sort
50 Loafs around
51 "Wheel of Fortune" star White
53 Tackle a bunny slope
56 Pack for a copier
57 Undomesticated beast
59 "Anything ___?"
60 Fingernail shape
61 Disruptive blog visitor
62 Hatchling's sanctuary
63 "Child's play!"
64 Wise ones

### DOWN

1 Chews the fat
2 Fairy tale beast
3 Jogging pace
4 Chop down
5 Submits
6 The Pleistocene Epoch, e.g.
7 ___-purpose (having two uses)
8 Slips up
9 Some magazine pages
10 "Yeah, right"
11 Beer brand
12 Climbing plants
13 Office subs
18 Rice accompaniment
22 Face parts
24 Portable bed
25 Indonesian island
26 Molecule part
27 Avoids a subject, perhaps
28 ___-cap stocks
29 Unwise undertaking
30 On the ___ (fleeing)
34 Finished
35 Tanning salon fixtures
37 Yellowstone Park grazer

**38** Relay segment
**40** Knotted accessories
**41** Division of a play
**42** ___ Prince (Wonder Woman's alter ego)
**43** Young children
**45** Host of an annual May gala
**46** Nice way of remembering something
**47** "Wee-ooh-wee-ooh" source
**48** "Rumour Has It" singer
**51** "___ Mexico!"
**52** "If only . . ."

**53** Air problem
**54** Veggie with tough stems
**55** Problems
**57** Great misery
**58** Savings plan initials

# 198
## AT THE PLAYGROUND
By Stella Zawistowski

**ACROSS**

1 Bread with a pocket
5 Stickers on license plates
9 Top grade
14 It turns litmus paper red
15 Stole or boa
16 Poetry's counterpart
17 Drop in the mail
18 Trickle slowly
19 Baby food, often
20 Physics model for neutrino masses
23 What a sheep says
24 Flamenco shout
25 Skewered treat with peanut sauce
28 Key in computer combinations
30 "Amanpour & Company" network
33 Desert water source
34 Edinburgh young'un
35 Second-largest branch of Islam
36 Old-school presentation aids
40 "Downton Abbey" title
41 Compete like Eliud Kipchoge
42 Contents of gloves
43 Poem of praise
44 Feature of Rome's Pantheon
45 Quartet on a car
46 Drink slowly
47 Not feel so hot
48 Makes a failed attempt
57 Summer camp vessel

58 Vein underground
59 Bowlful in Brazil
60 Unpleasant scents
61 Plaza payment
62 Go the distance
63 Core belief
64 Toe the line
65 Sequoia National Park sight

**DOWN**

1 Not fail
2 Frozen drink brand
3 One of four on a fork, usually
4 Throws in
5 Like some streets and radios
6 Pleasant scent
7 Female ___ (film theory concept)
8 Word before "sheet" or "script"
9 Shock and dismay
10 Plum, after dehydrating
11 ___ Grimes ("The Walking Dead" character)
12 Gets some mileage out of
13 Give the impression of being
21 "If life has ___ that it stands upon . . ." (Woolf)
22 Swarm of people
25 Dish with croutons, perhaps
26 "All kidding ___ . . ."
27 Neat
28 Make an exact copy of
29 ___ Mahal

**30** Device for texting
**31** Aviary residents
**32** Mouth off to
**33** Capital of Norway
**35** Have the biggest role
**37** Stage items
**38** ___ raisin ice cream
**39** Cook-off dish
**44** Summary
**45** Punctual
**46** Boring thing
**47** Confuse
**48** Edinburgher, e.g.

**49** Make use of hip boots
**50** Privy to
**51** The "A" in SATB
**52** Novice, informally
**53** Pepper's partner
**54** Villain voiced by Chiwetel Ejiofor in 2019's "The Lion King"
**55** Difficulty's opposite
**56** On-___ inspection

# 199
## CUT THE DECK
By Brooke Husic & Evan Kalish

**ACROSS**

1 Wrapped garment
6 Wrapped garment
10 Genre for The Bodysnatchers
13 Bicker
14 Pictures on a desktop
16 Little ___ (pop group)
17 Reverify
19 Wonderment
20 Green Chemistry Challenge org.
21 Youngster
22 Combination of two things
24 Mythology, e.g.
25 Orchestra's place
26 Football player covering a wide receiver, often
32 Sans-___ font
34 "Number the Stars" author Lowry
35 "Parasite" actress Jung-eun
36 Is the target of successful revenge
37 Shampoo bottle promise
39 Depend
40 Full-screen exit key
41 Sound of impatience
42 Accords
43 USPS vehicle
47 Prefix for "conscious"
48 Pinkish
49 Blazer accompaniment
52 "For sure"
53 ___ Paulo

56 Prefix for "factor"
57 "Unsquare Dance" composer
60 Word in a World Cup chant
61 It's less important in a game of chance
62 Word before "bear" or "opposite"
63 Halsey's "___ at Love"
64 Small Business Saturday event
65 Coppola who won Best Director at Cannes in 2017

**DOWN**

1 Band with the debut album "Diamond Life"
2 Farm output
3 Oceano liquid
4 Tofu steak coating
5 Made one's Spidey sense tingle
6 Make upset, in a way
7 Feeling in one's heart (or other muscles)
8 Poke bowl topping
9 One of more than 1.6 million in a marathon
10 Know-it-all
11 Fruit similar to pitaya
12 Terminated
15 Maintains a long-distance friendship, maybe
18 Bronte protagonist
23 Race runner's identifier
24 Garlands given as gifts

## Crossword Grid

| 1 | 2 | 3 | 4 | 5 | | 6 | 7 | 8 | 9 | | | 10 | 11 | 12 |
|---|---|---|---|---|---|---|---|---|---|---|---|---|---|---|
| 13 | | | | | | 14 | | | | 15 | | 16 | | |
| 17 | | | | 18 | | | | | | | | 19 | | |
| 20 | | | | 21 | | | | | 22 | | 23 | | | |
| | | 24 | | | | | | | | 25 | | | | |
| | 26 | | | | | 27 | 28 | 29 | | | | | 30 | 31 |
| 32 | 33 | | | | | 34 | | | | | 35 | | | |
| 36 | | | | 37 | 38 | | | | | 39 | | | | |
| 40 | | | 41 | | | | | | 42 | | | | | |
| 43 | | | 44 | | | | | 45 | 46 | | | | | |
| | 47 | | | | | | 48 | | | | | | | |
| 49 | 50 | | | 51 | | 52 | | | | | 53 | 54 | 55 | |
| 56 | | | 57 | | 58 | | | | 59 | | | | | |
| 60 | | | 61 | | | | | 62 | | | | | | |
| 63 | | | 64 | | | | | 65 | | | | | | |

**Down**

26 Washed without water
27 Like a frog
28 Electrolyte component
29 "C'est la ___!"
30 Boston hooper, for short
31 Tab and Caps Lock, e.g.
32 Hightailed it
33 Relieve
37 With 38-Down, pronoun pair
38 See 37-Down
39 Risque
41 Dodges
42 Some taekwondo conditioning

44 "Eww!"
45 ___ clef
46 Engine sound
49 Radio part
50 Spanish greeting
51 ___ Fifth Avenue
52 Shout
53 "The Source of ___-Regard" (Morrison collection)
54 South American berry
55 Bhindi bhaji ingredient
58 By means of
59 Halloween sound

# 200
# BROKERAGE
By Zhouqin Burnikel

**ACROSS**

1 Passionate partner dance
6 Ariana Grande song about needing space
10 Programs on mobile devices
14 Shy away from
15 Moisturizer brand
16 Takeover
17 It can be caused by a hailstorm
19 Spare, e.g.
20 "You're on your ___"
21 Diagnostic aids
22 Slight coloration
23 "Very funny!"
24 Had a hunch
25 62, for many Americans
30 Eschew nuptial formalities
31 MIT Sloan degrees
32 Prefix for "cycle" or "athlete"
35 Trees with coarse-grained wood
36 Pleasure trip, informally
38 "That's just the way ___"
39 National Donor Day mo.
40 Plumbing piece
41 Flared dress style
42 Economic aid measure
46 Like western Alaska's population
48 Commits a faux pas
49 Contaminate
50 Place for a hibachi
52 "Not a huge fan"

55 Bad-mannered
56 Traditional side dish for sauerbraten
58 Brewpub selections
59 Meat inspector's org.
60 Cady's "Mean Girls" love interest
61 Segment
62 The majority
63 Long lock of hair

**DOWN**

1 ___ cake (dim sum item)
2 State with conviction
3 Time for a lunch break, often
4 Format for some memes
5 "In all likelihood . . ."
6 Polite response
7 Astronaut Shepard
8 Loses firmness
9 Yes vote
10 Emma Watson skill
11 Plant associated with Christmas
12 Remove
13 Sprinter's forte
18 Persistent pain
22 Lapsang souchong and pu'er, e.g.
23 "___ Don't Lie" (Shakira song)
24 Stick around
25 Great Barrier ___
26 "Maleficent" actress Fanning

USA TODAY

**27** Franchise whose main character is Lara Croft
**28** Host
**29** Org. in which Becky Hammon coaches
**33** Toe accessory
**34** "Now it's clear"
**36** "Miami ___"
**37** Satyajit Ray protagonist
**38** Sorts
**40** Sibilant attention-getter
**41** Tightrope walker, for example
**43** Serious-sounding name
**44** Scratching post user
**45** Oratorio solo
**46** Helmet attachment
**47** "Forever Your Girl" singer Abdul
**50** Manila currency
**51** Tacks on
**52** Female zebra
**53** Senses of self-importance
**54** Female pheasants
**56** Mojito ingredient
**57** ___ none

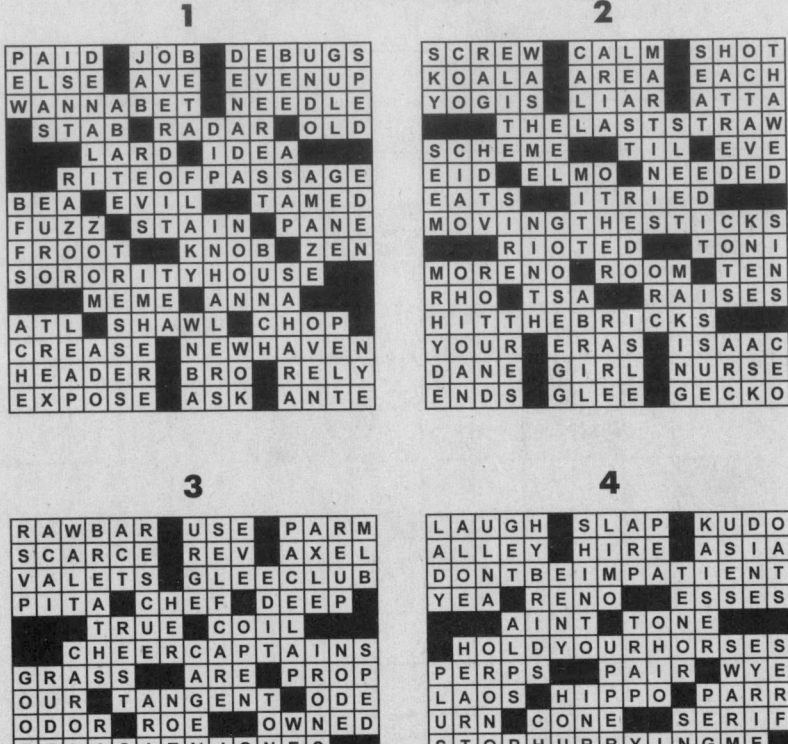

## 6

RIFT FLU SABERS
OKRA RAN ELEVEN
DEALTOUT LATINO
EATER GOOFS LOW
NOAH LIKE
SALTOFTHEEARTH
ALI PLEA SNARES
RING RNA SELL
AVERSE ODIN ALA
EDUCATIONALTOY
BORE PAVE
AHA OWLET ENJOY
LOSTTO DIALTONE
BOOMER GOD INCA
AFFIRM END LIES

## 7

AGENT FENG ODE
DALAI COCOA POR
SHINETHEORY PUN
AGUA NAIROBI
TAP ABIT CASTE
GLIMMEROFHOPE
ISSUE PAINT
FOAM WATTS UHOH
BRASH TRYME
FLASHINTHEPAN
SLEEP SOAR ERS
WINDSOR OLES
ABC TWINKLETOES
RYE AIDES PARTY
MAS REST MYBAD

## 8

COMMA KFC ANGLO
CRUEL OAR COOED
SAYNO RIO ADDED
BUTTERFLIES
LEI WASTE ERA
AYEAYE SCONES
SENSORS PSANDQS
PUPPYLOVE
OVER SIREN ARMS
FEDON TSA ATEAT
FRAMES SLANGY
SMITTENKITTEN
BAAS EVENT IWAS
ACME MIMIC META
DEED SLOTH EDEN

## 9

WELSH TWAS AGES
EXILE HINT SUMO
TIMORLESTE STAR
STAG UMPIRE FIT
ARTS EASELS
HANNAH FORCE
ACE KOALA ALAS
THEPERFECTCRIME
HYDE RETRO NBA
TEMPO ORIGIN
SCORER CUED
YAK HOTDOG ICON
NINA TIETHEGAME
TROT IDLE PILES
HOWL PETS STINI

## 10

STUB ASTER TSK
OHNO STAGE POLO
FAMOUSAMOS AFAR
TIE GENE PINUPS
STRAND LOSES
ANT RANTRACK
BAYED MOPS ALOE
ADO AROUSES AMY
LAUD ANNE CODES
IMSOGLAD SUN
AGILE REBELS
STINGY TOGA YAP
AIDA CIRCUSACTS
GRIP ALIKE IRIS
SET PLOYS RANT

## 11

```
CHIC   TAPAS   HEAD
LENO   AGENT   OGLE
ORAL   GHANA   TOOL
GOLDSTAR   DAMSEL
 SLOPES   SIRI
   PLATINUMCARD
 DREAM   MOM   RAY
MEANT   APB   PRICE
ALI   PIE   SUEDE
SILVERLINING
  EROS   INKING
INSERT   LEADFOOT
SOUR   EDICT   TOTE
LORE   CIDER   ENOS
EKED   TESSA   DENT
```

## 12

```
 APE   SASHA   AQUA
ODOR   ACHOO   DULY
THIRDWHEEL   DINE
TON   EYED   JONAS
OCTAVE   IWONT
  BIRTHDAYSUIT
SKILL   WOLFS   PAW
ANTE   ZIPIT   OLGA
YES   SAXON   OREOS
SEARCHENGINE
  LOANS   REMAKE
ALLOT   WHOA   LAT
MISS   GREENLIGHT
MEET   OHARE   LALA
OUTS   TONED   LEO
```

## 13

```
SITUP   ELATE   STL
OHARE   NOLAN   TOE
SOUNDADVICE   ANN
OPT   ALOE   OMANIS
  BLEW   TBIRD
APPLES   TREEFARM
CLOUD   TOOLS   LEE
MUIR   SWILL   COPS
ESS   SPILL   CANES
SHORTAGE   BARELY
  NORMS   TART
REDTEA   SILL   ACE
ERA   ELECTIONDAY
FIR   TOTAL   ADAGE
SET   STARE   NAMED
```

## 14

```
GASUP   SNAG   SCAB
ALINE   HOLE   HILL
BENDS   ALOT   AVIA
  GOODNIGHTKISS
COL   UKE   ERECTS
OPENIT   PLY
MEMORYCHIP   REAM
IRONS   LET   SELMA
CAME   KARAOKEBAR
  BAY   PYLONS
ARCTIC   ABE   WAH
PARACHUTEDROP
ADAM   ISEE   OHARA
RITE   NEAT   MIDAS
TOES   ARTS   POSTS
```

## 15

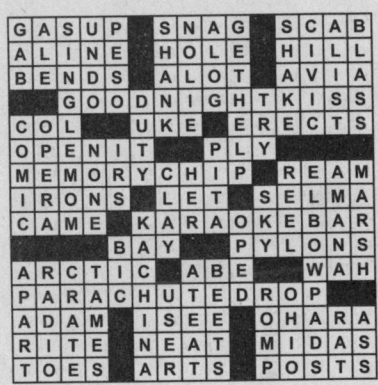

```
CAPE   DART   GYRO
ASIA   OHNO   LAUD
SHARONOSBOURNE
EON   DAY   APED
STOPIT   AGE   ICE
  SINEADOCONNOR
ATL   SOD   MEDIA
PROAM   LEG   GAINS
EMOTE   DOT   TAS
SOLEDADOBRIEN
ORS   CAN   INNOUT
  MALT   PDF   CSI
SHAQUILLEONEAL
PERU   NOUN   SAID
AREA   GUST   ANNE
```

## 16

```
D A B   A C T N O W   U S S R
A L A   C O R O N A   N A P A
H O B O S P I D E R   B U R N
L U A U     U S B   I D I G
      S A T C H E L P A I G E
S P O T T E R   C E O S
I O N   F L E D   D E L T A
F L I P   L E A D S   D A W N
T O T E M   M E N U   S O N
      P A C T   F I N E S S E
C L U T C H H I T T E R
H U L A   U R N   M P A A
I N T L   T O T E B O A R D S
L A R K   E A R N E D   O A K
I R A S   S T A T E D   P M S
```

## 17

```
P I B B   D E P A R T   B R A
A R I A   I S A Y N O   E O N
P O N Y E X P R E S S   S I T
I N G R A I N S   T I T L E
      U T E   R O A D S
P A D M A   S P I N Y E E L S
A D E   T E A A C T   A L O E
R I P E   A N C H O   S L O G
T E E N   S T E E P S   E M U
B U N N Y E A R S   T E R S E
    D U E L S   T A X
T R A I L   B A R R I E R S
W E B   L E M O N Y E L L O W
I L L   E V E N T S   E M M A
N Y E   D A R N I T   S O A P
```

## 18

```
B E A M S   M A C   C H A M P
E M C E E   A L A   A U D I O
T I T A N   R I V E R B A N K
S T I N T S   I O L D   G E E
    V I O L A   R B I   E R R
C H I E F O F S T A F F
I M S   F O A L   F I S T S
T O T S   P R I M A   G M A N
E S S A Y   C A L C   E L I
      C O A T E D T A B L E T
M A S   U T E   D E V I L
O C T   K O N O   R E S A L E
C H A I N M A I L   S T R A W
H E L L O   N B A   I R A T E
A S K E W   T E X   N O T E S
```

## 19

```
G A D O T   T U N E   E C H O
A L A M O   E G A N   N O O K
P I N G P O N G P A D D L E S
E S C   P R O S   M A I D
S T F E L E R   D O N T A S K
      T I S   F O R K   S H E
    A T O N   N U D E   I A N
D I N G D O N G D I T C H
P I G   R O D E   G O E S
H E H   S U N S   A U G
O U T C O M E   F L E A B A G
    K I A S   O A T S   L I L
K I N G K O N G C O S T U M E
A S I A   L O R E   S I R E N
L O T R   O W E S   O A S E S
```

## 20

```
H I S S   L E S S   O S C A R
M O A T   E X P O   B L U T O
M U N I C I P A L C O U R T S
    T R A C E   P E R S I A
E V A   B A R C A R   E R R
L E A K   T O M   M O S E Y
M E N A C E   L E V I S
    P A P A L C O N C L A V E
      O N I O N   R E G A L E
S K E W S   L E O   E M M A
T E X   P A L M E D   P O T
R E P A I R   E M O J I
E P I S C O P A L C H U R C H
E E R I E   E P E E   D E E M
P R E S S   P E T E   O S L O
```

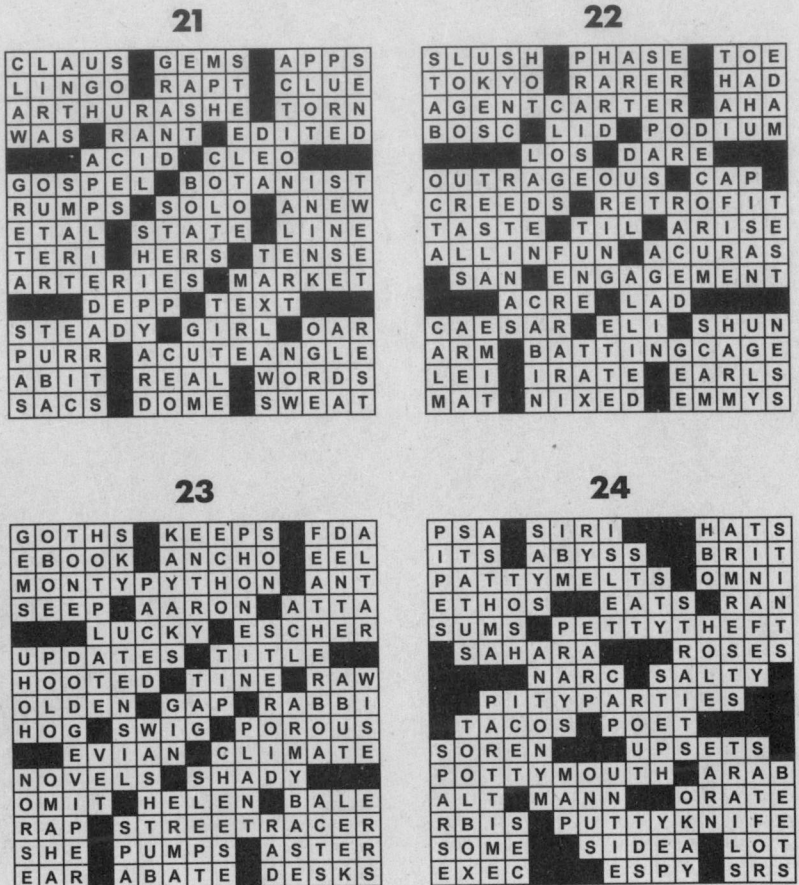

## 21

| C | L | A | U | S | | G | E | M | S | | A | P | P | S |
| L | I | N | G | O | | R | A | P | T | | C | L | U | E |
| A | R | T | H | U | R | A | S | H | E | | T | O | R | N |
| W | A | S | | R | A | N | T | | E | D | I | T | E | D |
| | | A | C | I | D | | C | L | E | O | | | | |
| G | O | S | P | E | L | | B | O | T | A | N | I | S | T |
| R | U | M | P | S | | S | O | L | O | | A | N | E | W |
| E | T | A | L | | S | T | A | T | E | | L | I | N | E |
| T | E | R | I | | H | E | R | S | | T | E | N | S | E |
| A | R | T | E | R | I | E | S | | M | A | R | K | E | T |
| | | D | E | P | P | | T | E | X | T | | | | |
| S | T | E | A | D | Y | | G | I | R | L | | O | A | R |
| P | U | R | R | | A | C | U | T | E | A | N | G | L | E |
| A | B | I | T | | R | E | A | L | | W | O | R | D | S |
| S | A | C | S | | D | O | M | E | | S | W | E | A | T |

## 22

| S | L | U | S | H | | P | H | A | S | E | | T | O | E |
| T | O | K | Y | O | | R | A | R | E | R | | H | A | D |
| A | G | E | N | T | C | A | R | T | E | R | | A | H | A |
| B | O | S | C | | L | I | D | | P | O | D | I | U | M |
| | | | L | O | S | | D | A | R | E | | | | |
| O | U | T | R | A | G | E | O | U | S | | C | A | P | |
| C | R | E | E | D | S | | R | E | T | R | O | F | I | T |
| T | A | S | T | E | | T | I | L | | A | R | I | S | E |
| A | L | L | I | N | F | U | N | | A | C | U | R | A | S |
| | | S | A | N | | E | N | G | A | G | E | M | E | N | T |
| | | A | C | R | E | | L | A | D | | | | | |
| C | A | E | S | A | R | | E | L | I | | S | H | U | N |
| A | R | M | | B | A | T | T | I | N | G | C | A | G | E |
| L | E | I | | I | R | A | T | E | | E | A | R | L | S |
| M | A | T | | N | I | X | E | D | | E | M | M | Y | S |

## 23

| G | O | T | H | S | | K | E | E | P | S | | F | D | A |
| E | B | O | O | K | | A | N | C | H | O | | E | E | L |
| M | O | N | T | Y | P | Y | T | H | O | N | | A | N | T |
| S | E | E | P | | A | A | R | O | N | | A | T | T | A |
| | | | L | U | C | K | Y | | E | S | C | H | E | R |
| U | P | D | A | T | E | S | | T | I | T | L | E | | |
| H | O | O | T | E | D | | T | I | N | E | | R | A | W |
| O | L | D | E | N | | G | A | P | | R | A | B | B | I |
| H | O | G | | S | W | I | G | | P | O | R | O | U | S |
| | | E | V | I | A | N | | C | L | I | M | A | T | E |
| N | O | V | E | L | S | | S | H | A | D | Y | | | |
| O | M | I | T | | H | E | L | E | N | | B | A | L | E |
| R | A | P | | S | T | R | E | E | T | R | A | C | E | R |
| S | H | E | | P | U | M | P | S | | A | S | T | E | R |
| E | A | R | | A | B | A | T | E | | D | E | S | K | S |

## 24

| P | S | A | | S | I | R | I | | H | A | T | S |
| I | T | S | | A | B | Y | S | S | | B | R | I | T |
| P | A | T | T | Y | M | E | L | T | S | | O | M | N | I |
| E | T | H | O | S | | E | A | T | S | | R | A | N |
| S | U | M | S | | P | E | T | T | Y | T | H | E | F | T |
| | S | A | H | A | R | A | | R | O | S | E | S |
| | N | A | R | C | | S | A | L | T | Y | | |
| | P | I | T | Y | P | A | R | T | I | E | S | |
| | T | A | C | O | S | | P | O | E | T | | |
| S | O | R | E | N | | U | P | S | E | T | S | |
| P | O | T | T | Y | M | O | U | T | H | | A | R | A | B |
| A | L | T | | M | A | N | N | | O | R | A | T | E |
| R | B | I | S | | P | U | T | T | Y | K | N | I | F | E |
| S | O | M | E | | S | I | D | E | A | | L | O | T |
| E | X | E | C | | E | S | P | Y | | S | R | S |

## 25

| O | R | C | A | | M | E | L | T | S | | S | M | O | G |
| F | E | E | L | | O | L | I | V | E | | C | A | V | E |
| F | A | L | L | E | N | S | T | A | R | | I | K | E | A |
| | L | L | A | M | A | | E | D | E | N | | E | R | R |
| | | Y | O | L | K | | S | N | U | B | S | | |
| A | S | I | | I | O | S | | A | D | L | I | B |
| R | A | M | | A | S | H | E | S | | G | A | T | E | S |
| M | U | S | I | C | A | L | E | N | S | E | M | B | L | E |
| S | N | O | O | T | | S | T | O | P | S | | I | L | L |
| | A | S | T | I | N | | O | U | R | | G | E | L |
| | C | A | N | E | S | | T | A | I | L | | |
| S | P | A | | G | P | A | S | | I | D | I | O | M |
| P | E | R | M | | A | L | L | E | N | S | C | R | E | W |
| A | R | E | A | | L | E | A | V | E | | K | A | T | E |
| N | U | D | E | | I | M | M | A | D | | S | L | E | D |

## 26

```
TADA  SMOG  SPURT
AGED  HOME  HANOI
LUAU  ASIN  ANIME
CARBONATEDWATER
    AUDI    ELM
AMP  TYCOONS  SIS
LEAVE   TNT  BAMA
GENERALHOSPITAL
ATIT  SEE  ADAGE
ESC  CHARMIN  YES
   RAO   AMEN
SQUIRTINGFLOWER
OUNCE  TONI  RAMI
HADES  EDEN  TRIP
ODORS  METE  HERE
```

## 27

```
ACHES  DOTS  SMOG
DRANK  IDEA  HAWN
WEDDINGDAY  IKEA
ATE  WOES  SPENT
RESEEDS  RIOTS
   WASTEOFMONEY
AFTER  CAFE  IRA
VIE  SCARY  CAM
OJS  POOR  CRESS
WITHOUTDELAY
  PURRS  DETESTS
WRIST  FINS  ART
HILT  WALTDISNEY
IDOL  ALOE  TOTAL
PETE  NEED  SPADE
```

## 28

```
DEBT  DARE  TOPS
AMID  SINEX  ISEE
WAGS  PENNE  PLEA
NIP  METEORSTORM
SLIPONS  CEO
  CLOD  PRICEWAR
GOTON  CLASS  OHO
ABUT  PEACE  CREW
PER  BUNNY  PALMS
EYETESTS  WORD
  ITS  TENTPEG
BISCAYNEBAY  ODE
LOOK  COLOR  IWIN
AWOL  AGONY  SECT
BANE  TONE  ARTS
```

## 29

```
RATON  SMELT  TAB
EVADE  EAGER  HUE
FIXEDINCOME  ARE
 DIS  MDS  ONSTAR
   SAGS  ENDED
PLANO  TVS  ROIL
DRE  TOMEI  VENI
VESTEDINTERESTS
DOSE  ATARI  IRA
SPEX  PMS  ALITA
  RADII  USED
THESIS  ABE  UGH
REV  STATEDINNER
AKI  COLOR  SNARE
PAL  SLAMS  TOILED
```

## 30

```
MAPS  CHAFF  BOAS
IRAN  RADII  UMNO
CECEWINANS  MIND
ESTEEMS  ICEDTEA
   RBI  STALE
OWNS  NENELEAKES
RHO  PALL  CLOUT
EAT  ILK  APT  ORA
CLONE  EGOS  KOI
KEKEPALMER  USSR
  MARIO  RUN
SILENTK  SINATRA
OPUS  FEFEDOBSON
FARE  USING  LAST
ASKS  LORDE  ERAS
```

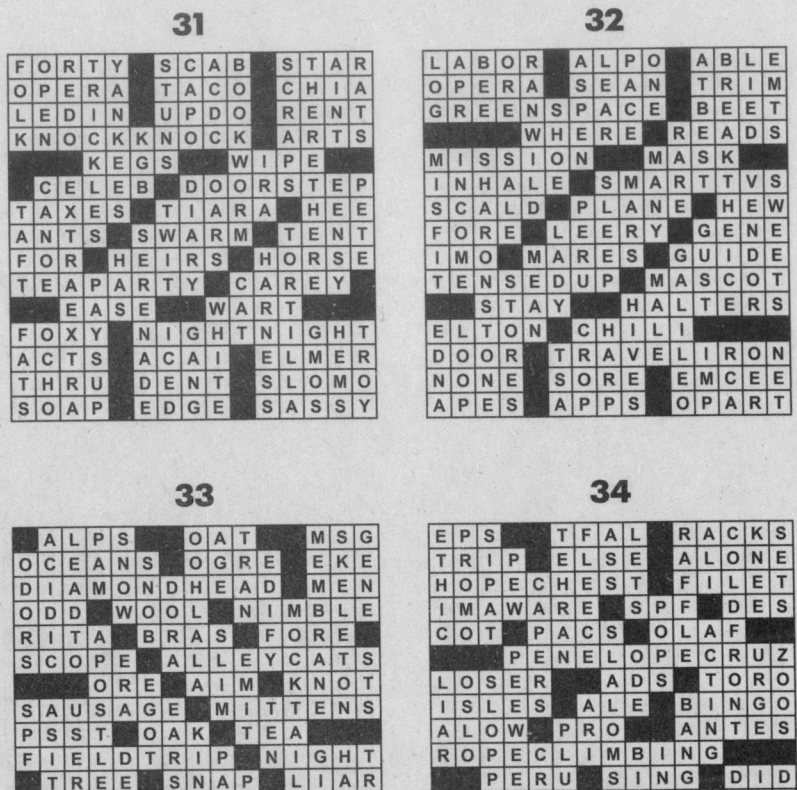

**31**

| F | O | R | T | Y | | S | C | A | B | | S | T | A | R |
| O | P | E | R | A | | T | A | C | O | | C | H | I | A |
| L | E | D | I | N | | U | P | D | O | | R | E | N | T |
| K | N | O | C | K | K | N | O | C | K | | A | R | T | S |
| | | K | E | G | S | | | W | I | P | E | | | |
| | C | E | L | E | B | | D | O | O | R | S | T | E | P |
| T | A | X | E | S | | T | I | A | R | A | | H | E | E |
| A | N | T | S | | S | W | A | R | M | | T | E | N | T |
| F | O | R | | H | E | I | R | S | | H | O | R | S | E |
| T | E | A | P | A | R | T | Y | | C | A | R | E | Y | |
| | | E | A | S | E | | | W | A | R | T | | | |
| F | O | X | Y | | N | I | G | H | T | N | I | G | H | T |
| A | C | T | S | | A | C | A | I | | E | L | M | E | R |
| T | H | R | U | | D | E | N | T | | S | L | O | M | O |
| S | O | A | P | | E | D | G | E | | S | A | S | S | Y |

**32**

| L | A | B | O | R | | A | L | P | O | | A | B | L | E |
| O | P | E | R | A | | S | E | A | N | | T | R | I | M |
| G | R | E | E | N | S | P | A | C | E | | B | E | E | T |
| | | | W | H | E | R | E | | R | E | A | D | S | |
| M | I | S | S | I | O | N | | M | A | S | K | | | |
| I | N | H | A | L | E | | S | M | A | R | T | T | V | S |
| S | C | A | L | D | | P | L | A | N | E | | H | E | W |
| F | O | R | E | | L | E | E | R | Y | | G | E | N | E |
| I | M | O | | M | A | R | E | S | | G | U | I | D | E |
| T | E | N | S | E | D | U | P | | M | A | S | C | O | T |
| | | | S | T | A | Y | | H | A | L | T | E | R | S |
| E | L | T | O | N | | C | H | I | L | I | | | | |
| D | O | O | R | | T | R | A | V | E | L | I | R | O | N |
| N | O | N | E | | S | O | R | E | | E | M | C | E | E |
| A | P | E | S | | A | P | P | S | | O | P | A | R | T |

**33**

| | A | L | P | S | | O | A | T | | | M | S | G | |
| O | C | E | A | N | S | | O | G | R | E | | E | K | E |
| D | I | A | M | O | N | D | H | E | A | D | | M | E | N |
| O | D | D | | W | O | O | L | | N | I | M | B | L | E |
| R | I | T | A | | B | R | A | S | | F | O | R | E | |
| S | C | O | P | E | | A | L | L | E | Y | C | A | T | S |
| | | R | E | | A | I | M | | K | N | O | T | | |
| S | A | U | S | A | G | E | | M | I | T | T | E | N | S |
| P | S | S | T | | O | A | K | | T | E | A | | | |
| F | I | E | L | D | T | R | I | P | | N | I | G | H | T |
| | T | R | E | E | | S | N | A | P | | L | I | A | R |
| O | W | N | S | I | T | | D | R | O | P | | V | I | E |
| P | E | A | | C | O | U | R | T | O | R | D | E | R | S |
| A | R | M | | E | L | S | E | | H | O | U | N | D | S |
| L | E | E | | | D | A | D | | | S | O | S | O | |

**34**

| E | P | S | | T | F | A | L | | R | A | C | K | S | |
| T | R | I | P | | E | L | S | E | | A | L | O | N | E |
| H | O | P | E | C | H | E | S | T | | F | I | L | E | T |
| I | M | A | W | A | R | E | | S | P | F | | D | E | S |
| C | O | T | | P | A | C | S | | O | L | A | F | | |
| | | | P | E | N | E | L | O | P | E | C | R | U | Z |
| L | O | S | E | R | | A | D | S | | T | O | R | O | |
| I | S | L | E | S | | A | L | E | | B | I | N | G | O |
| A | L | O | W | | P | R | O | | A | N | T | E | S | |
| R | O | P | E | C | L | I | M | B | I | N | G | | | |
| | | | P | E | R | U | | S | I | N | G | | D | I | D |
| S | L | Y | | A | M | P | | G | R | U | Y | E | R | E |
| C | A | J | U | N | | E | U | R | O | P | E | C | U | P |
| A | C | O | R | N | | A | R | E | A | | S | O | L | O |
| T | E | E | N | Y | | K | I | D | D | | | Y | E | T |

**35**

| A | L | P | S | | M | E | S | A | | L | A | M | B |
| N | O | O | K | | O | N | I | C | E | | O | D | O | R |
| T | O | N | I | C | W | A | T | E | R | | C | A | V | E |
| E | N | D | | R | I | C | E | | R | O | A | M | E | D |
| | | | F | O | N | T | | P | A | U | L | | | |
| T | A | P | I | N | G | | M | E | N | T | O | R | E | D |
| I | T | A | L | Y | | S | E | E | D | | F | E | A | R |
| T | E | R | M | | S | C | A | R | S | | F | U | S | E |
| L | I | S | T | | C | O | T | S | | R | I | S | E | S |
| E | T | E | R | N | I | T | Y | | R | E | C | E | S | S |
| | | | A | B | E | T | | H | E | R | E | | | |
| M | E | D | I | A | N | | I | O | W | A | | P | E | P |
| O | R | A | L | | C | O | T | T | O | N | B | A | L | L |
| T | I | N | E | | E | A | G | E | R | | A | L | S | O |
| H | E | A | R | | F | O | L | K | | H | E | E | D | |

## 36

```
AMBER   RAPS   RIMS
LAILA   BALI   IDEA
BIRMINGHAM   NORM
UNDONE   SNUGGLE
MES   FAD   BLAB
    SATIN   ARETHA
SHAWL   VAST   ARAL
NOBELPEACEPRIZE
ONCE   ORCA   HEXES
BESTOW   PRIOR
    THEM   EON   GRR
  FLOORED   WEENIE
ALSO   FREEATLAST
BEAT   UCLA   ALTER
SETH   LILT   GASSY
```

## 37

```
GALA   STRUT   SLOB
PIER   AROSE   KIWI
AROUNDANDAROUND
      BODY   ABAR
SESAME   ATTHAT
COO   ONSTAGE   IRA
INFER   LES   DETER
  AGESANDAGES
BORG   ONTOP   LAGS
IRS   RUG   IPA   TRA
CLOSER   ENTRAP
  AGAINANDAGAIN
SNOB   OREOS   KPOP
IDOL   TITLE   ELLA
RODE   EASED   SEAL
```

## 38

```
MADRE   ROMP   TOP
ARIEL   MINOR   EGO
PERFECTCUBE   ART
SAG   COVES   FARES
  SEETO   TABS
  VOLCANICCONE
AMBER   LFONE   PEA
SEAN   BASRA   BEER
AND   PINOT   FENDS
PUBLICSPHERE
  RUNS   TAPAS
SIEGE   BEAST   WHO
USA   FOODPYRAMID
ELK   OLDIE   OHARE
YES   REST   WANTS
```

## 39

```
SPAN   POEM   ACHED
TACO   ACRE   SHEAR
AILS   TEAS   HEAVY
BLUEGRASSSTATE
    CMON   TOT
BEMOAN   IRAN   FCC
OMANI   ATOM   MARA
WIRELESSSPEAKER
ELKS   DOME   LIETO
DES   RIFE   TINSEL
    PET   SITS
  CLASSSECRETARY
WAIST   AURA   ALOE
EMOTE   GRAD   YOWL
TONED   SOME   STEP
```

## 40

```
BLUE   SPAT   BOARD
RING   PLIE   ARRAY
OCTO   HORN   LATTE
WHISKEYSTILL
SEE   ERS   PSA   AVA
ENDUSE   COLDSNAP
  PHSCALE   HOSE
DELTA   ORE   AUNTS
ALSO   CLASSES
SLAPSHOT   TSHIRT
HAT   PAS   BAO   DUE
PAISLEYPRINT
ERROR   EELS   IDOL
KIOSK   UGLI   PINE
EPEES   MOAN   ETSY
```

## 41

```
A R I D   P I C S   O L D I E
F E T E   D R O P   H E A D Y
L A S T   F A M I L Y T R E E
A C T E D     E R I E   T A S
C H O C O L A T E L A B
    O T T E R     T H E S E
A I L   S N O R T     A W E S
S C A N   S M I R K   D E L I
K E T O     A G A I N   E S P
  D E A N S     I N E P T
    H O L D I N G W A T E R
S R S   S O O N     S L O M O
P I T C H B L A C K   L O O M
I C A R E   E L S A   E T T A
T O N Y S   S L I T   T H E N
```

## 42

```
D I N G   S L O B   S E E M S
U S E R   P E A R   A N G I E
C A M E R A S H Y   W R O T E
K Y O T O   U N E D I T E D
      A T M S     L U C
L A G   C A N V A S S H O E S
I L L   S O O N   T E R R A
L O O T   T R U T H   D A R N
A H O Y S   E C H O     T O T
C A M P E R S H E L L   E R A
      E V E     M E A D
G R A C E F U L     Z E S T S
R E R A N   C A N D Y S H O P
A N G S T   L I E U   K I L O
B O O T H   A N T E   S A L T
```

## 43

```
R O O S T   O A S I S   S U M
P H A I R   W H O R L   I M S
M O R G A N L E F A Y   T A N
    M I A S M A     L I M B
E R R A N T   S A T A N I C
L E O   S E T S   C O B
M I N I     A I R D R O P S
  K A N G A R O O C O U R T
  I N F A M O U S     R I O T
    U M P   X E N A   M A E
C L O S E S T   E S T A T E
H A Z E   R I V A L S
A G O   P L A N E T E A R T H
M E N   S A C K S   E R N I E
P R E   I D E S T   P S A L M
```

## 44

```
C A P E R   D O T   I D L E D
E L I T E   I D O   N E E D Y
D U T C H O V E N   S T A G E
E M T   E R A S   P U R R E D
      D A D S   P O L O
A S S U R E   A T T I M E S
P E T A   R O L L   S T O N E
H E E L   S T E E D   L O D E
I M A C S   T I D E   I D I D
D E M I L L E     F R O S T S
      T I E R   P E E N
N A T I V E   L E N A   A D A
A M A Z E   D E A D L Y S I N
B O X E R   E A R   L E A S T
S K I N S   N F L   Y A N K S
```

## 45

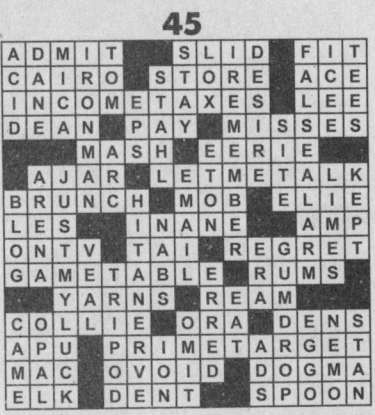

```
A D M I T   S L I D   F I T
C A I R O   S T O R E   A C E
I N C O M E T A X E S   L E E
D E A N   P A Y   M I S S E S
    M A S H   E E R I E
  A J A R   L E T M E T A L K
B R U N C H   M O B   E L I E
L E S   I N A N E     A M P
O N T V   T A I   R E G R E T
G A M E T A B L E   R U M S
  Y A R N S   R E A M
C O L L I E   O R A   D E N S
A P U   P R I M E T A R G E T
M A C   O V O I D   D O G M A
E L K   D E N T   S P O O N
```

## 46

| K | A | S | H | A |   | A | D | D | S |   | C | O | A | X |
| E | L | M | E | R |   | L | O | O | P |   | H | A | V | E |
| P | O | U | R | C | O | L | D | W | A | T | E | R | O | N |
| T | E | T | E |   | M | O | O | N |   | Y | E | S | N | O |
|   |   |   | G | R | I | T |   | V | O | L | T |   |   |   |
| A | F | L | O | A | T |   | P | O | R | E | O | V | E | R |
| D | R | I | E | D |   | H | A | T | E | R |   | O | N | E |
| R | O | T | S |   | M | O | P | E | S |   | R | I | D | E |
| E | Y | E |   | H | O | N | E | S |   | P | O | L | E | S |
| P | O | R | F | A | V | O | R |   | F | A | C | A | D | E |
|   |   |   | E | V | E | R |   | S | A | N | K |   |   |   |
| A | S | T | R | O |   | A | S | T | I |   | S | A | C | K |
| P | O | O | R | C | I | R | C | U | L | A | T | I | O | N |
| P | A | G | E |   | S | I | A | M |   | C | A | R | G | O |
| S | P | A | T |   | H | A | R | P |   | T | R | Y | S | T |

## 47

| A | D | U | L | T |   | A | L | L | S |   | A | B | B | A |
| M | E | N | U | S |   | R | E | U | P |   | C | R | A | B |
| I | N | I | G | O |   | F | I | V | E | S | T | A | R | S |
| G | A | S |   | A | S | S |   | L | O | S |   |   |   |   |
| O | L | E | O | L | E |   | U | R | L | S |   | P | I | T |
| S | I | X | F | I | G | U | R | E | S | A | L | A | R | Y |
|   |   |   | N | O | I | S | E | S |   | A | S | A | P |   |
| A | L | F | O | N | S | O |   | T | H | A | T | O | N | E |
| S | E | A | T |   | P | L | E | A | S | E |   |   |   |   |
| S | E | V | E | N | D | E | A | D | L | Y | S | I | N | S |
| T | S | A |   | E | O | N | S |   | L | E | T | O | U | T |
|   |   |   | T | A | U |   | T | A | S |   | D | R | E |   |
| E | I | G | H | T | B | A | L | L |   | A | R | I | S | E |
| A | C | R | E |   | L | I | E | S |   | P | A | N | E | L |
| T | E | R | M |   | E | R | G | O |   | T | H | E | S | E |

## 48

| A | T | O | M |   | S | H | A | L | L |   | A | C | M | E |
| M | E | G | A |   | H | I | R | E | E |   | S | L | I | T |
| M | E | R | C | H | A | N | T | V | E | S | S | E | L | S |
| O | N | E |   | A | N | T | S | Y |   | C | U | R | L | Y |
|   |   |   | H | U | T | S |   | M | A | R | K | S |   |   |
| L | A | T | E | L | Y |   | S | P | I | R | E |   |   |   |
| I | G | O | R |   | D | I | A | N | E |   | I | A | N |   |
| M | E | R | E | C | O | I | N | C | I | D | E | N | C | E |
| A | D | O |   | H | I | N | G | E |   | G | O | R | E |   |
|   |   |   | R | I | L | E | S |   | P | H | O | N | E | D |
|   | I | T | E | M | S |   | B | A | T | S |   |   |   |   |
| A | D | E | L | E |   | S | T | O | R | M |   | A | R | K |
| M | E | R | E | D | I | T | H | W | I | L | L | S | O | N |
| E | A | R | N |   | P | E | A | L | S |   | A | I | D | E |
| S | L | A | T |   | A | M | I | S | H |   | B | A | S | E |

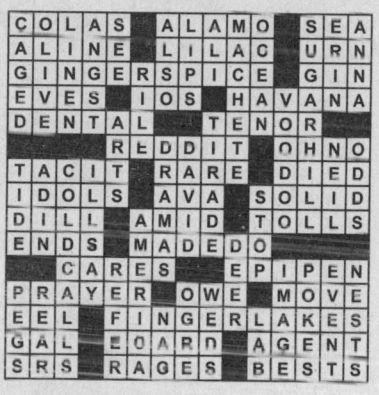

## 49

| C | O | L | A | S |   | A | L | A | M | O |   | S | E | A |
| A | L | I | N | E |   | L | I | L | A | C |   | U | R | N |
| G | I | N | G | E | R | S | P | I | C | E |   | G | I | N |
| E | V | E | S |   | I | O | S |   | H | A | V | A | N | A |
| D | E | N | T | A | L |   | T | E | N | O | R |   |   |   |
|   |   |   | R | E | D | D | I | T |   | O | H | N | O |   |
| T | A | C | I | T |   | R | A | R | E |   | D | I | E | D |
| I | D | O | L | S |   | A | V | A |   | S | O | L | I | D |
| D | I | L | L |   | A | M | I | D |   | T | O | L | L | S |
| E | N | D | S |   | M | A | D | E | D | O |   |   |   |   |
|   |   |   | C | A | R | E | S |   | E | P | I | P | E | N |
| P | R | A | Y | E | R |   | O | W | E |   | M | O | V | E |
| E | E | L |   | F | I | N | G | E | R | L | A | K | E | S |
| G | A | L |   | E | O | A | R | D |   | A | G | E | N | T |
| S | R | S |   | R | A | G | E | S |   | B | E | S | T | S |

## 50

| E | L | M | O |   | D | A | R | E |   | S | W | I | S | S |
| G | O | O | N |   | O | V | A | L |   | W | I | N | C | E |
| G | O | O | S | E | N | E | C | K |   | I | N | C | U | R |
| O | M | N | I | V | O | R | E |   | A | N | G | O | R | A |
|   |   |   | D | A | R | T |   | E | N | D |   | M | V | P |
| S | T | E | E | D | S |   | E | A | G | L | E | E | Y | E |
| A | W | A | K | E |   | D | A | M | S | E | L |   |   |   |
| N | O | R | I |   | B | E | S | E | T |   | L | A | N | E |
|   |   |   | C | A | R | V | E | S |   | M | I | S | E | R |
| D | U | C | K | T | A | I | L |   | C | O | P | P | E | R |
| A | N | O |   | T | I | L |   | G | L | U | T |   |   |   |
| M | U | D | R | U | N |   | H | A | I | R | I | E | S | T |
| A | S | I | A | N |   | R | A | V | E | N | C | L | A | W |
| G | E | N | R | E |   | O | V | E | N |   | A | L | I | A |
| E | D | G | E | D |   | B | E | L | T |   | L | A | D | S |

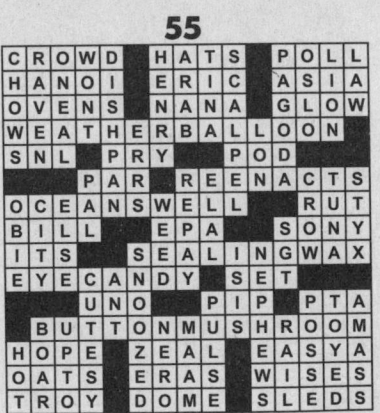

**51**

```
O M E N   B A T H S   C A P E
D O V E   O N S E T   A L O E
D R A W I N G P A D   L U L L
S E N D S   U S D   E M M Y S
      A P B S   L U G E
T O L D Y A   R I N G D I N G
I P A S   S T A N D S   D O O
E R R   S A V E R   E T A
R A G   S E C E D E   T A I L
S H O R T T O N   S M E L T S
      H U T T   T S A R
A P R O N   R L Y   M A P L E
L A I D   B U I L D A B E A R
S I D E   A C M E S   I S S A
O N E S   S K O R T   T O T S
```

**52**

```
A C I D   T E M P   E C I G
S O T O   E R I E   M A N E T
H U S T L E A N D B U S T L E
  G A S U P   U S E   T E A R
B A D   G A G S   A G E N T S
O R E   E D U   A C A   T O E
A S A P   I M D O N E
    L I T T L E A N G E L
      E A R T A G   L O K I
P O D   P A Y   E R R   S I N
U N E V E N   I S E E   T S K
R I P A   C A N   P L O T S
G O O G L E A N A L Y T I C S
E N S U E   R E B A   I M A C
  S E E D   P R E Y   S E M I
```

**53**

```
R A P S   E L I O T   L A B
A L O T   S U S H I   V A L E
B A L L E T S H O E   I N O N
I M O   L E T   A D D E D
D O S A G E   N I C E R
    B A M B O O S H O O T S
A N G E R   E A R L Y   V I A
R O U T   I S S U E   H E R S
A L I   A N T E S   M A R E S
B A L A N C E S H E E T
  T R E A D   I T S A G O
B E L O W   E G O   X E R
A R E S   B A D S H O W I N G
W I S E   E G Y P T   H O R A
L E S   T E E N S   O M E N
```

**54**

```
A L T O   C E L I A   B A K E
R O O T   G O U R D   O W E S
C U R T A I N R O D   D E E P
S T E E D   E N E M Y S P Y
      R A I L   O N U S
C V S   G R O U N D C H U C K
H O E   E A R N   H O P O N
I C E D   S E A T S   P O L O
C A D E T   P R O S   N O W
A B S T R A C T A R T   E R S
    A U R A   P E R M
C O N C E A L S   A I M A T
O H O H   F I L T H Y R I C H
S I T E   A C U R A   E C R U
T O E S   T O R A H   D E E D
```

**55**

```
C R O W D   H A T S   P O L L
H A N O I   E R I C   A S I A
O V E N S   N A N A   G L O W
W E A T H E R B A L L O O N
S N L   P R Y   P O D
    P A R   R E E N A C T S
O C E A N S W E L L   R U T
B I L L   E P A   S O N Y
I T S   S E A L I N G W A X
E Y E C A N D Y   S E T
    U N O   P I P   P T A
  B U T T O N M U S H R O O M
H O P E   Z E A L   E A S Y A
O A T S   E R A S   W I S E S
T R O Y   D O M E   S L E D S
```

## 56

```
TUBA  STARK  TOW
OPENS OHGEE  AHA
ADAGE HEADY  CAR
DOMEASOLID  BIRD
   LSU ANIMATES
LISA  MRS  TAT
OOPS  SITS  YARDS
STRAP NFL  ONION
SAYSO GRAD ELLA
  HOO  OWE  YELP
PETERPAN  ATE
LAOS  ACTEDALONE
AGO SQUID  CAREY
ILL PUREE  OSCAR
DES YEARN  HARE
```

## 57

```
AMEN  MAGMA  ORAL
BAKE  EUROS  DUNE
EYEWITNESS  ENDS
LOSESIT  ETC  DRS
   RAMSAY  ROMEO
AYEAYE  BONESCAN
SAM   LAVASH
HYUNDAI  ESTATES
  AIMFOR   AGE
REARVIEW  PARROT
ALICE  FEMALE
WOO RIO  ONATEAR
BILK WRISTWATCH
ASIA OCCUR  KALE
REST NEELY  ELSA
```

## 58

```
PITCH HISS  OLAF
ACHOO OMIT  POPE
REALESTATE  POOL
TEND  ETC  PROMPT
  FAME  DOES
SPECIALEFFECTS
THREES OAFS  LIE
GAIT  BOD  BORE
IRE GMOS  OBEYED
FEDERALEXPRESS
  MATT  REAP
CINEMA EAR  BETA
ODOR  DENTALEXAM
LONG OWIE  PEPUP
ALOE REDD  SPOTS
```

## 59

```
AWGEE  SPA  PORT
3INCE HOOD  AREA
SMALLWORLD  TEAL
PTA ANTI  TROLL
  IAGO  SHOO
LARGERTHANLIFE
PULSE  RUT  SNIT
EGO SCRAPES  PET
LENS LAD  ELENA
TREASUREISLAND
  FLEE  DEFT
ABBEY BIEL  EMO
SLAB  FINALDRAFT
KOBE IRKS  NOLIE
SCAT TDS  ANITA
```

## 60

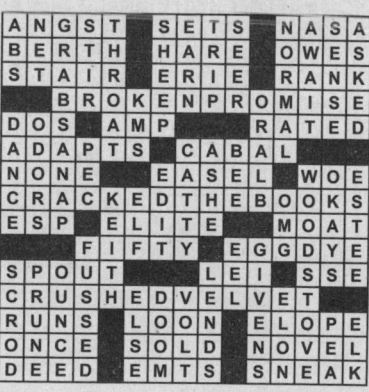

```
ANGST SETS  NASA
BERTH HARE  OWES
STAIR ERIE  RANK
  BROKENPROMISE
DOS AMP  RATED
ADAPTS  CABAL
NONE  EASEL  WOE
CRACKEDTHEBOOKS
ESP ELITE  MOAT
  FIFTY  EGGDYE
SPOUT LEI  SSE
CRUSHEDVELVET
RUNS LOON  ELOPE
ONCE SOLD  NOVEL
DEED EMTS  SNEAK
```

## 61

```
ADDS  ABBA  AMBER
DROP  MAUL  LEAVE
VICEVERSA   LATEX
EVENING   SLIT
RENTS ARKIN EBB
BLT   VIRALVIDEO
   TWINS   ANITA
MISHAPS   CRITTER
OTHER   DRANO
VROOMVROOM   BLU
EYE   CHESS GREEN
   LOSE TARIFFS
AFOUL VOICEVOTE
NEATO EINE  ARIA
DETER SLID  LENT
```

## 62

```
MEDAL ROCK  TANG
AMUSE ALOE  OBEY
DUSKTODAWN  PURR
EST SPAY TATTOO
   SEAR SUMO
TOTAL DECIBEL
MONET SULK  OMEN
GRIM  ENEMY TIVO
MOOT  LALA  STREW
SNORERS CLOSE
SAVE  SHAM
JUSTME SEAL  LAT
ONCE  NINETOFIVE
STAR  TOOK  MIMIC
HORN  HUBS  STASH
```

## 63

```
THIRD DESK  ISLE
RENEE ERIN  SKIN
ALTER EURO  TIED
PERFECTPITCH
SNO  LOST  PACKS
   BIT   MARTINI
BLOC  AWOL  TVAD
FRONTWHEELDRIVE
LOOS  EATS  RULE
ITSABET   AYE
THEIR  FAIL  LPS
TORTILLACHIP
STAR  AHEM  KOALA
PACE  NANA  EPSOM
ANTE  TIDY  SEATS
```

## 64

```
SMOTE HIT   TSAR
HOPIN UNUM  ULNA
OMENS LONI  NATE
PACKUPANDLEAVE
   LEAH  REAM
WERE  YOGA  GEARS
ATE   COO  ILLBET
SHACKUPTOGETHER
TOPHAT HUN   OVA
ESSAY ASTO  CREW
   RAMP  TRAY
BACKUPTHETRUCK
TACO  SLOE  TAHOE
ANNA  HERR  INONE
PEEL  SEE   COHEN
```

## 65

```
POSH  MACYS  ACTS
ANNE  ALLAN  SOOT
SMILEYFACE  SURE
TEPID  ASHE  ANEW
   PAN  STRAIT
PAJAMAS   CLYDE
STUD  DEGREE  SIA
ASS  PIGPENS  ETS
LET  ERASED  GATE
MAINE   DORITOS
   NOLESS  WAR
ANTI  SLOE  GAVEL
LEIS  SINGLEFILE
TOME  AMIGO  FLAG
ONES  YEAST  EELS
```

## 66

```
P R A D A   T A R P     B R A
S I T I N   I C O N S   E A R
S P A R T A N R A C E   A T M
T A P E   C C E D   G A T E S
    C U T A   S A U L
  S E T T I N G T H E P A C E
B A L S A   L E E   O N L Y
O W E   H U M O R M E   T O E
T U N A   S E A   R A I N S
S P A G H E T T I S A U C E
    R O S A   S U S S
B A B A R   D O T E   T H I N
E W E   S P A N I S H R I C E
T E A   E A T E N   M I N E R
A S K   T A S K   M A T E D
```

## 67

```
O O P S   L A M B   O D E S
S P A T   S E P I A   B E T A
H E I R   P A S T S   A B U T
A N N U A L F E E S   M A D E
    T R A Y   O R A T E S
I G E T I T   C H O O S E
R O V E D   C H A N T   T M I
A G E D   R O A R S   H E A R
S O N   A E S O P   P I A N O
  N O C U T S   M A D M E N
S H U C K S   S I N E
T A M E   A V A N T G A R D E
A B B A   B E F I T   B O R E
G L E N   L E A P S   E D E N
E A R S   E R R S   D E W Y
```

## 68

```
D R A W L   B E T S   B E L T
J U L I E   E X I T   O D I E
S M E L T   R E N O   S I N S
    D I R E C T O R S C U T
M U D   T U I   D I E T S
E N R O B E   B A I L S
S T E W E D P R U N E   O W E
S I G N   L A D   F L A X
Y E S   L E A D I N G E D G E
    C A N N Y   O O Z I E R
  B O O S T   S I T   E S T
F I G H T I N G T R I M
E L L E   C O L A   N A V E L
U B E R   E V E R   T I A R A
D O S E   S A N K   O N T A P
```

## 69

```
C A M P   T H A I   C R I M P
O R E O   H O S T   H E C K A
W E E K N I G H T   I D E A L
S A T E E N   E Y E T O E Y E
    R A G U   S O N
E C G   L I G H T S W I T C H
N O O B   E L I E   N O B L E
A B B A   S I L A S   N O E L
C R A B S   E L S E   S N A P
T A G Y O U R S E L F   E T S
    T A S   S T O W
G R E E N D A Y   Z O I N K S
O O Z E D   S W E E T R O L L
B A R T S   A C E R   E P E E
I D A H O   P A L S   S E E D
```

## 70

```
A S T O   E R I E     B I B
C H U M   B R E A K   C A N E
T O N G U E R I N G   A N N A
S P A   P R O   A N T E S
    S U P E R I O R C O U R T
T E A S E T   C H O S E
I D L E D   P I G S   S A R A
L E A   L A C E S   S A D
E N D S   I S L E   R A P I D
    I R A T E   I O W A N S
C O U N T R Y S I N G E R
L U N G E   S T U   T A D
A T I E   N A T U R E W A L K
M E T S   E R I C A   A M E N
P R E   T I C K   S E X Y
```

## 71

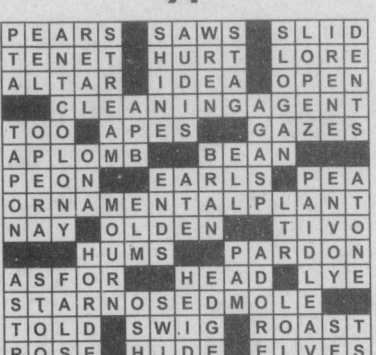

| P | E | A | R | S | | S | A | W | S | | S | L | I | D |
| T | E | N | E | T | | H | U | R | T | | L | O | R | E |
| A | L | T | A | R | | I | D | E | A | | O | P | E | N |
| | C | L | E | A | N | I | N | G | A | G | E | N | T | |
| T | O | O | | A | P | E | S | | G | A | Z | E | S | |
| A | P | L | O | M | B | | | B | E | A | N | | | |
| P | E | O | N | | E | A | R | L | S | | P | E | A | |
| O | R | N | A | M | E | N | T | A | L | P | L | A | N | T |
| N | A | Y | | O | L | D | E | N | | T | I | V | O | |
| | | H | U | M | S | | | P | A | R | D | O | N | |
| A | S | F | O | R | | H | E | A | D | | L | Y | E | |
| S | T | A | R | N | O | S | E | D | M | O | L | E | | |
| T | O | L | D | | S | W | I | G | | R | O | A | S | T |
| R | O | S | E | | H | I | D | E | | E | L | V | E | S |
| O | D | E | S | | A | M | I | D | | S | L | E | E | K |

## 72

| L | I | T | H | E | | C | L | A | D | | W | E | P | T |
| A | S | H | E | N | | H | E | R | O | | A | L | A | I |
| S | H | E | E | T | M | U | S | I | C | | T | I | L | T |
| | | P | L | I | E | R | S | | D | E | C | A | L | |
| A | C | E | | C | A | N | | C | L | A | R | I | C | E |
| D | R | A | P | E | D | | T | H | I | R | S | T | E | D |
| D | I | R | E | | F | O | A | M | Y | | | | | |
| | B | L | A | N | K | E | T | P | O | L | I | C | Y | |
| | | E | A | V | E | S | | | B | L | A | B | | |
| P | U | M | M | E | L | E | D | | T | A | M | A | L | E |
| O | N | O | R | D | E | R | | M | A | V | | S | E | E |
| P | E | T | T | Y | | C | O | C | O | A | S | | | |
| T | A | R | O | | P | I | L | L | O | W | T | A | L | K |
| A | S | I | A | | O | R | A | L | | E | M | C | E | E |
| B | E | N | D | | D | E | N | Y | | D | O | T | T | Y |

## 73

| T | A | B | S | | S | T | A | R | | I | D | I | N | A |
| A | C | R | E | | C | O | C | A | | S | I | L | O | S |
| R | E | A | L | | A | N | T | I | | U | N | I | T | Y |
| | F | A | R | E | I | N | C | R | E | A | S | E | | |
| P | A | I | N | | | F | O | E | | | D | O | T | |
| D | E | L | E | T | E | S | | O | N | C | E | | | |
| I | R | E | | G | O | E | R | | A | T | T | I | C | |
| S | I | X | F | I | G | U | R | E | I | N | C | O | M | E |
| C | L | A | R | A | | L | A | S | S | | | W | A | D |
| | | O | D | D | S | | T | H | I | N | I | C | E | |
| T | A | G | | M | O | I | | | N | I | T | S | | |
| R | A | R | E | I | N | S | T | A | N | C | E | | | |
| E | R | E | C | T | | T | A | C | O | | C | L | E | F |
| S | O | C | H | I | | E | X | I | T | | E | A | R | L |
| S | N | O | O | T | | R | I | D | E | | S | P | R | Y |

## 74

| R | E | F | I | | S | A | F | E | | S | T | U | N | T |
| I | R | A | N | | I | D | O | L | | H | A | N | O | I |
| O | N | C | E | I | N | A | L | I | F | E | T | I | M | E |
| T | I | E | R | S | | D | O | O | R | | T | E | D | |
| S | E | T | T | L | E | D | | T | U | B | S | | | |
| | | | E | X | I | T | | R | E | C | K | O | N | |
| R | A | N | T | | E | V | E | S | | T | O | N | K | A |
| A | M | E | R | I | C | A | N | H | I | S | T | O | R | Y |
| T | O | X | I | C | | N | O | O | N | | T | W | A | S |
| E | S | T | E | E | M | | R | E | F | S | | | | |
| | | | S | P | E | W | | S | O | O | N | E | S | T |
| A | P | T | | A | R | I | D | | | S | O | R | E | R |
| C | H | A | N | C | E | D | I | S | C | O | V | E | R | Y |
| D | I | D | O | K | | T | R | I | O | | A | C | T | S |
| C | L | A | W | S | | H | E | R | O | | S | T | A | T |

## 75

| | W | H | O | A | | S | E | A | T | | | C | O | W |
| C | H | A | R | M | | A | R | L | O | | G | O | N | E |
| R | A | B | B | I | T | H | O | L | E | | E | M | I | T |
| A | L | I | | D | E | A | D | | S | L | E | E | T | S |
| B | E | T | H | | A | R | I | A | | A | N | A | | |
| | | | O | R | L | A | N | D | O | M | A | G | I | C |
| | A | B | L | E | | G | A | R | B | | A | D | D | |
| I | S | A | I | D | N | O | | M | E | A | N | I | E | S |
| N | I | T | | T | H | A | T | | D | A | N | A | | |
| C | A | S | U | A | L | F | R | I | D | A | Y | | | |
| | | I | M | P | | S | I | R | E | | S | A | G | S |
| P | I | G | P | E | N | | B | O | B | A | | B | R | A |
| A | C | N | E | | C | O | U | N | T | S | H | E | E | P |
| T | O | A | D | | I | N | T | O | | I | O | T | A | S |
| S | N | L | | | S | E | E | N | | F | E | S | T | |

## 76

| S | U | G | A | R |   | C | C | E | D |   | S | I | B | S |
| T | H | O | S | E |   | A | U | R | A |   | T | R | I | O |
| J | U | M | P | F | O | R | J | O | Y |   | E | R | R | S |
| O | R | E |   | A | M | O | S |   | C | R | E | D | O |   |
| E | A | R | A | C | H | E |   | P | E | G | S |   |   |   |
|   |   | B | O | U | N | C | E | A | R | O | U | N | D |   |
| I | K | N | E | W |   | O | W | L |   | L | E | I |   |   |
| M | E | A | T |   | L | A | P | E | L |   | M | A | S | S |
| P | E | R |   | O | P | T |   | E | A | R | T | H |   |   |
| S | P | R | I | N | G | T | O | M | I | N | D |   |   |   |
|   | S | O | D | A |   |   | U | S | E | D | C | A | R |   |
| T | O | W | I | T |   | S | A | P | S |   | O | N | E |   |
| O | P | E | D |   | S | K | I | P | A | G | R | A | D | E |
| T | E | S | S |   | P | I | L | E |   | A | N | T | E | D |
| O | N | T | O |   | A | S | S | T |   | S | A | S | S | Y |

## 77

| D | R | A | W |   | S | C | O | P | E |   | I | T | E | M |
| I | O | T | A |   | O | H | H | E | Y |   | R | A | G | U |
| M | A | T | T |   | P | E | A | C | E |   | S | C | O | T |
| E | D | I | C | T |   | E | R | A |   | W | A | I | S | T |
|   |   | C | H | I | C | K | E | N | S | O | U | T |   |   |
|   |   |   | L | E | I |   |   |   | T | E | D |   |   |   |
| M | I | D | I |   | C | I | R | C | A |   | I | C | A | N |
| I | C | U | S |   | A | D | E | E | R |   | T | R | U | E |
| S | E | C | T |   | D | R | E | A | M |   | S | O | D | A |
| T | S | K |   | R | A | I | L | S | A | T |   | W | I | T |
|   |   | S | W | I | S | S |   | E | P | I | C | S |   |   |
| F | A | D | E | D |   | E | L | F |   | M | A | O | R | I |
| I | R | O | N |   | F | L | A | I | L |   | S | V | E | N |
| L | E | W | D |   | A | B | O | R | T |   | T | E | A | K |
| M | A | N | Y |   | B | A | S | E | D |   | E | R | R | S |

## 78

| C | A | B | A | L |   | H | A | S |   | P | S | S | T |   |
| A | L | O | H | A |   | P | I | C | K |   | E | L | L | A |
| W | I | S | H | Y | W | A | S | H | Y |   | R | E | U | P |
| E | C | O |   | E | E | N | S | Y |   | S | I | E | G | E |
| D | E | M | U | R | E |   | A | P | O | P |   |   |   |   |
|   |   | F | I | D | D | L | E | F | A | D | D | L | E |   |
| B | Y | R | O | N |   | R | O | A | R |   | E | E | L |   |
| L | E | I |   | G | R | O | T | T | O | S |   | B | A | S |
| I | T | O |   | I | O | T | A |   | H | A | T | H | A |   |
| P | I | T | T | E | R | P | A | T | T | E | R |   |   |   |
|   | G | I | G | I |   |   | C | R | E | E | D | S |   |   |
| T | O | R | S | O |   | B | A | M | B | I |   | L | E | T |
| E | R | R | S |   | D | I | L | L | Y | D | A | L | L | Y |
| E | C | R | U |   | O | K | O | K |   | A | L | E | V | E |
| M | A | L | E |   | G | E | E |   | N | I | N | E | S |   |

## 79

| M | O | R | A | Y |   | S | P | R | Y |   | S | L | A | B |
| A | D | E | L | E |   | E | R | I | E |   | H | A | L | O |
| R | E | P | O | S |   | I | O | T | A |   | I | R | O | N |
|   | L | E | M | O | N | M | E | R | I | N | G | U | E |   |
| A | V | E |   | O | R | E | O |   | D | E | E | D | S |   |
| R | E | N | A | M | E |   | S | E | T | S |   |   |   |   |
| U | N | I | T |   | S | E | L | M | A |   | M | O | O |   |
| B | U | S | T | O | U | T | L | A | U | G | H | I | N | G |
| A | S | H |   | P | S | A | L | M |   | U | S | E | R |   |
|   |   | L | I | A | R |   | V | I | R | T | U | E |   |   |
| S | P | A | I | N |   | A | B | E | T |   | L | P | S |   |
| T | U | R | K | E | Y | V | U | L | T | U | R | E |   |   |
| O | G | L | E |   | A | I | D | E |   | N | O | T | E | S |
| R | E | E | L |   | K | N | E | E |   | F | B | O | N | Y |
| E | T | S | Y |   | S | E | N | D |   | S | E | E | D | S |

## 80

| C | L | I | M | B |   | C | A | M | P |   | N | O | S | Y |
| R | A | C | E | R |   | A | M | O | R |   | O | R | C | A |
| I | T | A | L | I | C | T | Y | P | E |   | T | E | A | M |
| B | E | N |   | D | O | H |   | S | C | I | O | N | S |   |
|   |   | I | G | G | Y |   | G | U | A | M |   |   |   |   |
|   | L | A | N | E | S |   | S | E | M | P | E | R | F | I |
| S | O | L | O | S |   | S | A | N | E |   | T | O | R | N |
| A | T | I | T |   | S | P | U | R | S |   | O | D | I | N |
| U | T | A | H |   | N | I | C | E |   | E | D | I | T | S |
| L | O | S | E | F | A | C | E |   | A | M | I | N | O |   |
|   |   | R | A | K | E |   | A | C | M | E |   |   |   |   |
| B | L | O | N | D | E |   | R | A | Y |   | S | L | O |   |
| C | U | B | E |   | P | E | A | S | I | N | A | P | O | D |
| C | R | O | W |   | I | N | T | O |   | O | V | I | N | E |
| S | E | E | S |   | T | E | E | N |   | D | A | T | E | S |

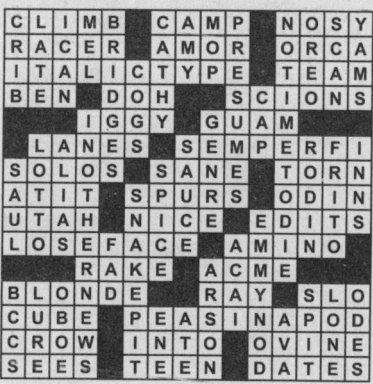

## 81

```
ABLE  RAGU    DIVE
BOOM  CLIPS   ERIN
BASEBALLDIAMOND
ASTRO    TANLINES
    GOOP  TSA
KATESPADE    REACH
IDO  TRUE   AMELIA
TORN  ALLOW   RODS
TROUGH  TAGS  HEN
YESNO   TAKEHEART
    UGH  SEAL
ASKEDOUT    PEPSI
DOLLARSHAVECLUB
ALUM   ELOPE  TOME
MEMO    YURT  SPOT
```

## 82

```
 SOFA   BARB   ABLE
FARIS   AFAR   GAIN
AREAS   TOGO   EMMA
BASSETHOUND   BBC
    CREST  TOBOOT
ROBOTS    RETRO
AKA  STORE  SIZES
FANS  SHOES  ELBA
TYKES  MEDIA   EAT
  RELAY    TIEDYE
DOODAD   SWIRL
ILL  BABYONBOARD
NILE  PURR  APNEA
EVER  TRIM  LENNY
REDS  SPAS  LSAT
```

## 83

```
ALGAE   DIPS   BOT
BEAST  SODOI   OLE
BOYISHLOOKS   ODE
ASST  EARLE   AKIN
   WENT   MAPLES
 OBEYS  PRONTO
SHORE  BLAND   VAC
RIDER  RAN   TREND
SOY  OWING  HORNS
  LILACS   LEASE
SLOWLY    BOND
TOTO   CHAOS  WAGS
ARI  BOUGHTLOCAL
IDO  ROMEO  ORATE
DEN  ALPS   SKIED
```

## 84

```
ACTS   LEAP   SMURF
BOOT   ERGO   TAPER
SOFA   TIAS   ECONO
PUBLICSERVANTS
     SET  PRIED
OMG  MIT   GNAWED
PANAMAHATS   MAMA
ERASE   ECO  BISON
DIRK  PELLGRANTS
SOLACE   DUO   TEE
    RATED  ETC
PANORAMICSHOTS
ONCUE  BRAS   MEAT
STANS  ETRE   MAKE
HEADS  DYED   AREA
```

## 85

```
HOLI   SODAS   STAG
OPEN   AKITA   ZULU
PEAK  GREENPARTY
ERRED   ASADA   NOS
SANDER    TRIBE
     COMB  ANYDAY
BLACKBALL    NONO
LACES   NEO  YOUNG
OVAL   YELLOWTEA
TAPING   PLAY
   PEARL   BORING
ARE  MAILS  SAVOR
GOLDENGALA   POLO
ELLA   THROW  IRIS
SLAM   STATE  DYES
```

## 86

```
ANDES   STU     FCC
LAUGH   LANA  REAL
BINGEWATCH  AERO
ALE  PIN  LASTLEG
  DANGLE   LOAD
SCOURS  ASSENT
ERRED   SAID  HAN
NOEL  BEAMS  DORA
TWO  DOGG   CUMIN
  CARBON  MADEDO
  COCA  MATURE
GEORGIA  ALA  SPA
RAKE  ONTHEMONEY
ASIS  NINO  ERODE
BEE    ATE  LEWIS
```

## 87

```
COATS   TITLE   TAB
OPRAH   EMAIL  ARE
PARTYPEOPLE  KIA
SLOT  INKS  CLEAT
 SWEPT    RTES
  RESPONSETIME
ONSET  SHOVE  DAN
REED  LAYUP  TEND
ERA  RITES  ROSES
OFTHEESSENCE
  BOND    EATAT
CREPE  BEAM  ODOR
AOL  GOODFORTUNE
VAT  ELDER  POLKA
ERS  SAYNO  METAL
```

## 88

```
HANS   VEG   SHAFT
IMOK  FARE  CAIRO
JURYTRIAL  INNER
ASS  WINS  WENTTO
BEEPED    ANA
  REALITYCHECK
PLOT  INANE  MAO
POOF  UNDUE  AIMS
EMO  STEIN  UNTO
APTITUDETEST
  NOR  DUSTED
PATTON  GAGA  ALE
SCRAP  FINALEXAM
SHAKE  EVER  VETO
TYPED  DEW   EDEN
```

## 89

```
RAT  MESSES  COPS
AGE  IMPALA  HARP
PASTASALAD  ASIA
TILE  COT  WRIST
 NASA  ENE  ITSME
  TOMB  SAFE
BOATLOAD  CIRCLE
ARCH  IRISH  MOAT
DETERS  GOODEGGS
  WITS  LOOM
GLOAT  IPO  EBAY
LATTE  MAC  ERAS
ASHE  MINUTERICE
DEER  OLDPAL  AHA
ERRS  BEASTS  SIL
```

## 90

```
LASER  AMUSE  FAT
ADIEU  MINOR  RUE
BACKSLIDING  EDS
SMS  SUNS   SNIT
  PILOTS  DECOY
SOCIAL   TOUCH
ONAN  SNOWGLOBE
ACRE  SHOWN  UPON
RESTROOMS   DENY
  ERASE  AGENDA
SCREW  DAYOLD
LOVE  LENA  MFA
ALI  DOUBLEDOORS
MAC  INKUP  EBOOK
SSE  POEMS  SINGS
```

## 91

| A | P | P | | K | N | I | C | K | S | | A | C | I | D |
| D | O | E | | H | U | M | A | N | E | | Z | E | R | O |
| D | O | T | | A | T | O | M | I | C | | A | D | A | M |
| S | H | R | E | K | | S | G | T | | L | A | T | E | |
| | | I | C | I | N | G | | H | O | V | E | R | E | D |
| R | E | D | O | | A | U | S | T | R | I | A | | | |
| I | M | I | N | | D | I | O | R | | A | S | C | O | T |
| S | I | S | | F | A | L | L | I | L | L | | A | H | A |
| E | T | H | E | R | | T | I | D | Y | | P | R | I | M |
| | | | T | O | O | R | D | E | R | | A | T | O | P |
| P | O | L | I | S | C | I | | R | E | A | I | R | | |
| E | R | I | C | | T | D | S | | | I | D | I | N | A |
| P | E | C | K | | A | D | L | I | B | S | | D | O | S |
| P | O | K | E | | N | E | U | R | A | L | | G | E | O |
| A | S | S | T | | E | N | G | A | G | E | | E | L | F |

## 92

| P | U | M | A | S | | N | O | W | | A | P | A | R | T |
| A | L | E | X | A | | A | H | A | | L | I | N | E | R |
| I | T | A | L | Y | | T | O | N | | O | L | D | I | E |
| L | A | T | E | N | I | G | H | T | S | H | O | W | | |
| | | | O | N | E | | | P | A | T | H | S | | |
| | B | A | D | | D | O | G | M | A | | | A | T | E |
| P | U | R | I | T | Y | | L | A | M | B | S | T | E | W |
| E | L | E | N | A | | C | O | Y | | A | N | N | I | E |
| L | O | W | E | R | J | A | W | | U | N | I | O | N | S |
| E | V | E | | U | P | S | E | T | | P | T | S | | |
| | A | C | T | I | N | | | S | A | D | | | | |
| | | L | U | C | K | O | F | T | H | E | D | R | A | W |
| G | E | E | N | A | | A | L | E | | E | R | A | S | E |
| O | N | A | I | R | | T | E | E | | T | E | C | H | S |
| T | E | R | S | E | | H | E | M | | S | W | E | E | T |

## 93

| B | A | L | S | A | | M | O | P | E | | B | L | A | H |
| A | S | I | A | N | | O | R | A | L | | L | I | N | E |
| S | T | O | C | K | C | L | E | R | K | | A | N | T | I |
| S | O | N | | L | I | E | S | | H | A | C | K | E | R |
| | | | B | E | T | S | | F | O | R | K | | | |
| D | E | P | U | T | Y | | C | R | U | M | P | E | T | S |
| E | V | I | L | S | | G | A | I | N | | E | L | I | E |
| C | A | L | L | | E | R | R | E | D | | P | A | G | E |
| O | D | E | S | | N | E | E | D | | O | P | T | E | D |
| R | E | S | E | N | T | E | D | | S | N | E | E | R | S |
| | | | S | O | R | T | | B | E | E | R | | | |
| T | R | U | S | T | Y | | P | O | E | M | | E | L | F |
| R | O | N | I | | F | L | E | A | P | O | W | D | E | R |
| A | L | T | O | | E | A | S | T | | R | A | N | G | E |
| P | E | O | N | | E | G | O | S | | E | R | A | S | E |

## 94

| G | L | O | O | M | | P | R | O | V | E | | P | G | A |
| A | E | T | N | A | | L | O | R | E | N | | U | R | N |
| P | E | T | E | R | R | A | B | B | I | T | | R | U | G |
| E | R | O | S | I | O | N | | S | L | I | P | P | E | R |
| | | | I | N | L | E | T | | | R | A | L | L | Y |
| A | P | P | E | A | L | | I | M | H | E | R | E | | |
| C | R | U | S | T | | H | A | I | M | | E | R | R | |
| T | O | E | | E | R | A | | S | O | L | | A | I | D |
| | P | R | Y | | A | L | D | O | | I | W | I | S | H |
| | | | T | O | G | G | L | E | | S | L | I | N | K | S |
| S | C | O | U | R | | S | W | A | Y | S | | | | |
| T | E | R | R | A | C | E | | A | T | P | E | A | C | E |
| A | L | I | | P | A | L | M | R | E | A | D | I | N | G |
| S | E | C | | E | N | S | U | E | | D | U | M | B | O |
| H | B | O | | S | E | E | D | S | | S | P | E | C | S |

## 95

| I | N | C | A | | S | K | E | W | | A | R | M | O | R |
| S | O | O | N | | D | E | L | I | | D | O | I | L | Y |
| L | I | S | T | | C | A | L | L | | L | O | R | D | E |
| E | S | T | I | M | A | T | E | D | T | I | M | E | | |
| S | E | A | | I | R | S | | G | O | B | I | | | |
| | | R | O | A | D | | S | U | N | | E | T | T | A |
| O | P | I | U | M | | F | L | E | E | | H | A | G | |
| V | I | C | T | I | M | L | E | S | S | C | R | I | M | E |
| A | L | A | | O | O | P | S | | H | O | S | E | S | |
| L | E | N | T | | D | O | T | | C | A | N | I | | |
| | | | U | B | E | R | | G | R | R | | S | I | S |
| | | C | L | I | M | A | T | E | I | M | P | A | C | T |
| S | T | A | I | R | | R | A | T | S | | F | L | O | E |
| T | E | M | P | T | | E | R | I | C | | F | I | N | N |
| Y | E | E | S | H | | A | S | T | O | | T | E | S | T |

## 96

```
A S I A   T M I N U S   S I R
R O M E   R A M O N A   O R E
A L A S   I N A D A Y   R O W
B O X O F F I C E   S O B A
    P I L L   O U T R O S
P S I   L E A P O F F A I T H
R I N S E   R E T O R T
O A T H   P O D   V I B E
  R A P I D S   S E E R S
T O O K O F F E N S E   S A P
R A V E N S   E L L A
O X E N   J O B O F F E R S
J A R   D R U M U P   T R A P
A C T   R E S A L E   E G G O
N A S   E X T R A S   R O U T
```

## 97

```
T A G S   H U G S   D A F F Y
B L O W   A B E T   A G I L E
A G U A   H E R E   M E N U S
L A D Y M A R M A L A D E
L E A S E     K E G   P B S
      T A O S   S E E O U T
A A S   E R R O R   V I S A
B L U E R I B B O N P A N E L
O O P S   S E V E R   T S K
E E R   N A P   M A U L S
  S P O T O F T R O U B L E
A T T I C   K I W I   R O A D
S H A C K   E V I L   A L M A
P E R K S   R E N E   S T A N
```

## 98

```
M A L L   S A U N A   V I P
S T O O P   O R S O N   A N A
G E T W E L L C A R D   N U N
    P E A S     H E I S T
T A C O B A R   G O O G L E
I R O N O N   G O A W O L
D I C E Y   P A T H   S A P S
E S O   S T A D I U M   B I T
S E N T   R I O T   E L E N A
  U R G E N T   T R E A T Y
  S T A R E S   D O M I N O S
T A M P A   M A R A
A B E   D R E A M T I C K E T
B R A   E E R I E   D O G M A
S E T   S C A N S   X B O X
```

## 99

```
N E M O   G R A S P   A D D S
A R A B   N O F E E   T R O T
P A S S M U S T E R   T I N E
E S T E E   S E M I   A V O W
    S T A I R   S K I E R S
L A P S E D   C H I N A
I R A   A L T O   D E P T H
F I R S   M U R A L   D A R E
T A K E N   G A L A   R U M
  A T O M S   I N S T E P
S A V O R Y   S T R A W
E D E N   S L O E   T E M P E
D O N E   T U R N T O D U S T
A R U N   I S T O O   E L S A
N E E D   C H A R T   N E I S
```

## 100

```
E Y E S   M A S S   O P E R A
L I M E   A P O P   D E L I S
K N U C K L E S A N D W I C H
    E E L   O R A L   C H E
G O D D E S S   S T Y M I E S
S L E E P   L I E U   E T S
A D A   S T A R   R P M
  E L B O W M A C A R O N I
    U N O   T A L E   A R M
  M U G   T I E R   S A M O A
P E N S I O N   S T I P E N D
A G T   N E S T   A D O
S H O U L D E R T H E L O A D
S A L S A   C I A O   L O R E
E N D O W   T O R E   O P E N
```

## 101

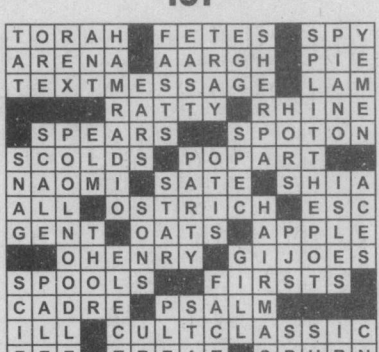

```
TORAH  FETES  SPY
ARENA  AARGH  PIE
TEXTMESSAGE   LAM
    RATTY  RHINE
 SPEARS   SPOTON
SCOLDS  POPART
NAOMI  SATE  SHIA
ALL  OSTRICH  ESC
GENT  OATS  APPLE
   OHENRY  GIJOES
SPOOLS   FIRSTS
CADRE  PSALM
ILL  CULTCLASSIC
FEE  TREAT  SPURN
IOS  SLAYS  KAREN
```

## 102

```
ZAPS  ABCS   MOPE
ELLA  SORE  HADES
SCAN  LOOM  OZONE
TONGUETWISTER
YAK  NESS  ATSEA
    LIP   LIU  ADO
  OBIT  NAILBITER
THEM  HULAS  PELE
EYEOPENER   RARE
DEN  HAS   MAD
 STARR  STEP  WHO
  HEADSCRATCHER
MEETS  PAID  HANG
VERNE  ALTO  ULNA
PLEA  SPEW  MEAN
```

## 103

```
HEROS   ORAL  RAT
AVATAR  AUTO  EMU
GENTLETHEMS  REF
URGE  EAU  SPENT
EYEROLL  WHEEL
   SELFRESPECT
GOCOLD  LAY  PALO
IDAHO  SIP  PESOS
SONS  YEN  BERETS
TRENDSETTER
  SAILS  HAUNTED
COUPS   SUV  OHNO
ORG  BECHDELTEST
MEA  ACHE  RESCUE
POR  ROAD  TOWED
```

## 104

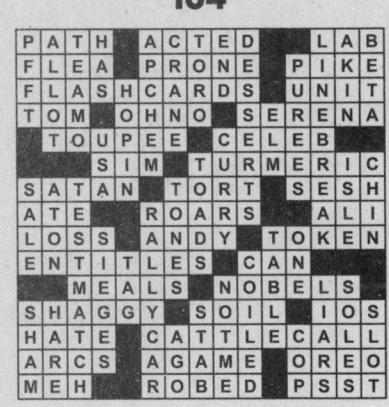

```
PATH  ACTED   LAB
FLEA  PRONE  PIKE
FLASHCARDS   UNIT
TOM  OHNO  SERENA
 TOUPEE  CELEB
   SIM  TURMERIC
SATAN  TORT  SESH
ATE  ROARS   ALI
LOSS  ANDY  TOKEN
ENTITLES   CAN
  MEALS  NOBELS
SHAGGY  SOIL  IOS
HATE  CATTLECALL
ARCS  AGAME  OREO
MEH  ROBED  PSST
```

## 105

```
BASS  SLAP  MOCKS
EMIT  HAUL  ALONE
ETTA  ANNA  LEVEE
COOKINGTIME   EEK
HONEST   DECOR
   PINT  TANNED
ARCS  EARL  TIARA
BOOT  SNAIL  OMAR
BALES  ACAI  NEST
ARDENT  TROD
  FLOWS  NORMAL
CAR  COLORSCHEME
ALAMO  IPOD  OLEG
ROMAN  NATE  NONO
DEERE  GLEN  ENDS
```

## 106

```
BOLD   DATE  SHOP
ERIE TIBIA  HUMS
ACES AGING  ALES
DASKAPITAL  RANT
  JUAN  EVES
MAJORS  BREWSKIS
ARUBA SLAYS  IRA
MISS FLAME  BRAG
BET MIAMI  BUTTE
ALACARTE SENSES
  SHOE   SPED
MAKE HASKITTENS
ALOE OUTIE  PLEA
MESS STAND  ASAP
ACHE EONS   NATS
```

## 107

```
CRABS UMPS    BLT
HIHAT POSIT  LEI
ACEHARDWARE  OWN
RCA ROAST  ROWDY
MIDWEST  GRAD
   ASSEMBLYHALL
ALEXA  ARE  URGE
BIN TIPTOES  TBS
BOUT MAC   CASTS
ANNEHATHAWAY
  CRAM  LINESUP
SWIMS  SCALD  UNO
MIA  ATLANTAHAWK
OPT NAOMI  LEVEE
GEE   TWOS  SHEDS
```

## 108

```
EBB CHUMP   BALSA
SEA EERIE   AVAIL
PAR DANCEAROUND
NUGGET  APP  IDEA
  AIDE   SPUD
AVID DIN  EPSOM
LINDT TOGAS  NEW
BABYONEMORETIME
ALI NOMAS  TROOP
 SNEER DST  INST
   ARTS  ROAR
SONG OTC  UGLIER
WHOLENUMBER  NDA
INLET NOISE  GIG
GOADS KNOTS  SEE
```

## 109

```
SWIM ASPIC  DEFT
CAVE CHINA  ERIE
AVON THUMBDRIVE
METUP  SILENCE
PIE IAM  NEW
INDEXCARDS  DATA
  NERVE  NEPAL
MIDDLESCHOOLERS
ARIES  OUGHT
NEED RINGLEADER
   SIN EEL  ODE
 VIETNAM  PARIS
PINKYSWEAR  CITE
ANTE EATME  ETON
LEOS DYSON  SORT
```

## 110

```
TOSS AFAR  SALAD
AREA NOSE  ELITE
LEAN GRID  LATTE
COLDCOMFORT  HIM
  MARS  AZTECS
SAHARA  SPIES
LIONS  COOLRANCH
EDU POURS   OUI
WARMHEART  PLOTS
  PESTS  QUAKES
TARGET  BULB
ELI HOTPROPERTY
NINJA ALOT  LARA
ENDOW MAKE  EVER
TESTS EYES  DEED
```

## 111

| P | E | A | | | E | C | A | R | D | | I | M | A | C |
| E | A | R | S | | M | O | V | I | E | | F | A | V | A |
| G | R | E | E | N | O | N | I | O | N | | S | N | O | W |
| S | N | A | R | E | | C | A | T | | D | O | G | I | E |
| | | T | A | L | L | | E | L | I | | O | D | D | |
| G | R | E | A | T | O | U | T | D | O | O | R | S | | |
| R | E | V | | O | D | E | | B | R | I | T | S | | |
| O | D | I | N | | S | E | A | T | S | | G | E | N | E |
| | S | L | O | P | E | | M | A | T | | | E | A | T |
| | G | R | A | N | D | O | P | E | N | I | N | G | S | |
| A | P | E | | U | S | E | | D | R | A | M | | | |
| F | I | N | A | L | | A | L | A | | T | H | E | S | E |
| R | A | I | L | | G | L | A | N | C | E | O | V | E | R |
| O | N | U | S | | M | E | C | C | A | | T | E | A | R |
| S | O | S | O | | C | R | E | E | P | | S | R | S | |

## 112

| T | O | T | | | S | A | F | E | S | | C | L | E | O |
| A | P | O | P | | A | T | L | A | S | | L | O | A | N |
| P | E | R | U | | L | E | A | S | E | | O | U | R | S |
| A | N | I | M | O | S | I | T | Y | | A | G | I | L | E |
| | | P | L | A | N | T | | D | I | G | E | S | T | |
| S | T | O | K | E | S | | E | L | U | D | E | | | |
| P | A | R | I | S | | P | R | O | S | | D | R | A | B |
| I | R | A | N | | W | A | I | S | T | | G | O | R | Y |
| T | A | L | C | | O | W | N | S | | J | U | D | G | E |
| | A | L | O | N | G | | M | E | T | E | O | R | | |
| S | H | E | R | Y | L | | C | R | E | S | T | | | |
| H | A | L | V | E | | R | O | A | D | T | E | S | T | S |
| A | N | T | I | | S | O | L | I | D | | R | O | O | T |
| N | O | O | N | | A | T | O | L | L | | S | A | G | A |
| K | I | N | G | | T | E | R | S | E | | P | A | R | |

## 113

| H | A | W | T | | G | A | S | T | R | O | | A | S | L |
| A | R | E | A | | M | R | T | O | A | D | | T | H | E |
| S | M | A | R | T | C | O | O | K | I | E | | T | E | T |
| H | O | R | S | E | | S | P | E | D | | B | E | E | S |
| T | I | S | | A | L | E | S | | R | O | M | P | S | |
| A | R | O | U | S | E | | B | A | D | A | P | P | L | E |
| G | E | N | Z | | B | U | Y | S | I | N | | T | E | E |
| | | O | U | R | S | | I | A | G | O | | | | |
| B | M | W | | T | O | E | T | A | P | | H | A | I | L |
| E | Y | E | C | A | N | D | Y | | E | R | M | I | N | E |
| S | L | A | S | H | | P | U | R | E | | R | V | S | |
| T | I | L | T | | G | R | I | N | | P | E | D | I | S |
| B | E | T | | C | O | U | C | H | P | O | T | A | T | O |
| U | G | H | | A | S | S | A | I | L | | A | T | E | N |
| D | E | Y | | P | H | E | L | P | S | | T | E | S | S |

## 114

| S | E | G | A | | S | C | R | E | W | | A | R | C | H |
| O | A | R | S | | P | H | O | N | E | | R | I | C | O |
| D | R | O | P | L | E | A | V | E | S | | A | C | E | S |
| A | T | V | | A | C | N | E | | A | B | O | D | E | |
| S | H | E | L | T | I | E | | C | Y | N | I | C | | |
| | L | O | C | A | L | B | R | A | N | C | H | E | S | |
| | N | H | L | | L | A | M | E | | E | T | S | | |
| L | U | T | E | | J | A | B | | S | T | A | N | | |
| E | R | R | | T | H | U | S | | P | R | Y | | | |
| E | L | E | P | H | A | N | T | T | R | U | N | K | | |
| | F | L | A | S | K | | R | E | D | C | A | R | D | |
| F | L | O | A | T | | M | U | S | E | | B | E | E | |
| R | U | I | N | | G | R | A | S | S | R | O | O | T | S |
| A | B | L | E | | M | A | T | T | E | | F | O | R | K |
| T | E | S | S | | C | H | E | S | S | | A | M | O | S |

## 115

| T | A | D | A | | R | I | P | S | | O | H | H | I |
| O | R | E | C | K | | A | N | E | W | | R | E | A | R |
| R | O | M | E | O | | N | O | R | I | | D | A | T | A |
| C | L | O | S | I | N | G | N | U | M | B | E | R | | |
| H | E | N | | P | I | E | | M | O | R | M | O | N | |
| | D | O | T | | L | I | E | D | | E | W | E | | |
| | L | Y | O | N | | V | I | N | E | | T | O | E | S |
| T | H | A | T | D | O | E | S | N | T | C | O | U | N | T |
| R | A | C | E | | V | E | T | S | | A | N | T | S | |
| A | S | H | | C | A | P | S | | D | R | Y | | | |
| P | A | T | R | O | L | | F | I | T | | Z | A | P | |
| | C | E | N | T | R | A | L | F | I | G | U | R | E | |
| A | B | L | E | | I | O | T | A | | E | L | M | E | R |
| L | O | U | D | | N | O | O | K | | R | A | B | A | T |
| L | A | B | S | | E | M | M | Y | | D | A | S | H | |

## 116

```
. M I S O . O A T . . T H E M
H A T E R . F I R . R A M I .
W R E N C H F R E E . A L M A
Y A M A H A . A V I D L Y . .
. . T A T . A S I D E . . . .
. B E R T . G U L L I B L E .
E P A . D E F E R . E N J O Y
D A Y . R I L E D . O R E . .
G L O A T . R E R U N . R E D
E M U L A T E S . R I S K . .
. C L A W S . I C E . . . . .
. A P O L L O . A E R A T E .
S L A V . C R O W N J E W E L
H O P E . K I A . O N E A M .
E T A S . S L Y . B A S S . .
```

## 117

```
. B U F F . V I A . Z I N C
M O R E L . S E N D . A C A I
E A G L E . T E A L . P E S T
G R E T A G E R W I G . S A Y
A D D . B A N . E B O O K . .
. . N A R C S . T R A C Y .
N O T A G A I N . L O A T H E
E M I T . G L A R E . N E A L
S I M I L E . G E T A G R I P
S T E V E . S T O N E . . .
. Z E S T S . R U T . P I E
W H O . S E C R E T A G E N T
I O N S . A R I A . C A R E S
F L E E . R A P T . I V O R Y
E A S T . S P A . D E N T .
```

## 118

```
O H A R F . F I R E . A C E
L A C E D . N I C E R . R A M
A I R P U R I F I E R . M R I
F R E E . E P E E S . B O A T
. . I P S . R E P O R T S . .
. H A S H T A G . S L O P .
R E F . A S S E S . A T L A S
C A T E R . A A H . C H A M P
A L E X A . P R I D E . T I A
. R I O T . S N U B B E D .
T O P T H A T . R O E . . .
E R A S . S Y R I A . E A S T
S I R . A S K I N G P R I C E
L O T . W E E P S . A M M A N
A N Y . E L S E . N E S T S
```

## 119

```
E A G E R . F E N G . T E E S
T E R R E . A S I A . R A G E
C R E A M . S P A R . U R G E
H O E S . C O N . T A I L O R
. . N E M O . U S E R S . . .
L A S E R S . T R E M B L E
S A C . G N O M E S . S L A M
A I R . T W E E T . A I M .
F L E A . O I L R I G . C R Y
E A S T E R N . S T O C K S
. L E T G O . C L I P . . .
S O M A L I . L A H . N O L A
E V E R . L O I N . S E W E D
R A N G . L O V E . A M E N D
B L U E . A F E W . Y A R D S
```

## 120

```
F R E E S . S T A S H . S O S
L E A V E . T I B I A . U R L
O B S E R V E L E N T . N I A
P A Y . V I A . C A N O N .
. . T R A C K L I G H T I N G
A S H E N . A T R E E . . .
C H E A T S . T I E S . A C T
H A R D . T H E S E . T R I O
E W E . G E A R . N A S C A R
. S O N I A . T A H O E . .
M O N I T O R L I Z A R D .
A R U B A . M I L . U S E .
T A R . W A T C H P O C K E T
E T S . A L I B I . S P E W S
S E E . Y E A S T . S A S S Y
```

# 121

| M | I | S | T | S |   | L | A | S | T |   | L | A | R | D |
| A | S | W | A | N |   | E | C | H | O |   | U | S | E | R |
| Y | E | A | R | O | F | T | H | E | M | O | N | K | E | Y |
| S | E | T |   | C | A | S | E | D |   | R | A | I | S | E |
|   |   | T | A | N | G |   | G | A | R | N | E | R |   |   |
| L | I | G | H | T | S | O | C | K | E | T |   |   |   |   |
| I | D | L | E |   |   | L | I | N | E |   | P | A | R |   |
| S | E | E | M |   | S | C | O | N | E |   | A | U | T | O |
| T | A | N |   | S | H | A | W |   |   | P | R | O | S |   |
|   | C | O | R | N | C | O | B | P | I | P | E |   |   |   |
| C | A | B | B | I | E |   |   | A | W | E | S |   |   |   |
| A | L | O | O | F |   | M | A | R | I | A |   | W | A | S |
| F | E | R | T | I | L | E | C | R | E | S | C | E | N | T |
| E | X | E | C |   | I | N | T | O |   | T | O | R | T | E |
| S | A | S | H |   | D | U | S | T |   | S | T | E | E | P |

# 122

| D | A | R | T |   | E | L | S | A |   |   | B | O | S | S |
| A | R | A | B |   | V | E | E | R |   | D | E | N | C | H |
| D | E | M | I | M | O | O | R | E |   | I | N | T | R | O |
|   | A | P | R | I | L |   | U | N | I | T |   | H | E | W |
|   |   | D | A | V | E | M | A | T | T | H | E | W | S |   |
| T | W | O |   | M | E | X |   | S | O | I | L |   |   |   |
| H | A | N | O | I |   | I | N | N | O |   | N | O | D | S |
| I | S | I | T |   | G | L | E | A | N |   | D | O | O | K |
| S | H | O | T |   | N | E | O | N |   | S | U | S | H | I |
|   | N | E | M | O |   | A | K | A |   | E | A | T |   |   |
| D | E | B | R | A | M | E | S | S | I | N | G |   |   |   |
| A | C | A |   | R | E | N | T |   | S | T | O | P | S |   |
| R | O | G | E | R |   | D | A | N | M | A | R | I | N | O |
| E | L | E | G | Y |   | E | R | I | E |   | G | N | A | T |
| S | I | L | O |   | D | E | L | T |   | E | G | G | S |   |

# 123

| E | D | G | E |   | T | A | S | T | E |   | A | F | A | R |
| D | O | E | S |   | A | L | L | I | N |   | S | U | M | O |
| I | R | I | S | H | P | O | U | N | D |   | K | N | E | W |
| E | M | C | E | E |   | E | G | G | O |   | S | S | N |   |
|   | S | O | N | I | C |   | S | E | W | S | U | P |   |   |
|   |   | C | R | O | P |   |   |   | I | P | O | D | S |   |
| R | O | B | E |   | C | O | D | I | N | G |   | N | I | L |
| A | M | I |   | P | O | K | E | M | O | N |   | G | P | A |
| G | A | G |   | R | A | Y | B | A | N |   | P | E | S | T |
| U | N | C | L | E |   |   | Y | O | G | A |   |   |   |   |
|   | H | A | Z | A | R | D |   | S | I | L | K | S |   |   |
|   | D | E | N |   | L | A | R | K |   | R | E | A | C | T |
| H | E | E | D |   | O | Z | O | N | E | L | A | Y | E | R |
| E | A | S | E |   | N | O | V | E | L |   | L | A | N | E |
| S | L | E | D |   | G | R | E | E | K |   | E | K | E | S |

# 124

| C | H | I | V | E |   | M | O | T | H |   | L | I | M | B |
| R | A | K | E | S |   | E | C | H | O |   | O | V | A | L |
| O | V | E | R | S |   | O | H | I | O |   | T | O | R | O |
| W | E | A | S | E | L | W | O | R | D | S |   | R | I | O |
|   |   | A | N | O |   | D | E | L | A | Y | E | D |   |   |
| A | M | P |   | C | U | E | S |   | D | A | R | T |   |   |
| P | E | R | C | E | I | V | E |   | W | O | O | D | S |   |
| P | E | A | R |   | S | E | E | D | S |   | S | W | A | P |
| S | K | I | E | S |   | P | E | T | P | E | E | V | E |   |
|   | R | E | N | E |   | S | E | E | R |   | R | E | D |   |
| C | L | I | P | O | N | S |   | R | O | O |   |   |   |   |
| R | Y | E |   | B | A | C | K | I | N | G | B | A | N | D |
| A | C | D | C |   | M | A | I | D |   | R | A | T | I | O |
| P | R | O | B |   | E | L | S | E |   | A | M | I | N | O |
| S | A | G | S |   | L | E | S | S |   | M | A | T | E | R |

# 125

| G | E | R | M |   | C | A | R | B |   | P | L | O | D |
| A | R | I | A |   | G | O | N | E | R |   | L | O | R | E |
| P | I | C | K |   | O | R | T | H | O |   | A | R | E | A |
|   | C | H | E | R | O | K | E | E | N | A | T | I | O | N |
|   |   | M | E | D |   | A | X | L | E |   |   |   |   |   |
| D | U | K | E | I | T | O | U | T |   | M | A | T | S |   |
| O | N | E |   | D | I | L | L |   | L | A | U | R | E | L |
| T | W | I | N |   | M | E | T | R | O |   | S | A | G | A |
| S | E | R | A | P | E |   | R | A | S | H |   | C | U | D |
|   | D | A | M | E |   | M | A | S | T | E | R | K | E | Y |
|   |   | E | A | S | Y |   | P | I | E |   |   |   |   |   |
| C | E | N | T | R | A | L | A | M | E | R | I | C | A |
| A | V | I | A |   | T | O | W | I | T |   | N | E | T | S |
| S | I | N | G |   | O | V | E | N | S |   | I | D | O | L |
| A | L | A | S |   | N | E | S | T |   | N | E | M | O |

# 126

```
L E O P A R D   A N G S T
O M N I V O R E   B E L T E D
S T A K E O U T   S C U R R Y
    E N T I C E   T E A S E
I R S   G E D   M B A   Y E S
T O L L E D   S C A R F
S P I E S   A P E S   A S A P
M E M O   S L E E K   L P G A
E D E N   A M A S   S C O R N
    E R R O R   S H O R E S
R V S   A A S   F E E   K E Y
I O W A N   T I A R A S
S W I N G S   S K E T C H U P
K E N N E L   H E N H O U S E
    L E E R Y   S E E T H A T
```

# 127

```
S A R I   B E A C H   E A S E
O B I T   D E L H I   X R A Y
N A P A V A L L E Y   C E D E
A T P L A Y   A R O S E
R E L I T   C G I   T R A P
  S E C   G R E E N A P P L E
    S H E S   O N T O U R
G E M   W A D   E T D   P G A
S E E S I N   M R I S
A N N A P A Q U I N   B A A
  Y U L E   U S C   F U G U E
    T R E A T   N I N E P M
B A L I   G I N G E R S N A P
E D E N   G L O R Y   E D I T
D O S E   O S T E O   N A R Y
```

# 128

```
E D I T   B O G   W A D E
D I S H   R N A   A R E N A S
U S H E R O U T   S I E R R A
    R A I S E T H E R O O F
S H T E T L   D R E   E L S E
P A R   E S C   A D O   L E S
A R I A   U N F U R L
M O T H E R O F P E A R L
    M A L A W I   B O A T
R ! H   M E T   C A P   U S E
A M O S   M O P   S O O T H E
B E A C H E R O S I O N
B A R R E N   E I T H E R O R
I N S E R T   M R I   A I D Y
    E W E S   S I S   L O D E
```

# 129

```
S T R I P   I D E A   L E E
I R A Q I   M A R C   B A C K
F A S T C A S U A L   A S H E
T Y P E   L O B S   O R T O
    S W I G   E A R T H
  P I T A   L O S T C A U S E
T E N   S P A M   L A B R A T
H S N   I D I N A   R U T
A T E A S E   T E S S   A T A
W O R S T C A S E   A C H E
    C L U E S   D A T A
W H E N   T O L D   N C A A
E R I E   N U D I S T C A M P
Y E L P   A T O N   A E S O P
E N D   B E R G   G L A S S
```

# 130

```
L L A M A   S N O T   I C U
O O H E D   T A L E   S C A M
T R A S H P A N D A   L A R A
S E T A D A T E   M E L T S
    N U T   O O D L E S
G A R B A G E T I M E
O R E O S   E R A   R E P O
D E A D S E A   A N Y I D E A
S A P S   M R S   A T I L T
    L I T T E R M A T E S
H A C K E R   E V E
A F O O T   R O A D R A C E
S L A B   J U N K D R A W E R
T A T E   I S E E   A T O N E
E T S   M A R S   B E L T S
```

## 131

```
USES   FAIRY   SECT
TODO   OLDIE   PILE
ASIF   RIOTS   AGUA
HOTTAMALES   CHER
    BIAS     IBET
IMPART   FORESTS
TOOLS   BOOED   RUT
EVIL   GAUZE   LASH
MEN   CARNE   MOCHA
  STEAMED   SANKIN
   TATE   SONG
DRAT   FATTUESDAY
JOKE   APRON   HIDE
EVER   COULD   OVAL
DENY   EPEES   TEMP
```

## 132

```
GAL   ALTAR   SOFAS
ONE   MOOLA   AWARE
EGG   PARISHILTON
SERPENT   SOD   CUD
PLEAD   IDLE   EASE
ROSY   FLEE   OTTER
OUT   GILA   OAT
  SANAALATHAN
   BUT   TUTU   ASK
TOMBS   TITO   PIPE
ORCA   OHNO   DELAY
SIA   MAR   SPECTRE
SOFIARICHIE   RED
ELECT   FRONT   IMO
SEEKS   TYPES   MEN
```

## 133

```
   FLOW   RIFF
INS   OSLO   AWAIT
MET   RAGU   PISCES
SWEETTALK   NOTRE
OYVEY   DII   IRA
LEEK   BANANABOAT
DAN   WENT   WREN
  RULING   MACAWS
  NORI   MARS   RED
DAILYGRIND   DINE
REV   NED   TOTAL
IRENE   FLATWHITE
PIRATE   ISEE   NOT
  ESSAY   FINE   GRE
  EASE   EAST
```

## 134

```
GAG   ALIAS   CARS
IVE   POSTIT   ASIN
FIRSTWATCH   BOHO
TAMES   IKEA   CAW
STAR   SECONDWIND
EON   NON   DIANA
TRY   ANEMIC   SLAY
   THIRDWAVE
APES   COSINE   PSI
LILAC   LAX   LIN
FOURTHWALL   DASH
AND   REEL   OUTTA
LEIA   FIFTHWHEEL
FEND   TRIBAL   ARE
ARGO   DEANS   USD
```

## 135

```
SPAM   MEAL   SHRUB
AUTO   INCA   QUOTA
BRAINSTEM   UNDER
EEL   ITIS   SAGEST
RELAXER   POLO
   CORETRAINING
AGAIN   WORD   COO
GOLD   SHIPS   VOTE
ESP   UPON   HANES
SHOWSOMESKIN
   HERE   TIMELAG
DOCILE   DRNO   ALA
AMUSE   SEEDMONEY
MARKS   PEAL   KARL
PRESS   ARMY   CITE
```

## 136

| S | I | T | U | P |  |  | G | P | S |  | N | I | P | S |
| I | M | A | G | E |  | S | O | H | O |  | O | S | L | O |
| B | A | R | G | A | I | N | B | I | N |  | R | E | E | L |
| S | C | A | B |  | C | O | I | L |  | S | U | E | D | E |
|  |  |  | O | D | O | R |  | L | I | E | S |  |  |  |
|  |  | M | O | U | N | T | A | I | N | C | H | A | I | N |
| S | P | A | T | E |  |  | L | E | N | T |  | C | O | O |
| K | E | D | S |  | I | P | A | S | S |  | C | O | T | S |
| I | R | A |  | S | T | I | R |  |  | A | R | R | A | Y |
| P | U | M | P | K | I | N | M | U | F | F | I | N |  |  |
|  |  |  | R | I | S | E |  | S | A | L | T |  |  |  |
| K | U | D | O | S |  | T | H | A | W |  | E | L | M | O |
| I | T | E | M |  | B | R | A | I | N | D | R | A | I | N |
| T | A | M | P |  | M | E | N | D |  | A | I | S | L | E |
| S | H | O | T |  | W | E | D |  | B | A | S | E | S |  |

## 137

|  | E | A | R | S |  | I | C | A | L | L |  | D | I | S |
| C | R | O | A | T |  | N | O | K | I | A |  | U | S | E |
| H | A | R | D | L | A | N | D | I | N | G |  | S | E | A |
| A | S | T | I |  | N | S | Y | N | C |  | S | T | E | M |
| R | E | A | S | O | N |  |  | T | O | T | E | M |  |  |
|  |  | H | A | I | R | C | O | L | O | R | I | N | G |  |
| B | U | G |  | R | E | A | L |  | N | E | U | T | E | R |
| A | L | O | G |  | M | U | D |  |  | M | E | S | A |  |
| S | T | E | E | R | S |  | E | U | R | O |  | S | T | Y |
| H | A | S | T | Y | P | U | D | D | I | N | G |  |  |  |
|  |  | A | T | E | I | T |  | N | O | O | D | L | E |  |
| H | A | L | O |  | N | O | O | K | S |  | L | O | U | D |
| I | L | L |  | H | A | P | P | Y | E | N | D | I | N | G |
| P | S | I |  | A | R | I | A | L |  | H | I | N | G | E |
| S | O | N |  | S | T | A | L | E |  | L | E | G | S |  |

## 138

| G | E | N | E |  |  | E | A | C | H |  | L | O | L |  |
| I | T | O | N | Y | A |  | O | A | H | U |  | O | U | I |
| G | A | R | D | E | N | S | N | A | I | L |  | A | T | M |
|  |  |  | L | A | T | E |  | C | A | R | D | I | B |  |
|  | H | E | R | E | T | I | C |  | U | S | E | S |  |  |
| U | R | I | S |  | S | O | R | E | A | T |  |  |  |  |
| T | E | N | S | E | D |  | W | A | T | C | H | D | O | G |
| A | D | D |  | D | I | V | E | B | A | R |  | I | P | O |
| H | O | U | S | E | F | L | Y |  | L | E | A | N | E | D |
|  |  | O | N | F | O | O | T |  |  | R | E | D | S |  |
| C | H | I | A |  | G | U | I | T | A | R | S |  |  |  |
| H | A | R | P | E | D |  | L | A | V | A |  |  |  |  |
| U | Z | O |  | D | A | N | C | E | M | O | N | K | E | Y |
| G | E | N |  | G | R | I | D |  | E | N | G | A | G | E |
| S | L | Y |  | E | E | L | S |  |  | E | T | O | N |  |

## 139

| M | I | N | D | S |  | A | R | A | B |  | Y | E | W | S |
| I | M | O | U | T |  | N | O | V | A |  | O | A | H | U |
| C | A | T | B | U | R | G | L | A | R |  | U | S | E | D |
| A | C | E |  | D | I | R | E |  | S | P | R | E | E | S |
|  |  |  | T | I | D | Y |  | P | O | R | E |  |  |  |
| B | A | R | R | E | S |  | C | R | A | Y | O | L | A |  |
| A | L | O | U | D |  | D | R | I | P |  | N | I | N | O |
| C | L | U | E |  | O | R | E | O | S |  | F | L | I | T |
| K | A | T | O |  | N | E | A | R |  | M | I | A | M | I |
|  | H | E | R | E | I | A | M |  | F | O | R | C | E | S |
|  |  |  | F | R | O | M |  | R | I | S | E |  |  |  |
| O | H | D | A | R | N |  | M | I | N | A |  | D | U | A |
| R | E | A | L |  | D | E | A | D | S | I | L | E | N | T |
| A | R | M | S |  | I | D | L | E |  | C | O | N | D | O |
| L | O | P | E |  | P | U | T | S |  | S | P | Y | O | N |

## 140

| U | S | E | D |  | T | M | I |  |  | S | A | G | S |  |
| G | W | E | N |  | M | A | I | N | E |  | P | U | R | E |
| G | A | R | A | G | E | B | A | N | D |  | E | T | A | L |
| S | P | I | T | E | D |  | M | E | G |  | C | O | I | L |
|  | S | E | E | N |  | F | I | R | E | S | I | G | N | S |
|  |  |  | S | E | A | L |  | S | E | A | R |  |  |  |
| L | O | F | T |  | D | A | N | K |  | L | L | A | M | A |
| A | I | R |  | B | A | K | E | O | F | F |  | P | O | D |
| G | L | O | B | E |  | E | T | T | A |  | T | H | I | S |
|  |  |  | N | E | S | S |  | E | R | I | E |  |  |  |
| E | S | T | A | T | E | T | A | X |  | M | E | T | A |  |
| M | A | S | T |  | R | U | M |  | P | A | N | E | R | A |
| A | L | E | S |  | F | L | A | S | H | C | A | R | D | S |
| I | M | A | M |  | S | I | Z | E | D |  | G | R | O | K |
| L | A | T | E |  | P | E | W |  |  | E | A | R | S |  |

## 141

```
S W A R M   S O A P   W A R S
C O C O A   C U R L   I R O N
A K I O M O R I T A   F E T A
R E D T A P E   G M I N O R
        E A T O U T   A R K
A L F R E D M O L I N A
L U A U S   S E E N   F L E D
P R I M E R   G A T E A U
S E R B   E P I C   L E A S E
    A N G E L A M E R K E L
P U P   B U C K L E
A N I M A L   I M I T A T E
N I N E   A L I C E M U N R O
T O T O   R E N O   A D D O N
S N O W   S O N S   N E S T S
```

## 142

```
L I M A   T I P S   A G E D
O R A L   I D E A   T O G O
C A R M E N S A N D I E G O
A T E A M       D A T A
L E S   I N G L E S   S P A T
      P L O W E D   K Y O T O
P H I   M E A   V I O L E T
G R A C E A N D F R A N K I E
O I N K E D   S A O   M A N
S M E L L   T O C O M E
H O S E   C I N E M A   E V A
      B A S E     N A M E D
S T A R T R E K P I C A R D
P A L M   E V I L   T I D E
A I L S   D E N Y   S L E D
```

## 143

```
J A D E   C A M E L   B E N
A W O L   A N I M E   H I R E
W O R K I N G M O M   E G G O
S K I   V A S E   M O R M O N
  E S C O R T   T E A M O
    P R Y   P A S T E U R
A M W A Y   G E R E   S T U D
N O R   I R A T E   H E R
D O O M   C A R S   S A S S Y
  D N A L A B S   A L L
    G R I N S   C L A I M S
U S M I N T   S H I N   A H A
N O O N   W A N I N G M O O N
D I V E   I G I V E   T R O T
O L E   N O T E S   V I S E
```

## 144

```
T O O L   P A S T A   M I C
E U R O S   U P P E R   A P E
A S C O T   N S Y N C   R O D
S T A K E   S O F A   B I D E
      I M F     I M P R E S S
I C O N   O P E C   A O C
D O U G   A L I T   S K U L K
E A T S   M A G I C   E R I E
A L O H A   T H O R   N I N E
    F A N   E T N A   R E E L
F L O R I D A   B Y E
A A R P   O R A L   O C E A N
L S D   R U M B A   D O D G E
S E E   A L O U D   A R G U E
E R R   P A R T Y   D E A D
```

## 145

```
F I R S T   R O M P   T A P S
A D E L E   O V E R   O B O E
C L E A N S L A T E   Y U L E
T E L L   I L L   H O O T E D
      O G R E   W E S T
  C O M M E R C I A L A R T
M O N E T   O N T O   O A F
O W E D   P E N D S   L U L U
B L U   M I D I   S I T O N
  S P R I N G C H I C K E N
      I S E E   O D I E
A D O P T S   A T E   A M P S
G I V E   F A S T A S L E E P
E V E N   O W I E   T O R T E
D E N S   R E A R   S T E E D
```

## 146

| M | O | S | T | | | A | D | E | P | T | | C | H | I |
|---|---|---|---|---|---|---|---|---|---|---|---|---|---|---|
| A | L | I | A | S | | M | O | L | E | S | | R | A | M |
| C | A | L | C | I | U | M | R | I | C | H | | E | S | P |
| | F | L | O | T | S | A | M | | I | R | A | T | E | |
| | | P | E | N | | C | A | R | A | M | E | L | | |
| R | A | W | B | A | R | | F | A | L | T | E | R | | |
| A | B | O | R | T | | C | O | R | P | S | | I | C | E |
| V | E | R | A | | P | O | U | R | S | | S | N | I | T |
| E | L | M | | S | U | N | N | Y | | P | E | S | T | O |
| | R | E | A | R | E | D | | | S | A | T | E | E | N |
| S | T | I | R | F | R | Y | | K | E | N | | | | |
| P | A | D | R | E | | I | N | E | E | D | I | T | | |
| E | N | D | | B | O | T | T | O | M | R | I | G | H | T |
| A | G | E | | E | D | I | C | T | | A | L | G | A | E |
| R | O | N | | T | E | C | H | S | | | L | Y | N | X |

## 147

| A | C | T | S | | A | C | D | C | | T | I | N | E | S |
|---|---|---|---|---|---|---|---|---|---|---|---|---|---|---|
| L | O | R | E | | S | H | E | A | | E | M | O | T | E |
| O | P | E | N | | C | O | N | S | | C | H | E | A | T |
| H | E | A | D | F | O | R | T | H | E | H | I | L | L | S |
| A | D | D | | A | T | E | | S | N | I | T | | | |
| | | B | U | S | | G | A | T | E | | S | P | A | |
| E | A | S | E | L | | S | O | L | E | | S | H | O | P |
| R | U | N | A | T | E | M | P | E | R | A | T | U | R | E |
| A | T | O | N | | J | A | R | S | | D | A | T | E | S |
| S | O | W | | H | E | R | O | | B | O | Y | | | |
| | P | A | C | T | | E | A | R | | D | U | O | | |
| D | I | R | E | C | T | M | A | R | K | E | T | I | N | G |
| I | N | I | N | K | | O | G | R | E | | H | A | I | L |
| S | C | O | N | E | | V | E | E | R | | A | N | T | E |
| C | A | T | E | R | | E | D | D | Y | | W | E | E | D |

## 148

| L | I | D | S | | J | O | B | | P | H | T | E | S | T |
|---|---|---|---|---|---|---|---|---|---|---|---|---|---|---|
| O | D | I | N | | U | N | I | | L | A | R | G | E | R |
| A | L | S | O | | L | O | G | | A | N | Y | O | N | E |
| D | E | C | O | D | E | | B | O | Y | D | | S | T | Y |
| | | Z | I | P | | I | N | D | Y | | | | | |
| M | U | L | E | S | | D | R | E | A | M | L | E | S | S |
| A | S | O | F | | P | E | D | | T | A | I | L | O | R |
| S | E | N | E | G | A | L | | J | E | N | K | I | N | S |
| T | U | G | S | O | N | | B | U | S | | E | T | A | L |
| S | P | I | T | F | I | R | E | S | | E | M | E | R | Y |
| | | | A | C | H | E | | A | L | I | | | | |
| R | O | T | | S | M | O | G | | W | I | N | K | A | T |
| O | P | E | N | T | O | | E | M | O | | D | I | C | E |
| S | T | A | Y | E | D | | E | E | K | | E | L | M | S |
| A | S | S | U | R | E | | S | H | E | | D | O | E | S |

## 149

| S | E | C | T | | I | S | H | | | D | A | V | I | D |
|---|---|---|---|---|---|---|---|---|---|---|---|---|---|---|
| U | T | A | H | | N | E | I | L | | A | D | E | L | E |
| C | O | M | E | | S | A | G | E | | N | O | N | O | S |
| K | N | O | W | N | O | T | H | I | N | G | | T | S | K |
| | | | H | E | M | | E | S | E | | K | I | T | S |
| | A | B | O | U | N | D | S | | O | R | A | L | | |
| P | S | A | | R | I | O | T | | E | L | A | T | E | |
| L | A | B | C | O | A | T | | T | U | B | E | T | O | P |
| S | P | Y | O | N | | M | E | N | U | | T | R | A | |
| | | | S | O | S | O | | E | N | L | I | V | E | N |
| D | A | H | L | | N | A | S | | E | L | I | | | |
| I | D | O | | B | A | G | S | N | A | T | C | H | E | R |
| N | E | W | E | R | | T | I | E | D | | T | A | D | A |
| O | P | E | R | A | | S | A | V | E | | O | V | E | N |
| S | T | R | A | Y | | H | E | D | | R | E | N | T | |

## 150

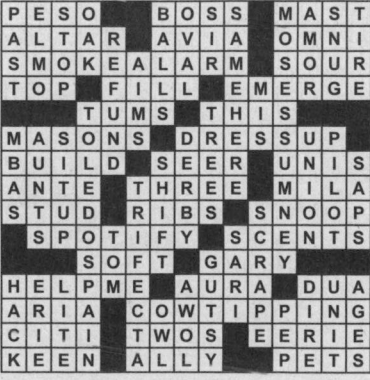

| P | E | S | O | | B | O | S | S | | M | A | S | T |
|---|---|---|---|---|---|---|---|---|---|---|---|---|---|
| A | L | T | A | R | | A | V | I | A | | O | M | N | I |
| S | M | O | K | E | A | L | A | R | M | | S | O | U | R |
| T | O | P | | F | I | L | L | | E | M | E | R | G | E |
| | | T | U | M | S | | T | H | I | S | | | | |
| M | A | S | O | N | S | | D | R | E | S | S | U | P | |
| B | U | I | L | D | | S | E | E | R | | U | N | I | S |
| A | N | T | E | | T | H | R | E | E | | M | I | L | A |
| S | T | U | D | | R | I | B | S | | S | N | O | O | P |
| | S | P | O | T | I | F | Y | | S | C | E | N | T | S |
| | | S | O | F | T | | G | A | R | Y | | | | |
| H | E | L | P | M | E | | A | U | R | A | | D | U | A |
| A | R | I | A | | C | O | W | T | I | P | P | I | N | G |
| C | I | T | I | | T | W | O | S | | E | E | R | I | E |
| K | E | E | N | | A | L | L | Y | | | P | E | T | S |

## 151

| A | T | L | A | S | | E | G | G | O | | O | A | H | U |
| H | A | I | K | U | | M | A | T | H | | T | R | A | P |
| A | T | E | A | M | | B | L | A | C | K | H | O | L | E |
| B | A | D | | A | C | R | E | | O | N | E | M | A | N |
| | | S | T | A | Y | | E | M | E | R | A | L | D | |
| P | O | L | A | R | V | O | R | T | E | X | | | | |
| A | V | E | D | A | | I | T | O | | P | I | S | A | |
| S | A | I | L | | S | E | D | A | N | | A | K | I | N |
| S | L | A | Y | | T | A | G | | A | R | E | N | T | |
| | | C | A | R | E | P | A | C | K | A | G | E | | |
| P | E | T | S | I | T | S | | I | N | C | A | | | |
| O | R | A | N | G | E | | A | L | T | O | | E | G | O |
| P | A | P | A | S | M | U | R | F | | U | P | D | O | G |
| U | S | E | R | | A | T | E | E | | N | I | N | E | R |
| P | E | R | K | | P | E | A | R | | T | E | A | S | E |

## 152

| S | C | H | I | S | M | | B | U | D | S | | D | A | D |
| N | U | A | N | C | E | | A | S | I | A | | E | C | O |
| L | E | S | S | O | N | | N | U | T | S | | T | O | N |
| | | | Y | O | U | N | G | A | T | H | E | A | R | T |
| | P | A | N | T | | O | S | L | O | | X | I | N | G |
| D | E | S | C | E | N | T | | | | A | L | S | O | |
| I | D | O | | R | O | M | A | | N | H | L | | | |
| G | I | F | T | E | D | E | D | U | C | A | T | I | O | N |
| | | | O | D | E | | S | P | A | N | | T | W | O |
| A | M | E | X | | | L | A | S | E | R | E | D | | |
| M | A | N | I | | S | H | U | I | | B | A | Y | S | |
| B | L | A | C | K | P | A | N | T | H | E | R | | | |
| I | A | M | | E | R | I | C | | O | R | N | E | R | Y |
| E | W | E | | P | E | R | U | | P | R | E | M | E | D |
| N | I | L | | T | E | S | T | | S | Y | R | U | P | S |

## 153

| B | A | D | P | R | | A | B | B | I | | C | H | I | |
| O | R | A | T | E | | W | O | R | M | S | | L | O | O |
| C | A | N | A | D | A | G | O | O | S | E | | I | N | N |
| A | B | E | | T | I | E | S | | C | R | I | E | D | |
| | | | B | A | L | E | | H | A | V | A | N | A | |
| I | N | C | A | P | S | | P | A | R | E | N | T | | |
| C | E | A | S | E | | R | U | L | E | R | | B | A | T |
| E | A | R | S | | S | I | R | E | D | | J | A | N | E |
| E | R | R | | P | A | N | S | Y | | P | A | S | T | E |
| | | O | R | A | N | G | E | | C | A | V | E | I | N |
| | S | T | I | N | T | S | | T | A | R | A | | | |
| I | N | D | I | A | | A | I | R | S | | S | A | D | |
| J | L | O | | C | H | E | C | K | P | L | E | A | S | E |
| O | K | S | | S | A | Y | H | I | | E | V | I | A | N |
| B | Y | E | | T | E | E | S | | Y | E | L | P | S | |

## 154

| R | O | W | S | | R | A | F | T | | T | I | B | E | T |
| I | K | E | A | | I | D | E | A | | A | G | A | T | E |
| C | A | R | G | O | H | O | L | D | | R | E | N | A | L |
| A | Y | E | S | H | A | | L | A | S | | T | A | L | L |
| | | | I | N | S | | | P | A | I | N | | | |
| | C | O | L | O | N | E | L | M | U | S | T | A | R | D |
| C | A | R | E | | A | R | I | A | N | A | | P | A | Y |
| H | I | D | E | S | | E | N | D | | P | E | E | V | E |
| I | R | E | | T | U | N | D | R | A | | R | E | E | D |
| C | O | R | P | O | R | A | T | E | W | O | R | L | D | |
| | | | F | A | W | N | | | S | N | L | | | |
| N | O | O | N | | S | A | T | | I | A | G | R | E | E |
| O | P | R | A | H | | C | O | R | N | F | I | E | L | D |
| S | U | M | M | A | | R | U | N | G | | G | A | L | E |
| E | S | S | A | Y | | E | R | A | S | | S | P | A | N |

## 155

| A | L | U | M | | O | V | A | L | | | D | R | O | P |
| L | E | N | A | | K | A | T | I | E | | N | E | A | R |
| B | A | R | D | | R | I | T | Z | Y | | A | N | T | E |
| U | N | O | R | G | A | N | I | Z | E | D | | A | M | P |
| M | I | L | E | Y | | | C | O | D | A | | M | I | A |
| S | N | L | | R | I | M | | | D | A | I | L | Y | |
| | | C | O | H | E | R | E | S | | I | N | K | S | |
| | | D | O | S | O | M | E | T | H | I | N | G | | |
| S | P | I | N | | P | O | P | T | A | R | T | | | |
| C | R | E | S | T | | | A | G | O | | S | Z | A | |
| R | O | T | | E | D | G | E | | | N | O | T | E | S |
| I | N | S | | T | R | E | S | P | A | S | S | E | R | S |
| P | O | O | L | | U | N | T | I | L | | A | L | O | E |
| T | U | D | E | | G | R | E | T | A | | G | L | E | N |
| S | N | A | G | | | E | R | A | S | | E | A | S | T |

## 156

| O | D | D | S |   | A | D | A | G | E |   | A | P | B |   |
| A | U | R | A |   | R | I | P | U | P |   | P | L | U | S |
| K | E | Y | L | I | M | E | P | I | E |   | R | A | S | H |
|   |   | A | R | O | D |   | L | E | D | I | N | T | O |   |
| H | A | M | M | E | R | A | N | D | S | I | C | K | L | E |
| E | L | V | I | S |   | W | A | S |   | D | O | S | E | S |
| L | I | P | S |   | D | A | B |   | T | N | T |   |   |   |
| M | T | S |   | H | A | Y |   | J | E | T |   | S | S | N |
|   |   |   | P | E | N |   | H | A | D |   | S | H | O | O |
| S | W | I | L | L |   | P | A | Y |   | E | T | U | D | E |
| P | E | D | A | L | T | O | T | H | E | M | E | T | A | L |
| R | A | U | C | O | U | S |   | A | R | I | A |   |   |   |
| A | N | N | A |   | L | E | G | W | A | R | M | E | R | S |
| T | E | N | T |   | S | U | L | K | S |   | E | V | I | L |
|   | D | O | E |   | A | R | O | S | E |   | D | E | M | O |

## 157

| W | A | L | K |   | O | P | A | L |   | D | A | T | H |   |
| A | R | L | O |   | H | A | V | E |   | D | E | B | R | A |
| F | R | A | I | D | Y | C | A | T |   | A | T | B | A | T |
| T | O | M |   | J | E | T |   | I | T | S | T | I | M | E |
|   | W | A | D | E | S |   | N | O | A | H |   |   |   |   |
|   |   | I | D | I | O | M |   | O | N | E | D | G | E |   |
| A | B | B | A |   | A | L | E | C |   | I | R | O | N | Y |
| S | E | E | M |   | M | A | D | A | M |   | A | J | A | R |
| A | L | T | O | S |   | F | A | M | E |   | N | O | T | E |
| P | L | A | N | T | S |   | L | O | G | I | C |   |   |   |
|   | D | A | I | S |   | A | C | H | E | S |   |   |   |   |
| R | O | T | H | I | R | A |   | A | S | K |   | T | E | A |
| A | L | I | E | N |   | P | A | R | T | Y | W | H | I | P |
| G | A | L | A | S |   | P | L | E | A |   | H | A | Z | E |
| E | Y | E | D |   | Y | E | A | R |   | O | N | E | S |   |

## 158

| T | E | M | P | O |   | R | O | W | S |   | S | P | R | Y |
| A | L | O | O | F |   | I | M | A | C |   | T | R | U | E |
| F | L | A | T | F | I | N | I | S | H |   | R | O | L | L |
| T | A | N |   | M | O | S | T |   | E | N | A | M | E | L |
|   |   | L | I | N | E | S |   | D | O | I |   |   |   |   |
| C | R | E | E | K | S |   | B | U | R | G | L | A | R |   |
| H | E | A | V | E |   | T | O | L | L |   | H | U | G | O |
| A | C | R | E |   | R | O | U | T | E |   | T | R | I | P |
| T | A | L | L |   | A | N | T | S |   | S | M | I | L | E |
| S | P | Y | W | A | R | E |   | S | P | A | D | E | S |   |
|   | I | K | E |   | A | L | L | A | N |   |   |   |   |   |
| G | O | S | T | A | G |   | R | E | A | R |   | E | M | T |
| A | R | C | H |   | E | V | E | N | B | E | T | T | E | R |
| R | E | A | M |   | M | I | N | D |   | L | O | T | T | O |
| B | O | N | E |   | S | P | A | S |   | Y | E | A | S | T |

## 159

| B | O | L | D |   | O | F | F | A | L |   | B | A | S | S |
| O | V | E | R |   | A | L | I | N | E |   | I | D | L | E |
| G | I | N | N | I | F | E | R | G | O | O | D | W | I | N |
| E | N | D | O | W |   | E | E | L |   | R | E | A | M | S |
| Y | E | S |   | O | U | T | D | O | E | S |   | R | Y | E |
|   |   |   | I | N | N |   |   | D | O | E |   |   |   |   |
|   | M | A | R | T | I | N | A | H | I | N | G | I | S |   |
| D | O | H | A |   | S | P | L | I | T |   | O | N | T | O |
| A | L | A |   | D | O | R | I | T | O | S |   | D | U | D |
| D | A | M | P | E | N |   | R | E | F | U | N | D |   |   |
|   | R | O | A | R |   | C | A | P |   | M | A | L | T |   |
|   | M | I | N | D | Y | K | A | L | I | N | G |   |   |   |
| W | H | E | N |   | O | N | I | C | E |   | F | E | T | A |
| A | U | N | T |   | C | I | T | E | S |   | I | M | A | C |
| G | E | T | S |   | S | C | A | R | S |   | C | E | D | E |

## 160

|   | B | A | R |   | C | H | O | S | E |   | S | P | A | T |
| T | O | D | O |   | H | E | N | N | A |   | K | A | L | E |
| A | X | E | L |   | A | L | T | A | R |   | A | S | I | A |
| B | U | L | L | E | T | P | O | I | N | T |   | T | A | R |
| S | P | E | E | D |   | P | L | E | A | S | E | S |   |   |
|   |   | R | U | S | H |   | R | P | M |   |   |   |   |   |
| O | P | E | D |   | H | E | A | D |   | E | A | T | A | T |
| F | A | R | E | W | E | L | L | A | D | D | R | E | S | S |
| F | L | A | R | E |   | M | E | N | U |   | T | A | S | K |
|   | B | L | T |   | G | O | B | Y |   |   |   |   |   |   |
| W | A | Y | T | O | G | O |   | A | P | T | L | Y |   |   |
| S | A | M |   | S | U | R | F | A | C | E | A | R | E | A |
| P | L | U | G |   | R | A | T | I | O |   | N | O | E | L |
| A | L | S | O |   | E | V | E | N | T |   | T | O | R | E |
| M | E | E | T |   | D | E | N | T | S |   | S | P | Y |   |

## 161

```
L O S S _ S O O T _ _ W I G
I N K Y _ E B B E D _ H I L L
B A I L _ A G I L E _ O S L O
Y I E L D _ Y E L L O W C A B
A R R A I G N S _ _ R I O T _
_ _ B A O _ D R E _ N E T _ _
I N D U S T R I O U S _ S A O
D U O S _ C E N T S _ H I S S
L I N _ R H I N E S T O N E S
E S T _ I A N _ E A T _ _ _ _
_ A P E S _ _ L A T T E A R T
S N A K E E Y E S _ A L G A E
A C N E _ T O V A H _ B A K E
L E I S _ A R E N A _ A M E N
E S C _ _ E R A S _ R E D S _
```

## 162

```
A S S E T _ I S E E _ U P T O
C L O N E _ O P A L _ N E O N
H A R D A T W O R K _ F A R E
E P E E _ O A T _ H O U S E S
_ _ A M E N _ H O U R _ _ _ _
_ P R E S S Y O U R L U C K _
C A R E T _ _ O W N S _ N O R
A C I D _ P O K E D _ S I R I
L E D _ S A K E _ M E T E S _
F R E E T R A D E Z O N E _ _
_ _ D U T Y _ F E E D _ _ _ _
S A T I N Y _ S I R _ S H O T
A L O T _ H A L L O F F A M E
G E N E _ A L O E _ R O L E S
A X E D _ T I P S _ I R O N S
```

## 163

```
S P E C _ P L A N S _ A C E S
E U R O _ D E P O T _ C O E N
C R I B _ F O O D R E C A L L
T R E A D _ _ P E A N U T S _
_ _ L O S T _ A Y E S _ _ _ _
F A I T H H I L L _ W E I R D
A R F _ A U D I _ S O L A R _
T E A M _ T E N O R _ F I D O
A N N O Y _ D I E S _ A I L _
L A Y L A _ F A L S E I D O L
_ _ A C T I _ S T A G _ _ _ _
_ D O S H O T S _ L E T I N _
F I R S T O F A L L _ T A M E
I C E E _ T U L S A _ I R A S
N E S S _ S L E D S _ T A C T
```

## 164

```
A R T S _ S L O T H _ S L A P
L E I A _ L O T S A _ N A T O
E N V Y _ E V I A N _ E R O S
_ T O U P E E S _ D R E A M T
_ _ N I P S _ W H I Z _ _ _ _
_ T A C K Y _ T I E D Y E D _
S I D L E _ W E L L S _ D O C
E R I E _ G R E E D _ P I P S
T E E _ S L A M S _ F A C E T
_ D U G O U T S _ M I S T Y _
_ _ R U T H _ C U S S _ _ _ _
O C C U L T _ B A S H F U L _
C R A M _ O D O R S _ A R E A
H A R P _ N U D G E _ I D O L
O B E Y _ Y O Y O S _ L U S T
```

## 165

```
A C T E D _ B E N D _ S T A T
R E A D Y _ A R E A _ T A L E
T O X I N _ G R I T _ A X L E
_ _ S T A T E E L E C T I O N
O D E _ M O L D _ _ O U S T S
R E A S O N _ C A M E _ _ _ _
E L S E _ H A I T I _ M O C _
C H O C O L A T E E C L A I R
K I N _ R O M A N _ I D L E _
_ _ D A B S _ N E P H E W _ _
A S S E T _ H O A X _ A D S _
W H I T E E L E P H A N T _ _
F A R E _ R A R E _ L E T B E
U K E S _ A V O N _ T R E A T
L E N T _ S A S S _ S O R T S
```

## 166

```
DAZED  IMAC  GRIP
ECOLI  COCO  RAZE
BROKENOPEN  EGOS
TEM HENS  SPEEDO
    HATS  LOAN
TAPERS  HOLYSEE
IFOLD  SITE  CLAP
ELLE  PUTTS  RATE
RAIN  LIMO  GETIT
 COMPETE  PREENS
   IRAS  CLAN
ASTROS  NOUN  ERA
POUR  EVENSTEVEN
PANE  DEAD  EVENT
SPAN  OGRE  DARTS
```

## 167

```
SCATS  APOP  PAGE
ARBOR  DEAR  EXIT
PUBLICDEFENDERS
 DIE  ILKS  ODDLY
    RAVES  STL
 ATARI  PUREST
SCENICDRIVE  LOT
PUNT  EYE  AURA
ART  GENERICDRUG
 ASSESS  RAMPS
   ETC  UMAMI
EGRET  SNIT  RAN
MNEMONICDEVICES
MANE  ELLA  INNIE
AWED  WOES  AGENT
```

## 168

```
SHOT  PEG  FOURS
TODO  RAE  KRISTI
ALEX  OUTFIELDER
BASIL  LAWNS
  CATHOLIC  VAT
DJS  SHAWL  HEIRS
MAC  TRY  HATRACK
CRISCO  RANON
 FLABBERGAST
RIAL  ATV  STEMS
FAMILYCREST  DAL
IRON  AHOST  PITA
REV  BRA  TAKEOUT
ELI  ANT  TENURE
DYE  TSA  SASSED
```

## 169

```
 HES  SHAG  CLEAT
PEAK  TARO  HELLO
EASY  ORAL  ANKLE
PREMIUMBLEND
ATLAST  SYNC  FAR
  PLEA  DEFINE
SOB  ESTEE  EGGS
CHRISTIANMINGLE
AJAR  TRYON  YET
MOSAIC  ANEW
SYS  MAYA  TRISHA
 ALTERNATEMIX
RHINO  SMUG  NONE
AUNTS  NOME  EKGS
TENET  ORBS  RYE
```

## 170

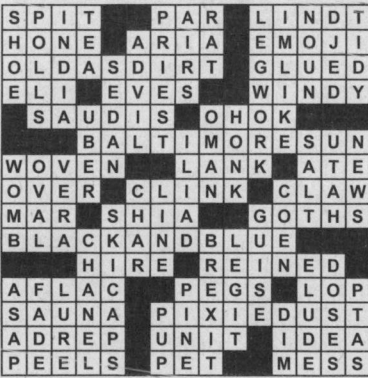

```
SPIT  PAR  LINDT
HONE  ARIA  EMOJI
OLDASDIRT  GLUED
ELI  EVES  WINDY
 SAUDIS  OHOK
 BALTIMORESUN
WOVEN  LANK  ATE
OVER  CLINK  CLAW
MAR  SHIA  GOTHS
BLACKANDBLUE
 HIRE  REINED
AFLAC  PEGS  LOP
SAUNA  PIXIEDUST
ADREP  UNIT  IDEA
PEELS  PET  MESS
```

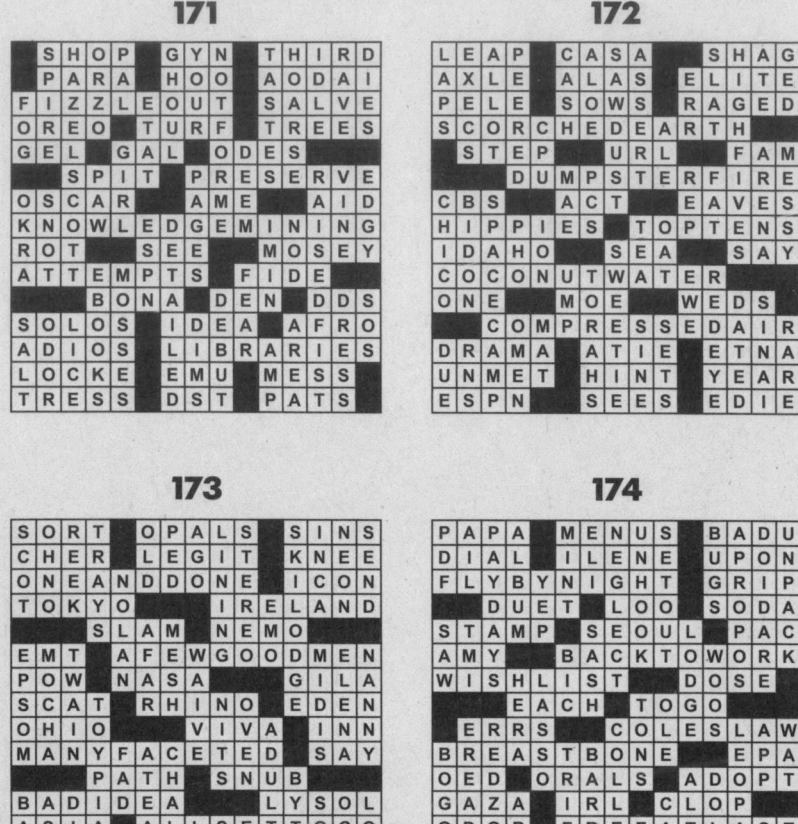

**171**

| | S | H | O | P | | G | Y | N | | T | H | I | R | D |
| | P | A | R | A | | H | O | O | | A | O | D | A | I |
| F | I | Z | Z | L | E | O | U | T | | S | A | L | V | E |
| O | R | E | O | | T | U | R | F | | T | R | E | E | S |
| G | E | L | | G | A | L | | O | D | E | S | | | |
| | | S | P | I | T | | P | R | E | S | E | R | V | E |
| O | S | C | A | R | | A | M | E | | | A | I | D | |
| K | N | O | W | L | E | D | G | E | M | I | N | I | N | G |
| R | O | T | | | S | E | E | | | M | O | S | E | Y |
| A | T | T | E | M | P | T | S | | F | I | D | E | | |
| | B | O | N | A | | D | E | N | | D | D | S | | |
| S | O | L | O | S | | I | D | E | A | | A | F | R | O |
| A | D | I | O | S | | L | I | B | R | A | R | I | E | S |
| L | O | C | K | E | | E | M | U | | M | E | S | S | |
| T | R | E | S | S | | D | S | T | | P | A | T | S | |

**172**

| L | E | A | P | | C | A | S | A | | | S | H | A | G |
| A | X | L | E | | A | L | A | S | | E | L | I | T | E |
| P | E | L | E | | S | O | W | S | | R | A | G | E | D |
| S | C | O | R | C | H | E | D | E | A | R | T | H | | |
| | S | T | E | P | | U | R | L | | | F | A | M | |
| | | D | U | M | P | S | T | E | R | F | I | R | E | |
| C | B | S | | A | C | T | | E | A | V | E | S | | |
| H | I | P | P | I | E | S | | T | O | P | T | E | N | S |
| I | D | A | H | O | | S | E | A | | | S | A | Y | |
| C | O | C | O | N | U | T | W | A | T | E | R | | | |
| O | N | E | | M | O | E | | W | E | D | S | | | |
| | | C | O | M | P | R | E | S | S | E | D | A | I | R |
| D | R | A | M | A | | A | T | I | E | | E | T | N | A |
| U | N | M | E | T | | H | I | N | T | | Y | E | A | R |
| E | S | P | N | | S | E | E | S | | E | D | I | E | |

**173**

| S | O | R | T | | O | P | A | L | S | | S | I | N | S |
| C | H | E | R | | L | E | G | I | T | | K | N | E | E |
| O | N | E | A | N | D | D | O | N | E | | I | C | O | N |
| T | O | K | Y | O | | | I | R | E | L | A | N | D | |
| | | S | L | A | M | | N | E | M | O | | | | |
| E | M | T | | A | F | E | W | G | O | O | D | M | E | N |
| P | O | W | | N | A | S | A | | | G | I | L | A | |
| S | C | A | T | | R | H | I | N | O | | E | D | E | N |
| O | H | I | O | | | V | I | V | A | | I | N | N | |
| M | A | N | Y | F | A | C | E | T | E | D | | S | A | Y |
| | P | A | T | H | | S | N | U | B | | | | | |
| B | A | D | I | D | E | A | | | L | Y | S | O | L | |
| A | S | I | A | | A | L | L | S | E | T | T | O | G | O |
| B | O | O | N | | M | E | E | T | S | | E | R | R | S |
| A | F | R | O | | S | T | O | U | T | | S | E | E | S |

**174**

| P | A | P | A | | M | E | N | U | S | | B | A | D | U |
| D | I | A | L | | I | L | E | N | E | | U | P | O | N |
| F | L | Y | B | Y | N | I | G | H | T | | G | R | I | P |
| | D | U | E | T | | L | O | O | | S | O | D | A | |
| S | T | A | M | P | | S | E | O | U | L | | P | A | C |
| A | M | Y | | B | A | C | K | T | O | W | O | R | K | |
| W | I | S | H | L | I | S | T | | | D | O | S | E | |
| | | E | A | C | H | | | T | O | G | O | | | |
| | E | R | R | S | | C | O | L | E | S | L | A | W | |
| B | R | E | A | S | T | B | O | N | E | | | E | P | A |
| O | E | D | | O | R | A | L | S | | A | D | O | P | T |
| G | A | Z | A | | I | R | L | | C | L | O | P | | |
| O | D | O | R | | F | R | E | E | A | T | L | A | S | T |
| T | E | N | T | | L | E | G | O | S | | C | R | E | E |
| A | R | E | S | | E | L | E | N | A | | E | D | E | N |

**175**

| C | A | M | P | S | | O | B | O | E | | D | A | T | A |
| O | C | E | A | N | | F | O | A | M | | I | R | O | N |
| B | A | L | L | O | F | F | I | R | E | | P | E | O | N |
| S | I | T | | R | E | E | L | | R | E | L | A | T | E |
| | | | G | E | A | R | | H | A | L | O | | | |
| R | E | S | O | R | T | | D | E | L | I | M | E | A | T |
| O | R | A | L | S | | B | O | L | D | | A | L | S | O |
| W | O | R | D | | L | A | M | P | S | | M | E | S | A |
| E | D | G | E | | U | S | E | S | | L | I | N | E | S |
| R | E | E | N | A | C | T | S | | G | O | L | A | S | T |
| | | | B | I | K | E | | H | A | U | L | | | |
| F | A | I | R | L | Y | | B | O | R | N | | S | K | I |
| I | N | S | O | | D | A | I | L | Y | G | R | I | N | D |
| S | T | E | W | | O | G | R | E | | E | E | R | I | E |
| T | E | E | N | | G | O | D | S | | S | P | I | T | S |

## 176

| C | A | V | E |   | G | Y | M | S |   | F | L | O | A | T |
| A | R | E | A |   | R | A | R | E |   | R | A | B | B | I |
| D | O | N | T | P | A | N | I | C |   | E | X | I | L | E |
| E | M | T |   | I | C | K |   | T | W | E | E | T | E | D |
| T | A | I | P | E | I |   |   | A | B | S |   |   |   |   |
|   | D | R | A | M | A | C | R | I | T | I | C |   |   |   |
| C | A | L | F |   | S | E | S | A | M | E |   | D | U | H |
| A | R | I | S | E |   | R | I | B |   | S | M | O | R | E |
| R | I | M |   | L | O | C | A | L | E |   | A | L | E | X |
|   | D | A | T | E | L | I | N | E | N | B | C |   |   |   |
|   |   |   | U | M | A |   |   | J | E | S | T | E | R |   |
| E | V | I | L | E | Y | E |   | A | O | L |   | I | V | E |
| R | E | R | A | N |   | D | E | F | Y | L | O | G | I | C |
| G | R | A | N | T |   | A | C | R | E |   | F | E | T | A |
| O | A | S | E | S |   | M | O | O | D |   | T | R | A | P |

## 177

| R | E | C | A | P |   | A | M | P |   |   | F | A | M | E |
| A | D | O | B | O |   | M | O | O |   | R | I | C | E | S |
| F | I | R | S | T | D | A | T | E |   | O | N | T | A | P |
| T | E | N |   | H | U | S | H |   | O | D | D | I | T | Y |
|   |   |   | F | O | E | S |   | T | R | I | O |   |   |   |
|   | S | P | I | L | L |   | P | R | E | N | U | P | S |   |
| C | H | A | S | E |   | C | H | I | C |   | T | H | A | W |
| R | O | T | H |   | S | H | O | C | K |   | M | A | T | E |
| Y | E | T | I |   | H | U | N | K |   | R | O | S | I | E |
|   | S | Y | N | E | R | G | Y |   | S | I | R | E | N |   |
|   |   |   | G | N | U | S |   | A | C | N | E |   |   |   |
| D | O | G | L | E | G |   | D | R | A | G |   | S | I | T |
| O | P | I | U | M |   | F | I | R | M | P | R | I | C | E |
| L | A | R | R | Y |   | U | N | O |   | O | H | G | E | E |
| E | L | L | E |   |   | N | E | W |   | P | O | N | D | S |

## 178

| B | I | B |   | C | R | A | B |   |   | T | R | A | I | L |
| E | M | O |   | R | E | A | L |   | L | I | A | I | S | E |
| G | A | Z | P | A | C | H | O |   | A | P | P | L | E | S |
| S | C | O | O | T |   | C | A | M | P | U | S | E | S |   |
|   |   |   | D | E | E | P |   | B | E | E | N |   |   |   |
|   | A | D | S |   | G | R | O | U | N | D | Z | E | R | O |
| B | R | R |   | L | O | O | P |   | T | O | E | C | A | P |
| O | B | A | M | A |   | M | E | H |   | F | L | A | K | E |
| R | O | M | A | N | S |   | R | E | E | F |   | R | E | D |
| G | R | A | N | D | P | I | A | N | O |   | A | D | D |   |
|   |   |   | G | L | E | N |   | S | N | A | P |   |   |   |
| W | E | A | R | I | E | S | T |   | N | E | S | T | S |   |
| A | L | M | O | N | D |   | G | U | E | S | S | W | H | O |
| G | L | O | V | E | S |   | I | S | L | E |   | A | I | R |
| E | A | S | E | S |   | F | A | I | L |   | T | N | T |   |

## 179

| P | A | S | S |   | A | R | A | B |   |   | P | A | T | S |
| A | C | H | E |   | R | O | V | E |   | D | I | X | I | E |
| C | H | E | E | S | E | L | O | G |   | E | X | I | L | E |
| T | O | E |   | A | N | E | W |   | R | A | I | S | E | D |
| S | O | N | A | T | A |   |   | H | E | R | E |   |   |   |
|   |   |   | C | A | S | H | R | E | G | I | S | T | E | R |
| C | H | U | R | N |   | E | E | R | I | E |   | E | Y | E |
| H | O | P | E |   | R | A | I | D | S |   | J | A | R | S |
| I | P | O |   | F | U | D | G | E |   | C | O | M | E | T |
| C | I | N | N | A | M | O | N | R | O | L | L |   |   |   |
|   |   |   | I | C | O | N |   |   | P | O | T | A | T | O |
| Z | I | P | P | E | R |   | T | I | E | S |   | L | O | L |
| A | D | A | P | T |   | H | I | T | R | E | C | O | R | D |
| P | O | L | E | S |   | I | K | E | A |   | A | N | T | E |
| S | L | E | D |   | D | I | M | S |   | P | E | E | R |   |

## 180

| H | I | J | A | B |   | L | A | P |   | I | F | F | Y |
| A | R | U | B | A |   | C | O | M | E |   | M | A | L | I |
| L | O | N | E | R | A | N | G | E | R |   | F | L | A | P |
| O | N | E |   | R | U | N | O | N |   | H | U | S | K | S |
|   |   |   | L | I | N |   | D | O | Y | L | E |   |   |   |
|   | S | C | O | O | T | E | D |   | W | E | L | C | H | S |
| E | C | H | O |   | G | R | A | I | N |   | L | O | U |   |
| T | E | E | N | C | H | O | I | C | E | A | W | A | R | D |
| A | N | A |   | R | E | S | E | T |   | A | I | D | S |   |
| S | T | P | A | U | L |   | S | I | L | L | Y | M | E |   |
|   |   |   | T | H | E | M | E |   | I | O | S |   |   |   |
| A | P | R | I | L |   | A | F | L | A | C |   | S | H | U |
| L | O | I | S |   | G | R | A | Y | M | A | T | T | E | R |
| O | N | C | E |   | E | L | S | E |   | L | E | A | R | N |
| T | Y | K | E |   | M | E | T |   | E | D | G | E | S |   |

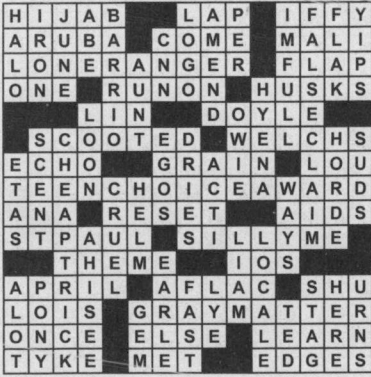

## 181

```
P S S T   I D E D   S P L I T
O A H U   S O L O   O H A R A
S L A B   L O S T   L O N E R
T I M E S A W A S T I N G
A V E   H M O   O D E S S A
L A S S O   P F F T   S T O P
  A W E   L O T S   O O P
N E W M A N A G E M E N T
P O M   E R A S   R U M
E S P N   T Y K E   D U N S T
W H O O S H   L A G   U A E
  R O M A N N U M E R A L S
A B I D E   A U D I   O N I T
P A U L A   I D E S   A C N E
T A M E R   L E S S   D E E D
```

## 182

```
O T T O   O R B I T   C A T S
A A R P   F I R M A   A R I A
F R I E D F O O D S   T A N G
S P O R E   S O T H E B Y S
    A N T S   W E A R
T H E   S A T I N S H E E T S
H I N T   T A R   A D M I T
A N D A   S T I N T   T A T A
I D O L S   S E A   O I L Y
S U N K E N S H I P S   L E S
    S L O T   L A P S
T R E E F R O G   E A S E L
Y A R N   M O N E Y C L I P S
K I A S   A G A P E   A R E A
E L S E   L E T A T   D I E T
```

## 183

```
W I S H   F R A M E   S C A M
E C H O   L I N E S   C H I A
T H E R M O S T A T   R E N T
    C O O K S   D I E T S
  T H O R   A L U M S
  W E A R   T H R E E P E A T
B E S T S   H Y M N S   C G I
U L T A   P E E P S   J U A N
T S K   S U N N I   W O R M S
T H I C K C O A T   H Y D E
  T R I E D   O O H S
R A C E D   T U L S A
A C H E   T H U N D E R C A T
P R E P   N O R T E   J A V A
T E N S   T E N O R   O P E N
```

## 184

```
  O F F   F L A T   P U P S
S H I E S   L O R I   A S A P
C A R B O   I A M M A L A L A
A R E   U S E D   E V E
R E C A N T S   S C O O P S
  A L D A   L O A N   O T S
R E P O S T   Y U P   F L E A
A T T N   E V I L S   L A R K
S H A G   C A N   U T U R N S
P O I   D A N G   L O K I
  S N O O P S   D E T E C T S
  C G I   R O S A   E A T
L O S E S T E A M   L Y C R A
I D E A   A C N E   S O A P Y
D E A N   L O T S   U P S
```

## 185

```
R A P T   T E A   S M U R F
A L S O   E A S Y   H O N O R
F L Y O F F T H E H A N D L E
T A C T I L E   S A M E O L D
S H H   G O N G   V E T
    F U N   R E A D   P A W
  C H A R   L A W N   B A N E
D R I V E H O M E A P O I N T
R E N E   A R M S   A X L E
Y E T   T R E Y   P R Y
    P H D   S A R I   A H A
S T E E R E D   N E S T L E S
W A L K O N E G G S H E L L S
A L L E N   N I L E   S O L E
T E A S E   N E T   T W O S
```

## 186

```
S L I M   S M A S H   W A D E
T O R E   P A R T Y   E R I E
I C O N   A D O R E   N E O N
F A N T A     S A N I T A R Y
F L Y O N T H E W A L L
    R O S E     S H O O T
O A R     A R E   A N N I E
F L O W E R A R R A N G I N G
F E V E R   R E C   T A G
  S E A R S     B L A B
    P O L E V A U L T I N G
I M P O L I T E   T E N O R
D A R N   C U R S E   A S I A
L A I R   E D G A R   M E S S
E M M Y   S E E Y A   S T E P
```

## 187

```
S T A S H   B R A D   E M T S
P A S T A   R E N O   Q U I P
E X H U S B A N D S   U C L A
D I Y   S A V E   S P I K E S
      E L S E   R I O T
T I T L E S   D O E E Y E D
A R A B S   P O U R   F L I P
L O B O     L U G   U S E S
K N O W   R U S H   S N I T S
  S O S U E M E   M O D E S T
    T R U E   L A O S
I N F A N T   A U N T   K I A
M O A N   E M P T Y H A N D S
A V I D   R I P E   E C O L I
C A R S   S A S S   S E X E S
```

## 188

```
S T I G M A   N A S A   P D F
M A D R I D   O P E N W I D E
U P L A T E   D E A D H E A T
T E E N   L E S S   E A S Y A
    T I E D   M A T
  S P E D   A L I E N S H I P
G O U D A   M A C S   T O S S
A U R A   G A T E S   H U L A
S T E M   A M I D   G E N E S
P H E N O M E N A   A D D S
    E V E   M A Y A
A R I S E   M O S S   M E M O
M U S T R E A D   S C A L E D
P L A Y D A T E   E A G L E D
S E W   O R E S   T W E E T S
```

## 189

```
A L I S T   A B B A   R I N D
S O N I A   L O A N   F R I E
S T A R T   O U S T   P O E T
    S I T O N T H E F E N C E
O D E   L E G S   L A Y E R
C Y C L E D     S H O T
A L O E   P A P E R   B R A
L A N D R E S T O R A T I O N
A N D   U P S E T   E G G O
    B R A T   L E A S E S
A T S E A   B O O M   I R E
S E T T L E F O R L E S S
Y E A R   D A N A   R A T E S
E T T A   G L U T   G R E E K
T H E Y   E L S E   F A R L Y
```

## 190

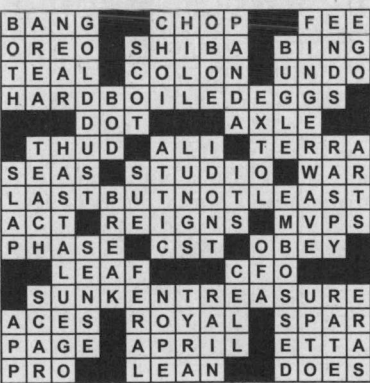

```
B A N G     C H O P     F E E
O R E O   S H I B A   B I N G
T E A L   C O L O N   U N D O
H A R D B O I L E D E G G S
    D O T       A X L E
  T H U D   A L I   T E R R A
S E A S   S T U D I O   W A R
L A S T B U T N O T L E A S T
A C T   R E I G N S   M V P S
P H A S E   C S T   O B E Y
  L E A F     C F O
  S U N K E N T R E A S U R E
A C E S   R O Y A L   S P A R
P A G E   A P R I L   E T T A
P R O   L E A N     D O E S
```

## 191

| D | R | A | B | | C | E | L | L | | M | I | M | E | S |
| O | O | Z | E | | O | R | E | O | | I | L | A | N | A |
| H | O | T | E | L | M | A | I | D | | M | O | L | D | Y |
| A | T | E | | I | F | S | | G | L | O | V | E | S | |
| | S | C | H | M | O | | L | E | A | S | E | | | |
| | | E | E | R | I | E | | P | A | Y | N | O | W | |
| N | U | L | L | | T | O | G | A | | S | O | A | M | I |
| A | S | A | P | | S | W | E | L | L | | U | N | I | T |
| D | E | N | I | M | | A | N | T | E | | M | A | T | S |
| A | R | E | N | A | S | | D | O | G | M | A | | | |
| | | G | R | I | D | S | | C | A | N | I | T | | |
| | T | A | H | I | N | I | | B | U | N | | G | A | G |
| S | A | R | A | N | | J | E | R | R | Y | R | I | C | E |
| O | P | I | N | E | | O | V | A | L | | A | V | O | N |
| B | E | A | D | S | | N | A | G | S | | N | E | S | T |

## 192

| H | E | L | P | | M | O | O | S | E | | B | U | S | T |
| A | C | A | I | | E | R | R | O | R | | O | N | T | O |
| W | H | I | Z | | H | O | C | U | S | P | O | C | U | S |
| | O | R | Z | O | | A | L | A | S | K | A | N | S | |
| | | A | I | R | | | T | A | R | P | S | | | |
| R | A | Z | Z | L | E | D | A | Z | Z | L | E | | | |
| P | R | E | Z | | F | E | T | A | | M | C | A | T | |
| M | A | R | | R | A | D | | | | | M | O | B | |
| | B | O | A | T | | E | R | I | E | | S | O | N | Y |
| | | W | A | L | K | I | E | T | A | L | K | I | E | |
| | C | E | A | S | E | | | A | C | E | | | | |
| F | O | L | K | T | A | L | E | | T | E | X | T | | |
| L | O | V | E | Y | D | O | V | E | Y | | P | O | O | H |
| A | K | I | N | | I | R | E | N | E | | E | X | P | O |
| T | E | S | S | | N | E | R | D | S | | R | O | S | Y |

## 193

| H | E | R | O | | W | A | I | T | | O | P | R | A | H |
| A | V | O | W | | A | M | M | O | | S | A | U | N | A |
| V | I | O | L | I | N | B | O | W | | M | I | N | T | Y |
| E | L | M | | N | I | L | | S | P | O | N | G | E | |
| | | L | A | N | E | S | | A | N | T | | | | |
| S | A | R | O | N | G | | H | U | N | D | R | E | D | S |
| A | D | O | B | E | | T | I | M | E | | O | X | E | N |
| G | U | T | S | | P | R | E | P | S | | L | I | P | O |
| A | L | O | T | | E | E | L | S | | A | L | L | O | W |
| S | T | R | E | S | S | E | D | | S | W | E | E | T | S |
| | | R | H | O | | S | P | E | A | R | | | | |
| | H | O | P | E | S | O | | I | R | K | | B | R | O |
| B | O | W | I | E | | M | O | V | I | E | C | L | I | P |
| E | L | E | C | T | | A | L | O | E | | A | U | N | T |
| D | E | S | K | S | | N | E | T | S | | P | E | G | S |

## 194

| I | M | A | C | | S | H | A | R | P | | T | E | R | M |
| S | A | G | A | | T | U | B | E | R | | H | A | I | R |
| S | O | A | P | B | U | B | B | L | E | | A | R | C | S |
| A | R | I | E | L | | Y | I | D | D | I | S | H | | |
| | I | N | R | O | A | D | | V | I | E | | | | |
| | | S | O | L | A | R | E | C | L | I | P | S | E | |
| A | B | S | | P | I | T | A | | T | I | M | I | N | G |
| N | O | P | E | | E | B | B | | | P | L | U | G | |
| T | H | E | L | M | A | | B | I | A | S | | E | G | O |
| S | O | C | I | A | L | C | I | R | C | L | E | | | |
| | | | S | I | A | | D | E | A | D | E | N | | |
| | M | U | S | T | A | N | G | | P | I | V | O | T | |
| M | A | N | E | | S | O | L | I | D | S | T | A | T | E |
| A | R | I | A | | E | L | U | D | E | | O | D | E | S |
| N | E | X | T | | S | A | T | O | N | | R | E | D | S |

## 195

| | A | I | D | | A | L | B | A | | C | R | I | B | |
| | B | R | A | G | | L | I | O | N | | P | O | I | S | E |
| | B | I | B | L | E | B | E | L | T | | L | I | N | E | N |
| | A | S | S | U | R | E | | D | E | B | U | N | K | E | D |
| | | E | A | R | L | | E | M | T | | | | | | |
| | G | I | F | S | | T | A | S | T | E | | O | R | G | S |
| | A | H | A | | B | A | T | H | I | N | G | S | U | I | T |
| | R | E | U | S | E | | E | A | T | | E | S | S | A | Y |
| | B | A | N | A | N | A | S | P | L | I | T | | S | N | L |
| | O | R | A | L | | S | T | E | E | D | | T | O | T | E |
| | | | A | M | I | | | S | E | T | H | | | | |
| | S | A | N | D | R | A | O | H | | A | R | I | S | E | S |
| | A | L | I | B | I | | B | I | L | L | Y | G | O | A | T |
| | I | O | T | A | S | | O | P | A | L | | H | O | S | E |
| | D | E | E | R | | E | S | P | Y | | | N | E | W | |

# Play these other fun puzzle books by USA TODAY

USA TODAY Sudoku

USA TODAY Everyday Sudoku

USA TODAY Crossword

USA TODAY Logic Puzzles

USA TODAY Word Roundup

USA TODAY Word Roundup and Word Search

USA TODAY Jumbo Puzzle Book

USA TODAY Picture Puzzles

USA TODAY Jumbo Puzzle Book 2

USA TODAY Don't Quote Me®

USA TODAY Picture Puzzles Across America

USA TODAY Word Finding Frenzy

USA TODAY Crossword 2

USA TODAY Logic 2

USA TODAY Sudoku 3

USA TODAY Up & Down Words Infinity

USA TODAY Crossword 3

USA TODAY Sudoku Super Challenge

USA TODAY Crossword Super Challenge

USA TODAY Logic Super Challenge

USA TODAY Jumbo Puzzle Book Super Challenge

USA TODAY Sudoku Super Challenge 2

USA TODAY Crossword Super Challenge 2

USA TODAY Logic Super Challenge 2

USA TODAY Jumbo Puzzle Book Super Challenge 2

USA TODAY Sudoku Super Challenge 3

USA TODAY Crossword Super Challenge 3

USA TODAY Logic Super Challenge 3

USA TODAY Jumbo Puzzle Book Super Challenge 3

USA TODAY Sudoku and Variants Super Challenge

USA TODAY Word Fill-In Super Challenge

USA TODAY Picture Puzzles Across America 2

USA TODAY Sunshine Sudoku